PRODIGIOUS BIRDS

*Moas and moa-hunting in
prehistoric New Zealand*

Pl
da
·y

.

WV

FRONTISPIECE: Otago University medical students, Wi Repa and Te Rangi Hiroa (later Sir Peter Buck), posed as hunters beside a 'restored' moa in the Woodhaugh Gardens, Dunedin. Photograph by Augustus Hamilton, 1903, reproduced courtesy of the National Museum, New Zealand.

PRODIGIOUS BIRDS

Moas and moa-hunting in prehistoric New Zealand

Atholl Anderson

CAMBRIDGE UNIVERSITY PRESS

CAMBRIDGE   NEW YORK   PORT CHESTER   MELBOURNE   SYDNEY

PUBLISHED BY THE PRESS SYNDICATE OF THE UNIVERSITY OF CAMBRIDGE
The Pitt Building, Trumpington Street, Cambridge, United Kingdom

CAMBRIDGE UNIVERSITY PRESS
The Edinburgh Building, Cambridge CB2 2RU, UK
40 West 20th Street, New York NY 10011–4211, USA
477 Williamstown Road, Port Melbourne, VIC 3207, Australia
Ruiz de Alarcón 13, 28014 Madrid, Spain
Dock House, The Waterfront, Cape Town 8001, South Africa

http://www.cambridge.org

First published 1989
First paperback edition 2003

A catalogue record for this book is available from the British Library

Library of Congress cataloguing in publication data

Anderson, Atholl.

   Prodigious birds: moas and moa-hunting in prehistoric New Zealand/
Atholl Anderson.

     p. cm.
   Bibliography: p.
   Includes index.
   ISBN 0 521 35209 6 hardback
   1. Maoris–Hunting. 2. Moa. 3. Hunting, Prehistoric – New Zealand.
   4. New Zealand – Antiquities. I. Title.
DU423.H8A53 1909   89-7197
993.01 – dc20   CIP

ISBN 0 521 35209 6 hardback
ISBN 0 521 54396 7 paperback

To the memory of Sir Julius von Haast (1822–1887),
father of research on moas and moa hunting in New Zealand

CONTENTS

ILLUSTRATIONS

TABLES

PREFACE

Since the first reference to moas and moa-hunting appeared in print, more than 150 years ago (Polack 1838), an extensive literature has accumulated about these aspects of New Zealand's past. Until recently, though, it was curiously polarised and incomplete. On the one hand, moa bones propelled a zoological interest in phylogenesis and systematics; on the other hand, artefacts from moa-hunting sites sustained a similar preoccupation with the classification and antecedents of material culture.

In the last 20 years, however, both biological and archaeological approaches have converged towards the broad domain between these fields. Investigations of certain functional aspects of moa morphology and inferences about the behaviour and ecological relationships of moa species have provided some of the basic data upon which a more searching analysis of the nature and consequences of moa-hunting could be founded. In writing this book, therefore, my first intention has been to describe the results, as I understand them, of this work.

Since no comprehensive review of moa research has been published, it also seemed appropriate to set the recent studies in the context of a broad historical summary which aimed to show how knowledge of moas and moa-hunting developed out of zoological, archaeological and ethnographical investigations. In pursuing these objectives I have confined my attention to moa biology, and not the wider significance of moas in New Zealand's natural history, and to moa-hunting as an activity, but not the role of it in the broader pre-European economy or other aspects of the society and culture to which moa-hunters belonged. I hope that this book will be seen as an introduction to the natural and cultural history of moas and as a contribution to moa-related research which will help us to see where we have been, are now, and where we could profitably proceed.

Many people responded generously to my requests for information, even those who were somewhat surprised at how far I was prepared to presume beyond my disciplinary caste. For assistance with information relevant to moa biology I thank: R. McNeill Alexander (University of Leeds), Ian Atkinson (DSIR, Lower Hutt), Sandy Bartle (National Museum), David Butts (Internal Affairs), Graeme Caughley (CSIRO, Canberra), John Darby (Otago Museum), Michael Forrest (Southland Museum), Ewen Fordyce (Otago University), Richard Holdaway (Canterbury University), Beverley McCulloch (Canterbury Museum), Matt McGlone (DSIR, Christchurch), Chris McGowan (Royal Ontario Museum), Mike Pole (Otago University), Ellen Prager (University of California, Berkeley), Pat Rich (Monash University), Ron Scarlett (Canterbury Museum), Charles Sibley (Yale University), Cyril Walker (British Museum, Natural History) and Trevor Worthy (National Museum). I am also grateful to Holdaway, Rich, Scarlett, Worthy and the late Sir Charles Fleming for reading some of the chapters and offering valuable comments. I am particularly indebted to Worthy for supplying new data and ideas about moas.

For assistance with information relevant to moa-hunting I thank: Brian Allingham (Seacliff), Sally Burrage (Canterbury Museum), Richard Cassels (Otago Museum), Roger Fyfe (Taranaki Museum), Peter Gathercole (Darwin College, Cambridge), George Griffiths (Dunedin), Jill Hamel (Dunedin), Wendy Harsant (Auckland), Brian

Kooyman (Calgary University), Kevin Jones (DOC, Wellington), Hardwicke Knight (Broad Bay), Helen Leach (Otago University), Foss Leach (Wellington), Les Lockerbie (Dunedin), Bruce McFadgen (DOC, Wellington), Rick McGovern-Wilson (Otago University), Graeme Mason (Otago University), Reg Nichol (Auckland University), Nigel Prickett (Auckland Institute and Museum), Ron Scarlett (Canterbury Museum) and Michael Trotter (Canterbury Museum). Foss Leach gave particular help with the radiocarbon chronology, and Brian Allingham with compiling data on ulus and teshoas. Michael Trotter and Beverley McCulloch kindly read the chapters on moa-hunting and offered comment.

For assistance with illustrations I thank Martin Fisher and Les O'Neill (Otago University). For providing figures, or permission to publish, I thank D. V. Avery (New Plymouth), the Canterbury Museum (Christchurch), Richard Cassels, Charles Higham (Otago University), the Hocken Library (Dunedin), Hardwicke Knight, Les Lockerbie, Beverley McCulloch, the National Museum of New Zealand, the Otago Museum (Dunedin), the Polynesian Society, the Royal Society of New Zealand, Charles Sibley, the Taranaki Museum (New Plymouth), and the Zoology Department Museum, Cambridge University. Chris Gaskin (Dunedin) drew figures 1.3 and 1.4. For assistance with the manuscript I am particularly grateful to Jennifer Evans (Otago University), subeditor Marilyn Little (Thora, NSW) and Karen McVicker (Cambridge University Press, Melbourne).

I began this book in 1986 as a Visiting Fellow at Clare Hall, Cambridge University, and I thank the President and Fellows for their hospitality.

Above all, I thank Rosanne Anderson – for unfailing practical assistance and encouragement and for doing much more than her share of managing the family.

1

INTRODUCTION

The first Europeans to land in New Zealand, in 1769, came to determine whether the country coasted briefly by Tasman in 1642 was part of a great southern continent inhabited by people, plants and animals of appropriately rich diversity. This hypothesis, which Joseph Banks, the principal naturalist on the expedition and a self-confessed 'continent-monger' hoped to verify, sank irrecoverably in the wake of circumnavigation only six months later. New Zealand was proven to be an oceanic archipelago, and Banks was left to reflect, with some disappointment, that an observed 'scarcity of animals upon the land' (Banks 1770 in Morrell 1958:124) would probably stand the test of subsequent exploration.

In the event, he was quite right. New Zealand did have an unusually impoverished fauna of terrestrial vertebrates. The only mammals were two species of small bats (*Mystacina* spp.). There were also one genus of frogs (*Leiopelma* spp.), two families of lizards (Gekkonidae, Scincidae), one rhyncocephalian reptile (the tuatara, *Sphenodon punctatus*) and less than 80 species of land and freshwater birds. Amongst the latter, flightless species were unusually numerous, but Banks had not seen any and so missed the first portent of a remarkable discovery.

Evidence of the new birds did not come to light suddenly, and no living representatives of them were ever found, although the probability of their contemporary existence remained tantalisingly long in legitimate doubt. Yet even without that ultimate triumph, remains of them startled the Victorian world of natural history and sent a thrill of half-fearful excitement through the colonial community of European settlers.

The revelation of New Zealand's greatest faunal secret began to unfold more than 60 years after Banks' visit – curiously enough, in almost the same place where he had first stepped ashore. In the winter of 1834 the trading cutter *Emma*, badly damaged by storms off the East Coast of New Zealand, put in to Tolaga Bay for repairs. There, Joel Polack, its owner, was shown 'several large fossil ossifications' by the Maoris, who also mentioned that 'very large birds had existed' long ago, and had been exterminated by excessive hunting. Polack concluded that 'a species of emu, or a bird of the genus Struthio' had once lived in New Zealand. This shrewd deduction, which appeared in 1838 (Polack 1838i:303), is the earliest reference to the giant, flightless birds of New Zealand. Since Polack, however, had neither bones to show nor a name to report, it fell to others to bring these to notice.

The first bone to reach an osteological authority had actually been collected, between 1831 and 1836, by another East Coast trader, John Harris, but it was not until 1839 that the brilliant comparative anatomist, Richard Owen, saw the 'unpromising fragment' and deduced that it had belonged to a flightless bird, probably extinct, which had been heavier than an ostrich (Owen 1839, 1879ai:iv). He later named the bird *Dinornis Novae Zealandiae* (Owen 1843a), meaning the prodigious or surprising bird from New Zealand. Meanwhile, by virtue of further investigations amongst the East Coast Maoris, the bird was already becoming widely known by a Polynesian word 'moa', which meant, amongst other things, 'domestic fowl or chicken'.

1

Interest in moas

News of the moas (there soon proved to be a number of different kinds) had an immediate and sustained impact on natural scientists and public alike. The monstrous size of the large species attracted wide attention, in part, perhaps, because it was often substantially exaggerated (some early guesses had the tallest moa towering to 5 m in height, about twice the real maximum), and moa skeletons were enthusiastically reconstructed to conform with popular belief (Fig. 1.1). Nevertheless there were other very large, flightless birds still manifestly in existence such as the ostrich, emu, cassowaries and rheas, and others thought to be not long extinct such as the elephant birds of Madagascar, so size, as such, was not the issue which captured scientific attention.

Rather it was the fact that such large flightless birds came from one of the most isolated landmasses on earth; from a small archipelago located near the centre of the world's water hemisphere.

FIG. 1.1   An early attempt to reconstruct a moa skeleton. The anonymous collector has added numerous supernumerary vertebrae. (By courtesy of Hocken Library.)

As Owen (1879aɪ:iv) observed, all other large ratites were confined to continents, though some ranged to islands nearby. That initial interest was then amplified by the developing realisation that there were more kinds of moas than of any other ratites, and by the evidence that they had been, uniquely amongst birds, entirely wingless. It was an extraordinary puzzle. 'All analogy seemed against it' as Owen (1879b:273) remarked, and Oliver later (1949:1) suggested that New Zealand had been 'the locus of a grand experiment in evolution'.

Another matter of great interest was the question of whether any moas still lived (a claim which still attracts proponents). Owen had observed at once that the first bone he saw was quite unfossilised, and there were soon numerous stories in circulation asserting, successively, that Maoris had hunted moas within living memory, that some moas remained in remote mountain ranges and that European explorers had actually seen them. The earliest of the latter was the 'mechanic's tale' (Colenso 1846:90), told in 1842, about two Americans who ventured into the Marlborough mountains to a place that their Maori guide knew a moa to visit; 'presently they saw the monster majestically stalking down in search of food: they were, however, so petrified with horror at the sight as to be utterly unable to fire on him. Had they commenced the combat, it is, I think [said Colenso], highly doubtful how it might have terminated'. Excitement ran high for a time, and then subsided into a general optimism that moas might soon be 'seen striding among the emus and ostriches in the Regent's Park' (*The New Zealand Journal* (London) 30 March 1844).

This proved, if slowly, a vain hope, and interest in the period to which moas survived became transferred to the rapidly accumulating field evidence of Maori moa-hunting. In this, as in other respects, the story of moas was quite unusual. Other large ratites were hunted in modern times and their bones turned up occasionally in prehistoric middens, but only moas had been hunted on a scale sufficient to leave remains comparable with those of such classic examples of the big-game hunters' art as the bison kill sites on the high plains of North America. Furthermore, moa-hunting was so utterly unlike the subsistence activities of the historically known Maoris that the question was begged of whether it had occurred in a more remote antiquity than Maori accounts of it suggested and represented, perhaps, the tenure of a different people altogether.

These various considerations, fitted together, formed an exotic and compelling story. Archaic birds, remarkable in size and diversity, had survived into modern times as the common prey of a lost race of Polynesian hunters at the very margins of human colonisation, and were possibly still to be found in some remote mountain valley. Moas became surrounded, consequently, by an aura of romance which so appealed to New Zealanders that the birds were, for much of the 19th century, as common a symbol in public imagery as the kiwi, which succeeded them, is today (Sinclair 1983). Even much later Buick (1931:2) could remark that of all the ratites, past and present, 'the Moa is indisputably the bird shrouded in the greatest mystery and steeped in the richest glamour'.

Behind the facade of popular romance, however, scholarship continued to quarry inexorably, if sometimes erratically, at the face of the early enigmas, and it is the progress of this research which forms the core of the present work.

Principal research themes

The early surprise at birds such as moas being discovered in an isolated oceanic archipelago, turned, not unexpectedly, into the main theme around which research on moas and moa-hunting has continued to centre. This can be stated, briefly, as an investigation of the consequences of island colonisation. Here was a large, temperate landmass of considerable environmental variety in nearly all respects, but it was an archipelago and it had a peculiarly impoverished fauna which, in particular, was utterly destitute of cursorial mammals. For flightless birds this was a uniquely inviting evolutionary canvas and much of the study of moas has dwelt, if not often very explicitly, on the consequences of that situation. It has concentrated, in particular, on the question of how many moas there were and how they were related to each other; an issue which is fundamental to other matters of island colonisation and adaptation such as how moas got to New Zealand and when, how they developed into different shapes and sizes and how these different types were distributed according to variations in the topography and vegetation.

The adaptation of moas to their unusual island environment has been the main theme in research on moa-hunting as well, especially since it has concentrated very substantially upon the question of extinction. Patterns of morphology and behaviour, developed in insular conditions, and which facilitated the evolution of moas, have been seen as subsequently rendering them peculiarly vulnerable to the entry of new and very capable predators –

people in particular. Equilibrium patterns of behaviour which had been the most efficient strategies, such as low breeding rates, fatally depressed the resilience of moa populations under predation; the absence of other large land animals, which had reduced competition for moas, now narrowed prey choices and focussed the attention of predators upon them, and so on. It was, in addition, insular isolation which ensured the lateness of contact between moas and people, so that a traditional memory of the former reached, if barely, into the period of European colonisation.

In discussing these and related issues this book is divided into two parts. Chapters 2 to 6 outline the discovery and biological nature of moas. In the second part, Chapters 7 to 10 outline the discovery and nature of moa-hunting sites and aspects of their archaeological evidence, while important questions arising from that evidence are considered in Chapters 11 to 13. Since a wide variety of issues and data – ranging from zoological taxonomy to use-damage on stone tools – are involved in these matters it may prove helpful to sketch, at the outset, the main questions which I tackle, some of the answers which I prefer and the order of dealing with these in the book.

How many kinds of moas were there?

The discovery of moas is described at greater length in Chapter 2. As an extended, piecemeal process marked by uncertain communications between antipodes, and intense rivalry between the main participants, it provides a useful introduction to the atmosphere in which interests in moas, which essentially meant in their systematics, were pursued during the first century of research.

Systematics, or taxonomy, concerns the arrangement of living things into classes which express degrees of relatedness, as in a family tree. In the case of extinct animals, the discrimination of relationships is necessarily inferential, and it requires a fine judgement of differences in size and shape between bones of the same anatomical element. Does a tibiotarsus which is 15 per cent longer than any others of the same shape require the establishment of a new species? Should all moas which had blunt beaks be classed together? These, and many other such questions, have been the consuming passion of moa research since the beginning.

Owen's investigations demonstrated that there were two broad groups of moas, but he could not find the characters with which to define them. Increasingly large samples of material compounded the difficulty by appearing to indicate that moa limb bones, the main source of evidence, exhibited more or less continuous variation in size and shape. It was only with systematic research on moa crania, which began at the end of the 19th century, that the family and generic relationships of moas came to be sorted out. The number of species, however, remained as high as 24 to 28 until 1976 when Cracraft reduced it, by analogy with the amount of variation in kiwi bones, to 13. Subsequent minor revisions have reduced it further to 11. There are, however, several species, retained by some current workers, which I have also kept as a matter of convenience: *Euryapteryx gravis* and *Dinornis torosus*, although the case for doing so is becoming weaker. The historical development of moa systematics is discussed in Chapter 3 and the classification which is used here is shown in Table 1.1.

TABLE 1.1   The taxonomy of moas used in this book (see Chapter 3 for comment)

Order: Dinornithiformes	
Family: Anomalopterygidae	Family: Dinornithidae
Anomalopteryx didiformis	*Dinornis struthoides*
Megalapteryx didinus	*Dinornis torosus*
Emeus crassus	*Dinornis novaezealandiae*
Euryapteryx curtus	*Dinornis giganteus*
Euryapteryx geranoides	
Euryapteryx gravis	
Pachyornis mappini	
Pachyornis australis	
Pachyornis elephantopus	

How did moas get to New Zealand and develop?

Moas, and other ratites (so-called from their common possession of a flat breastbone), are more usefully defined as 'palaeognaths', a term referring to a fused, inflexible arrangement of bones in the roof of the mouth. This palatal condition seems to have been the original or primitive form in birds, but amongst the majority of birds, which later evolved the light, flexible, 'neognathous' palate, some subsequently reverted to the older form. The significance of this fact is that whereas it once seemed an inescapable conclusion that the southern hemisphere palaeognaths (emu, ostrich, cassowaries, rheas, moas, kiwis, etc.), were descended from an ancient stock of flightless birds on Gondwanaland, and became divided by continental

drift, it is now possible that there is no such close relationship at all. Palaeognaths could have diverse origins, including as flying neognathous birds, and may have developed their similar features by convergent evolution. Unfortunately there is very little fossil evidence to assist in deciding the matter. No moa remains are more than a few million years old, whereas New Zealand was last separated from other landmasses more than 80 million years ago. I prefer the view that moa ancestors flew to New Zealand, but cannot claim strong grounds for it.

Similarly it is possible only to speculate about the development of different kinds of moas in New Zealand, by reference to major environmental events which might have encouraged evolution within an ancestral stock: the Oligocene reduction of the landmass to an archipelago; uplift of the Southern Alps; fluctuations of climate during the Pleistocene; the subsequent formation of Cook and Foveaux Straits, and so on. All that can be said is that the modern moa species existed by about 25,000 years ago, and that no remains belonging to other species have yet been described.

But although we know very little about the speciation process, we do have some evidence of the way in which species were distributed in the late Holocene environment. Comparison of species distributions through time in a changing environment, where deposits from both Pleistocene and Holocene can be found in the same area, and comparison of species distributions with the broad variation of late Holocene vegetation patterns, both point to the same conclusion: a different suite of species occupied humid forests than those that occupied dry forest, scrub or open ground. The smaller *Dinornis* species and *Anomalopteryx* occupied the former habitats, while *Dinornis giganteus* and all the remaining moas occupied the latter habitats. Amongst the latter, there was also some variation in species with altitude.

All these matters are canvassed in Chapter 4.

How did moas differ in morphology and ecology?

Opinions have varied considerably over the years about how 'the moa' might have appeared in life, and it is only quite recently that the idea of obvious morphological variation has begun to inform artistic reconstructions (Fig. 1.2). This is quite strange considering the early, and enduring, belief that moas belonged to two quite different groups. It is now commonly expressed as a division into two families: Dinornithidae and Anomalopterygidae. Dinornithids were tall, comparatively slender

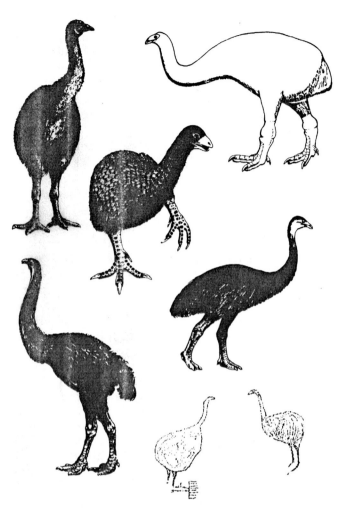

FIG. 1.2 Previous images of moas: *Dinornis* (*Palapteryx* in Hochstetter 1867:176), top left; *Dinornis maximus* according to Augusta and Burian (n. d., pl. 41), bottom left, and Temple and Gaskin (1985, frontispiece), centre right; medium-sized moa, top right and smaller moa, centre left (in McCulloch 1982:7, cover); probable pre-European drawings of moas in Craigmore Shelter, bottom right (Kreuzer and Dunn 1982:176).

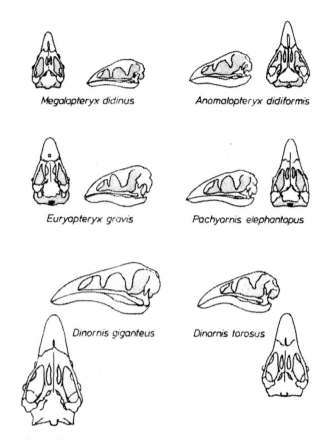

FIG. 1.3 Outlines of cranial morphology in moas, side and palatal views. Note variations in size, and in length and shape of beak (minus keratinous sheath, which seldom survives).

birds with long lower legs, flat, wide skulls and relatively long, downcurved beaks. It was species of this family which, mounted in museums as massive frames of peat-black bones, promoted the impression that moas, in general, had looked like giraffes from which the front legs had been lopped (Kennedy 1876:201). Anomalopterygids were much more variable. The small genera, *Anomalopteryx* and *Megalapteryx*, contained rather gracile birds with limb bones similar, in some ways, to those of *Dinornis*, but the larger genera contained heavy, robust birds with short, stout limbs. Beak forms were variable, and included the sharp *Pachyornis* and blunt *Euryapteryx* forms (Fig. 1.3).

Moas ranged in weight from about 20 kg to more than 200 kg. Stature is a more problematical matter. If any birds stood with legs and necks extended to a more or less vertical position they would have reached about 3.5 m in height. Recent evidence indicates, however, that moas as a whole stood with their leg bones arranged into a reversed-Z position, as amongst birds in general, and that they held their necks in the looped manner common amongst other large flightless birds (Fig. 1.4). This would have reduced the range of stature amongst moas to about 0.5 to 2 m (Chapter 5).

Do Maori stories about moas provide reliable evidence?

The short answer here is 'no'. The numerous purported Maori accounts of moa biology, ecology and behaviour (also hunting, Chapter 11), which were published between about 1870 and 1930 were described bluntly, but accurately, by Elsdon Best

FIG. 1.4   Some examples of moas as they may have appeared in life: *Megalapteryx didinus* and, for comparison, Brown kiwi (*Apteryx australis*), top; *Euryapteryx gravis*, centre; *Dinornis giganteus*, bottom. To right, are the leg bones shown in mean positions of rotation as determined by Worthy (pers. comm.).

(1942:182), as 'a remarkable quantity of puerile data'. He objected, as other scholars have done, to the general anonymity of the alleged informants or the circumstances of transmission, and to the frequent obvious flaws, such as descriptions of moa wings. In addition, it is clear that many Maoris, if indeed they were much implicated in these tales at all, were quite familiar with the appearance and habits of emus and other large ratites from as early as the 1860s, in some cases from the 1840s. There may be some pure metal of genuine pre-European recollection about moas in these stories but it is now impossible to extract it from the dross.

Another, and perhaps more serious, difficulty lies in the use of the word 'moa'. It was first recorded in connection with a giant bird in 1838 when Colenso (1846:81) heard it as the name of a mythological creature of part-avian, part-human characteristics which lived in a cave on the East Coast and was guarded by giant reptiles. Whether this 'moa', the relics which came to be known as moa bones and the birds identified as *Dinornis* were all held to be manifestations of the same entity, in the original Maori perception, is open to question. Furthermore, early Maori phrases or sayings which include the word 'moa' are peculiarly non-specific in terms of such obvious features of moas as their remarkable size. Conversely, the word can often be plausibly traced to a Polynesian phrase or saying where it clearly refers to the domestic fowl. There have been various attempts to get around this longstanding problem by putting forward other words alleged to have been genuine Maori names for moas; none are at all convincing. These and related issues are discussed further in Chapter 6.

Who were the moa-hunters?

Chapter 7 opens the section on moa-hunting with an historical survey of the long and often contentious debate about the identity of the moa-hunters. This canvassed three main sources of uncertainty: stratigraphical evidence of the age of moa-hunting, a problem which arose with the first discovery of moa-hunting remains at Waingongoro, south Taranaki, in 1843; the contents, and their cultural implications, of the moa-hunters' artefactual assemblage, a lightning rod of dissent erected by Haast in 1871; and the credibility of certain Maori traditions, brought to light in the early 20th century, which alleged a non-Polynesian ancestry of the moa-hunters. A substantial consensus on these matters, not achieved until the 1950s, was that the moa-hunters were exclusively east Polynesian by ancestry (and Maori by retrospective ascription), and had arrived about 1200 years ago, bringing with them a distinctive aceramic, neolithic material culture.

The most persuasive arguments in reaching this conclusion had come from comparative analysis of artefactual styles, but when Duff (1956a) attempted to capitalise on that research by proposing a formal nomenclature for the assemblages he raised another problem of identification altogether. For the early assemblage Duff revived Haast's term 'Moa-hunter' which, by implication, inverted the proposition that people who hunted moas had a certain kind of material culture. In fact, whichever way the proposition was turned, it could not define accurately a relationship between artefacts and economy which had never been a perfect match. Furthermore, the constant repetition of 'Moa-hunter' as if moa-hunting had been the predominant activity of the early Maoris and was, by extension, a major focus of archaeological interest, served only to obscure the fact that nothing could have been further from the case.

What is the archaeological evidence of moa-hunting?

This is a deceptively complex issue. It might seem to involve only matters of fact – such as the numbers, distribution and contents of moa-hunting sites – but the lack of systematic research on moa-hunting and processing as activities, and not merely as cultural markers, has meant that even basic issues of definition, or the adequacy of archaeological sampling, have hardly been considered.

How, for instance, should we define a moa-hunting site? If the emphasis was placed on hunting, so that only places where moas had been successfully hunted were included, that is, kill sites, there would be no more than a handful currently recorded. If presence of moa remains was the criterion, then many sites in which the moa bone was only introduced as an industrial raw material would be included. I regard as an essential criterion of a moa-hunting site the existence of non-artefactual remains of moas.

However this also raises questions. One of these is whether the quite frequent description of moa bone in North Island sites as 'subfossil' (i.e. either pre-existing on the site, or brought in to it as old bone) is determined less by any tangible evidence of that condition than by an assumption about the scarcity of moas. It might also be true, of course, that assumptions about moa abundance in the South Island have swept aside a proper consideration of whether specific remains had been of subfossil origin. There is here, as well, a question only briefly discussed, for want of data, about possible regional variation in the survival of moa bone, and thus of our perception about the distribution of sites as a whole.

These, and other issues in relation to the data base, are discussed in Chapters 8 to 10 which present the data, otherwise not available in a single place, and much of it previously unpublished, about the archaeology of moa-hunting. This includes, for each region, the number and distribution of sites, moa taxa identified and numbers represented, and for major sites, evidence of stratigraphy, moa processing and relevant structures and artefacts. Two sites which have been comprehensively investigated in recent times, Kaupokonui in the North Island and Hawksburn in the South Island, are considered in most detail.

How were moas hunted and processed?

Chapters 11 and 12 investigate two important issues in the archaeology of moa-hunting: how the birds were hunted and what lithic technology was associated with processing of carcasses.

Moa-hunting can be considered at two levels: the means by which moas were detained and killed, and the strategic organisation of hunting and processing in terms of such factors as the selection of hunting grounds, seasonality and the transportation of products. In regard to the first, the unreliability of alleged traditional accounts of moa-hunting, and the lack of any tangible evidence of hunting weapons, throw the matter wide open to speculation. Frequently repeated episodes of small-scale hunting, though, seem more probable than large-scale drives, in the light of inferred moa behaviour and an absence of mass-kill sites.

At a strategic level there is rather more to go on. It is clear that moas from fairly open habitats were sought preferentially (notably *Euryapteryx* species), and in the South Island, where moa-hunting occurred most intensively, it is possible to perceive a difference in the distribution of hunting sites in these habitats which may be explicable in terms of the comparative shape of catchments and the usefulness of their rivers for rapid transport to the coast. These differences also bear on questions of seasonality and flesh preservation, although neither can be clearly answered at this stage.

The processing of carcasses once they reached the sites, a matter described in terms of the representation of bones in Chapters 8 to 10, is considered in terms of lithic technology in Chapter 12. The nature of the stone artefact assemblage associated with moa-hunting is not the same, of course, as that associated with 'Moa-hunters', in the sense defined by Duff (1956a); rather it comprises those tools which were actually used in processing recently killed moas.

Use-damage and other evidence concerning the functions of tools in moa processing is examined at some length, in relation to blades in particular. The questions which are considered include the influence of raw material type and distribution on geographical variations in assemblages, and what inferences can be drawn from the functional attributes of used and retouched blades. Few firm conclusions emerged from this investigation. Availability of silcrete was certainly a major factor in the proportion of blades to other tools in different moa-hunting assemblages, but blades were much less common than is often assumed and cannot be unequivocally shown to have been moa-butchery implements.

When did moas become extinct and why?

No question about moas, or about the significance of moa-hunting, has attracted more attention than that of why moas became extinct. Whatever answers are proposed depend in the first instance, though, upon the chronology of the event. If it could be shown on the one hand that some species were already extinct before the arrival of Polynesians, that others were very rare, and that extinction of the remaining moas occurred very soon after human colonisation, then explanations which emphasise such non-cultural factors as evolutionary senescence, or an inability to adapt adequately to post-glacial environmental changes, would gain in plausibility. Evidence on the other hand that all moas survived into the human era (as we now know), and of widespread moa-hunting, swings the balance of explanation towards cultural factors such as habitat destruction, introduction of predators, and over-hunting.

The main emphasis in Chapter 13 is on the impact of hunting. The precise chronology of moa-hunting, however, cannot be easily established because of questions about the reliability of some classes of radiocarbon dates. Nevertheless the broad picture is that moa-hunting occurred between the 11th and 17th centuries but peaked as early as the 13th century in most areas. Whether the early decline in moa numbers, implied by that view, can be accounted for by over-exploitation, is a question which depends very much upon which numbers are entered into a model of the relationship between moa population density and human consumption rates. Within the likely ranges of those variables, however, overkill seems a credible explanation of moa extinction in the main hunting areas and with respect to the more common species. However, a wider variety of cultural factors, including habitat destruction and the introduction of quadripedal predators, was implicated in the extinction of moas as a whole.

These eight questions, and all the ancillary matters which they raise, by no means exhaust the range of moa-related research. There are, for instance, questions about the symbolism associated with moas by early European settlers (Anderson n.d.b), and the significance of moas portrayed in Victorian fiction, paintings and cartoons. In both, moas seem to have been metaphors for a wilderness in which, many thought, they might still exist. It is not what moas came to mean, but what they were, how they were exploited by people and what became of them, which are the subjects of this book.

I

DISCOVERY AND BIOLOGY OF MOAS

2

DISCOVERY

The word 'moa' first came to light in January 1838 when the missionary William Williams, accompanied by a mission printer, William Colenso, travelled to the East Coast (Fig. 2.1). They evidently had no knowledge of Polack's discovery, and the moa described to them at Waiapu (Fig. 2.2) was a peculiar creature indeed. It resembled a huge domestic rooster, but had the face of a man, and it lived on air in a cave on Whakapunake Mountain where it was guarded by a pair of giant tuatara. No Maoris actually claimed to have seen the moa, but they did tell Colenso about bones, larger than those from cattle, which they collected to use in making fish hooks.

In early 1839, Williams returned to the East Coast (Fig. 2.2) with the Rev. Richard Taylor. Williams recalled offering a reward for any remains of the moa and was eventually handed a large bone which was so water-rolled that he could not determine anything useful about it (Owen 1879ai:75–6). Taylor's recollections were somewhat different. Writing to Richard Owen, in February 1844, he said that he had procured a moa's toe at that time, but in 1873, the last year of his life, he outlined a quite different set of events in support of his claim 'to have been the first discoverer of the Moa' (Taylor 1873:98). Finding the fragment of a large bone in the ceiling of a Maori house at Waiapu Pa he passed it to Williams, and remarked that its cancelled structure suggested that it was a bird bone. Williams laughed at the idea, but the local Maoris confirmed that it was indeed a bird bone and that it came from a 'tarepo'. One of these, they said, still lived on Hikurangi Mountain, and they described it in the same terms as the moa had earlier been portrayed.

It is difficult to accept Taylor's version of the events at Waiapu. For one thing, there is too much

FIG. 2.1 Four important figures in the discovery of moas (Buick 1931:52, 68): John Williams Harris (top left), William Williams (top right), Richard Taylor (bottom left), and William Colenso (bottom right). (By courtesy of D. V. Avery.)

coincidence begged by the fact that a similar incident involving the identification of a fragment of 'extremely cellular' bone had earlier been described by Taylor to Owen (Owen 1879ai:75–6) as occurring at the 'Whaingaihu' river mouth near

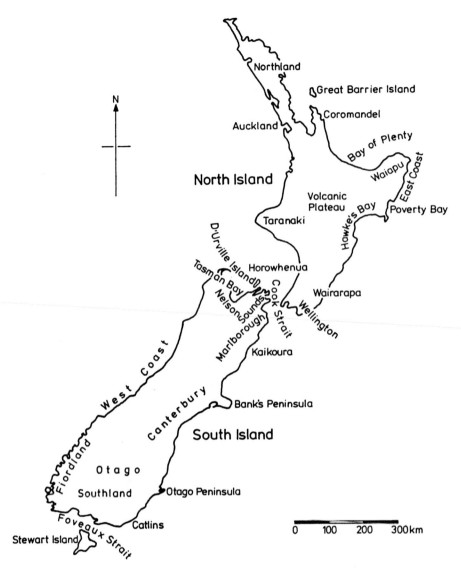

FIG. 2.2   New Zealand: main islands, districts and places (other than sites) referred to in text.

Turakina, just south of Wanganui in 1843 (in fact, it was at the mouth of the Waingongoro River in South Taranaki). For another, Colenso (1880) asserted that he could recall Taylor arriving at Paihia, in the Bay of Islands, on his way home from the East Coast in 1839, and that Taylor had only the moa toe or claw. Colenso, in a vigorous attack upon the deceased Taylor, suggested that even this relic 'resembled a bit of water-worn and rolled Obsidian more than anything else' (ibid.:106). As for the tarepo, this had also appeared, but in a very different context, in Taylor's early letter to Owen (1879a1:135–6), 'the Kakapo or Tarepo, which is about the size of a turkey . . . seems so closely to resemble the Dodo, as to lead me to suppose it is the same'.

Colenso's anger at Taylor's belated claim to have been the first to identify a moa bone was very largely generated by his fervently held belief that the honour had been shared by himself and Owen, and specifically that he was the first person in New Zealand to identify moa bones as the remains of struthious birds (Colenso 1846:85, 101, 1892:472). The basis of this assertion lay in Colenso's journey to the East Coast district in the summer of 1841–42. Colenso was looking for the living moa, but found that at each place at which he was positively assured of its current existence, 'the people had never seen a Moa, although they had always heard of, and invariably believed in, the existence of such a creature at that place' (Colenso 1846:88). At Waiapu, however, he had been given seven moa bones. When he reached Poverty Bay, where Williams was by then residing, he gave him a pair of femora to add to the tibiotarsus which Williams was about to send to the Rev. Dr Buckland at Oxford University. Colenso returned to the Bay of Islands in the autumn of 1842 where he wrote his first paper on the moa.

In it Colenso (1846) argued that moa bones had belonged to large, wingless, gallinaceous birds which had legs about 2 m long, stood about 5 m tall, and were extinct. He assigned them to Struthionidae and observed that the name 'moa' was Malay for the cassowary, and Polynesian for the domestic fowl. On this perceptive article, and its date of submission (November 1842), rests Colenso's claim. But how much of what he wrote did he owe to others?

One such was Dr Ernst Dieffenbach who had been warned by Taranaki Maoris in November 1839 to watch out for the moa and giant ngarara (lizardlike monsters) which were living on Mount Egmont (Mt Taranaki). Dieffenbach lived close to Colenso at Paihia in 1841 and they often discussed moas. He, as well as Colenso, had also inspected Taylor's moa 'toe' and he was already writing of the 'struthious Moa' in 1843 (Dieffenbach 1843I:140).

The possibility that Colenso had heard about Owen's first paper (1839) on *Dinornis* was also raised later in Colenso's career, and strenuously denied by him (Colenso 1892), but the evidence is not as clear as he concluded it to be. Colenso may not have seen a copy of Owen's paper until 1843, but the conclusions of it were being discussed as early as July 1842 when Williams was visited by the Rev. William Cotton, who had arrived at the Bay of Islands with Bishop Selwyn in June (Owen 1843a:1–2, 1879aI:v; Hill 1914:334). Since others to whom Owen recalled giving copies of his paper had been in New Zealand since 1841 it is not impossible that Colenso had heard something even if he did not know its source. It should also be noted that *The New Zealand Journal* (London) of 4 April 1840 published a summary of Owen's first paper, and that copies of this issue had probably reached New Zealand within a year from that date.

More important than these speculations, however, is the evidence in Colenso's paper that much of the vital information came to him from William Williams. After Colenso left Poverty Bay Williams induced local Maoris to engage in an enthusiastic search of the nearby riverbed, during which numerous moa bones were recovered. These were divided into two consignments for Buckland. The

largest, and some smaller, specimens were sent out through Port Nicholson (Wellington), but the other consignment may have gone initially to Colenso at Paihia. Certainly the illustrations to his paper are all of bones from Poverty Bay, whereas he possessed, at the time, only the remaining relics from Waiapu and some fragments sent to him by Maori teachers on the East Coast (Colenso 1880:70, 102; Williams 1842 to Buckland, in Owen 1879aI:75–6). Colenso (1846) also refers to a letter from Williams which seems to have been the same as that written to Buckland on 28 February 1842, much of the information given being the same as can be found in Colenso's paper. It is, of course, quite likely that Williams and Colenso had canvassed all the essential points appearing in Williams' letter and Colenso's paper during their journeys and correspondence prior to May 1842, but, on the face of it, all except the proposal to refer the birds to Struthionidae might be more accurately credited to Williams. His letter certainly impressed Owen (1879aI:76), who readily conceded to Williams 'a just claim to share in the honour of the discovery of *Dinornis*'.

But if Colenso was less than generous to Williams in his later papers (Colenso 1892:476), he was implacably hostile to the claims of Polack when they were at last drawn to his attention by Augustus Hamilton, in 1892. Writing to Walter Mantell several years later, Colenso said that no useful information could have been obtained from Polack, or from his book, because,

it is evident he never saw a moa bone. Had he done so he would have grabbed it. He did not, for he could not, write his book. He supplied the rough materials and the booksellers of London got them licked into shape. I knew Polack well; a Jew of the lowest grade and type. I have often seen him in his rum store on the Kororareka beach . . . Polack was never at East Cape, nor at Poverty Bay, the two known deposits, then, of Moa bones (Buick 1936:44).

Perhaps the savagery of Colenso's reaction to Polack, who had died in 1882, reflected the realisation that he could no longer sustain a claim he had cherished for decades. Yet his contribution was at least as important as Polack's discovery. Williams wrote very little about moas, and Taylor was careless or confused in his recollections. It fell to Colenso to describe the early results of the East Coast research, both osteological and ethnographical. As Duff (1977:293) later wrote of Colenso's paper, 'if the discussion had then closed we would scarcely know less on the subject than from the spate of papers during the following one hundred years'.

In the event it was neither Colenso nor Polack who was to be credited with the major honours of discovery, but rather the Professor of Comparative Anatomy at the Royal College of Surgeons, Richard Owen (Fig. 2.3). The sequence of events which led to his formal announcement of the discovery of a giant struthious bird in 1839 has been reconstructed by Buick (1936), who refers to an important letter written by J. W. Harris on 28 February 1837. Harris, about to return to New Zealand after a brief visit to Sydney, wrote to his uncle, Dr John Rule, describing some articles of interest which he was leaving for him to collect. Amongst them was a bone, of a kind about which the Maoris had 'a tradition that it belonged to a bird of the Eagle kind, but which has become extinct – they call it "A Movie". They are found buried on the banks of rivers' (Buick 1936:108).

Rule kept the bone for two years, evidently realising that although it was only a broken shaft fragment, about 15 cm long, it had belonged to quite an unusual animal (Fig. 2.4). In 1839, he returned to England and began comparing his specimen with bird bones in various London museums. Finding nothing to match it he eventually wrote to Owen, offering to sell the bone for ten guineas. His letter described it as 'part of the femur of a bird now considered to be wholly extinct', and then went on to describe the Maori tradition that it had belonged to a flying bird which seasonally left the forest to visit the rivers. He pointed out that inspection showed that the bone was from a bird and not any other kind of animal, but a bird of great size and strength (Buick 1936: 111–13).

When Owen, interrupted in the course of writing a lecture, was shown the bone by Rule and told that it was probably from a gigantic flying bird, he saw at once that the heavy construction of the bone precluded this interpretation and remarked that it was probably 'a marrow bone . . . like those brought to table wrapped in a napkin' (Owen 1879b:273). Persisting, Rule pointed to the cancellous structure in the interior of the bone, a feature common in bird bones but not in ungulate bones. He then told Owen that the specimen had

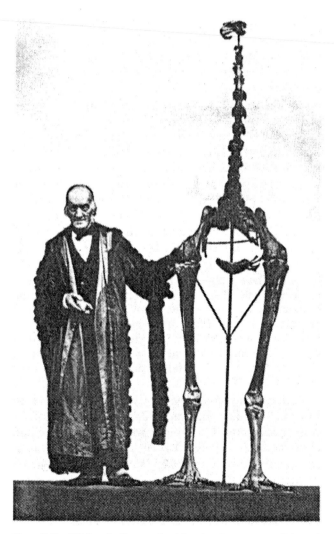

FIG. 2.3   Richard Owen beside the important *Dinornis robustus* (now *novaezealandiae*) specimen from Tiger Hill (see Chapter 5). In his right hand is the femoral shaft brought to him by Rule (Buick 1931: 244). (By courtesy of D. V. Avery.)

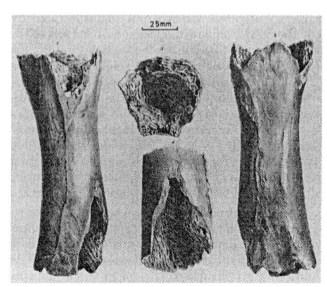

FIG. 2.4   The femoral shaft which John Rule took to Owen in 1839 (Owen 1879a1:pl. 3).

come from New Zealand and laid upon the desk, as if to confirm the point, a nephrite *mere* (club) which had come to him from Harris at the same time as the bone. By now Owen was sufficiently curious to ask Rule to leave the bone with him so that he might have a good look at it after his lecture.

Turning initially to the mounted skeleton of an ox, Owen saw that his first impression had been wrong, and as he checked the bone against the skeletons of other large domestic animals he found nothing to match it. While doing so, however, he noticed surface markings on the bone which were similar to those he recalled on certain large bird bones, and when he compared Rule's fragment with an ostrich femur he was at last convinced that a hitherto unknown giant bird, but not a bird of flight, was represented by the bone he held (see also Rule's (1843) account).

On 12 November 1839 Owen (1839:170) exhibited the bone before the Zoological Society of London and outlined his deductions about its origin.

The texture of the bone, which affords the chief evidence of its ornithic character, presents an extremely dense exterior crust . . . [which] degenerates into a lamello-cellular structure . . . This coarse cancellous structure is continued through the whole longitudinal extent of the fragment and immediately bounds the medullary cavity of the bone. There is no bone of similar size which presents a cancellous texture so closely resembling that of the present bone as does the femur of the Ostrich; but this structure is interrupted in the Ostrich at the middle of the shaft, where the parietes of the medullary, or rather air-cavity are smooth and unbroken. From this difference I conclude our extinct bird to have been a heavier and more sluggish species than the Ostrich; its femur, and probably its whole leg, was shorter and thicker.

His colleagues were not at once convinced – some arguing that New Zealand was too small and isolated to sustain such large species of birds – and the publication of his short paper by the Society was delayed but then approved with the addition of a statement that responsibility for it rested exclusively with its author (Owen 1879b:273; Buick 1931:70). Owen had 100 copies printed and distributed, some of them to people whom he knew were leaving for New Zealand, in the hope that further information or specimens would, in due course, be produced.

Rule, meanwhile, was still anxious to sell the bone. Owen had recommended that it be purchased by the Royal College of Surgeons, but their Museum Committee turned him down. Soon after

Rule sold it to a private collector, Benjamin Bright of Bristol, from whose estate it passed in 1873 to the British Museum.

Rule was not treated as generously by Owen in the matter of discovery as he might have been. Although Owen mentioned Rule in his address to the Zoological Society he did not acknowledge that the basic character of the bone, and a valid argument in support of that, had been first established by Rule, who had then been obliged to urge it upon him. In later years Owen referred to Rule, who had been a member of the same Royal College of Surgeons which Owen served, as merely 'an individual' or 'the vendor' of the bone as if it had been, indeed, the 'tavern delicacy' he first perceived it to be (Owen 1873, 1879b:272–3).

It was to be three years before Owen received evidence in support of his brief announcement. It came in a letter from William Cotton who had visited Williams in 1842 (above) and whose remarks seem, like Colenso's paper, to have been based on Williams' letter to Buckland, although it concluded with a currently popular story of the sighting of a 16 ft (4.8 m) tall moa in the South Island and the hopeful observation that 'I should not be surprised if the Zoological Society were to send out an army to take the monster alive, for alive he most certainly is in my opinion' (Owen 1843a:2).

Soon after, the first case of Poverty Bay bones arrived in England and Buckland invited Owen and W. J. Broderip, a Fellow of the Royal Society, to examine the contents with him. They found 29 bones, mostly femora and tibiotarsi, and began a systematic study comparing these with the skeletons of ostrich, emu, rhea and kiwi. Taking first a femur Owen observed that, as in the kiwi, but unlike in the other ratites, it had no air-hole at the back of the femoral neck, and therefore it confirmed the suspicion he had implied in 1839, that marrow and not air had been the contents. Turning to the best tibiotarsus, he observed that it was twice the length of the femur, as in the large ratites, but unlike in the kiwi, and that it differed from all of them in the existence of a complete distal anterior canal for the passage of an extensor tendon.

These preliminary observations brought Owen and his colleagues to the tarsometatarsal, '*the* bone and the key to the whole', as Broderip remarked (Buick 1931:80). This showed that the bird had been three-toed and that the tarsometatarsus had been only half the length of the tibiotarsus, as in the kiwi, but unlike in the other ratites. Yet any suggestion that the bird might have been a giant species of *Apteryx* was able to be rejected by the additional observation that no articular surface for the small hind-toe, found in the kiwi, could be discerned.

Adding these observations together, and noting the unusually broad pelvis, Owen could justify the establishment of a new genus and species: *Megalornis Novae Zealandiae*. Hardly had he disclosed these results to the Zoological Society, however, than he found that the generic name had already been claimed. He was thus obliged to change his manuscript, in press, to incorporate a new name, *Dinornis* – from the Greek *deinos*, meaning 'prodigious' or 'surprising'.[1] One of his colleagues, Sir John Herschel, immediately protested against Owen's spelling of *Dinornis* on the grounds that 'the French, who never learn Greek and have no notion of what deinos means, will from our spelling pronounce it deenornis'. Owen replied that spelling it Deinornis would simply encourage the English to do the same thing! (Owen 1843a:19, 1843b:8–10; R. S. Owen 1894ɪ:228.)

With the benefit of hindsight it is obvious that

the discovery of moas was not, and hardly could have been, the single event which some of those involved perceived it to have been. Nor, indeed, did the early evidence come exclusively from the East Coast. Dieffenbach in Taranaki in 1839, the Rev. James Watkins (n.d., 28 September 1841) and Edward Shortland (1851:137–9) at Waikouaiti in Otago, from 1841 to 1843, independently embarked along the same course. It was, nonetheless, the East Coast evidence which threaded together the beads of discovery.

Harris may have been the first to secure a moa bone, but it came with a misleading or misunderstood interpretation. Polack reported a remarkably clear and accurate tradition and speculated shrewdly upon the struthious nature of the birds, but produced no bones in evidence. Colenso tested the traditions of contemporary moa survival and, together with Williams – who first wrote of 'moa' – and Taylor, sought the osteological remains upon which an initial sketch of the biological nature of moas could be outlined. Rule claimed credit for the earliest comparative examination of a moa bone, while to Owen, who undertook the first osteological analysis, went the honour of announcement. 'Happy dinornis, whose bones and giant strides will not be unknown to posterity . . .' wrote Buckland to Owen (quoted in Owen 1894: 211), in congratulation.

---

[1] In Owen (1843c) 'deinos' is given as 'prodigious', but in Owen (1849b:235) as 'surprising'. Hutton (1892c:108) suggested 'terrible' which is, in fact, the more common meaning.

3

SYSTEMATICS

At a very early stage in their research on moa bones it became apparent to Williams and Colenso that there were considerable differences in size between specimens representing the same anatomical element. Williams' explanation of this was quite simple; bones of different sizes belonged to birds of different age. Colenso was more cautious about this inference, but accepted it in the absence of a better explanation, and remarked upon the longevity of birds.

In some instances, of course, the missionaries would have been correct in their assumption, but in most cases significant size differences, particularly in mature bird bones, reflect the former membership of the birds in different populations or species. Just how many species or subspecies of moas there were and their interrelationships, however, is a matter still to be satisfactorily resolved after 150 years of periodic investigation.

The literature of moa systematics is extensive and much of it is written in language which the non-specialist is likely to comprehend only with difficulty, but the history of moa classification is important and is therefore reviewed here at some length, because what was assumed about systematics, at any stage, provided the essential support from which contemporary researchers reached towards their understanding of moa evolution, ecological adaptations and behaviour, or the interactions between moas and people.

In picking a way through the taxonomic history of moas I have avoided most of the details of morphological description and mensuration in favour of the broader themes of methods and results. Certain other relevant issues – such as whether any moas possessed wing bones – are also discussed here, but the systematic relationships of moas to other birds are left to the succeeding chapter. It is possible to recognise several broad styles of classification research, but there was great variation in individual approaches, and this is best understood by discussing the subject in terms of such contributions.

Owen: descriptive classification

His brief notes of *Dinornis* in 1839 and 1843 established Owen as the undisputed authority on moas, a position he maintained for nearly 40 years by the publication of 30 papers and, in 1879, a two-volume collection of some of them, *Memoirs on the Extinct Wingless Birds of New Zealand*. Owen's long preeminence ensured for his taxonomic studies – and the methods which produced them – a profound influence upon the future of moa research. It is important, therefore, to understand something of Owen's approach before considering his results.

The theoretical underpinning of Owen's analytical methods was derived largely from the thinking of Lorenz Oken and Geoffrey St Hilaire of the late 18th century 'Naturphilosophie' school of natural history. In explaining the development of vertebrate anatomy they postulated the existence of an archetype which was expressed, if imperfectly, in all vertebrate forms and which remained perceptibly immune from environmental and inheritable influences. The power behind it was, as Owen explained, 'a polarising force pervading all space, and to the operation of which . . . the repetition of parts, the signs of the unity of the organisation may be mainly ascribed'. These somewhat vaguely expressed views were elaborated at length by Owen in language that not even his eminent contemporaries seemed able to fully comprehend;

T. H. Huxley characterising them as 'a series of metaphorical mystifications' (R. S. Owen 1894II: 315–16).

But whatever philosophical meaning Owen took from them the central doctrine of repeated or homologous forms lay at the heart of his osteological methods. This concept carried a powerful predictive capacity for the analysis of fossil collections; missing elements within or between individuals or species could be predicted by appeal to homologies and, indeed, whole skeletal frames could be hypothesised by understanding a single part.[1] Since, in addition, the 'distinctive characters are most strongly developed in the peripheral parts of the body', the lower limb bones were the focus of attention in defining differences between species or in inferring functional characteristics, as Broderip's remark about the tarsometatarsus (above) indicates (Owen 1849b:240).

These principles of osteological practice had been sharply focussed for Owen by three months spent in Paris, in 1831, as an assistant to the brilliant comparative anatomist and palaeontologist, Baron George Cuvier. Owen (in R. S. Owen 1894I:248) later described him as 'the great teacher from whom I received my final instructions . . . in the sciences I have since cultivated'. From Cuvier, Owen also adopted a style of analysis consisting of minutely described observations upon the form of bones – which was laboriously pursued to the substantial exclusion of any other matters except provenance and taxonomy. His devotion to the Cuvierian method was doubtless greatly reinforced by the clear confirmation of his (perhaps Rule's) very first inferences about moas and by the terms in which even his adversaries appraised this success. Thus Gideon Mantell (1848a:225), Vice-President of the Geological Society, wrote that:

if I were required to select from the numerous and important inductions of palaeontology, the one which of all others presents the most striking and triumphant instance of the sagacious application of the principles of the correlation of organic structure enunciated by the illustrious Cuvier – the one that may be regarded as the experimentum crucis of the Cuvierian philosophy – I would unhesitatingly adduce the interpretation of this fragment of bone. I know not among all the marvels which palaeontology has revealed to us, a more brilliant example of successful philosophical induction – the felicitous prediction of genius enlightened by profound scientific knowledge.

Owen's work on moas did not begin in earnest until the second case of bones sent by Williams arrived in 1843. Looking at all his material he began with tarsometatarsi, and assigned the smallest, which was about the size of that in a dodo (then *Didus ineptus*), to a species named, accordingly, *Dinornis didiformis*. The next largest, from his earlier *D. Novae Zealandiae* material, was about the size of the same bone in an ostrich (*Struthio camelus*), and became *Dinornis struthoides*. The largest became *Dinornis giganteus* (Fig. 3.1). Turning to the tibiotarsi, Owen found a small, slender

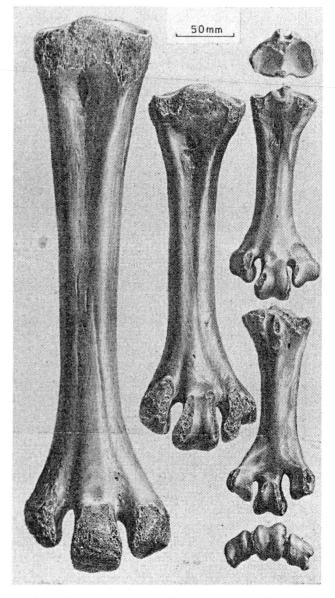

FIG. 3.1   Comparative size of tarsometatarsi: left to right, *Dinornis giganteus*, *Dinornis struthioides*, *Dinornis didiformis* (now *A. didiformis*) (Owen 1879aII:pl. xxvii).

[1] See also Mivart (1893), Woodward (1893).

specimen comparable to that in the Great Bustard (*Otis tarda*) which he could not match with any tarsometatarsus. For it he proposed *Dinornis otidiformis*. Another tibiotarsus, also from *D. Novae Zealandiae*, was too large to fit any tarsometatarsus and was assigned to *Dinornis ingens* (i.e. vast), a specific name he had taken, along with *giganteus*, from the names of giant Triassic birds (Ornithichnites) from North America.

Owen's analysis of the small femora provides a good illustration of his style of argument. Left with three specimens which could not belong to any of the five species already defined, he set out to test the propositions that they were either from immature individuals of *D. struthoides* or the larger sex of *D. didiformis*, the two closest species in size and shape, or were a distinct species again. One femur, he concluded, was an immature example from *D. struthoides*. The other two femora appeared mature but were thinner and had muscular ridges and concavities of different shape or depth than those of *D. struthoides* or *D. didiformis*. Since he knew that sexual differences in the femora of ostriches and kiwis were expressed only in size and not in shape, it followed that his unknown femora could not be sexual variants. This left only the third proposition and, observing that the femora were similar to those in the emu (*Dromaeus* sp.), he created a new species, *Dinornis dromaeoides* (Owen 1843d, 1849b).[2]

Seeking further comparative material Owen then wrote to Colenso appealing to his patriotism, 'for the honour of our country the scientific account of the rarities of our remote colonies should emanate from England. We have too often been indebted to foreigners for such information' (Hill 1914:337). By 1846 he had received a much larger collection of moa bones from Colenso and other sources which included, notably, remains from a coastal swamp site at Waikouaiti in Otago, where a bone deposit had come to light in 1843 (Shortland 1851). From this new material Owen (1846) defined three additional species and a variety. *Dinornis casuarinus* (cf. cassowary, *Casuarius* sp.) had limb bones comparable in length to those of *D. struthoides*, but they were significantly thicker, with broader extremities and more developed surface sculpturing. A second species, *Dinornis crassus* (i.e. fat), had the strongest and most robust bones Owen had yet seen. He characterised it as

representing 'the pachydermal type and proportions in the feathered class' (Owen 1849c:325). The third category – bones intermediate in size between *D. didiformis* and *D. otidiformis*, but thicker than the latter – were assigned to *Dinornis curtus* (i.e. short). Except possibly for *D. crassus*, this species had proportionately shorter tibiotarsi and tarsometatarsi than any other species. Of the total of nine species, Owen observed that the three smallest – *D. didiformis*, *D. curtus* and *D. otidiformis* – were confined to the North Island, and that the most thickset (*D. crassus*) and the most robust specimens of the largest species were found in the South Island. Amongst the latter Owen singled out the bones of *D. ingens* as especially notable and referred them to a variety 'var. *robustus*' (see p.23).

If his resorting to this varietal distinction suggests that Owen's early classification was beginning to creak, then his creation immediately thereafter of a second genus, *Palapteryx*, split it apart. The tortuous history of *Palapteryx* is outlined below.

A large collection of bones sent by Walter Mantell in 1848 enabled Owen (1848) to add a small, thickset moa, *Dinornis geranoides* (i.e. crane-like) to his list, but compelled him to delete one of his first described species.[3] The bones had been collected from Waingongoro in South Taranaki and were mostly, if not entirely, from an archaeological site (p. 98). They included eight tarsometatarsi with very prominent articular surfaces for a hind-toe. Owen saw that these were not from *Dinornis* but resembled, rather, those of a dodo. Because they fitted the tibiotarsi he had assigned to *D. otidiformis* he was obliged to create a new genus, *Aptornis* (a contraction of *Apterygiornis*) *otidiformis*, the extinct 'giant rail' (Owen 1849d:347). Some years later, in 1856, he had to rectify two further early errors in this connection: the tibiotarsus assigned to *D. didiformis* in 1843 and a skull to *D. casuarinus* in 1848 were seen to belong to *Aptornis* as well (Owen 1866b:395).

In 1850 Owen (1862a) distinguished robust examples in the collection of small phalanges from Waikouaiti as belonging to a rhea-like moa, *Dinornis rheides*. Four years later he received some bones from W. E. Cormack, who had recovered them from an archaeological site at Opito, on the Coromandel Coast. Amongst them were remains from a species of about the size of *D. struthoides*, but of

---

[2] *Struthoides* became *struthioides* in 1854, and *dromaeoides* became *dromioides* in 1846. *Struthoides* Owen 1844, was reinstated in 1954 (see notes in Appendix A).

[3] *D. geranoides* was founded in such a confused way that Archey (1927:152) advocated assigning the cranial remains to a new species, *D. expunctus*.

more slender proportions. Owen (1862c) named it, therefore, *Dinornis gracilis*. Two years on, and bones from another archaeological site, Awamoa near Oamaru, were received from Walter Mantell. Included were remains from a very heavily built species which Owen (1862d, e) named *Dinornis elephantopus* (Figs 3.2, 3.3). By 1858 he was becoming aware that there might be a still larger species of moa than any he had described, but it was 1867 before he was able to define it. The bones, which came from Glenmark swamp in Canterbury, were of such a size that Owen (1869b, 1874) was confident in assigning them to a new species, *Dinornis maximus*. Further South Island material, from Kakanui, prompted Owen (1874), with some apologies for adding yet another species, to describe a heavy, medium-sized moa, *Dinornis gravis* (i.e. heavy), in 1872.

Yet this was not the last of Owen's species. In the same paper he perceived within the tarso-metatarsi of *D. maximus* a group of longer and

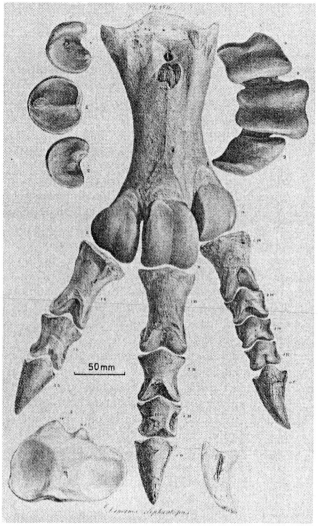

FIG. 3.3   The stout foot bones of *Dinornis* (now *Pachyornis*) *elephantopus* (Owen 1879aII:pl. lvii).

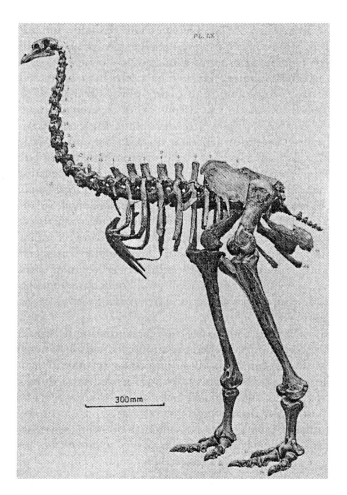

FIG. 3.2   Skeleton of *Dinornis* (now *Pachyornis*) *elephantopus* (Owen 1879aII:pl. lx).

more slender specimens which were referred to *Dinornis altus* (i.e. high or tall) (Owen 1874:376). In 1879, North Island tibiotarsi corresponding to the South Island *D. didiformis* were assigned to *Dinornis Huttonii* (Owen 1879aI:430), and three years later he described two of the smallest moas. The first was a Bustard-sized species with, comparatively, the largest skull of all the moas, *Dinornis parvus* (Owen 1885b), (Fig. 3.4). The second, described from the mummified head, neck and legs of a moa found in a cave near Queenstown, was similar to *D. didiformis* but had a larger hind-toe and was assigned to a similarly named but separate species, *Dinornis didinus* (Owen 1885b) (see Appendix A).

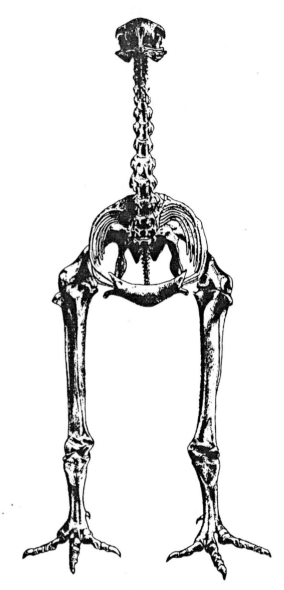

FIG. 3.4   *Dinornis parvus* (Owen 1885a:pl. 51).

A second genus

I turn back now to an issue which generally concerned Owen, and many who followed him: whether the kiwi, New Zealand's other 'struthious' bird, had giant ancestors, or whether there were small moas which in size and other characteristics filled the gap between *Dinornis* and *Apteryx*. In the early stages of research one of the perceived differences lay in the existence of a hind-toe on the kiwi. Therefore, when Owen (1849c:322) found a rough tract above a concave depression on the posterior surface of a *Dinornis ingens* tarsometatarsus in 1846, he recognised the resemblance to the hind-

toe attachment area in the kiwi and tentatively referred *ingens* to a new genus, *Palapteryx* (i.e. ancient kiwi). The Waingongoro material allowed him, several years later, to pursue the matter further, for not only were marks of hind-toe articulation discerned on the bones of other species, but several moa skulls seemed to illustrate a difference as well. The broad, low-domed *Dinornis* cranium bore clear signs of a powerful musculature and had a broad, down-curved beak, while the *Palapteryx* cranium was more like that of the kiwi and bore a sharper, emu-like bill (Owen 1849d: 348). The species *geranoides*, *struthoides*, and *dromioides* were thus added to *ingens* in the genus *Palapteryx*.[4]

Once convinced of the difference, however, Owen found himself doubting the fundamental struthious nature of the remaining *Dinornis* species. In the lack of a fourth toe, the shape of the pelvis and the 'adze-like beak and crocodilian cranium', *Dinornis* resembled the bustards. It was only the shape of the rostral part of the beak which gave him cause to hesitate, in 1848, 'in pronouncing *Dinornis* proper to have been a gigantic form of the Otididae or bustard family'. Even so, while he regarded *Palapteryx* as a struthious form lying somewhere between the kiwis and emu, *Dinornis* appeared 'to have but little immediate affinity to any of the struthious or other known birds in the rest of the world' (Owen 1849d:374–5).

Notwithstanding these views, Owen had returned at least *dromioides* and *struthoides* to *Dinornis* by 1854, and in 1856 declared that he had a strong impression of the generic affinity of the species which he had referred to *Palapteryx* and *Dinornis* (Owen 1862c). The problem was not clearly resolved, and Owen allowed it to dangle for 12 years before dismissing the perceived difference between *Palapteryx* and *Dinornis* skulls as unsupported by later evidence. Resting the generic distinction upon the existence of a hind-toe, however, begged the question of whether osteological evidence of that digit need always exist; an unusual argument for Owen. He thus admitted that 'of late years I have practically dropped "*Palapteryx*" and described additional facts and evidences of these extinct birds under the old generic term of *Dinornis*' (Owen 1872a:119).

But this explanation merely cleared the way for an attempt to restore *Palapteryx* upon different grounds. Observing the broad sterna with flared

---

[4] Owen (1849d:372) regarded his two genera as 'most fully and satisfactorily confirmed'.

lateral processes in the stout-legged species *elephantopus*, *crassus* and *robustus*, he adduced these features as evidence which 'might justify the restitution of the term *Palapteryx*', and he promptly transferred them into that genus (Owen 1872a:119). Yet six months later, in 1869, Owen (1872b:145) was again on the side of a single genus arguing that 'the degree of development of the abortive and functionless back toe, which I cannot regard of generic importance, and the proportions of sternum, limbbones and rostral part of the beak-bones [are] all more or less gradational'. This conclusion stood until the end of 1875 when he again reviewed the morphology of sterna and concluded that those of *elephantopus* and *crassus* were indeed sufficiently different to warrant a generic or subgeneric status for these species. In his uncertainty he returned to the ambiguous forms '*Dinornis (Palapteryx)*' and '*Palapteryx (Dinornis)*' (Owen 1877:173), but by the end of the same year had discarded '*Palapteryx*'. He never used it again, although he recognised that there was a generic distinction to be made, somehow, between tall, slim and short, broad species.

Searching for wings

Another issue which Owen pondered was whether *Dinornis* had wings. Initially he thought wings were lacking because cancellous bone extended along the entire shaft cavity of Rule's femur – an argument for a heavy, marrow-filled bone. But if this disposed of any possibility that moas could fly, which was highly unlikely on other grounds as well, it did not rule out the retention of small, vestigial wings represented by fragile or insignificant bones. Owen noted that forelimb bones were entirely absent from the collections he possessed in 1843, despite there being more bones in the avian fore- than hindlimb. Unsatisfied, however, he turned to an homologous argument based on the degree to which air was admitted to the skeleton of birds. Owen found that in the winged rhea and ostrich air was admitted to the skull, vertebrae, ribs, sternum, coracoids, pelvis and femora. In emu and cassowary, which have much smaller wings, the circulation is less but still reaches the femur. In the kiwi, which has only rudimentary wings, no air reaches beyond the chest cavity. Since there were pneumatic foramina in the vertebrae of moas, but not in the femora, Owen inferred the existence of small moa wings intermediate in size between those of emu and kiwi. As to why he had not received any, he appealed to both their probable size and fragility and the fact that he had also not received larger

thoracic bones such as ribs and sterna (Owen 1849b:261–3).

In 1850 the issue seemed to be settled by an 8 cm long fragment of bone which Owen (1862b:66) identified as the proximal portion of a tiny moa humerus. This had come to him in a collection of bones from Governor George Grey; a fact of some significance, it might be thought, in the light of a letter which Grey had sent to Owen two years earlier describing the moa bones he had lost in a house fire. Amongst them were said to be wing-spurs of moa 'and, I am almost afraid to say it, but bones which we all regarded as the rudimentary wings of the moa, to which the spurs corresponded' (Grey to Owen March 1848, in R. S. Owen 1894II:319). It may have been this suggestion, rather than any compelling osteological facts about a fragment that, as Owen admitted, was similar to a fibula, which was the real basis for his conclusion. In any event, the identification was promptly disregarded, and no other humeri were discovered.

Owen still had some regard for his original hypothesis, however, and he commented on the existence of small air-holes in the femora of *D. struthioides* (new spelling) in 1854 (Owen 1862c:141) and also in a femur of *D. parvus*, reported in 1882 (Owen 1885a:249). But the question had been very largely settled in 1864 by his analysis of scapulo-coracoid remains from *D. robustus*. These showed that there was no glenoid cavity for the attachment of a humerus, so that if any wing had existed it must have been suspended by ligaments. Owen (1866a:356–7) concluded that the scapulo-coracoid arch in the moa was retained solely as a lever for the respiratory muscles.

Taxonomic problems

The continually changing direction of Owen's views on genera, wings and other issues is understandable to the extent that he was a pioneer in the field of moa studies. Without precedents to appeal to he had to make what he could of small samples, often unsystematically collected, which arrived unpredictably over a period of four decades. Yet, if only by the benefit of hindsight, it is evident that many of his difficulties owed as much to deficiencies of method.

In taxonomy the problems extended further than those associated with the generic question, and began earlier. In a move which presaged later quirks of classification, Owen (1849b:244, 247) totally deleted his first species, *D. Novae Zealandiae*, when he found that the original specimens belonged to separate species, which he then named

D. ingens and *D. struthoides*.[5] Soon after began one of the more complicated episodes of Owen's taxonomic career, the development of the species *Dinornis robustus* (Fig. 3.5).

When the Waikouaiti material was examined in 1846, Owen (1849c:320–1, 327) recognised robust varieties of *D. giganteus* and *D. ingens*, the latter of which he named *D. ingens* var. *robustus*. At the same time he transferred his North Island *ingens* to *Palapteryx*, so that when the Waingongoro material was found to disclose robust specimens of *ingens* in 1848 these became *P. ingens* var. *robustus* (Owen 1849d:346, 348). Several years later, however, he removed the varietal name from his South Island material and transferred it to the bones of a different and larger species of moa in the Waikouaiti collection. Here it was raised to specific status and attached to the second genus as *Palapteryx robustus* (Owen 1862a:2). This new *robustus* seems to have come from his earlier *Dinornis giganteus*, because that species was deleted from the South Island list but retained in the North Island for bones less stout than those of *P. robustus* but of comparable length (Owen 1862d:156, 1869b:498). The specific name then followed the changing fortunes of *Palapteryx* and *Dinornis* until finally coming to rest in *Dinornis* in 1874 (Owen 1872a: 119, 1874, 1879aɪ:428).

Owen also exploited his inductive approach by simply shifting his ground when thwarted – as exemplified by his quite different attempts to establish a second genus. He was also vague about how much observed difference in bone characters was taxonomically significant. The usual basis seems to have been a judgement about the degree to which differences in moas matched those in other struthious or cursorial birds (Owen 1874: 361). He took some measurements of course, but they were used merely to illustrate conclusions which had been already derived by inspection and never to make objective the process of size or shape discrimination.

Underwriting these deficiencies in analytical technique was Owen's faith in Cuvier's system. The use of homologous arguments was, and remains, basic to the practice of phylogenetic taxonomy, but Owen carried it to unusual lengths. He seldom hesitated to pronounce upon the most fragmentary evidence and would build a superstructure of predictions upon such speculative conclusions. In the final analysis this was the weakness of his moa

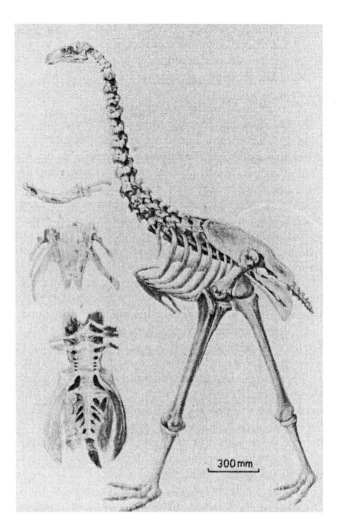

Fig. 3.5 Skeleton of *Dinornis robustus* (now *novaezealandiae*) (Owen 1879aɪɪ:pl. xcvi).

research: belief in the detailed application of the comparative method overrode any readiness to profit from mistakes or informed criticism. By the time he died, in December 1892, respected but not much liked, his ideas about the development of vertebrate anatomy were widely ridiculed and to him was attributed the major part, however unwittingly, in discrediting the Cuvierian method.[6]

Haast: *Palapteryx* again

As early as 1852 Owen's classification of moas had been reorganised into seven genera by the German naturalist Reichenbach.[7] Owen (1862d:152) commented tartly on this effort that it involved 'no

---

[5] *D. ingens* was added between Owen's lecture (1843d) and publication. Rule's femur was assigned to *D. struthoides* (Owen 1849b: 264).

[6] Woodward (1893:130–1), Mivart (1893:20, 23), Sherborn (1893: 18) and editorial comment in *Natural Science*, July 1893.

[7] *Anomalopteryx* and *Emeus* are Reichenbach genera.

other facts or characters being assigned for that multiplication of generic names than those which are to be found in the pages or plates of the Memoirs in the Zoological Transactions'. That meant, of course, only his own papers.

A more substantial contribution was made by the Austrian geologist Julius Haast who, as the newly appointed Director of the Canterbury Museum in 1869, turned his attention to the rich moa-bone deposits in the province. By 1874 he was convinced that *Palapteryx* should stand as a second genus. Of the vital hind-toe or hallux, he wrote, 'I am more convinced than ever that it is of great importance, and that the principal division of our extinct struthious birds has to be based upon this, as I believe, constant character' (Haast 1874:210). Other distinguishing features were the existence or otherwise of a bony scapulo-coracoid, the shape of sternum and beak and a difference which he perceived in the toughness of the bone surface of *Palapteryx* remains compared to those of *Dinornis*.

These differences added up to a more than generic importance, in Haast's view, and he thus created two families, Dinornithidae and Palapterygidae, each with two genera, and between which were distributed 11 species (Appendix A). Dinornithidae contained long-legged, slender, narrow-beaked moas which lacked the hind-toe (Fig. 3.6). Palapterygidae included short-legged, broad, round-beaked moas bearing the hallux. Haast distinguished the genus *Dinornis* from *Meionornis*, largely on the former having a bony scapulo-coracoid structure. This element was a source of some concern to him because, like Owen, he believed it to be an integral part of the respiratory system, and its absence in his other three genera was difficult to explain except by proposing that they had possessed a cartilaginous equivalent. Only such an explanation might also account for the weak development or even absence of coracoid-articulating depressions in the sterna of many of his specimens. The genus *Palapteryx* was distinguished from the other new genus, *Euryapteryx*, by stouter, bowed legs and a broader sternum and pelvis.

Haast's short list of species was not the result of combining Owen's species, but of simply setting aside those for which he had insufficient material to enable the venture of an informed opinion. Relying upon leg bones from South Island collections, and leaving aside cranial evidence, Haast accepted *D. maximus* as the southern equivalent of the North Island *D. giganteus* and said that he could

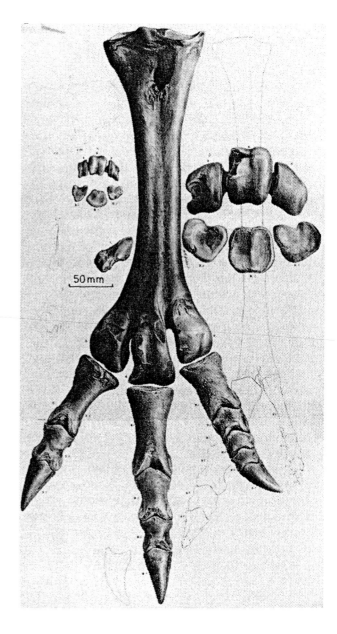

FIG. 3.6   The foot bones of *Dinornis robustus* (now *novaezealandiae*) showing the long tarsometatarsal characteristic of the genus. Left of it are shown the first phalanx of the hind toe (Haast was wrong about this) and, for comparison of size, the articular surfaces of ostrich bones (Owen 1879aII:pl. xlix).

see a gradation of size and robustness in his material which extended to the smaller species once designated *D. giganteus* in the South Island. *Dinornis robustus*, which Owen had regarded as equivalent to the northern *D. giganteus*, was distinctly smaller and more robust than *D. maximus*, and within it Haast saw two size ranges which he attributed to sexual dimorphism, the larger probably representing female birds as amongst kiwis.[8]

Inter-specific gaps in size and two distinct size ranges within each species were also apparent, according to Haast, in *D. ingens*, *D. gracilis* and *D. struthioides*. Four ranges of size in *Meionornis casuarinus* indicated that two sexually dimorphic subspecies were probably included, and the same was apparent in *M. didiformis* and *P. elephantopus*. In each of the three remaining species two ranges of size were evident.

Owen was less than enthusiastic about Haast's classification. The two men had been in sufficiently close communication by 1874 to be reaching similar conclusions in other matters, and Owen's paper of 1872 had, of course, specifically suggested a generic distinction between tall, slim *Dinornis* species and short, broad *Palapteryx* species in which the presence or absence of the hallux was a vital distinction. The difficulty for Owen, however, was that he had already concluded that the existence of this feature was not reliably indicated by osteological evidence. When he came to comment on Haast's scheme, therefore, Owen (1874: 377, 1877:174) was prepared to entertain *Palapteryx* as a genus based upon the robustness of the limb bones and flaring sternal processes, but not the family Palapterygidae based upon the hallux. Owen was sceptical about Haast's remaining genera, but neither his nor Hutton's urgings could prompt Haast to publish the measurements on which the classification was allegedly based. Hutton's (1875:276, 1892c:102) later analysis of Haast's material disclosed little support for it.

In 1885 Haast described a new species of small moa, *Dinornis oweni*, from a nearly complete skeleton found in a cave in the Pataua Valley near Whangarei. The skull was virtually identical to one which Owen had wrongly assigned to *D. dromioides*, a species of twice the size. The new species had the flat cranial profile and evidence of a powerful jaw musculature characteristic of *Dinornis* and it appeared closely allied to Owen's *D. curtus*, although it was a smaller and comparatively more gracile form than the latter (Haast 1890a).

In the same year Haast proclaimed that he had, at last, found a giant fossil kiwi. A set of bones in the Nelson Museum's moa bone collection so convinced him that, without reference to kiwi bones, he immediately named them *Megalapteryx hectori*

(Haast 1884:557). A later and more considered analysis raised some questions. For example, on the anterior surface of the tarsometatarsus there was a foramen in the groove between the inner and central condyles which was typical of *Apteryx* but absent in all the moas. The perforation passed, however, through only a thin flange and not the whole bone wall. Similarly the tibiotarsus, and especially the femur, also exhibited apterygian characteristics which were not beyond question. It was difficult for Haast to be certain whether some of the features were simply those of *Dinornis* rendered morphologically similar to those on kiwi bones by a high degree of gracility or whether a true affinity was in evidence. Nevertheless Haast (1890b) concluded that *Megalapteryx*, if not a direct ancestor of kiwis as he had first argued, at least came much closer to *Apteryx* than it did to *Dinornis*.

Hutton: division by size

Haast's classification was fairly widely accepted abroad despite its inadequacies having been promptly exposed by Frederick Hutton, Director of the Otago Museum. Hutton argued that there was not sufficient variation in moas, compared to other struthious birds, to warrant a separation at the family level, and he dismissed the presence or absence of either hind-toes or the scapulo-coracoid structure as having any taxonomic significance. Moreover he had specimens of *Dinornis* in his museum collection (including *D. ingens*, *D. casuarinus* and *D. gravis*) which exhibited evidence of the hallux, and had not Owen, in any case, shown the existence of a hind-toe on *D. robustus* more than 20 years before? As to an alleged family difference in bill shape, Hutton pointed out that although *D. robustus* had a blunt bill, *D. elephantopus*, which Haast assigned to the broad-beaked Palapterygidae, actually had a narrow bill. In fact, if the shape of the beak was critical to classification, then Haast's *P. elephantopus*, *E. rheides* and *M. didiformis* would have to go together in one group and *P. crassus*, *M. casuarinus* and *E. gravis* in another. Point by point, Hutton (1877) demolished Haast's scheme and concluded, as had Owen, that one genus was sufficient for all of the moas.

It is therefore somewhat ironical that when Hutton had moved to the Canterbury Museum he proposed a classification which contained seven genera, two subgenera and 26 species (Appendix A). In Hutton's scheme the genera were based

---

[8] Owen (1869b) transferred the varietal name from *D. giganteus* var. *maximus* to *D. maximus* in 1867.

upon three cranial measurements and other characters with which the shape of sterna and pelves were said to generally agree (Hutton 1892c:100, 106). The essential aspects of skull shape which Hutton relied on were the elevation of the cranium, the visibility from top and side of the occipital condyle and the shape and strength of the beak. His genera were arranged in a broadly regular gradation from the flat *Dinornis* cranium to the moderately depressed *Palapteryx* and very elevated *Anomalopteryx* crania; all the others were variously convex in elevation. Beak shape varied from the very long, strongly curved and obtusely tipped *Dinornis* form, to a shorter, more compressed, and slightly curved *Palapteryx* form, to the short, round-tipped and straight beak of *Anomalopteryx*. There were permutations in these characters amongst the remaining genera, with the shortest, but round-tipped beaks being found amongst *Euryapteryx* species (Hutton 1892c:118, 120–35).

In distinguishing species, Hutton followed his predecessors in concentrating upon leg bones, but he bluntly rejected all morphological differences as a means of discrimination. Size was the essential criterion. He argued that those few common differences of shape which he noticed, such as variations in the distal breadth of tarsometatarsi or in the shaft curvature of tibiotarsi, were continuous, and thus probably referrable to factors such as age rather than any species difference (Hutton 1892c: 101).

The leg bone measurements from 16 species were used to map out a framework within which dimensions for the bones of other species, or of missing elements from the original set, were interpolated. There remained, however, 'much conjecture in placing the other bones of the skeleton with the legs' (Hutton 1892c:94). Hutton was concerned at the number of species that he ended up with and at the way many graded imperceptibly, by size, into others, but he took the view that it was better to accept later coalescence as the price of first expressing the great variety of size exhibited by the moas as a whole.

Hutton (1875:276) found no evidence of sexual dimorphism and observed that in some of Haast's examples the proposed sexes were synonymous with species which had been geographically separated by the length of the South Island, or even by Cook Strait. Of other contentious features, Hutton (1892c:105) found evidence of scapulo-coracoid bones in three genera and of a glenoid cavity in one, *Palapteryx*, to which he attributed a probability of wings.[9]

Hutton, Lydekker and Forbes

The classification section of Hutton's paper was presented to the Philosophical Institute of Canterbury in October 1891, about the same time as Richard Lydekker's (1891) catalogue of the fossil bird remains in the British Museum of Natural History reached New Zealand. Hutton's former colleague at Canterbury Museum, Henry Forbes (1893a:378), actually accused him of having already seen Lydekker's work and, by ignoring its differences in classification, of 'adding to the already hopelessly involved synonymy of Dinornithidae'. In a public exchange of letters which followed it became clear that Hutton had not seen Lydekker's catalogue until after reading his own paper but had, nonetheless, made no attempt to resolve the differences by altering the proofs of his paper before publication (Forbes 1893b:318; Hutton 1893c:317).

Lydekker's classification of moas was based largely upon material examined by Owen. In it he corrected several of Owen's errors. It was not as different from Hutton's classification as it first appeared (Appendix A). Lydekker thought Hutton admitted too many species to *Dinornis* and ought to have added *Megalapteryx*, but they agreed that Lydekker's lumping of species under *Anomalopteryx*, with the suggestion of a 'Celine' subgroup, did not radically disagree with Hutton's distribution of those species amongst *Anomalopteryx*, *Cela*, *Mesopteryx* and *Palapteryx*. The main point of difference concerned the species *elephantopus*. Lydekker followed Owen in taking a sharp-billed skull as the type and assigned it to *Pachyornis*, but Hutton argued, contrary to his position in 1876, that comparative material in the Otago Museum showed Owen's *elephantopus* skull actually belonged to *crassus* of *Syornis* (or *Emeus*). That left only the unresolved question of whether the two broad-billed species, *gravis* and, now, *elephantopus*, could be accommodated within *Euryapteryx*. Lydekker (1892:594) thought not, but he was prepared to consider changing his classification on both issues to meet Hutton's views.

At least part of the difference between these two contemporary and independent classifications can be attributed to the use of quite different samples:

[9] The scapulo-coracoid with apparent glenoid cavity was from Te Aute swamp. Forbes (1892b) figured a similar specimen, from *D. maximus*, found at Enfield. Hutton (1896a:632) dismissed these claims, remarking that 'several [scapulo-coracoids] have a depression on the inner side at the anchylosis of the two bones which might perhaps lead to a mistake'.

Lydekker mainly used the older Earl and Mantell collections, while Hutton used the new material from Shag Mouth, Te Aute, Glenmark and Hamiltons. But there were also differences of approach because Lydekker, unlike Hutton, followed Owen in a meticulous examination of osteological topography, apparently supplemented by few measurements. He also sought evidence of sexual dimorphism and held that much of his material varied on that ground.[10] As Hutton (1897b:541) later explained, another difference lay in Lydekker's conforming to the rule of priority in choosing the first described bone for each species, whereas Hutton took tarsometatarsi as the types in each case. He later changed to the conventional approach.

Yet, in their broader conclusions about the classifying of moa, they were as one. Hutton (1892c:101) wrote that 'so far as the leg bones are concerned, my examination has shown that several of the species pass gradually into one another, so that any line separating them must be an arbitrary one; and I should not be surprised if further knowledge showed that this applies to those species which at present appear to be distinctly marked off'. Lydekker (1891:221) discerned complete size transitions in the femora from Emeus, across four species of Anomalopteryx and amongst all of his Dinornis species, and suggested that 'some members of the various species, if not of the genera, may have occasionally interbred'.

Despite this, Hutton (1893b:7) developed a progressively self-reinforcing mode of species splitting; 'bones, which I formerly regarded as being merely varieties of one species, belong really to different genera; and the more I study the bones the more I see the necessity of limiting the amount of variation allowed to each species'. He justified this approach by arguing that moas, living in a favourable environment and unchecked by predators, were able to radiate into an extraordinarily wide range of morphological variation, and that to study the variation it was essential that species should be narrowly defined. This came close to being a self-fulfilling prophecy, because increasingly fine discrimination continually expanded the pool of variation from which new species were drawn.

Nevertheless Hutton saw more clearly than his contemporaries the full extent of the taxonomic difficulty which extensive size gradation presented. For any element there was inter-specific and inter-generic gradation in each collection. There was also gradation amongst distantly located but contemporary collections (Hutton 1892c, 1896a), and gradation in the same stock between collections distant in time (Hutton 1896b:645). Compounded by unsystematic collecting, and perhaps by sexual dimorphism, the problem of sorting out these sources of variation and of imposing on them a classification which reflected the relationships of moas in a biologically valid way was, Hutton (1893b:8) judged, almost hopeless.

In the case of his own attempt his pessimism proved well founded, as Forbes showed in a devastatingly precise dissection of Hutton's measurements. Nearly all the skull, pelvic and long-bone ratios for the subgenera Dinornis and Tylopteryx overlapped; some also overlapped with Palapteryx, Anomalopteryx measurements with Palapteryx, and so on, to the extent that it was evident 'that these ratios are valueless for differentiating the various bones into their proper genera by measurement alone' (Forbes 1893a:375–6). There were similar inconsistencies in Hutton's criteria for defining species. For instance, the long bones of D. ingens and D. firmus differed only in length, by about 13 mm, whereas bones differing in length by 38 mm, and in breadth by 30 mm, were included in the same species, D. validus.

Hutton's later classifications largely represent attempts to accommodate these and other criticisms from Lydekker and Forbes. In 1892 he introduced Pachyornis, and deleted Syornis in favour of Emeus (Hutton 1893b:7); and in 1894 he abandoned Palapteryx and both subgenera of Dinornis. He also brought Megalapteryx into Dinornithidae as Lydekker had done (Hutton 1895b:157–8). Soon after, on the grounds of priority of nomenclature, Emeus was amalgamated with Euryapteryx, Cela was dropped (but later tentatively replaced) and Mesopteryx and Anomalopteryx were changed to Meionornis and Anomalornis respectively (Hutton 1897b) (see Appendix A).

There had also been an important addition to Hutton's methods of discerning species. A large collection of bones from a single source, the Kapua swamp in south Canterbury, enabled him to adopt a 'method of averages' instead of relying upon identification by comparing specimens with a single, supposedly typical, skeleton. The basic assumption of the new method was that by examining large numbers of bones from a single genus one could identify which forms or sizes really were

---

[10] Lydekker (1891:224) has D. ingens Owen as male, and D. giganteus Owen as female, of D. novae-zealandiae; he also thought that the original and possibly smaller D. robustus Owen was the male of D. maximus Owen.

typical, and the range of variation about these. One result of the application of this technique was the reduction to varietal status, at best, of *Dinornis validus, potens* and *strenuus, Palapteryx plena, Euryapteryx compacta* and *Pachyornis valgus* (Hutton 1896a:630).

Parker: the importance of crania

Hutton's emphasis on moa skulls as the source of generic distinctions inspired one of the most important of the 19th century taxonomies. Jeffrey Parker, Professor of Biology at the University of Otago, greatly expanded Hutton's quantification of skull dimensions and concentrated upon this single element instead of attempting to derive taxonomic evidence from a number of bones which might not have come from the same species. It would be fair to say that this was an idea whose time had come. There was greater confidence in earlier identifications of crania as a result of corrections undertaken by Lydekker and others, and there was much more material available from the major swamp and cave deposits than there had been in the time of Owen, or even Haast. Just as important were the almost complete, single skel-

etons on which many questions of identification could be tested.

Parker examined some 200 skulls and found about 30 suitable for measurement. Wherever possible he took 29 chordal dimensions to the nearest mm. Of these he (1895:406–8) used 15 principal measurements in defining the relative shape of moa skulls (Fig. 3.7).

In order to compare shape free from the complication of size differences, Parker standardised his principal measurements against a unit length of the basis cranii. I have combined and plotted some of his results (Fig. 3.8). The three cranial width measurements (at paroccipital and squamosal protuberances and between the temporal fossae) have been reduced to single means and plotted against the length of the cranial roof. The length of the mandibular ramus against the width at the symphysis is also shown for each species.[11]

The values for the two species of *Dinornis* indicate a broad and comparatively short cranium to which was attached a long and moderately broad mandible (Fig. 3.9). At the other end of the scale are the two species of *Emeus*, which have narrow crania and short, comparatively broad, mandibles. In between are the remaining genera which have moderately broad crania and moderately long but narrow mandibles. Comparison with some of the modern ratites shows that moas had skulls significantly shorter and more variable in width, with much shorter mandibles.

Parker's additional evidence generally strengthened this tripartite division of moa skulls, particularly in distinguishing *Dinornis* and *Emeus* from each other and, less clearly, from the rest. Thus only *Emeus* had a flattened, plate-like maxillopalatine bone, a very strongly built jaw and a cylindrical nasal process. On the other hand, *Dinornis* had a thin nasal process, weak mandibular rami and a very strong downward deflection to the mandible (35–45 mm from horizontal as against 10–15 mm in the other genera – except *Anomalopteryx*, where it is almost straight).

On these and other criteria Parker (1895:414–15) came to the following important conclusions:

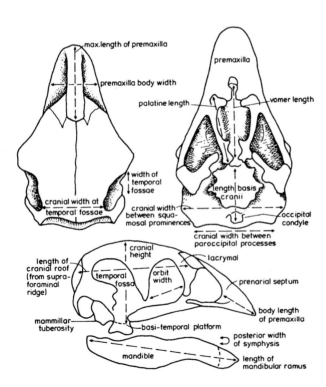

FIG. 3.7 The 15 principal dimensions of ratite skulls measured by Parker (1895:table B).

[11] Data from Parker (1895:table B). I added each end of the range and took a single mean. Small sample sizes and ranges render insignificant errors arising from differences of variance. Of other principal dimensions, cranial height ranges were all encompassed by a 15 mm range; premaxilla body dimensions were less variable than those of mandibles; lengths of vomer and palatines were seldom measured; there was no apparent pattern in orbital widths; and temporal fossae widths of *Mesopteryx* and *Emeus* were smaller than in other genera.

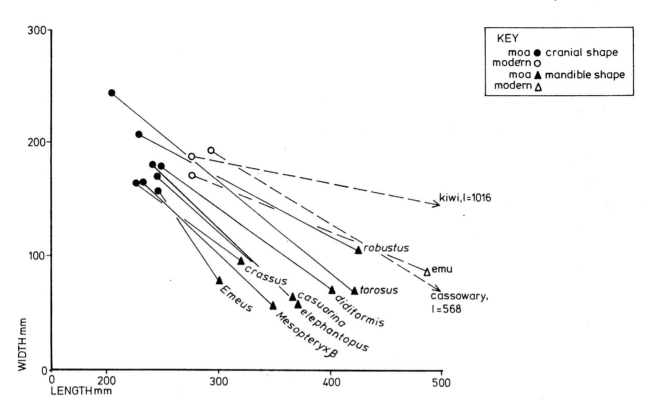

FIG. 3.8 Cranial and mandible shape in selected moas and modern ratites. Data from Parker (1895:tables A and B).

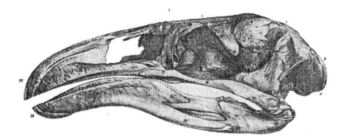

The tall, comparatively slender limbed forms, with broad skull and long, wide, deflected beak constitute a very natural and highly specialised group . . . which includes all the species placed . . . in the genus *Dinornis* . . . A second highly specialised or culminating group is constituted by heavy-limbed forms with strongly-built narrow skull, short broad beak and stout mandible [the *Emeus* group] . . . The remaining species together form a comparatively generalised group including forms of small or moderate height and of varying bulk, having narrow skulls and pointed beaks.

In the latter assemblage Parker made three subdivisions: an *elephantopus* group with the larger and broader crania of the three, large temporal fossae and a wide V-shaped mandible; a *casuarina* group which had similar but smaller features; and a *didiformis* group characterised by an unusually straight beak and immense temporal fossae.

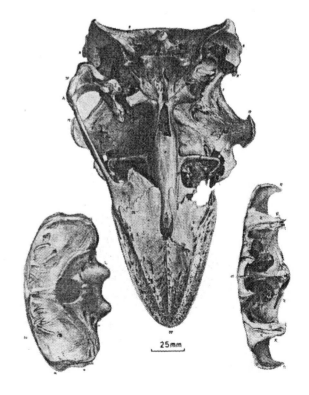

FIG. 3.9 The broad flat cranium and elongated beak of *Dinornis robustus* (now *novaezealandiae*) (Owen 1879a II:pl. lxiv, left; pl. lxv, above).

Turning to the kind of classification which these various divisions might represent, Parker saw little to choose between a scheme of three genera, one with three subgenera and his eventual choice of three subfamilies, one including three genera. The full classification is shown in Appendix A and Parker's (1895) two-dimensional model of ratite relationships in Fig. 3.10.

Parker's innovative analysis – which Oliver (1949:55) later described as the foundation of the modern classification of moas – brought to an end an unusually productive period of methodological experimentation in moa systematics. The compiling of different classifications, however, rolled steadily on. In 1900, Forbes (1900) came close to the lumping end of the road with a scheme of six monotypic genera. Seven years later, Rothschild (1907:xxiii) objected to the severity of this scheme and also called Forbes' (1892a) notice of his new

genus *Palaeocasuarius* 'a most pitiful and unscientific proceeding'. But Rothschild allowed none of his criticism to get in the way of adding Forbes' new types to what still stands as the longest classification at seven genera and 37 species.

Archey: difficulties of measurement

Thirty-five years after the publication of Parker's work, Walter Oliver (1930:28–54) tackled the same problem of generic and familial classification and managed to reduce Parker's three groups to two: the families Dinornithidae and Anomalopterygidae. This bipartite division, although flawed by a number of errors at the generic level – notably the assigning of *elephantopus* to *Euryapteryx* – nevertheless emphasised more clearly the considerable difference between dinornithids and all other moas (Appendix A).

In his monograph, Archey (1941) adopted Oliver's basic scheme but revised it to include two subfamilies of Anomalopterygidae and the genus *Pachyornis*. His research relied largely on the skull and leg bones. For the first, which provided the main evidence of generic differences, Archey was able to use a much-improved sample of beaks associated with crania, and skulls clearly associated with particular post-cranial skeletons. The new evidence came from his own collecting, particularly in caves in the Waikato and East Coast hill country and from contemporary excavations in the natural site at Pyramid Valley swamp, north Canterbury, where for the first time there had been recovered associated and almost-complete skeletons of the important and troublesome species *Pachyornis elephantopus* and *Emeus crassus*. Archey was now able to summarise the beak forms of the difficult stout-bodied genera as follows: *Pachyornis* had a sharp-pointed bill similar to but shorter and broader than that of *Anomalopteryx*; *Emeus* had a narrow bill moderately rounded at the tip, instead of pointed as Oliver had thought; and *Euryapteryx* had a broad, obtusely pointed bill (1941:9–10), (Figs. 3.11 and 3.12).

It was an analysis of leg bones, however, which provided Archey's main platform for classification. He recognised that there was a very difficult problem because 'many leg bones, taken by themselves, cannot be identified by their size or proportions as being of this or that species or genus, and sometimes even a careful study of their form will not help us' (1941:10). In ample illustration of the difficulties Archey undertook a detailed study of the leg bones from 43 individuals of *Anomalopteryx*

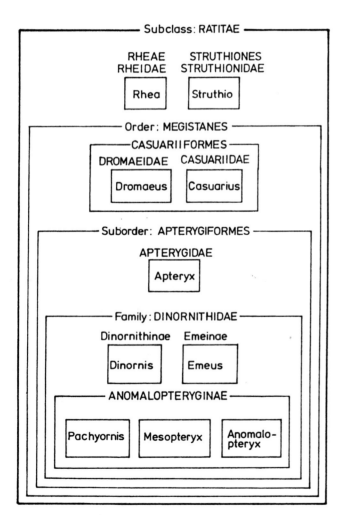

FIG. 3.10 Classification of ratites according to Parker (1895:426).

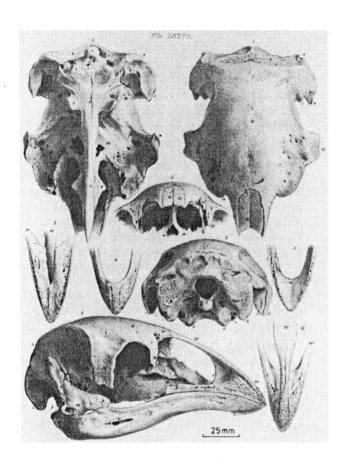

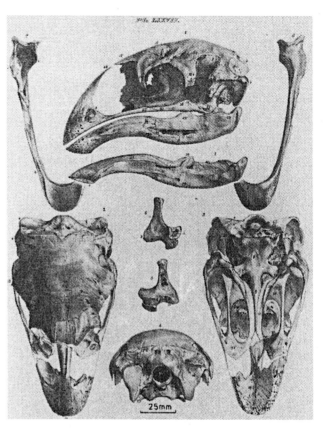

Fig. 3.11 Narrow-beaked skull of *Dinornis* (now *Pachyornis*) *elephantopus* (Owen 1879aII:pl. lxxvi).

Fig. 3.12 Broad-beaked skull of *Dinornis crassus* (Owen 1879a II:pl. lxxvii). Oliver (1949:108) assigned this to *Euryapteryx gravis*.

didiformis. He measured length, proximal and distal width and mid-point width and circumference. The results showed that there was considerable variation in each dimension. In length, for instance, the range of variation was 32 per cent of the mean in the femur, and it was scarcely less in the other two bones. Furthermore 'among individuals which, for instance, may have been grouped for their possession of a long tibia, some will be found to have the femur and metatarsus correspondingly long; in others both these bones will be relatively short; or the femur may be long and the metatarsus short, or vice versa' (1941:16). A table of measurements for any one bone, or dimension, was thus quite unreliable as a means of identifying species or genera. Archey also found that size variation in leg bones, skulls and pelves of this test-case species provided no evidence of particular groupings by sex or locality.

Faced with such unencouraging results, Archey sought an alternative measure of classification in the relative lengths of the main leg bones. The variation proved more or less consistent amongst

the genera, but was particularly marked at the familial level where Dinornithidae stood out in possessing a tarsometatarsus well over half the length of the tibiotarsus and a covariantly long femur. Throughout the Anomalopterygids the tarsometatarsus barely approached half the length of the tibiotarsus – often significantly less – and the femur was also correspondingly short.

As well as these differences, Archey found that Dinornithidae had single neural spines on the nape vertebrae, laterally compressed vertebrarterial canals, a scapulo-coracoid, distinct coracoid facets on the sternum and a broad, flattened skull. Anomalopterygidae, on the other hand, had bifid neural spines on the nape vertebrae, reduced or absent scapulo-coracoids and articular facets, uncompressed vertebrarterial canals and higher, rounded skulls.

Between the subfamilies, the existence of five phalanges to the outer toe in Anomalopteryginae (and also in Dinornithidae) set it apart from Emeinae. Other distinguishing characteristics were the short, broad sterna of the former, compared to the narrow sterna of the latter, sharp-pointed in contrast to round-tipped beaks, and an expanded, as against reduced, maxillary antrum (a cavity in the upper jaw), respectively.

The generic distinctions in Anomalopterygidae were founded on a variety of criteria such as the size of the temporal fossa, but the main differences concerned variations in stoutness which were, *inter alia*, expressed in somewhat different relative leg-bone lengths. Archey argued for a parallel development of shorter and stouter leg bones in each subfamily, with *Emeus* and *Anomalopteryx* only moderately different in this respect, but *Euryapteryx* and *Pachyornis* diverging from them in increased body breadth and massiveness of legs (1941:76–8).

In separating species, size of leg bones remained the essential criterion – unsatisfactory as it generally was; Archey (1941:12) observing that variation in leg-bone length in *Euryapteryx* and *Pachyornis* in North Island collections reached as high as 38 per cent and 40 per cent of the minimum length respectively. It was only the evidence of size clusters, albeit with perilously small gaps between them, which enabled him to define species ranges at all. Archey (1941:79) however remained suitably cautious, remarking that 'both the even and continuous gradation in size and proportionate thickness in a series of any one bone remarked by earlier workers, and the promiscuous and haphazard association of large and small bones in individual skeletons from the same locality recorded in this paper, make it difficult to define limits between many of the species that have been proposed' (Appendix A).

Some of the intraspecific variation was, Archey thought, probably due to sexual dimorphism, but he saw no means of isolating it. Geographic variation was evident however, despite his experience with *A. didiformis*. Archey recognised the long-standing inter-island species-pairs of *Dinornis* (*novae-zealandiae–torosus, ingens–robustus* and *giganteus–maximus*). Similarly he observed a marked difference in robustness between northern and southern species of *Euryapteryx* and *Pachyornis*. These differences he attributed not to the formation of Cook Strait, which was a comparatively late event, but rather to the earlier existence of the diagonal mountain barrier of the Main Divide through which the more gracile moas (*Dinornis, Anomalopteryx, Megalapteryx*, small species of *Pachyornis*, etc.) could pass, but which effectively maintained the stouter species to the south and east (1941:80).

Oliver: a duty to split

In 1949 Oliver published his second and more comprehensive analysis of moa remains. He retained the classification scheme devised earlier by himself, and revised by Archey, but made a number of changes to genera and species:

I have transferred *Pachyornis* from Anomalopteryginae to Emeinae and proposed a new genus *Zelornis* in the latter subfamily to take *haasti* and *exilis*. I have suppressed *Pachyornis pygmaeus* as a mixture and have transferred part of Archey's *P. oweni* to *Anomalopteryx* and the remainder to a new species of *Pachyornis*. Two other new species of *Pachyornis* are described. Archey's *Euryapteryx exilis* is in my scheme divided between *Zelornis exilis* and a new species of *Euryapteryx*. In *Anomalopteryx* I have restored *parvus* to specific rank and reinstated *oweni*. In *Dinornis* I have defined two new species (Oliver 1949:56) (see Appendix A).

The changes clearly reflected Oliver's penchant for splitting taxa. This began, at the generic level, with his observation that the preorbital plate (below) of *Pachyornis* (*Pachyornis*) *australis* exhibited a relatively primitive condition; the lacrymal and antorbital bones were not properly fused (1949:59). *Pachyornis* was therefore removed to Emeinae, a less developed subfamily in Oliver's view, but the variability of this enduringly difficult genus also prompted him to create three subgenera. These were distinguished by certain differences in the sternum (the angle between the front flange and the body), the ilia, the width of the postorbital processes and the shape of the culmen or medial ridge along the top of the beak. In his new species of *Pachyornis*, *P.* (*M.*) *septentrionalis* took the more gracile individuals of Archey's *P. mappini* and some of his *P. oweni*; *P.* (*P.*) *murihiku* was defined by a more markedly 'roman nose' shape in the upper beak than in any other species, while *P.* (*P.*) *australis*, in addition to the characteristics of its preorbital plate, had a comparatively broad cranium reducing sharply forward into a shorter and more pointed beak than in *P.* (*P.*) *elephantopus* (1949:61–80).

The new genus *Zelornis* was carved out of *Euryapteryx* largely on the basis of a broad, blunt-tipped premaxilla with a high, arched culmen, although the premaxilla in the latter genus is not especially dissimilar. *Euryapteryx tane* was a larger form of *Eu. curtus*, and the two *Dinornis* species, *gazella* and *hercules*, were defined as that part of the *novaezealandiae* and *giganteus* ranges, respectively, which exhibited shorter leg bones and greater curvature to the tibiotarsi (1949:105, 117–21, 164).

Oliver employed a wide range of criteria in defining taxa, including morphological features and simple numerical data. He rejected the number of phalanges in the outer toe as being anything other than a spasmodic characteristic of little taxonomic importance, and he did not emphasise the leg-bone proportions to the same extent as Archey, nor revive his own method from 1930 which stressed the proportionate widths of leg bones. Instead, sternal and pelvic characters were used to define genera and subfamilies, while untransformed length and breadth leg-bone data defined species. Often, however, the differences proved so subtle that he turned to beak and cranial characters to sort them out (1949:52–4). For the families he concentrated upon the skull, and in particular upon the shape and relative geometry of the preorbital plate (1949:33–5).

This structure, which arises out of the basisphenoidal rostrum, a keel in the palate, extends upwards and outwards to form a partition between the orbit and the nasal chamber. Amongst the various potentially diagnostic features of it, Oliver relied mainly upon the shape of the basisphenoidal rostrum and its triangular processes, the angle between the rostrum and the plate and the shape of the lacrymal and antorbital bones along with their alignment and vertical displacement relative to each other. In Fig. 3.13 are shown two examples of this structure in palatal and side view. The *Anomalopteryx* preorbital plate is fairly representative of all genera except *Dinornis*. It arises from the rostrum (strictly speaking from the intervening inferior aliethmoid bone) at an angle of about 45 degrees and diverges in a straight line. The lacrymal is produced to below the lower border of the antorbital and it ends in a hook-like process. Divergence angles of 30–60 degrees for the preorbital plate characterise all other Anomalopterygid genera, and all except *Pachyornis* exhibit a lacrymal hook and a tendency for the lacrymal to extend below the antorbital. The lacrymal and antorbital are also broadly in alignment, and the preorbital plate tends to be slightly bowed.

In Dinornithidae, however, the preorbital plate diverges at 90 degrees on a strong transverse bar, which then takes a sharp turn forward. The plate is comparatively narrow, and the lower antorbital border is at or slightly below the distal end of the lacrymal. There is no lacrymal hook, and the antorbital and lacrymal bones are set at right-angles to each other.[12]

[12] His confidence in the preorbital plate was, however, incomplete (Oliver 1949:118–21).

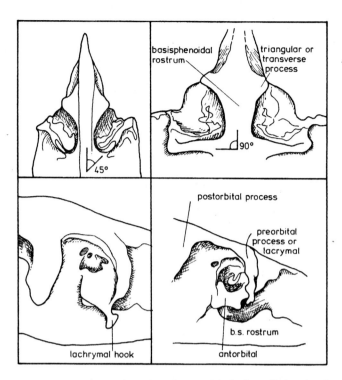

FIG. 3.13 Palate (above) and preorbital plate (below) of *Anomalopteryx didiformis* (left) and *Dinornis novaezealandiae* (right), after Oliver (1949:132, 133, 165).

Oliver's discrimination of species depended, as it had for so many others, upon variations in leg-bone size. His method, recently described by John Yaldwyn (1979), was the latest manifestation of the LPMD system which had originated in New Zealand with Haast 80 years earlier. The measurements, taken on each bone, were: maximum length (L), and proximal (P), mid-shaft (M) and distal (D) widths. In unpublished data he also took other measurements, including of depth (i.e. antero-posterior dimensions). Since Archey, earlier, and Ron Scarlett, later, had used essentially the same method and equipment, Yaldwyn (1979:19–22) tested its consistency by asking Scarlett to re-measure several of Oliver's samples. He found that there were only small variations of 1–2 mm (about 0.3–1.0 per cent depending on the dimension) in the results.

However even small errors and other minor sources of variation such as shrinkage, which Scarlett estimated as up to 3–4 mm in *Dinornis* tibiotarsal lengths for specimens taken from swamps, could assume some significance in Oliver's classificatory work because of the extremely small size differences in his species ranges. In Fig. 3.14 are plotted the tibiotarsal lengths for

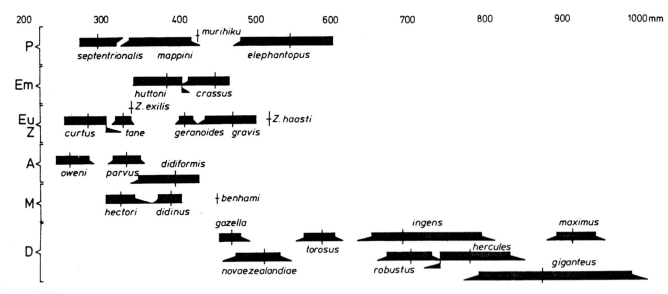

FIG. 3.14 Tibiotarsal length range of Oliver's (1949) species.

Oliver's species showing for each one the mean and range and, added as a spike at one or both ends, the mean difference between individual measurements. This latter is important because in most cases the sample size was very small (for 22 of his species $n = < 10$) and it is apparent that the addition of each new specimen had a significant effect on the range of variation. As the figure indicates, adding one new specimen in almost any case would thus almost or actually close the gap between it and its nearest neighbour. The figure also clearly illustrates the continuous overlap throughout the moas of any one dimension in any particular leg bone.

Oliver was much less worried by these problems than Archey had been. Indeed he argued that it was positively the duty of the systematist to chop continuous series into units and give those units specific names because it was probable that we would find, had we knowledge of the external characters, an even greater number of biological species (Oliver 1949:164). His emphasis upon speciation as the source of variance was accompanied, logically enough, by a general disregard for sexual dimorphism or intraspecific geographical variation. This argument flowed from his philosophical adherence to an orthogenetic position upon evolutionary processes (see Chapter 4).

Scarlett and Cracraft: means to lump

The classificatory schemes of Archey and Oliver, and their methods, prevailed up until the last decade, supported in their essentials by Charles Fleming, Robert Falla and Ron Scarlett – although Scarlett gradually deviated from Oliver's conclusions. In 1957 he (Scarlett 1957:17) noted the existence of a small species of *Euryapteryx* in material from Stewart Island, and later found remains of it in other collections from southern New Zealand. Scarlett (1968) also extended the range of *Pachyornis elephantopus* to the North Island with discoveries from Waipukurau and North Taranaki. In 1972 (Scarlett 1972) he published a full classification (Appendix A).

Scarlett relied only partly upon measurements of leg bones for identifying species. He used Archey's and Oliver's data and his own measurements on material from Pyramid Valley swamp, Wairau Bar and the Catlins sites, in particular. But:

measurement, alone, is unreliable, as the legs of different species can be of similar size. With broken bones the task is even more difficult. I have found that the blood-vessel markings on tibio-tarsi are a considerable help, when visible, in distinguishing fragmentary material, as although they vary somewhat between individuals, there is a constant pattern for each genus (Scarlett 1972:20).

Only Scarlett seems to have used these markings in a classificatory way, but he has not yet published any details of the technique.

The main points to notice about this classification apart from additional, and as yet undescribed, species of *Dinornis* and *Euryapteryx*, are the synonymising of Oliver's *Zelornis* with *Euryapteryx*, *E. huttoni* with *E. crassus* and the reappearance of Hutton's *P. pygmaeus* and *A. antiquus*. It must be said, however, that Scarlett expressed considerable doubt about whether a number of the species could stand much longer. *Dinornis hercules*, he thought, might be simply a bow-legged variant of *D. giganteus*; *P. mappini* and *P. septentrionalis* might eventually be united, so also *P. australis* and *P. elephantopus*, because in both cases there appeared to be only minor size-range differences; *Eu. haasti* could be a subspecies of *Eu. gravis*; and *A. antiquus* was, he thought, doubtfully distinct from *A. didiformis* (Scarlett 1972:20–2).

Scarlett was well on the way to arranging a classification which would probably have contained seven species of *Dinornis*, three of *Pachyornis* (of which there would be only *P. elephantopus* in the South Island), three or four species of *Euryapteryx*, one of *Emeus*, one or two of *Megalapteryx* and two of *Anomalopteryx*; that is to say, perhaps only 17 species overall, and only ten of these in the five non-*Dinornis* genera.

Scarlett's drift towards greater lumping since the time of Forbes was overtaken by events. The number of moa species which the 1970 checklist (Kinsky 1970:77) had brought down to 24 from Oliver's 28, and which Scarlett had split to 27 but thought might, in fact, be as few as 17, was reduced to only 13 species by Joel Cracraft (Appendix A).

Cracraft's revisions

When Cracraft tackled the systematics of the moa in the mid-1970s the paradox of identification created by increasingly comprehensive samples had become acute. Distinguishing between classes at the generic and higher levels had become more certain with the growing availability of skulls clearly associated with particular post-cranial remains. But almost the opposite had occurred in discriminating species. More material, particularly leg bones, simply added to an almost continuous range of variation so that creating species became a progressively subtle, indeed arbitrary, exercise.

The way forward clearly depended upon answers to two related questions. Having hypothesised species clusters in the data, how would these compare with clusters of similar data from known, accepted, biological species in comparable families? Or, to put it another way, how few such clusters would be needed, on that comparative basis, to account for all the variation within each genus? The second question was this: if no *a priori* assumptions were made about species and generic divisions, would appropriate statistical methods pick out the same classes hypothesised on other grounds? The second issue has yet to be tackled, but Cracraft (1976a) took on the first (and see Caughley 1977:24).

As a comparative measure of species variability

Cracraft (1976a:192–4) chose the leg bones of *Apteryx australis*, and for his moa samples the LPMD leg-bone data from Archey's and Oliver's tables and from his own measurements for four classificatory species likely to have been biological species: *Megalapteryx didinus*, *Anomalopteryx didiformis*, *Pachyornis elephantopus* and *Dinornis torosus*. Using LPD data only, he first established that the size-independent, coefficients of variation (CV) for the kiwi bones were in the range 4.7–7.6, which was comparable to values for some similar cases reported in the literature (CV values for emu leg bones were in the range 4.8–5.3). The CV values for intraspecific variation in the moa species, however, were mostly in the range 5.8–10.0, with some as high as 12.0, and the problem was potentially worse than it appeared because the classificatory moa species were each held to be of only one sex, thus removing this potential source of variation from the data.

Cracraft argued, however, that most of the variation was in bone breadth which was, in turn, largely a function of individual body weight; lateral bone expansion continuing for some time after the maximum bone length had been attained. If bone length was taken as a fairer measure of variation then the intraspecific CV values for the moas came down to the range 4.6–7.8 which was much more acceptable.

Turning to inter-specific variation and classification, Cracraft proceeded in the same manner and also took up a number of Scarlett's suggestions in cases beyond the availability of his own data. He followed Scarlett in merging *A. antiquus* with *A. didiformis*, and was able to synonymise *M. hectori* with *M. didinus* by showing that the CV values for the combined samples were inside the range for other moa species. The same proved true of *P. murihiku* and *P. elephantopus*, while *P. australis* was included because the cranium on which it had been described showed no morphological variation outside the *elephantopus* range. Oliver's allegedly gracile *P. septentrionalis* was synonymised with *P. mappini* when Cracraft performed a principal components analysis of the combined leg-bone data (LPMD) and found that there was no discrimination in the bone breadth. There was, though, a clear distinction in bone length which Cracraft put down to sexual dimorphism, although tentatively in view of the very high CV values for the combined sample (10.0–13.5).

In *Euryapteryx*, Cracraft followed Scarlett in synonymising *Zelornis*, and noted that the high-arched culmen which Oliver had emphasised as the crucial point of difference was on a broken and abraded specimen. *Euryapteryx exilis*, *Eu. tane* (both of Oliver) and *Eu. curtus* were merged by Cracraft after discriminant function canonical analyses of the five nominal species of *Euryapteryx* grouped these three, smaller species close together. *Euryapteryx tane* proved virtually identical to *Eu. exilis*, and the combined sample disclosed cv values in the range 10.0–11.8. This was comparable to *P. mappini* (above), and was possibly another case of sexual dimorphism. The canonical analysis maintained a clear distinction of more than two standard deviations between the three smaller 'species' and *Eu. geranoides*, and between the latter and *Eu. gravis*. Scarlett had suggested that *Eu. geranoides* might be united with *Eu. curtus* and Cracraft's results show it to be slightly closer to the smaller than the larger species in this genus. Cracraft argued, however, that the combined sample cv values of 9.3–11.6 for *Eu. geranoides* and *Eu. gravis* were acceptable in the light of those for *P. mappini* and *Eu. curtus* and that a *geranoides-gravis* union was more logical in the light of both forms being found on each island, whereas *Eu. curtus* is missing in South Island collections.[13]

In *Emeus*, Cracraft followed Scarlett in merging *E. huttoni* and *E. crassus*, because although there are two size ranges involved the geographical distributions are very similar and the combined sample cv values are 7.70–9.90 which is within the range for other species. Sexual dimorphism was thought probable.

In Dinornithinae, Cracraft recognised four species. Oliver's *D. gazella* was merged with *struthoides* (the more slender bones of the former were from immature individuals). *Dinornis torosus* was maintained separately from *D. struthoides*, to which it is very similar in size, by some cranial differences, a stouter and less-deflected mandible and an inflated basisphenoidal rostrum. On grounds of similarity in long-bone length, Cracraft united *D. robustus* and *D. hercules* with *D. novaezealandiae*. The combined sample cv values were only 4.4–7.3, rather less than in similar cases above. *Dinornis giganteus* and its South Island counterpart *D. maximus* were also merged, under the former name, with cv values of 5.4–8.0 (Cracraft 1976a:194–204).

The validity of Cracraft's pioneering study appears to depend upon two issues concerning the data: first, whether cv values calculated only on length are an adequate expression of intraspecific

leg-bone variation; and second, whether the species ranges taken into combination by Cracraft had actually been set at appropriate intervals in the data series by earlier workers. Only the first question has been attempted. Cracraft had argued that greater variability in bone breadth, and the probable reason for it (above), made this dimension less useful than length, but when he undertook a subsequent study of the moa leg by multivariate morphometrical techniques (below) he found that bone length proved to be the major source of intraspecific variability. One reason for this contrasting result is that the second paper looked at a wider range of moas, which included *Dinornis* species in which leg-bone length (as, in fact, in *D. torosus* in the first paper) is significantly more variable than breadth. The cv values, therefore, are bound to discriminate unequally between the genera, and it was this implicit problem which required the use of principal components analysis in comparing the North Island *Pachyornis* species (Cracraft 1976b: 502–5).

Nonetheless Cracraft's radical lumping has met with general approval, partly because it was the first classification of the moa to depend, in species discrimination, entirely upon objectively testable evidence, and partly, I suspect, because parsimonious systematics was the coming style, foreshadowed by Scarlett's apprehensions about a number of Oliver's species and the basis for them.

Towards a modern taxonomy

Among the changes which have been proposed to Cracraft's classification is the deletion of *Anomalopteryx oweni*. Cracraft had only retained it pending re-examination of the material, and when this had been accomplished by Millener (1982) it became clear that the type cranium should be synonymised with *A. didiformis*. *M. benhami* should also be deleted. Kooyman (1985) concluded that the material was in the right genus and, that being so, it can be regarded as simply an extension of the size range of *M. didinus* (*Megalapteryx* has, it is worth noting, the smallest size range of any of the genera). Cracraft was not prepared to go this far, but the leg-bone data (Oliver 1949:158) show that the Mount Arthur specimen is not much longer (10.5 per cent in the femur, 13.5 per cent in the tibiotarsus) than the largest *M. didinus* specimens. Such relatively small variation is well within that common to the moas. Furthermore there are a few instances of *M. benhami*, and all from the same small area of north-west Nelson; Worthy (1988)

---

[13] Scarlett (pers. comm.) insists on specific or subspecific status for *Eu. haasti*, arguing from better material than was available to Archey or others who rejected it.

argues that they are simply the Otiran (glacial age) ancestors of *M. didinus*.

Millener (1981) returned *P. elephantopus* to the North Island species list, with evidence of it from six localities. Analysis of a *Pachyornis* collection from Tangatupura swamp showed that there was no size gap between *P. elephantopus* and *P. mappini*, but that drawing a line between two weakly evident clusters in the data would provide, to each side, an acceptably small range of variation to fit the two nominal species. Millener also had strong misgivings about Cracraft's suggestion of sexual dimorphism as the cause of size variability in the *P. mappini-septentrionalis* synonymy. In 111 localities where *Pachyornis* of one or other of these species occurred, there were only 16 in which both were found. Furthermore he observed a north to south size cline in *P. mappini* with, in addition, a concentration of *P. septentrionalis* to the far north. Since the larger *P. mappini* were in the south and overlapped in size with the South Island *P. elephantopus*, the evidence suggested that a broad latitudinal size variation was the more likely explanation.

These views have recently been challenged by a re-examination of the Tangatupura material in which it has been shown that bones of both sizes of *Pachyornis* are morphologically distinct from *P. elephantopus*. They seem, instead, to represent marked sexual dimorphism within a population of large *P. mappini*. Worthy (1987) argues that the size of this species at Tangatupura is a function of temporal variation in which larger size was related to the greater extent of preferred habitat (open country for *Pachyornis*) during the late Pleistocene. Tangatupura dates, on moa bone, to 18,300 ± 600 bp (Worthy 1987). Differences in the relative representation of the two size ranges (*P. mappini = mappini*, *P. mappini = septentrionalis*), especially in swamp sites, are related by Worthy (1987) to the possibility that the larger size represented females which, on grounds of size and mobility, were at greater risk of entrapment (assuming males were smaller and often nest-bound, incubating eggs).

Fragmented remains of small individuals of *Pachyornis* in South Island archaeological sites were designated *P. cf. mappini* by Kooyman (1985), but they may turn out to be from *P. australis*, as implied by Worthy (n.d.a).

In *Euryapteryx* there remains an area of disagreement. Millener (1981) and Worthy (n.d.a) accept the Cracraft synonymy, although they note evidence of a significant size-cline in which the larger bones assigned to *gravis* are predominant towards the south. Scarlett's (pers. comm.) revised classification, however, retains a species division

between *gravis*, *haasti* and his new species. There are several grounds on which *gravis*, at least, might be retained.

First, as noted above, the *gravis* remains were as significantly different in size from those of *geranoides*, in Cracraft's (1976a:fig. 2) canonical analysis, as the group of smaller *Euryapteryx* species which he lumped together under *curtus*. Second, as Millener (1981:498–501) argued, the distribution of *gravis* and *geranoides* remains is at odds with Cracraft's explanation of sexual dimorphism for the size variation between them. Rather, the distribution suggests a size-cline for which a subspecific status might be appropriate. Millener's discussion of the *Pachyornis* data might be construed as another argument for subspecific recognition, but the argument for merging *septentrionalis* and *mappini* is stronger than in the *Euryapteryx* cases above and, in addition, the demonstration that a population of small *Pachyornis* (*mappini* or *australis*) existed in the southern South Island invalidates the size-cline thesis in this instance.

The lack of convincing evidence for *Emeus crassus* in the North Island leads me to follow Oliver and Scarlett in deleting *Emeus* from the list for this island until some more compelling data are brought forward.

At a broader level, the outstanding issue of distinguishing between the stout-bodied moas of *Pachyornis*, *Emeus* and *Euryapteryx* must still be regarded as unresolved. Despite examining very large samples Hutton (1875:277) could not distinguish between his *Dinornis crassus* and *D. elephantopus* tarsometatarsi; Oliver (1949:90) remarked on the similarities between *Emeus* and *Euryapteryx* crania, sterna, pelves and the number of phalanges in the outer toe; Archey (1941:10) observed the almost identical sizes and proportions of leg bones between *Euryapteryx* and *Pachyornis*; and recently Cracraft's (1976b:505–17) morphometrical comparison of leg bones grouped all three genera closely together and found *Emeus crassus* and *Euryapteryx geranoides* virtually indistinguishable. Kooyman (1985) encountered similar difficulties in comparing morphological traits amongst these genera.

Looking at *Dinornis*, Kooyman (1985) found six individuals of *D. struthoides* in South Island localities, thus strengthening the southern claim of this species which Cracraft had been obliged to regard as uncertain. Whether Worthy's (n.d.a) synonymising of *D. torosus* with *D. struthoides* will stand depends on further research (Appendix A).

Equally unresolved is whether moas should be assigned to two families, a recurrent proposal adopted most recently by Worthy (n.d.a) and here.[14] In addition to Worthy's species I would retain two others, *Eu. gravis* and *D. torosus*, as a working convenience.

Prospect and review

Looking ahead, it seems to me that to the degree modern classifications err, is it more likely to be on the side of splitting than otherwise. Millener's analogy in this respect is a telling one: the New Zealand rails, which exhibit a greater structural diversity than moas, and about the same range in body weight, are classified into barely a dozen species. Other analogies point the same way, suggesting that the number is still too high. The nearest large fossil birds in Australia, the Dromornithidae, peaked at five genera and eight species in the Miocene (Rich, pers. comm.), and then dwindled in taxa down to extinction some 20,000 years ago (Rich and van Tets 1984:433). Perhaps closer in ecological circumstances and certainly in phylogenesis were the Aepyornithidae of Madagascar, which are classified into three genera and seven species (Clements 1981:3). Less variable still are the large modern ratites in which no family exceeds two genera and three species despite the fact that all of them ranged until recently over greater areas than moas and had at least the same apparent opportunities for adaptive radiation.

A different kind of analogy produced a similar conclusion for Caughley (1977). He looked at the distribution of species of modern flying and flightless birds in New Zealand and found that species exclusive to either island were much fewer than those in common. In Oliver and Archey's moa classifications, however, the opposite was the case – there were about twice as many moa species attributed to each island as occurred on both. Caughley argued that this was an artefact of taxonomy, not a reflection of reality, and suggested that there should be fewer species and more subspecies reflecting differences in geographically separate populations. However re-arranging moa

taxonomy in such a way, as Cracraft has partly done, raises the question of whether there are perhaps too many genera. Certainly it would be no surprise to find that comprehensive multivariate analyses of a range of moa elements such as crania, pelves and leg bones conducted, as Caughley suggested, without prior judgement as to their appropriate taxa, had the effect of reducing the number of genera and expanding the number of subspecies.

Looking back over the history of moa systematics can, however, provide little cause for confidence, and it is worth concluding by enquiring briefly into why the classification of moas has been, and is, so uncertain. I think that there are at least three related answers.

The most obvious is that moa specimens have been, more often than not, collected in such a haphazard and poorly recorded way that essential questions about the individual, specific or generic associations of taxonomically crucial bones – notably crania and beaks – remained substantially unanswered until the 1940s. This problem was continually aggravated by a willingness to promiscuously associate material of uncertain provenance.

Second, there has been a longstanding belief that variability in moa osteology, particularly below the familial level, is unusually subtle and continuous. Whether true or not it has been manifested in a jumble-sale search for distinguishing criteria which, in retrospect, seems almost comical; a miscellany of esoteric landmarks from the deflection of the beak to the shape of the preorbital plate, from the disposition of pneumatic foramina in the sternum to the number of joints in the outer toe. Very few of these criteria were subjected to any objective tests of their ability to discriminate and some were neither adequately explained nor illustrated.

Third, there have been only two quite brief periods of active critical analysis and productive disputes in the history of moa classification. The first, mainly in the 1890s, involved Hutton, Parker, Forbes and Lydekker, and it was a time of considerable progress in breaking away from the long hegemony of Owen's comparative morphology and starting down a path towards a more objective and quantified style of analysis. The second did not begin until the 1970s when the widely accepted Archey–Oliver scheme and methods were challenged – tentatively by Scarlett, and more forcefully by Cracraft – thus opening the way to another round of useful questioning and methodological inventiveness. In both cases it is interesting to observe that there was a preference for attempting actual lumping instead of retreating to the primitive philosophy of 'split now, lump later' which prevailed at other times.

---

[14] After the manuscript was complete and revised, Worthy (pers. comm.) argued that the familial classification of moas ought to be into Dinornithidae and Emeidae, rather than the former and Anomalopterygidae, on the ground that Emeinae of Bonaparte 1854 has priority over Anomalopterygidae of Oliver 1930, as suggested by Brodkorb (1963:208). This would create two subfamilies in Emeidae; Emeinae to take the genera Emeus and Euryapteryx, and Anomalopteryginae to take the remaining non-Dinornis genera. The scheme, published in Brodkorb (1963), was seldom adopted, (but see Miller and Cassels 1985 for an example) and we must await Worthy's detailed argument. No matter of consequence in this book would be affected by adopting it.

4

ORIGINS AND DEVELOPMENT

Ratites and their phylogenesis

No issues concerning moas have attracted more contentious speculation than questions about the definition, origin and distribution of ratites, the group of large flightless birds to which moas belonged.

Merrem defined Ratitae in 1813 as birds lacking a keel, or carina, on the sternum, but Huxley (1867) introduced a crucial complication by arguing that the essential character of the group was its emu-like or dromaeognathous palate. On the basis of this feature he assigned all the large living or recent ratites, together with the kiwis (unknown to Merrem), to the order Ratitae, and all other modern birds, by their carinate sterna, to Carinatae. Some nominal carinates, however, were also palatally 'ratite', notably the small, volant tinamous (South America), and Pycraft (1901) resolved this contradiction by proposing that the palate should take precedence. All Huxley's ratites and the tinamous were thus assigned to Palaeognathae, and all other birds to Neognathae.

The precise nature of the palaeognathous (i.e. dromaeognathous) palate and the degree to which it can be recognised in, or is restricted to, the ratites has proved a fertile field of debate. Huxley's definition referred to a long and posteriorly broad vomer which prevented articulation of the palatine and pterygoid bones with the basisphenoidal rostrum, but this description was inadequate. An accumulation of criticisms over the years culminated in McDowell's (1948) claim that the palaeognathous palate could only be recognised in different approximations of it which corresponded to four separate ratite orders.

Bock (1963) later described it in a more comprehensive manner. He referred, in summary, to a complex arrangement of bones whereby the palatines and vomer held the pterygoids tightly between the quadrates and the basipterygoid processes to create a strong inflexible structure in which the parts were either fused or articulated by long sutures (Fig. 4.1). It was, thus, quite distinct from the typically light-boned, flexibly articulated, neognathous palate.

The existence of the palaeognathous palate became widely accepted, but whether it and other

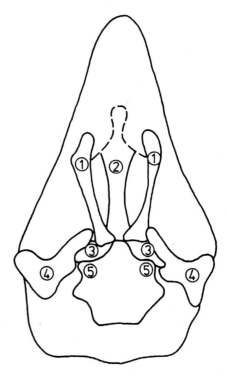

FIG. 4.1   Palatal bones of Anomalopterygid moa illustrating the palaeognathous arrangement. Simplified after Parker (1895:fig. 6): 1 = palatines, 2 = vomer, 3 = pterygoids, 4 = quadrates, 5 = basipterygoid processes.

anatomical features constitute evidence of a common ancestry, or monophyly, of the ratites is a matter which has been long and intricately debated.

The case for monophyly, as proposed by Cracraft (1974a), begins with the argument that ancestral affinity must be determined by finding uniquely shared characters which, being later evolved than characters held in common by a wider range of related groups, are relatively derived, as opposed to relatively primitive, in the evolutionary sense. By ranking the degree to which characters or character-states are shared it is possible to draw up a family tree (cladogram) of phylogenetic relationships within a group.

Comparing Palaeognathiformes with nearly all other non-passerine birds, Cracraft found that they exhibited three exclusive character-states; the palaeognathous palate (above), a unique rhamphothecal structure and a large ilioischiatic fenestrum (i.e. a gap) reflecting lack of fusion between the ilia and ischia. The rhamphotheca, or keratinous bill, had been studied by Parkes and Clark (1966) who concluded that there was a particular form of grooved rhamphotheca found only amongst ratites and tinamous.

Within the Palaeognathiformes Cracraft defined 25 characters the states of which were postulated to be either primitive or derived. Most concerned changes towards elongation or broadening in articulatory features of the leg bones. Others included a reduction in the number of toes, a narrowing of the pelvis, fusion of the scapulo-coracoid, reduction in the size of the wings and so on. A cladistic analysis of these showed that the tinamous shared no character-states with any particular ratite lineage and Cracraft (1974a:505) concluded that they were the most primitive group which 'probably had their origin relatively soon after the palaeognath lineage became defined within birds'. Amongst all the other lineages the moas and kiwis, which proved more closely related to each other than to any other group, were the next most primitive, and Cracraft found little evidence of a close relationship between them and either elephant birds, or cassowaries and emus, as earlier studies had variously suggested.[1]

Some biochemical analyses have also been argued to support the hypothesis of ratite monophyly. Prager et al. (1976) compared immunological distances by antiseral reactions to avian transferrins (a type of protein) and found that ratites and tinamous formed a single distinct assemblage; while analysis of somatic chromosome patterns for all the modern ratites, but not the tinamous, also showed them to be essentially identical (de Boer 1980).[2] Taking monophyly as an assumption, Sibley and Ahlquist (1981, 1983, 1984) then examined the relative tenacity of induced DNA nucleotide hybrids amongst living ratites and tinamous. The results of their 1981 study varied slightly according to the statistical means of presenting them, but Δ T50H values (which express the temperature, under normal frequency distribution conditions, at which 50 per cent of all unique (single-copy) DNA sequences have hybridised) are thought to provide the best estimates of distance between lineage divergence events (i.e. between internodal distances in cladograms). These data, subsequently revised (Sibley pers. comm.), are shown in Fig. 4.2. The most obvious differences from Cracraft's divergence sequence are the proximity of kiwis to modern Australian ratites and the position of both at the most recent end of the divergence sequence.[3]

The argument that ratites are monophyletic by derived characters has been attacked on various grounds. Gingerich (1976) proposed that Cracraft's three features defining the Palaeognathiformes were all primitive, a view now widely shared. On fossil evidence, Molnar and Archer (1984:417) have argued emphatically that the palaeognathous palate, the linchpin of ratite monophyly, was shared by all Cretaceous toothed birds and the theropod dinosaurs. It may, they argue, 'be a structural grade basic to all birds, and its loss in some [i.e. the neognathous birds] an indicator of their monophyly'. Olson (1985:101) also concluded 'that the characters defining the ratites and tinamous are *not* derived', and that discarding Cracraft's hypothesis left two others in contention: ratites are either survivors of an ancient

---

[1] The principal character-states which suggest a moa–kiwi relationship are enlargement and anterior projection of the internal condyle of the tibia, and development of a double-ridged hypotarsus.

[2] Prager (pers. comm.) found transferrin in moa bone but it was very degraded. She suggests application of mitochondrial sequencing techniques to mummified moa tissue may prove useful.

[3] Amongst older opinions Owen (1866c:II:12) thought the kiwis and the moas were allied to the megapodes; Mivart (1879) thought the kiwi and the moa were closely related to the emu (but there is a contradiction with his diagram on p. 52); Fürbringer (1888) thought ratites polyphyletic and morphologically convergent, and Pycraft (1901) thought ratites were essentially monophyletic. Beddard (1911) found the intestinal arrangements of kiwis and tinamous were similar to those of gallinaceous birds. Harrison (1916) suggested ratite parasites (*Malophaga*) indicated a ralline origin for kiwis. Chandler (1916) argued that ratite feathers are primitive and not derived from flying ancestors.

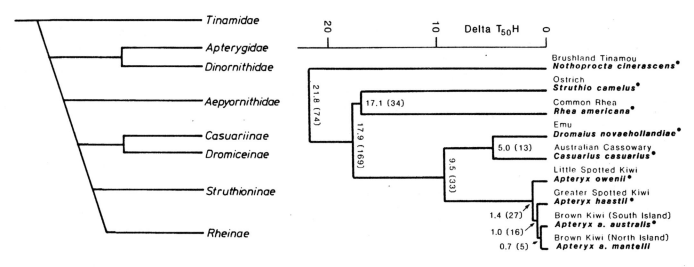

FIG. 4.2   Phylogenetic relationships amongst ratites and tinamous according to Cracraft (1974a), left, and Sibley and Alquist (Sibley pers. comm.), right.

lineage of palaeognathous birds, even if some are only secondarily palaeognathous through neoteny (below), or they all arose through neoteny in neognathous ancestors, amongst which no family connection need be implied.

Neoteny (arrested development leading to the retention of juvenile traits in adults) could explain the same phenomena emphasised by Cracraft, as Feduccia (1980) has argued. The ilioischiatic fenestrum, for instance, is found in the embryos of modern rails and is thus, Feduccia suggested, neotenic in adult ratites (since it is also found in various early birds, including the Cretaceous toothed bird, *Hesperornis*, it might be a primitive feature in modern birds as well). The palaeognathous palate, grooved rhamphotheca and the adult existence of cranial sutures were also considered by Feduccia to be neotenic in ratites. Since neotenic features need disclose no phyletic connections the ratites could thus be polyphyletic, deriving their similarity by neotenic convergence. Feduccia also cited various examples of differentiation in anatomical features as evidence against ratite monophyly; for example great variety in the shape of the pelvis, notably amongst the cursorial species, and the existence of diverse types of feathers amongst ratites claimed to be closely connected, such as after-shafted moa and single-shafted kiwi feathers.[4]

[4] Feduccia (1980) argues that kiwis are not closely related to moas and that moas shared few characteristics with other palaeognathous birds. They were wingless, lacked a pygostyle (cf. Owen 1862e:162, but see Archey 1941:84) and shared, uniquely amongst ratites, a feature of flying birds in the form of a tendonal canal in the distal tibiotarsus. See also Swinton 1975:63–4 on neoteny in ratites.

These competing hypotheses about ratite origins are difficult to test directly, but they can be investigated further in several ways. One involves the relationship between ratite distribution and the palaeogeography of the continents.

Palaeogeography and palaeognaths

Nineteenth-century views about how moas reached New Zealand and could be related to other ratites canvassed various propositions. Owen (1849c:328) first speculated that moas could be related to fossils of apparently similar birds in North America by proposing that New Zealand lay at 'one end of a mighty wave of the unstable and ever-shifting crust of the earth, of which the opposite end, after having been submerged, has again risen with its accumulated deposits in North America . . . [while] the intermediate body of the land wave along which the *Dinornis* may have travelled to New Zealand, has progressively subsided, and now lies beneath the Pacific Ocean'. He later abandoned this rather too facile suggestion in favour of an hypothesis about winged moa ancestors (Owen 1879ai:460–5).

Nevertheless the idea of a former great southern landmass proved a resilient concept. Mantell (1850), Thomson (1854), Buller (1869), Haast (1874), Russell (1877), Hutton (1892a) and Hector (1893) all subscribed to the view that moas had once inhabited a 'wide continent', although not necessarily one connected to any other, which had subsequently become reduced to the New Zealand archipelago and some southwest Pacific islands. However they were not prepared to go as far as Milne Edwards (in Haast 1948:693) who postulated the former existence of land connections between southern Africa and Australasia. Taking that idea to its logical conclusion, Haast (in Haast 1948:694) argued, would result in the improbable proposition that the southern landmasses must once have been connected! He suggested icebergs and floating islands as a means of transporting non-volant organisms, and convergent adaptation as the explanation of morphological similarities.

Hutton (1873, 1892a, 1892c:146–7) attempted to combine the various views by proposing that flying moa ancestors from South America reached a New Zealand landmass which extended almost to Norfolk Island, and that after the power of flight was lost a population of moas became isolated on a mobile portion of land which fetched up against the coast of Australia.

The ultimately triumphant view lay, however, in the notion of a super-continent. Forbes (1893d: 54) proposed that all the area within the 2000 fathom line in the southern ocean had once been dry land; a super-continent with land connections extending to Africa, South America and Antarctica. This idea, which in general terms goes back at least to Hooker (1853:xxi), was later given a geological basis in the theory of Gondwanaland and its dissolution by continental drift.

The sequence of continental separations still contains some problems but, according to an orthodox model (Fleming 1979, Archer 1984: 50–1), Gondwanaland began to separate about 140 mybp with the disconnection of a block comprising Africa, Madagascar and India, although Africa remained attached to South America which, in turn, remained a part of Gondwanaland until about 90 mybp. This latter date is therefore the latest at which, in Cracraft's (1974a) model, there could have been divergence between the ancestors of rhea and ostrich. Since this is the last divergence in his scheme the separation of the ratite–tinamou lineage, as well as divergence of all the ratite lineages, must have occurred at earlier stages. Pushing these events back to 100 mybp or earlier, i.e. the mid-Cretaceous, seems too early, however, in the light of avian evolution as it is currently known (although the data are comparatively few and enigmatic before the end of the Cretaceous).

New Zealand separated from Australia about 80 mybp, and from Antarctica at about the same time. This fits Cracraft's early divergence of the moa–kiwi lineage, and it also conforms with his argument that 'phyletically primitive species will generally be postulated as being near the centre of origin of the group in question, whereas phyletically more derivative or advanced taxa will tend to be peripheral to it' (Cracraft 1974b:221).

The separation of Madagascar from Africa at about 65 mybp is in the right place for Cracraft's sequence but presents several problems. First, since India had been attached to the east side of Madagascar, and probably remained so for a few million years after the separation of these areas from Africa, it is difficult to explain why it should not have supported its own ratite lineage. Second, the separation of Madagascar from Africa much later than the separation of both from Gondwanaland means that both elephant-bird and ostrich ancestors ought to have been available to colonise Madagascar (and India).

About 56 mybp Australia finally separated from east Antarctica. As Cracraft points out, the Australian ratites could not be derived from a divergence with the New Zealand lineages, but rather both from an ancestral South American or west Antarctican source.

Turning back to the ostrich problem, it seems probable that this lineage is out of sequence in Cracraft's model and ought to diverge first after the separation of ratites and tinamous, as some immunological and karyological data suggest (e.g. Prager et al. 1976:292). The elephant-bird lineage would then become the vicariant sister-group to the ostriches, and it is not difficult to imagine that an original graviportal stock continued to develop in the protected isolation of Madagascar, while the less secure and increasingly arid environment of southern Africa favoured evolution of cursorial ostriches (but see Houde 1986, below).

The Sibley and Ahlquist model also runs into some palaeogeographical problems. When the Δ T50H values were calibrated against an assumed 80 mybp separation date for tinamous and ratites (an average value of 5 my = 1 T50H), it was apparent that the Australasian ratite divergences ran into a snag: the kiwis diverged at about 40 mybp, or within the Eocene, which is some 40 mybp after the geological separation of New Zealand from Australia and Antarctica. Sibley and Ahlquist (1981) suggested that an archipelago, the 'Inner Melanesian Arc', persisted between New Zealand, New Caledonia and northern Australia until about this time and that it was sufficiently studded with islands to permit strong swimming ratites, but not marsupials, to pass along it. This explanation became less plausible, however, as Sibley and Ahlquist (1983:281, 1984:4, 12) recalculated their unit rate of DNA evolution from 5 my to 4.0–4.5 my, and unlikely when Helm-Bychowski and Wilson (1986) indicated that the rate ought to be 2.5–3.0 my. At the latter rates, and using the same calibration assumptions as Sibley and Ahlquist, the kiwi (and presumptively moa) divergence would be at 24–29 mybp, or the late Oligocene, which seems too young, on present geological evidence, to sustain the hypothesis of an 'Inner Melanesian Arc'.

The question these various geological considerations raise in reference to hypothesised divergence sequences of ratite monophylies do not invalidate the latter, but they do suggest that it is rather unlikely that it was only geotectonic vicariance which led to ratite dispersal. Flying ancestors must also be considered.

Volant ancestors

Rudimentary ratite wings were seen by Lowe (1935) and Oliver (1949:189) as the survival of 'airrowing' forelimbs which had existed in cursorial ancestors. Similar but less radical views held that ratites were descended from proto-carinates which had achieved a measure of flight but were not capable fliers (Pycraft 1901:266; Archey 1941:82–6; Prager *et al.* 1976), and a similar case has recently been advanced by McGowan (1982) who concluded that a suite of primitive features is characteristic of ratite wings (fewer muscles than in carinates, weak development of pectoral muscles and those required to lift the humerus, absent propatagium – a muscular structure on the carinate wing which facilitates flying – and triosseal canal in the coracoid, retention of forelimb claws and feathers unattached to the wing skeleton). These, and an ascending process to the astragalus, McGowan (1984) regarded as primitive features within birds.[5] In his view neoteny is a less-plausible explanation of these features on two grounds. First, many of the features can be found in fossil evidence of primitive birds and it stretches credulity to propose that degeneration from a fully volant status would coincidentally arrive at the same forms. Second, the loss of flight in modern carinates is accompanied by only minor anatomical changes in the wing. Owen (1879aı:463) had made this point in relation to the wing structure of the dodo which, save in size, was still 'the perfect instrument of flight in truly winged birds' (in this case doves, from which the dodo descended). Lowe (1928, 1935) had provided further instances of minimal change between the wings of flighted birds and their flightless conspecifics, and McGowan (1986)

has shown that the same is true of the weka (*Gallirallus australis*) wing – a species which may have been flightless as long as some ratites.

Nevertheless the modern, and historical, consensus is strongly on the side of ratite evolution from capable fliers. Anatomical indications of volant ancestors include fusion of the metacarpals, the existence of a pygostyle (the bone controlling tail feathers in flying birds), complex development of the cerebellar portion of the brain, an alula or slipstream slot in ratite wing feathers, flight quill feathers and, in Struthio at least, the presence of a metapatagium (Benham 1935:98–9; Swinton 1975: 64; Feduccia 1980:135; McGowan 1982:215).

Volancy amongst ratite ancestors does not, of course, mean that they colonised by flying, since flightlessness could have evolved prior to dispersal. Nevertheless several arguments can be advanced in favour of it. First, there is fossil evidence (*Lithornis* cohort) of a group of hen-sized palaeognathous carinates, potentially volant, from Palaeocene and Eocene deposits in North America and Europe. These seem to be closer to ratites than tinamous and to have given rise to a flightless ostrich ancestor by the middle Eocene in Europe – and very possibly to kiwi ancestors at an earlier stage as well (Houde 1986). It is conceivable that all other modern ratites are also descended from the *Lithornis* line, and colonised by flying from the northern hemisphere. Second, no other fossil remains of palaeognathous birds are older than the late Palaeocene (55–60 mybp). There were flightless ratites of this era in South America, and presumed rheas by the lower Miocene; tinamous go back to the upper Pliocene, and emus to the Miocene (Olson 1985:106–7). The fossil record of moas extends only to the Pliocene (Fordyce pers. comm.), and there is no confirmed Tertiary record of kiwis or elephant birds (Olson 1985). Although negative evidence, in this context, the fossil record does suggest that ratites may not have reached many of the areas in which they were subsequently found until after landmass separation was well advanced in the southern hemisphere. Third, while a monophyletic stock of volant palaeognaths on Gondwanaland could have dispersed either by flight or by continental drift after the evolution of flightlessness, the probability of flightlessness occurring after dispersal would seem to increase in proportion to the degree that ratites are polyphyletic, and on various grounds discussed above that seems more likely.

Post-colonisation flightlessness is a common enough phenomenon. Why it should occur deserves a brief comment. In reference to moas

---

[5] Martin (1983) argues, however, that the ascending process fuses with the calcaneum to form the pretibia, and is derived within birds. Whether it is anatomically primitive by descent or neoteny remains the problem (Feduccia 1986).

Owen (1879a1:460) appealed to Buffon's principle of transmutation by degeneration; 'by long disuse of the wings, continued through successive generations, those organs . . . ultimately atrophied to a degree affecting their capability to raise the body of the bird in the air'. But recent discussion about flightlessness has cast it in a more positive light. Loss of flight could enable a reduction of 20–25 per cent in muscular weight (the wing muscles) and a corresponding decline in the heavy energy demand needed to fly. Flightlessness also released constraints upon body size and shape so that, for instance, more robust legs, and feet fully adapted to walking, could be developed. Another option opened up is a fully herbivorous diet with its requirement of a long and heavy intestinal tract (Feduccia 1980:110, 122). No doubt flightlessness was a competitive strategy in Pacific environments, where there were often few terrestrial predators.

In the Pacific, flightlessness occurred across a wide range of classes, although particularly in the Gruiformes (notably rails). Furthermore the geological history of some islands is such that it must have occurred in much shorter periods than is generally thought (Feduccia 1980; Diamond 1981; James and Olson 1983). Impressed by the flightless birds in Hawaii, Olson has speculated that not only kiwis and moas but perhaps the two main groups of moas as well represent separate colonisations by flying ancestors (James and Olson 1983:40). Like Feduccia, he suggested that the Gruiformes are the most likely source of a paraphyletic group of moa ancestors, but that kiwis could possibly be descended from ibises since they bear an uncanny resemblance to the flightless ibises which developed in Hawaii.[6]

If this view takes us into the realm of speculation, the contrary assertion that 'the entire assemblage of living and extinct ratites of Australia, New Guinea, New Caledonia [*Sylviornis neocaledoniae* Poplin 1980; not, in fact, a ratite] and New Zealand must be viewed as the result of a single invasion into the Australasian region' (Sibley and Ahlquist 1981:322) also goes too far on present evidence. Various data indicate a comparatively close association of Australasian ratites; this is largely biochemical and molecular data from modern species although there have been some morphological arguments along the same lines (Mivart 1879: 51–2), and Semba and Mathers (in Sibley and Ahlquist 1981:302) observed that kiwi ocular pec-

ten, while uniquely structured, has probably been derived from the type found in the emu and cassowary rather than that found in other ratites and tinamous. But the only data upon which moas can be included are morphological, and these run into a number of problems, one of the most difficult being in excising convergence effects from the argument. Cracraft allowed that matter to remain an open question, but Feduccia (1980), Olson (1982:737) and Sibley and Ahlquist (1981:325) all thought that convergent adaptations, especially in ratite leg bones, were a strong probability.

What, then, can be concluded about the origin of moas? Strictly speaking, only that they were palaeognathous birds descended from volant ancestors. Beyond that the weight of evidence suggests, but does not demonstrate, that they were related to other ratites by neotenic convergence rather than phyletic derivation. If they were more closely related to other Australasian lineages than to ratites elsewhere (and following Rich and Balouet (1984), Olson (1985) and Rich (pers. comm.) I exclude the mihirungs or dromornithids from the Australasian palaeognaths), and particularly if they were closely related to kiwis (Sibley model (pers. comm.); Fig. 4.2; Gould 1986), then they probably reached New Zealand long after it became an archipelago, and subsequently became flightless.

Development in New Zealand

Almost nothing is known about the evolution of moas and kiwis within New Zealand, primarily because fossil remains dating to older than the Pleistocene are extremely scarce. Scarlett and Molnar (1984) described a late Cretaceous phalanx which is possibly from a terrestrial bird, but there is no particular evidence on it of ratite affinities. Amongst the oldest moa remains are those recovered in 1890 from a 'laterite' (probably burnt loess) horizon underlying a 14 m-thick lava flow near Timaru. Two small collections have been described. The Miller collection, examined by Forbes (1891a), included a femur of *Apteryx* cf. *australis*, a moa pelvic fragment inseparable from *D. oweni* and two tarsometatarsal fragments, one of which appeared to be from *D. curtus* and the other from that species or *D. didiformis*. The best specimens of the Stubbs collection (Hutton 1892c:144) were two tibiotarsal fragments which he assigned, on the grounds of their size, to a new species, *Anomalopteryx antiquus*. The Miller tarsometatarsal frag-

[6] Interesting possibilities also in Saiff (1982).

ments, seen only in photographs by Hutton (1893a), were added by him to this new species.

For several years Forbes and Hutton engaged in an ill-tempered debate about the nature and provenance of the remains and their age. Hutton (1892c:144) argued that the kiwi femur was actually from *Aptornis*, which Forbes (1893a:378, 1893c) vehemently denied, while for his part scorning Hutton's association of the tibiotarsal fragments and his estimate of the original bone length by claiming that the pieces came from quite different locations and were damaged. As for the age of the bones, Hutton (1893c:318) suggested Upper Miocene for the lava flow on Alexander MacKay's word, but Forbes (1893b:318), appealing to the same authority, insisted that the sediments under the lava flow were of Upper Pliocene or even Pleistocene age.

Although some tarsometatarsal features such as the comparatively unproduced middle trochlea and the small inner hypotarsal ridge have been used to support the retention of *A. antiquus*, notably by Oliver (1949:145, 185, 1955:183), more recent information suggests that the remains are probably *A. didiformis* and dated to the early Pleistocene, about 1.8–2.0 mybp (Cracraft 1976a:195). But it is just possible that the remains are much younger. Forbes mentioned loess-filled cracks and pockets in the lava which, in one case, extended entirely through it to the horizon beneath – from which the moa bones had been recovered.

A shaft fragment of a moa femur found in papa sediments at Nukumaru Beach, near Wanganui (Marshall 1919:253), was identified as *D. robustus* and the provenance as Upper Pliocene. Association with the last appearance of certain molluscan genera such as *Lutraria* indicates, however, that the provenance might be Lower Pleistocene (Fleming 1979:74), about 1.2–1.5 mybp. Millener (1981:450, 502) has recently described the moa remains as being from *D. novaezealandiae* (i.e. returning *robustus* through *ingens* to its original name) and possibly *E. crassus* and he suggests an Upper Pliocene to Lower Pleistocene date for these bones and also for remains of *Eu. geranoides* from Nga Rata and Hunterville (in the latter case, also bones of *D. novaezealandiae*).

Mineralised bones of *Pachyornis mappini* were reported from a Pliocene deposit at Maungapurua, on the Wanganui River, by Oliver (1949:65) but details of their provenance have not been published. Fleming (1974:62) thought that they appeared much more recent and were possibly accidentally associated with Pliocene strata by a landslip. Fossil feathers were said to have come from Pliocene deposits near Gisborne (Hill 1889). Moa footprints found near Gisborne (Williams 1872) were also thought to be of Pliocene age, but soon proved to be from later Pleistocene sediments, as were others found on the banks of the Manawatu, (Fig. 4.3) (Hutton 1892c; Hill 1895; Wilson 1913; Buick 1931:4–6; Millener 1981:450).

How moas developed in New Zealand is thus a matter of conjecture, though constrained by the main events of palaeobiogeography.

Palaeobiogeography

By the late Cretaceous New Zealand was a peneplained landmass lying at the eastern end of Gondwanaland where, because of seafloor spreading, it had been rotated poleward to about 80 degrees S

FIG. 4.3 Moa footprints exposed on the banks of the Manawatu River in 1912 (Wilson 1913:211). (By courtesy of Royal Society of NZ.)

(at 95 mybp). By the time the last land connections with Australia and Antarctica were lost, about 80 mybp, New Zealand lay at about 70 degrees S and was 'subject to relatively low temperatures, and long winter nights with a high rainfall and cloud cover' (Mildenhall 1980:203). The land was covered by a fern-rich podocarp forest containing a minor *Nothofagus* component.[7]

At the beginning of the Tertiary (65 mybp) New Zealand was a large Y-shaped landmass extending from near Campbell Island to Northland with another arm extending towards Norfolk Island. As New Zealand slowly returned northward a long phase of marine transgression set in. This covered half the area of modern New Zealand by the end of the Eocene and two-thirds by the early Oligocene. The early Tertiary climate was mainly warm-temperate, apart from a cooler period around the beginning of the Oligocene, and the forest had become increasingly dominated by *Nothofagus*.

In the late Oligocene and early Miocene (*c.* 18–26 mybp) there were rapidly rising temperatures, the beginnings of a new orogenic phase (still continuing), and of the West Wind Drift, once the separation of Australia and Antarctica was sufficiently well advanced. In the Lower Miocene, then, the main environmental characteristics of New Zealand – a mid-latitude position, mountains and westerlies – were achieved more or less together.

From the Upper Miocene (7–12 mybp) onward there was gradual cooling, and by the early Pleistocene (*c.* 1.3 mybp) subantarctic waters reached as far north as Hawke's Bay. *Nothofagus* forest grew at sea level in Auckland and the Subtropical Convergence Zone lay across the northern North Island (giving it a climate comparable with that of the present-day Chathams).

During the Pleistocene environmental changes were geologically abrupt and dramatic. The Pliocene Manawatu Strait closed by about 1.2 mybp, orogenic uplift increased rapidly and was accompanied by extensive volcanism in the North Island, while there occurred a succession of four or five phases of glacial expansion and lowered sea levels. During the glacial phases the South Island vegetation was mostly 'extensive shrublands dominated by Compositae and *Coprosma* species' (Fleming 1979:83) while *Nothofagus* forest grew extensively in the North Island. Low altitude grasslands were common in the South Island and, at the most severe glacial periods, there may have been only discontinuous coastal stands of forest in the south-

ern region. During interglacial phases conditions and vegetation returned to temperate, or even warm-temperate conditions, while high sea levels probably re-created the Northland archipelago of the Pliocene as well as separating the main islands.

During the Holocene, or post-glacial phase (*c.* 14,000 up to the present day), there was rapid marine transgression to create Cook Strait, by 10,000 bp, and Foveaux Strait soon after, while the climate had recovered to conditions which were probably slightly warmer than today by 5000 bp (Mildenhall 1980; Knox 1980; Stevens 1980).

Evolution and environment

Various of these environmental changes have been singled out as instrumental in the evolution of moas. Hutton (1892c:149–51) suggested that the formation of the Oligocene–early Miocene archipelago provided the most likely site of initial generic divergence from a common ancestor by isolation of populations upon islands. By the time a single landmass was re-formed in the early Pliocene the smaller genera subsequently found on both main islands had evolved. Hutton regarded the least specialised, and earliest, types as *Palapteryx* (for its wings) and *Anomalopteryx* (for its size, gracility and the evidence, in *A. antiquus*, of fossil ancestors). From *Palapteryx* evolved *Dinornis*, and from *Anomalopteryx* came *Euryapteryx* and *Mesopteryx* which subdivided into *Cela* and *Syornis*. Arguing from cranial characters, Parker (1895:424) took a similar view, although it was the large orbits of *Anomalopteryx*, together with its narrow beak, and narrow beaks in *Mesopteryx* and *Dinornis* which suggested to him that all these genera had diverged at about the same time from a ratite ancestor (ratites generally being narrow-beaked). *Pachyornis* and *Emeus* later diverged from *Mesopteryx*.

Hutton (1897b:543) suggested that the moas steadily increased in size during the Pliocene, a process facilitated by an abundance of food and a scarcity of predators. With the formation of Cook Strait, which Hutton believed to have occurred during the late Pliocene, all the island-specific species and genera (*Cela* in the North, *Euryapteryx* in the South) were evolved.

Archey (1941) did not accept the importance of Cook Strait. Noting that *Eu. gravis* occurred in the eastern South Island and southeastern North Island, that *M. didinus* had a western distribution, that *Anomalopteryx* was not developed into separate species, and similar evidence, he argued that speciation must have occurred prior to the origin

---

[7] But see also Fleming (1979:43) and Knox (1980:289).

of Cook Strait. Variations in species distributions seemed to Archey to reflect the existence of the main mountain divide which ran SW–NE across the South Island and southern North Island. This provided 'a semi-pervious, selective barrier to moa distribution . . . [which was] more readily traversed by the tall active species of *Dinornis*, and by *Anomalopteryx* . . . [but less frequently] by the heavier forms, *Emeus*, *Pachyornis* and *Euryapteryx*' (Archey 1941:80). Archey cited topography as a formative influence upon other aspects of moa evolution as well. Thus the tougher grasses and shrubs of the upland areas which could be exploited by the gracile *Anomalopteryx* and *Dinornis* genera may have operated a selective pressure upon the evolution of large mandibles and temporal fossae in these genera. Similarly he agreed with Hutton that wide and continuous size gradation in moas was an environmental effect and was not due, as Oliver (1930) had argued, to an innate or orthogenetic predisposition.

Oliver's (1949) discussion of moa evolution ranked the genera, primitive to advanced, as *Pachyornis*, *Emeus*, *Euryapteryx*, *Zelornis*, *Anomalopteryx*, *Megalapteryx*, *Dinornis*; almost opposite to the arrangement preferred by Hutton. Oliver's (1949:54) argument was based on a variety of morphological characteristics such as the unproduced lacrymal bone in *Pachyornis*, which put it at the bottom of the Anomalopterygidae, while the shape of the *Megalapteryx* pelvis, especially its escutcheon, put it at the top. The cursorial adaptations of *Dinornis* were, he thought, the most advanced moa features.

Oliver (1949:188) conceded that Cook Strait 'had the effect of separating the developing lines of moas and thus in some, but not in all, cases ensuring their evolving into different species and genera'. His refusal to grant any further role to geographic isolation in moa evolution did not arise on any evidential grounds but from a deeper philosophical opposition to evolutionary theory. Oliver had rejected the contemporary orthodoxy of evolutionary gradualism (the doctrine that speciation is a slow incremental process moulded by natural selection), disagreeing with both natural selection and genetic change by mutation. In earlier papers (Oliver 1930:29, 1945:68) he had set out the orthogenetic charter of his later work: through time, animals increased in size and degree of ossification, while projecting portions became more prominent.

Scarlett (1957:18) argued that New Zealand was split into three regions in the late Pliocene–early Pleistocene by the Manawatu Strait and the Manukau Strait, and he divided the moas, according to

their source areas, in the following way. In Northland the comparatively small species of *Z. exilis*, *Eu. curtus*, *Eu. tane* and *A. oweni* evolved. On the mainland North Island the northern species of the *Dinornis* species-pairs were evolved, along with *A. didiformis*, *Eu. geranoides* and probably *P. mappini* and *P. septentrionalis* (possibly also Northland). In the South Island the southern species of *Dinornis*, *Eu. gravis*, *Emeus crassus*, *P. elephantopus*, *Z. haasti* and *Megalapteryx* evolved, while in the southern region a small form of *Euryapteryx* developed and spread to Stewart Island before the formation of Foveaux Strait during the Holocene.

Fleming (1974:63) proposed an earlier framework of divergence. The 'Greater Moas' (*Dinornis*) separated from the 'Lesser Moas', and the latter into subfamilies, in the early Tertiary, and into genera by the later Tertiary. Speciation began in the Pleistocene, but occurred largely during the Holocene once Cook Strait existed. Later he proposed moa 'diversification and specialisation' (? subfamilial and generic divergence) during the Eocene, although why particularly then is not clear (Fleming 1979:98). Speciation began, he thought, in the Miocene, although why then is, again, not apparent. Fleming (1977:146) also observed that some moa species, particularly the species-pairs of *Dinornis*, might well be regarded as subspecies.

Millener (1981:472–3) subsequently returned, as Fleming almost had, to Hutton's argument that the evolution of moas into subfamilies and genera began during the Oligocene transgression, while speciation probably occurred during the Pleistocene.

This longstanding hypothesis of moa evolution contains two assumptions which are today rather questionable. The first is that allopatric speciation was induced only by major events of vicariance, and the second is that phyletic divergence as deep as the subfamilial level must have required a very long period of time to attain. In the case of the first there had been other vicariant events, notably during the late Pliocene and Pleistocene, and not all of them concerned marine transgressions. Climatic severity during the last glacial period was probably sufficient to create a lack of woody vegetation across the highly glaciated waist of the South Island thus isolating some southern species from their northern populations. But in addition to vicariance there were, beginning in the Oligocene, other processes which may have been just as influential. Two were the development of relief, with its consequences for climatic and botanical differentiation, and a marked increase in floral taxa, notably shrubs such as the *Coprosmas*, which first appear in Oligocene pollen spectra (Fleming 1979:84, 93; Mildenhall 1980:222).

In the case of the second assumption the 'punctuated equilibria' model of evolution does not require the precondition of long periods of time for speciation to occur. Instead of lengthy, incremental transformation, Gould (1980:15) argues that 'lineages change little during most of their history, but events of rapid speciation occasionally punctuate this tranquility'. Since the hypothesis works in conditions of sympatric speciation (i.e. within the same ancestral population), it is not dependent upon vicariance. Leaving aside island-specific subspecies or varieties, all the remainder of moa phyletic divergence might just as easily have occurred in the late Pliocene or well back into the early Tertiary during the 40 my before the Oligocene archipelago arose at the mid-point of the lineage's separate existence.

The consequence of these arguments is that our understanding of moa evolution, like ratite evolution in general, lies at the mercy of speculation. But more disquieting than that is the possibility that sufficient fossil evidence might never become available to establish moa evolution upon a firmer foundation – for there are few Tertiary terrestrial deposits, and no abundance of shallow-water strata.

Natural sites and geographic distribution of moas

Leaving unresolved the problem of moa evolution in New Zealand, and moving forward to the time when all the modern genera were in existence, the next major question concerns the relative abundance of the different kinds of moas and the factors involved in distribution patterns. The most pertinent data are those from natural deposits, of which the richest and best known are swamp sites. The others are sites in caves, dunes and similar sedimentary deposits. The distribution of these (Fig. 4.4) largely reflects the geography of alkaline sediments. Caves are mostly in areas of limestone, and the swamp sites, unlike peat swamps in general, contain layers of alkaline mud which form the principal bone-bearing horizons (Millener 1981: 452–4).

Swamp sites

Shortland (1851:137) recorded the first swamp containing moa bones in 1843. It was situated at the neck of the Waikouaiti peninsula, where a bed of black sand and rotted flax up to a metre deep extended for about 100 m along the low tide level. Containing numerous bones of moas and other birds, this layer was underlain by stiff blue clay. Important collections were made by William Davison, Dr McKellar, Percy Earl and Walter Mantell in the 1840s, but apart from one observation of the lower legs of a moa in a natural position, nothing has been recorded of the disposition of the remains (G. Mantell 1850, 1862). Mantell (1849) described the usual rough means of recovering and handling them as 'hunnish behaviour'.[8]

Glenmark swamp was the next major find (Haast 1869). The bones, many of them abraded, were found up to 4 m deep, resting upon gravel. Haast identified to species 138 adult moas, and also found six unidentifiable adults and 27 young birds in the bone collection. His MNI (Minimum Number of Individuals) figures are regarded as dubious by Scarlett (pers. comm.) who found Euryapteryx, in addition to Haast's genera, comparatively few Anomalopteryx and numerous Dinornis maximus (giganteus). Worthy's (pers. comm.) analysis of Haast's figures is shown in Table 4.1, but its value must be tempered by Hutton's (1897a: 558) observation that the Glenmark collection was so widely dispersed that it was impossible to arrive at any accurate results about the relative numbers of species.[9]

One of the best described sites was found in 1870 by B. S. Booth (1875) at Hamiltons, in Central Otago. Working with Hutton, Booth recovered more than 3 tonnes of moa bones from a semicircular area of swamp about 12 × 6 m and 0.6–1.2 m deep, which was set in a basin of blue clay. About half the bone was discarded as being too decayed,

[8] The possibility that the site was archaeological in whole or part was raised by Mantell's remark that seal and dog bones had been found amongst the moa bones (to G. Mantell 1850:337). With Cyril Walker (BMNH) I checked the extensive Waikouaiti collection remaining in the Natural History Museum. We found only a D. robustus tibiotarsus and a P. elephantopus tarsometatarsus which exhibited signs of cultural charring and damage. The mammal bone fragments, unlike nearly all the moa bone pieces, were dessicated and unmineralised. Inside one was written 'sand-hills' suggesting that these remains, and possibly the few culturally modified moa bones, came from the sand dunes which had partially covered the swamp site or from the archaeological site in the adjacent dunes (G. Mantell 1848a:229, 1850:334. See diagram in Oliver 1949:6).

[9] In transforming older data into modern taxa I have followed the synonymy in Archey (1941). D. crassus var. major has been equally divided, if arbitrarily, between P. elephantopus and Eu. gravis. Since I have corrected earlier errors in arithmetic and calculated MNI according to the most common element, some figures are quite different from those in earlier publications (e.g. Falla 1941).

Fig. 4.4   Distribution of important natural moa-bone deposits.

but it was estimated that the original deposit had contained at least 400 moa skeletons. Booth observed some signs of possible cultural activity such as split sticks and large stones in the deposit, as well as a rat mandible, but there were no obvious artefacts, cut bones or charcoal. The bones were less decayed at the top of the bed, although no bones from young moas were found there, unlike at deeper levels. Heaps of gizzard stones were common, indicating that moas reached the swamp as carcasses, but there was no eggshell.

Evidence of a spring was found beneath the deposit, and Booth concluded that moas had been attracted to a warm spring in which they had huddled together and starved to death during an episode of very cold climatic conditions. His con-

temporaries preferred the view that carcasses had been washed in to the site.

A second deposit of moa bones was found at Hamiltons in 1875 (Booth 1877). It contained twice as many bones, but in a more decayed condition, and it lay 2 m below the clay floor of the first deposit; the only recorded instance of natural sites being stratified in this fashion. Both sites had evidently been related to the same spring and the greater concentration of young moa bones near the bottom of the upper deposit was continued into the lower, with young moas as abundant as adults.

It is not clear what significance is to be attached to stratigraphic variation in the incidence of young moa bones. Hutton (1892c:151–4), noting the absence of eggshell and the probability of higher

TABLE 4.1   MNI of moa species in natural sites

North Island		Moa species									MNI total
		Anom. didif.	Pachy. mapp.	Pachy. eleph.	Eury. curtus	Eury. geran.	Din. struth.	Din. novaez.	Din. gigan.		
Northland Dunes		5	118	–	335	32	26	8	6		530
	%	1	22	–	63	6	5	2	1		
King Country Caves		343	42	2	56	38	61	43	22		607
	%	57	7	–	9	6	10	7	4		
Total		348	160	2	391	70	87	51	28		1137
	%	31	14	<1	34	6	8	4	2		

South Island		Anom. didif.	Mega. didin.	Pachy. eleph.	Eury. gravis.	Em. crassus	Din. toros.	Din. novaez.	Din. gigan.		MNI total
Canterbury/Otago Loess		2	–	5	10	8	3	1	3		32
	%	6	–	16	31	25	9	3	9		
South Island Caves											
Heaphy Valley		8	–	–	–	–	3	–	–		11
Oparara Valley		23	1	–	–	1	–	–	1		26
Nile Valley		14	3	8	5	–	9	4	2		45
West Coast Misc.		23	1	–	3	–	4	10	–		41
Takaka Valley		35	1	3	6	–	2	3	1		51
Nelson Misc.		8	–	–	–	–	–	–	–		8
Eastern South Is.		17	6	4	6	4	1	8	10		56
Takahe Valley		–	53	–	–	–	–	–	–		53
Total		128	65	15	20	5	19	25	14		291
	%	44	22	5	7	2	7	9	5		
South Island Swamps											
Molesworth		–	–	1	3	–	7	2	–		13
North Dean		1	–	3	8	6	–	–	1		19
Pyramid Valley		–	–	17	20	60	4	8	55		164
Glenmark		x	x	22	17	82	12	3	8		144
Albury Park		–	–	22	–	34	2	–	3		61
Kapua		2	3	44	12	254	28	20	15		378
Enfield		x	–	33	10	134	10	2	6		195
Hamiltons		–	–	45	12	27	9	4	x		97
Wanaka		–	–	–	2	–	5	3	–		10
Miscellaneous		1	1	1	4	1	–	–	1		9
Total		4	4	188	88	598	77	42	89		1090
	%	<1	<1	17	8	55	7	4	8		

Note: North Island data from Millener (1981:251, 255). South Island loess and cave data from Scarlett (pers. comm.), plus Hector (1872), Hutton (1892c), Hamilton (1893a, 1894), Ritchie (1982a). Swamp site data from Hutton (1875, 1896a, 1896b), Haast (1869), Scarlett (1969, pers. comm.), Burrows *et al.* (1984), Worthy (pers. comm.).

mortality in the colder months, thought the carcasses had been washed into the swamp during the autumn or winter, but there is no other evidence upon which to base a seasonal hypothesis.

Alexander McKay (1882) reported the discovery of a densely packed layer of moa bones in clay, overlain by gravel and 'peaty lignite', at Motunau.

The adult bones were in little apparent order, but the immature bones were generally found in an upright position. *Pachyornis elephantopus* seems to have been the main species.

Seven years later Augustus Hamilton (1889) recovered more than 1000 moa bones from the swampy margins of Te Aute Lake, the major

North Island discovery of this kind. Many of the leg bones were upright, indicating that the birds had walked into the swamp. The bones lay among the remains of a drowned forest and were underlain by blue clay. There was a spatial concentration towards the ends of low spurs extending into the lake as if the birds had been using these features as routeways. No quantitative results have been published for Te Aute swamp, but all the North Island *Dinornis* species, *Eu. curtus*, *A. didiformis* and *P. mappini* were represented. Hutton (1892c:127, 152) thought that *Cela [Euryapteryx] geranoides* was the most common species and that *D. struthioides* and *A. didiformis* were also plentiful amongst the remains. A recent re-examination of the material (Worthy pers. comm.) indicates that *Eu. curtus* was the main species, followed by *Eu. geranoides*. Remains of all the North Island *Dinornis* species were also common.

In 1891 Forbes (1892c) collected numerous moa bones from ploughed land at Enfield, and estimated that 800–900 moa skeletons had been deposited there. The site consisted of an area of peat about 11 m wide and 1.2 m deep lying upon blue clay. The bones were concentrated in the peat and were in positions which suggested that the birds had died with their legs folded. *Dinornis [Pachyornis] elephantopus*, *D. rheides [E. crassus]* and *D. ingens [novaezealandiae]* seemed to Forbes to be the main species, but Hutton's (1896b) examination of the bones remaining in the Canterbury Museum arrived at slightly different results.

At Kapua swamp Hutton (1895a:628) thought 800 moas had been represented (Fig. 4.5). These came from an area 6 × 9 m by 2.0 m deep in which blue clay packed with bones, below black peat containing few bones, was overlain by 1.2 m of soft yellow clay. The bones were undamaged and there were numerous remains of young moas, but no eggshell.[10]

These were the major 19th-century discoveries, but swamps rich in moa remains continued to be

[10] At Enfield, Kapua and Glenmark immature bones were not identified. At Kapua they were discarded.

FIG. 4.5   Excavations at Kapua swamp, October 1894. (By courtesy of Canterbury Museum.)

discovered. The bones of 40–50 birds, mainly
A. didiformis, *Eu. curtus* and *D. novaezealandiae* were
found in a mud-spring at Clevedon in 1912, and
about the same number of birds were represented
in the Herbert swamp excavated in 1941 by Oliver
(1949:12–18). Here the main species was
P. elephantopus. At Upokongaro numerous moa
remains were excavated in 1936 and proved to be
mainly of *Dinornis*, *Anomalopteryx* and *P. mappini*.
In deep peat above a spring at Albury Park,
Scarlett (1969) recovered moa remains in 1963, and
Trotter (1970d) found moa remains in a peat
swamp at Scaifes Lagoon, Lake Wanaka, in 1970.
At North Dean a small number of moa bones have
recently been recovered from a peaty earthflow
containing forest remains (Burrows *et al.* 1984). Of
all the swamp sites, however, none is more important to our understanding of them than that at
Pyramid Valley.

Found to contain moa bones in 1938, this North
Canterbury swamp was the site of systematic excavations by the Canterbury Museum in 1939–42,
1948–49, 1965 and 1973. The swamp had been a
shallow lagoon before European drainage and
extended over about 1.2 ha. The density of bones
in the excavated areas suggests that the site might
have contained 2000–2500 moas. The remains
were concentrated in a viscous, jellified, clay or
gyttja which underlay shallow surface peat and
overlay a thick peat layer resting upon stony silt.
The gyttja was 0.6 m thick near the margins of the
swamp but up to 1.2 m in the deepest areas excavated. The moa skeletons were found in small
clusters of individuals which Duff (1941) thought
might reflect load-bearing variations in the surface
peat (but see below). There were also spatial differences in the species composition. Smaller moas,
especially *E. crassus*, occurred in the shallow margins, while the *Dinornis* species were evidently able
to extricate themselves from these areas and were
mainly caught in deeper deposits towards the centre (Fig. 4.6). Most skeletons were found standing
in an upright position, although in the deepest
areas some had turned upside down in the water
and liquid mud. Trapped by sinking up to the back
had, in general, preserved the leg and trunk bones,
but heads and necks evidently decomposed or were
scavenged on the surface. There are, as a result, no
complete skeletons, and the association of loose
crania with particular leg bones was seldom
beyond doubt. *Emeus crassus* and *Dinornis
giganteus* were the main species recovered (Table 4.1).
Adults outnumbered young birds by two to one,
and all species were represented by immature individuals (Duff 1941, 1955; Gregg 1972).

FIG. 4.6 Jim Eyles, Ron Scarlett and Roger Duff (left to
right), with *Dinornis* legs and pelvis recovered from
Pyramid Valley swamp, March 1949 (Duff 1949:20).
(By courtesy of Canterbury Museum.)

Looking at the swamp sites as a whole it is clear
that they were not all formed in the same way.
There are mud-springs (Upokongaro, Clevedon,
Pukemata), lake-side margins (Te Aute), wet
earthflows (North Dean) and rich peat swamps in
clay basins, which are in the majority. In most
cases where the standards of excavation were sufficient to tell, moa leg bones tended to be found
standing upright indicating that the moas had been
trapped alive. At Hamiltons and Glenmark and
possibly some other sites, however, it seems that
the deposits, whatever their original form, had
been re-sorted. The fact of densely packed bones,

often commented upon by early observers, might reflect no more than the shrinkage of the mud or peat matrices as the original lagoons dried into shallow swamps.

Booth (1875:127), and on some occasions Hutton, thought that swamp sites had been formed during the last ice-age while, at the other extreme, Hector (1893:557) referred to cultural firing and claimed that 'among the moa-bones found in the swamps were great masses of charred bones'. This unsubstantiated remark perhaps suggests that Hector had misidentified the oxide staining on the bones, despite Booth's (1875) clear observations on the matter. The hypothesis of a late, post-human accumulation was also raised at Pyramid Valley, where it was argued that the moas had become trapped by breaking through surface peat into the gyttja below, and that this had occurred after about AD 1300 when swamp vegetation was thought to have spread over the lake sediments during a period of climatic dessication (Gregg 1966).

Hutton's (1897a) later opinion was that the three Canterbury swamp sites known to him were of different ages. Glenmark was regarded as the oldest since the *Meiornis* remains appeared relatively undifferentiated. Kapua, in which they were differentiated and the bones lay deep in blue clay, was younger, and Enfield, where the bones were in surface peat and both *Meiornis* species had increased in size, was the youngest. There might be something in this on stratigraphical grounds, as radiocarbon dates also suggest, but the argument about *Meiornis* is unconvincing. When the species are combined into the modern *E. crassus*, the fact that the smaller of the two (*Mei. didinus*) was found twice as frequently as the larger (*M. casuarinus*) at Enfield, whereas the larger form was four times or more as frequent at the other two sites, indicates that the actual trend would be a decline in size.

Radiocarbon dates from moa-bone swamp deposits are shown in Appendix B. Of the 21 Pyramid Valley dates, NZ609 is on bone carbonate and can be ignored, while details concerning the Y129 series are insufficient for much reliance to be placed upon the results. The remaining dates provide a very consistent series which shows that the lower peat was covered by a shallow lake at about 4000 bp and that the gyttja trapped moas from then until at least 2600 bp. In fact, judging by a gyttja accumulation rate of 0.45 mm per year, it may have been 1500 bp before the upper peat began to form (Gregg 1972:154–5). The other swamp dates range from the earlier Holocene at Pukemata and Albury Park, up to dates comparable to the upper

end of the Pyramid Valley gyttja accumulation at Glenmark, Enfield and Scaife's Lagoon, with North Dean and Clevedon at the end of the sequence. Poukawa swamp is a complex of several sites including a probable Pleistocene deposit in which there are numerous remains of large *P. mappini*, and a Holocene deposit in which other species, notably *A. didiformis*, are more common (Worthy pers. comm.).

The swamp sites as a whole form a quite homogenous and directly comparable series. They also bear out Fleming's (1979:97) view that the formation of modern peat swamps was largely a Holocene phenomenon which, along with the development of coastal sand dunes, was a consequence of rising post-glacial sea levels to their present position at about 5000 bp.

Cave sites

As cave sites I include vertical sinkholes, caves with horizontal entrances (which form together the majority of the cases) and rockshelters. If sufficient details were available it would be interesting to divide the sample into these various categories to see whether sinkholes, which acted only as traps, caught a different spectrum of moas than other caves and rockshelters which, in varying degrees, were also used as nesting and resting places by some moas, notably *Anomalopteryx*. A further potential source of variation in the data for this broad site type arises from the probability that rockshelters might also contain cultural deposits of moa remains which could easily be mixed, and mistaken, in loose floor sediments. The Hawke's Bay rockshelters investigated by Hartree (1960, n.d.) and the Takahe Valley shelters (Duff 1952) certainly contained deposits of both kinds and, as in sand dunes (below), it is a matter which demands rather greater attention than has been the case hitherto (see also Ambrose 1970).

Systematic collection of moa bones from caves began with Thomson's (1854) exploration of limestone caves in the Waipa Valley in 1849, and it was continued by Haast and Maling, excavating under Hochstetter's (1867:186) patronage, in the Aorere Valley caves in 1859. They found two caves with moa bones, from which 11 individuals were recovered. One was *P. ingens* (*D. novaezealandiae*), and the remainder were divided between *P. elephantopus* remains found in a semi-fossilised condition beneath up to a metre of stalactite and *A. didiformis* bones in a soft surface layer. Hochstetter concluded that a considerable time difference was involved, and it now seems likely that the lower deposit was formed during a glacial era (Worthy pers. comm.).

About 1871 moa remains were discovered at the Earnscleugh Cave, and these included the preserved *Emeus* neck (Chapter 5). Although there have been more accounts of research in this cave than any other it is still not possible to say with certainty whether it was, as most have supposed, a natural deposit. Fraser (1873:103) and Hutton (1875:139) had seen some signs of possible cultural activity – charred moa bones at the cave entrance and rat bones mixed amongst bones which were probably those of *Euryanas finschi* – but they rejected this interpretation. Thomson (in Hector 1872: 113), on the other hand, found charred moa phalanges in the interior chamber of the cave during the first rudimentary excavations there and he speculated upon cooking *in situ*, while Hector (1871:185) claimed that Fraser had told him that chert knives and flakes were found 'at the same place where the moa's neck was recently obtained'. In this connection the sharp, straight margin to the broken skin on the dorsal surface of the moa neck invites conjecture, but the matter will not be resolved until the site is relocated and investigated. Various other desiccated moa remains have been found in central Otago (e.g. Fig. 4.7 and see Chapter 5).

A few moa bones, mainly of *Anomalopteryx*, were found at Castle Rocks by Hamilton (1893a, 1894), but it was not until 1914 that a cave site comparable with the swamp deposits was excavated. This was at Coonoor, where 500 kg of bone representing some 50 moas and 30 *Aptornis*, as well as smaller birds, were dug out of a shallow sinkhole (Buick 1936:12–16). Most of the moas proved to be *A. didiformis*, and the remainder were *D. novaezealandiae*. There have been further cave sites located nearby (*The Evening Standard* (Palmerston North), 25 February 1984).

The next year the Martinborough Caves were discovered, but they were not excavated until 1920. Cave 1, a vertical sinkhole, contained numerous moa leg bones but Yaldwyn (1956, 1958), who later identified the remains, decided to rely upon crania. Of these, there were eight belonging to *Anomalopteryx*, seven to *Pachyornis* and one to *Dinornis*. In Cave 5, a crevice suitable for nesting, were the remains of an *Anomalopteryx* adult and chick and of several eggs.

During the 1930s and 1940s numerous caves in the King Country, East Coast hill country and Golden Bay districts were inspected, but few specific results have been published. Worthy's (pers.

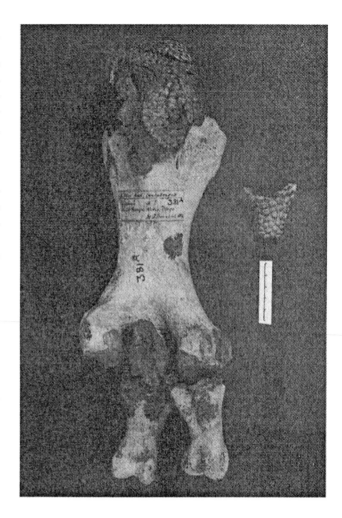

FIG. 4.7   Dessicated tissues on a foot of *Pachyornis elephantopus* found, presumably in a rockshelter, at Nevis (see Table 5.2). (By courtesy of Zoology Museum, Cambridge University.)

comm.) analysis shows that *A. didiformis* (56 per cent) was the main species in the King Country material, followed by *Dinornis* (21 per cent), particularly *D. torosus* and *D. novaezealandiae*. A series of caves at Lake Waikaremoana produced numerous moa remains, particularly of *A. didiformis*, *D. novaezealandiae* and *P. mappini*, while remains in a cave at Tarakohe proved to be largely of *P. elephantopus* (Archey 1941:5; Oliver 1949:14–18).

Since then many caves in the South Island interior and along the West Coast have been investigated (some results Table 4.1; there have also been recent discoveries of desiccated remains, Fig. 4.8). Amongst them may be noted the rockshelters in Takahe Valley which contained a large collection of *Megalapteryx* remains. Another very important site is the Oparara Caves complex – this is still

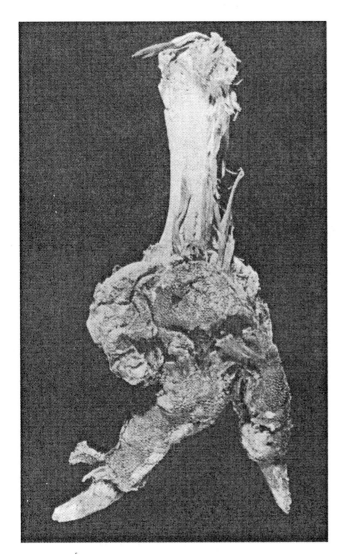

FIG. 4.8   Mummified foot (ventral view) of *Megalapteryx didinus* from cave at Mt Owen (see Table 5.2). (By courtesy of National Museum, NZ.)

under investigation and the figures in Table 4.1 refer only to the small sample of bones taken to the Canterbury Museum. There are hundreds of moas represented in the full collection, and they are distributed amongst some 50 discrete deposits which date from the late Holocene to about 60,000 bp. In general, remains of *P. elephantopus*, *P. australis* and *M. didinus* are prominent in deposits dating to the glacial era, while *A. didiformis*, *D. torosus*, *D. novaezealandiae* and *M. didinus* are typical species in Holocene deposits (Worthy pers. comm.).

More typical of eastern South Island sites are two small clefts in schist near Cromwell (Ritchie 1982a). The Firewood Creek deposit contained remains of two *Eu. gravis*, one *A. didiformis* and one

D. robustus (*novaezealandiae*), while the Station cleft contained at least six individuals of *A. didiformis*.

A marked predominance of *A. didiformis* is, as these cases would suggest, clearly revealed in the data for caves as a whole, and there is a striking overall similarity in the representation of genera for each island. One potential reason might be that cave deposits were generally formed at a particular time. The formation of limestone caves has been dated as early as 500,000 bp in New Zealand, and there is no apparent reason why bones should not survive for that length of time in such richly-calcareous environments. The earliest published date for cave deposits of moa bone, however, is only about 24,000 bp from Moa Cave in Waitomo. The other dates for such remains are fairly evenly spread up to 1000 bp, with seven earlier, and 11 later than 10,000 bp (Millener 1981:411, 848; Appendix B).

Sites in dunes and loess

Faunal remains in sand dunes can present a difficulty in distinguishing between natural and cultural deposition because there are frequent opportunities for cultural material to be lowered by deflation to horizons occupied by natural bone accumulations, or indeed for the reverse to happen. Distinguishing the former occurrence of such events can be exceedingly difficult, and opinions may differ with equal support about the status of such sites. In northern Northland, for example, Scarlett (1979) concluded that the bone deposits were generally middens, but Millener (1981:240), with the support of radiocarbon dates, argued that they were essentially of natural origin. Since the case must be made in each instance it is not possible to say to what extent the numerous moa-bone deposits in sand dunes at Doubtless Bay (Archey 1931), Pataua (Thorne 1876), Riverton Beach (Ewen 1896) or on the East Coast (Hill 1914), to take just four examples, are clearly of natural origin. In the circumstances the only data presented here are from sites in Northland which Millener (1981) regards as being of natural origin.

In line with Fleming's (1979) views about Holocene dune development, the sites are dated between 1000–5000 bp, with the main concentration about 2000–3000 bp. Only one date, NZ4608, might fall within the human era. The main species in these sites is *Eu. curtus* (63 per cent), with *P. mappini* at 22 per cent. These two small moas thus constitute 85 per cent of the total MNI sample.

Moa bones have been recovered from other open sedimentary deposits in at least one case with desiccated flesh attached (Fig. 4.9). Bones have been dredged from the floor of Cook Strait as well. They probably represent birds which had been living there during the last low sea level (Fleming 1963). Moa bones have also been found in Pleistocene loess deposits about Banks Peninsula, Timaru and North Otago. Some from Cape Wanbrow (*Emeus* and *Euryapteryx*) have been dated to the last glacial advance (Burrows *et al.* 1981:322). Moa remains of apparently similar age were found by Haast (1865) in glacial moraines and in lacustrine deposits formed immediately upon glacial retreat in Canterbury.

Moa ecology

In considering the evidence from natural sites it is apparent that there is, as ecological principles would predict, an inverse correlation between size and abundance. In the North Island small species of moas constitute nearly 80 per cent of the

numbers, while in the South Island medium and medium-large species are predominant, 75 per cent of the numbers, (Fig. 4.10). In an environmental context, small species constitute 71 per cent of the numbers in rugged hill country and 85 per cent of the numbers in the coastal dunes, while in downlands, most moas were from medium-sized (59 per cent) or medium-large (24 per cent) species. Leaving aside the Northland data which seem to reflect a latitudinal rather than topographical effect, there is an obvious and expectable difference between hill country and lowlands in the relative abundance of smaller and larger moas.

Amongst the different categories of natural sites (Fig. 4.11) the caves appear different from the rest. *Anomalopteryx* is the main genus, followed by *Dinornis* (although *Megalapteryx* is equally abundant in Fig. 4.11 by virtue of the Takahe Valley sample). In contrast, in loess and especially sand dunes, *Euryapteryx* is the main genus, while *Emeus* is predominant in swamps. If sample size is not a major factor what do these differences mean?

It is impossible to rule out a chronological effect. Cave and loess sites are quite likely to be of Pleistocene age, while swamps and sand dunes with moa bones are generally Holocene features dated

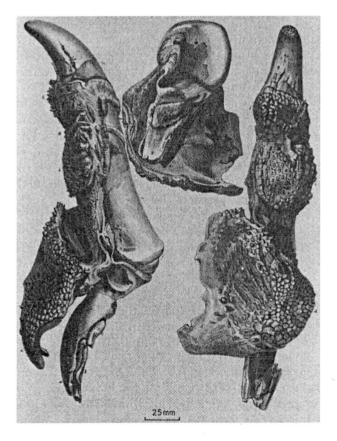

FIG. 4.9 Preserved tissues on a foot of the Tiger Hill specimen (see Table 5.2), found in alluvial sand (Owen 1879aII:pl. lxxi).

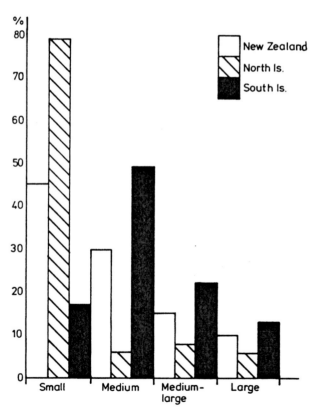

FIG. 4.10 Proportional distribution of moa MNI in natural sites by species-size and island.

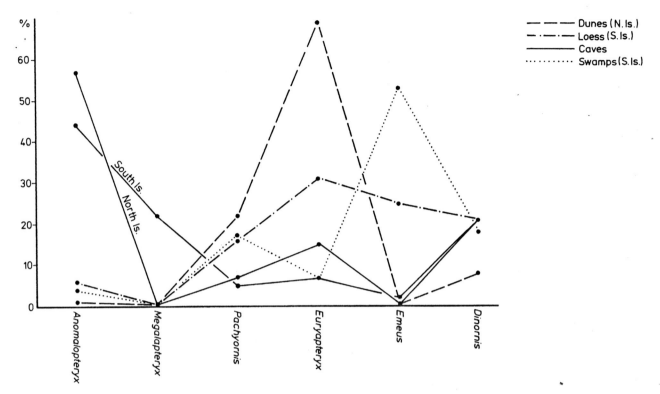

FIG. 4.11   Proportional distribution of moa MNI in natural sites by site type and genera.

to after 5000–6000 bp. Furthermore it is apparent from recent research, notably in the Oparara Caves, that there is a significant difference between species assemblages of the glacial era, dominated by *Pachyornis* in particular, and those of the Holocene, when *Anomalopteryx* became especially common.

Another possibility is that the site types operated in selectively different ways amongst genera of similar relative abundance. This could hardly be true of sand dunes or loess, but it is conceivable that *Anomalopteryx* was particularly prone to end up in cave sites – either because it chose to inhabit them more often than other genera, or because of some other behavioural idiosyncrasy, such as greater mobility. Similarly *Emeus* may have been more attracted to swamp-edge food resources than other genera, or more prone to being bogged. But examining such possibilities remains beyond the present evidence. The most likely explanation of the differences is that they largely reflect different distributions of genera in the environment.

Early observations in the eastern South Island remarked upon the scarcity of moa bones on plains (e.g. Haast 1872c; Hutton 1897a:557) as compared to the margins of plains (Hector 1872; Booth 1875; Pyke 1890), and such differences probably reflect variations in the former vegetation patterns which were significant for moas. Until the last millennium in Central Otago, for instance, forest existed around the hill slopes, although in some areas it had been cleared by natural fires as early as 2500 bp. . The lower fringes of the forest were largely determined by rainfall, and in most of eastern Central Otago the threshold lay along the lower slopes of the hills below which shrublands probably extended to about the hills–plains interface where they gave way to the dry open country apparent today. Examination of the locations of both natural deposits of moa bones and of moa-hunting sites (Anderson 1982a) demonstrates a correlation with the ecotonal area of the shrublands (Figure 4.12). Factors other than preferred habitat might, however, be involved. Recent surveys have encountered natural deposits of moa bone of unknown age in the driest areas of the basins, and it is possible that the distribution of natural deposits in general significantly reflects differential opportunities for preservation and subsequent exposure in the sedimentary landscape (Pole pers. comm.). In addition, moa-hunting sites might generally have been located at points below the hunting area, i.e. below the former forest, so that recovery of carcasses was always downhill. Even

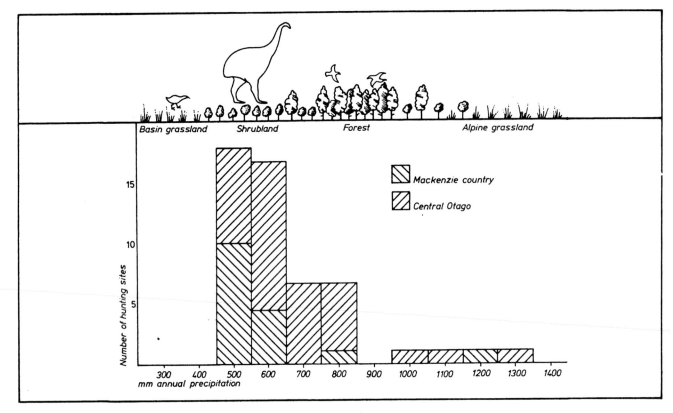

Fig. 4.12   Distribution of moa-hunting sites in the inland South Island in relation to precipitation and former vegetation patterns.

so the evidence suggests, at least, that moas were not as common on open plains as they were in woody vegetation at higher altitudes.

This does not mean, however, that moas generally lived in forest. Taking the evidence as a whole, there seems to be a broadly inverse correlation between moa habitat preference and closed forest throughout New Zealand, so far as moa-hunting sites are concerned, although some major sites were clearly on the edge of major tracts of forest, as in the Catlins. Natural deposits are rather more difficult to interpret in this regard since they have seldom been dated with sufficient precision to rule out accumulation during the last glacial period when the vegetation patterns were very different. Similarly 19th-century reports of moa bones being found amongst the remains of former forest in Otago, for example, could be explained by mortality in shrublands which replaced the forest. All that can be concluded is that evidence of moas is relatively scarce in beech forest and that moas as a whole seem to have been less abundant in the North Island – a more completely forested habitat than the South Island – during the early Maori era.

Recent research by Worthy (n.d.a, pers. comm.) has brought these earlier and tentative perceptions of pattern into much sharper focus. From the results of his fieldwork at Oparara Caves, and an extensive examination of material from many other natural sites, he has defined two broad ecological assemblages of moa species. One is an 'Anomalopteryx assemblage' comprising that genus together with the smaller Dinornis species. It is common to Holocene sites in areas of damp, lowland, podocarp–broadleaf forest. At higher altitudes, notably in beech forest or in cooler (Pleistocene) environments, Megalapteryx replaces Anomalopteryx.

In contrast, a 'Euryapteryx gravis assemblage' is typical of drier, lowland open forest, scrub and grassland, particularly where these communities form vegetation mosaics. It is an assemblage which was more extensively distributed during the last glacial era, and in addition to subsequent restriction of range there seems to have been some general diminution in the size of certain species, notably Euryapteryx (n. sp. of Scarlett) in coastal Southland where open country became very restricted, and

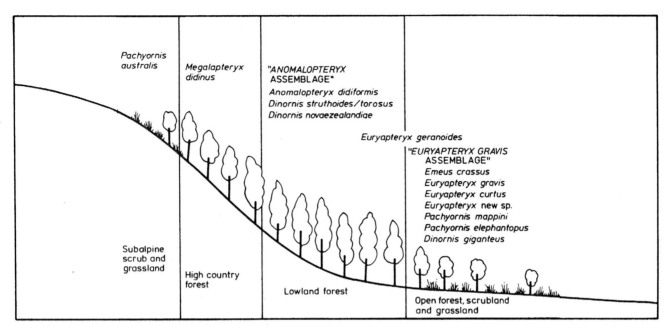

Pachyornis
australis

Megalapteryx
didinus

"ANOMALOPTERYX
ASSEMBLAGE"

Anomalopteryx didiformis
Dinornis struthoides/torosus
Dinornis novaezealandiae

Euryapteryx geranoides

"EURYAPTERYX GRAVIS
ASSEMBLAGE"

Emeus crassus
Euryapteryx gravis
Euryapteryx curtus
Euryapteryx new sp.
Pachyornis mappini
Pachyornis elephantopus
Dinornis giganteus

Subalpine
scrub and
grassland

High country
forest

Lowland forest

Open forest, scrubland
and grassland

FIG. 4.13   Model of moa ecological assemblages (data from Worthy pers. comm.).

P. mappini in the North Island. In subalpine scrub and grassland *P. australis* occupied a similar habitat. *Eu. geranoides* seems to have been widely distributed in lowland areas of the North Island but is too scarce in Holocene sites to define a clear pattern of ecological distribution. Worthy's model is shown in Fig. 4.13. It should also be noted that the transition from one ecological assemblage to another occurs not only at a regional level but also within local areas. For example, in Southland, there is an 'Anomalopteryx assemblage' represented at Castle Rock, but at sites on plains nearby are remains of a 'Eu. gravis assemblage', e.g. at Hamiltons near Winton (Worthy pers. comm., and see Millener 1981:480 on Northland).

5

MORPHOLOGY AND BEHAVIOUR

In studies of moa systematics and evolutionary history there is one point of common agreement: variability in the size and shape of moa bones is both considerable and difficult to characterise or subdivide. This is especially true of the post-cranial skeleton upon which most attention has been focussed over the years. Two papers by Cracraft (1976b, 1976c), however, now provide a quantified introduction to variation in moa morphology.

Sources of variability

Cracraft (1976b) analysed measurements of length, mid-point circumference and various dimensions of breadth and depth at each end for the three leg bones of his 13 species, plus *E. huttoni* recognised separately. The morphometrical techniques employed were principal components and canonical analyses.

Looking first at variation within species, Cracraft found that it was mostly expressed in size; 65–93 per cent of variability depending upon species and bone. The remainder, or non-size variability, was largely due to shaft thickness in the femur, but there were more complex relationships in the other two bones, particularly in the tarsometatarsus where the middle trochlea recedes with increasing length in *Dinornis* but becomes more prominent in all other genera.

Principal components analysis of interspecific variability also picked out size as the most important component (94 per cent of variation in the tarsometatarsus, 96 per cent in the tibiotarsus and 97 per cent in the femur). Most of the non-size variability was due to shaft thickness in the femur and tibiotarsus, with *Dinornis, Megalapteryx* and

A. oweni being noticeably gracile. In the tarsometatarsus those three genera also exhibited slender shafts and shallow middle trochlea, whereas the opposite qualities were evident in the remaining genera.

Canonical analysis similarly revealed size as the main source of interspecific variability, although it was more complex than simply overall bone length and included, for example, the internal condyle length of the femur. There was about 10 per cent non-size variability in the femur which was mainly due to variation in robustness and to distally narrow ends in *Anomalopteryx* and *Dinornis*, as against distally-broad ends in *Pachyornis* and *Euryapteryx*. In tibiotarsi, 86 per cent of the variability was due to size and the minor shape component distinguished between proximally narrow ends in *Anomalopteryx, Megalapteryx* and *Dinornis*, as opposed to proximally-broad ends in *Emeus, Euryapteryx* and *Pachyornis*. There were also differences in robustness. This consistent and simple pattern became more complex in the tarsometatarsi, where variability proved less easily divisible between size and shape. A relation between long bone length and a small middle trochlea in *Dinornis* formed one extreme of a continuum extending to species with short bone length and moderately developed middle trochleae (*Eu. curtus, P. mappini* and *E. huttoni*). However since overall bone length was a major factor, species with moderate bone length, but a large middle trochlea, occupied the central ground (*Eu. geranoides, P. elephantopus* and *E. crassus*). Most of the remaining 25 per cent of variability lies in the relative size of the proximal end, as might be expected, although again the influence of bone length is such that short tarsometatarsi with narrow proximal

ends (the small species of *Euryapteryx*, *Pachyornis*
and *Emeus*) sort towards the same pole as short
tarsometatarsi with broad proximal ends (the large
species of those genera).

Taking these analyses together, the variability in
moa leg bones can be sorted into two broad
groups. In the first, femora are slender and distally
thin, tibiotarsi are long and slender and tarsometatarsi are slender, proximally narrow and have
small, shallow, middle trochleae. In the second
group, femora are robust and distally thick, tibiotarsi are robust and proximally broad and tarsometatarsi are robust. The first group can then be
subdivided into two, largely on the basis of bone
size; the larger bones all belong to *Dinornis*, the
smaller to *Anomalopteryx* and *Megalapteryx*. Tibiotarsi are proximally narrow in the former and
proximally broad in the latter. The second main
group can also be subdivided into two, and again
largely according to bone size; the larger belonging
to the big species of *Euryapteryx*, *Pachyornis* and
Emeus, and the smaller to the diminutive species of
these genera. Tarsometatarsi have comparatively
large and deep middle trochleae in the former and
are also proximally broad, whereas they are proximally narrow in the latter. In Figs. 5.1 and 5.2
these relationships are illustrated. The degree of
overlap is largely caused by the size of individuals
at the top end of the *A. didiformis* range.

In a second paper Cracraft (1976c) used multiple
factor analysis to examine the patterns of morphological covariation amongst 42 variables measured
on the feet and leg bones, pelves and sterna of 32
'associated' skeletons (i.e. skeletons in each of
which all the bones are claimed to belong to the
same individual). He found that sternal breadth
was largely independent of hindlimb factors, as it
seems to be in flying birds, and that pelvic breadth
covaried with the breadth of leg bones, probably
because of their integration in structural support.
The relationship between body length (thorax plus
pelvis) and leg length disclosed the expected difference between *Dinornis*, with relatively long legs,
and the Anomalopterygines with relatively short
legs.

At the risk of obscuring important differences,
the common result of both studies could be summarised thus: there are two morphological models
of the moa hindlimb of which one comprises comparatively long, slender, narrow-ended bones with
small processes (*Dinornis*, *Anomalopteryx* and *Megalapteryx*) and the other comparatively short, stout,
thick-ended bones with more prominent processes
(*Euryapteryx*, *Pachyornis*, *Emeus*), Fig. 5.3.

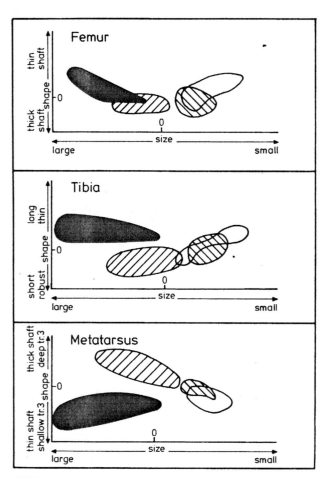

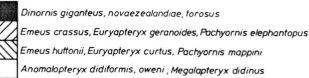

Dinornis giganteus, novaezealandiae, torosus

Emeus crassus, Euryapteryx geranoides, Pachyornis elephantopus

Emeus huttonii, Euryapteryx curtus, Pachyornis mappini

Anomalopteryx didiformis, oweni ; Megalapteryx didinus

FIG. 5.1   Principal components of size and shape for moa
          limb bones, adapted from Cracraft (1976b:Figs. 2
          (reversed), 4 and 6).

Two questions now arise. How was this variability expressed in stature and weight, and were
these morphological characteristics related uniformly amongst all species?

Stature and weight

Early popular estimates of stature suggested that
moas generally were nearly 5 m tall, and figures of
up to about 3.6 m are still commonly accepted.
One reason for these estimates was the way in
which moa skeletons were set up in museums. In
the 19th century mounted specimens of moas were
usually arranged with the pelvis and thoracic
vertebrae inclined upwards, and with the neck

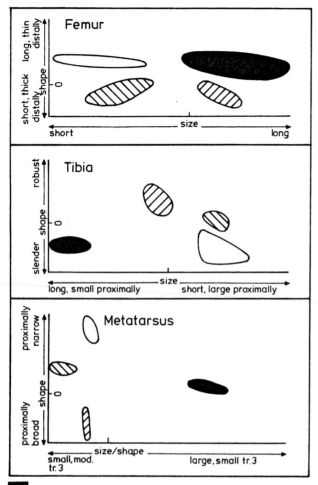

FIG. 5.2   Canonical analyses of size and shape for moa limb bones, adapted from Cracraft (1976b:Figs. 8, 10 and 12).

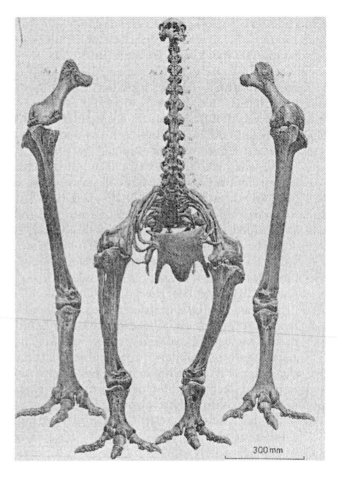

FIG. 5.3   Skeleton of *Dinornis* (now *Pachyornis*) *elephantopus*, compared with leg bones of *Dinornis robustus* (now *novaezealandiae*), illustrating differences in length and shape between Dinornithids and Anomalopterygids (Owen 1879aII:pl. lxi).

almost vertical and elongated by supernumerary vertebrae.

Even so, more realistically mounted specimens included some undeniably tall individuals. A *D. maximus* skeleton 'articulated in an easy standing position' (Owen 1877:184) in the British Museum stood 3.35 m tall, and Hutton's (1892c: 171) figures for *D. maximus* leg bones, converted to overall stature according to the method outlined below, would yield a bird 3.51 m tall. Since *D. altus* was assumed to be taller again, moas of 3.65 m tall are not impossible. But moas generally were much shorter birds. Owen's (1849b) early estimates (given the original imperial measures) by comparison of moa leg bones with ostrich and cassowary homologues, put *D. giganteus* at 10 ft (3.04 m) tall, *D. ingens* at 9 ft (2.5 m) and the remaining species known in the 1840s at between 4 ft (1.2 m) and 7 ft (2.1 m) tall.

Now that the preferred taxonomy of moas is so different it becomes desirable to calculate stature again. For comparative purposes, amongst ratites in general, the height of the back is the most useful measure, since some carried the neck upright and others in a looped horizontal manner.[1] For moas,

[1] How moas usually held their necks is an unresolved problem. The cervical vertebrae are comparatively short (cf. kiwi, cassowary) and massive dorsal spines on the thoracic vertebrae impressed Owen (1849b:260) as evidence of a powerful neck. Interlocking cervical vertebrae also suggest a looped posture (Halliday 1980:132; McCulloch 1982:13). Rock drawings, which show moas with the neck held upright (Teviotdale 1932a:104), are possibly modern drawings executed after the introduction of emus to North Otago in 1866. Alternatively, they may depict moas in an alarm posture, with heads raised.

the most direct way to obtain the height of the back would be to measure, on mounted specimens, the height above the feet of the dorsal spines on the thoracic vertebrae and add a small amount for flesh and feathers. The problem here is that there are very few accessible specimens and some contain bones from different species. Moreover, while *Dinornis* skeletons tend to be mounted with the leg bones aligned more or less vertically, and skeletons of other genera with the knee bent at an obtuse to right-angle, it has been argued by Alexander (1983a:229) that the shortness of the metatarsi in Anomalopterygids, and to a lesser extent in Dinornithids, probably required a standing moa to maintain the femur as well as the other leg bones in a more or less vertical position in order to keep the centre of mass over the legs. Whether this theoretical consideration worked out in practice is an issue on which Holdaway (pers. comm.) and Worthy (pers. comm.) adopt a different view. Study of the articular surfaces of the leg bones suggests to them that, in life, moa leg bones generally assumed a conformation more like a reversed Z, especially in Anomalopterygids (Fig. 1.4). This probably implies several locomotory modes – a running action in that family and a striding action in Dinornithids. In any event, the calculations below should be regarded as having a comparative rather than an absolute value.

The method I have adopted assumes that the height of the back was equivalent to the length of the leg, plus 10 per cent to allow for the height accumulated by the pelvic crest or dorsal vertebral spines above the acetabulum, the tissues of the feet and between the bones and the flesh and feathers of the back. The data shown in the bottom line of the first column (Table 5.1) are, for each species, the mean for the sum of the leg-bone lengths derived from the references shown and, in brackets, the minimum and maximum means of the summed leg-bone lengths from Oliver's (1949) tables, adjusted where necessary to fit the modern taxonomy. So far as the mean leg lengths are concerned, I have used the latest reference in which the measurements were taken as a single set (i.e. leaving aside data sets which combine measurements from different authorities, as in Cracraft (1976a), because it is likely that duplicated measurements are included). Comparison of reconstructed back heights for three species (in Fig. 1.4) suggests that the results in Table 5.1 exaggerate actual stature by 20–50 per cent.

The head-up stature, which I assume moas could adopt (below), is included as a basis for comparison with older estimates. It is simply the height of the back plus 33 per cent in each case. That figure was obtained by estimating the proportional height of the head above the back in illustrations of modern ratites (average 31 per cent), and from the top of the highest thoracic vertebrae to the top of the cranium in illustrations of mounted moa skeletons (average 36 per cent).

Compared with figures for the nearest large, living ratites, it is apparent that half of the moa species or subspecies were shorter than the cassowary or emu, three stood at about the same height and only the three large *Dinornis* species were significantly taller. In back height, the largest moa species was 2.7 times as tall as the smallest.

Turning to moa weight or mass, the figures shown in Table 5.1 arise from a variety of techniques. Amadon (1947:163) calculated the weight of *D. maximus* and *D. giganteus* at 230 kg and 242 kg respectively, by using proportions of femoral cross-sectional area to weight in the cassowary for the former, and body length to weight in the cassowary for the latter. Smith (1985:477) employed the cross-sectional method using the cassowary as a model for *Dinornis* and the rhea for the other genera. It is difficult to see why he should choose different analogues, particularly the rhea for moa species such as *Pachyornis*. Alexander (1983a) used four different techniques: scale models for which the volume was calculated by displacement in water and then converted to mass; the cube of a linear dimension, such as leg length; a method based on the assumption that trunk mass is proportional to body mass in which measurements of the trunk bones in moas were compared with those of the ostrich (and the ostrich mass was then used to estimate the moa mass); and calculation of body mass by assuming that it is about 14 times skeletal mass.

Taking up Alexander's method based upon the geometric relationship that mass scales as the cube of length, a relationship which seems to hold fairly broadly in biological terms, I have calculated the body weights of the moas according to the mean leg lengths shown in Table 5.1. The results have been plotted as the curve in Fig. 5.4.

It is difficult to choose between the various sets of results. The length cubed method expresses a physical constant and is therefore useful as a basis of comparison, but some estimates obtained by this method are very different from those obtained by others, amongst which there is a reasonable measure of agreement.

There is nothing to be gained by averaging these

TABLE 5.1   Estimated stature and mass of moas compared with other ratites

Species	Approx. height of back (cm)	Approx. head-up stature (cm)	Body mass (kg) By c/s femur Smith (1985)	By length³ (Author)	By scale model	By trunk mass	By skeleton mass	Preferred* single figure	Raw data source
					Alexander (1983a)				
A. didiformis	87 79 (50–89)	116	32	†46, 49	29	20	42	32	Archey (1941), Smith (1985), Alexander (1983a)
M. didinus	89 81 (65–95)	119	25	53				25	Cracraft (1976b), Smith (1985)
P. mappini	73 67 (54–81)	97	28	30				30	Cracraft (1976b), Smith (1985)
P. elephantopus	117 107 (86–121)	156	105	†119, 123 †163	129	115, 127	170	123	Cracraft (1976b), Smith (1985), Alexander (1983a)
Eu. curtus	70 64 (51–70)	93	22	26				22	Oliver (1949), Smith (1985)
Eu. geranoides	91 83 (79–85)	121	61	57				57	Oliver (1949), Smith (1985)
Eu. gravis	106 96 (90–103)	141	61	†66, 88			75	75	Oliver (1949), Smith (1985), Alexander (1983a)
Eu. crassus	94 85 (73–99)	125	51	61				61	Cracraft (1976b), Smith (1985)
D. struthoides	112 102 (93–112)	149	117	106				117	Oliver (1949), Smith (1985)
D. torosus	131 119 (113–124)	175	125	169				125	Oliver (1949), Smith (1985)
D. novaezealandiae	155 141 (131–166)	207	167	280				167	Cracraft (1976b), Smith (1985)
D. giganteus	189 172 (158–199)	252	230‡	242, 509‡	242	199		230	Cracraft (1976b), Smith (1985), Alexander (1983a)
Aepyornis maximus	183 166	237		457				Actual weight	Amadon (1947)
Rhea	87	116		66				20	Amadon (1947)
Ostrich	111	148		137				100	Alexander (1983a)
Cassowary	103 93	133		86				45	Amadon (1947)
Emu	112 102	145		106				35	Amadon (1947)
Kiwi	31 28	40		2.2				2.5	Cracraft (1976a)

Note: *Preferred in light of stature, body shape, etc.; †Alexander (1983a); ‡Amadon (1947).

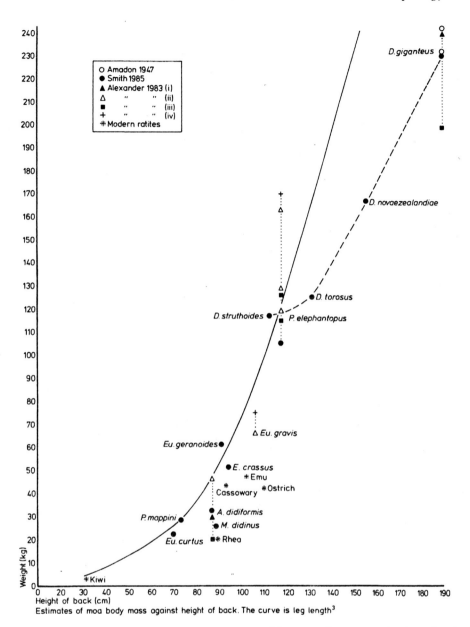

FIG. 5.4 Estimates of moa body mass against height of back (see Table 5.1). The curve is leg length cubed.

data. While I generally prefer Smith's figures (Table 5.1), I suspect that his results generally underestimate results for Anomalopterygids and overestimate them for Dinornithids.[2] In general terms they show that there were four lightweight species in the range 20–50 kg (*A. didiformis*,

M. didinus, *P. mappini* and *Eu. curtus*); three light-medium-weight species (*Eu. geranoides*, *Eu. gravis* and *E. crassus*) in the range 50–90 kg; four heavy-medium-weight species in the range 100–170 kg (*P. elephantopus*, *D. struthoides*, *D. torosus* and *D. novaezealandiae*); and one heavyweight moa (*D. giganteus*) of 200 kg or greater. The discrepancy between the weights for *Aepyornis*, compared with those for *D. giganteus*, arises largely because the femora in the latter have a very much smaller cross-sectional area. This difference may serve to introduce the fundamental issue of allometry in moa morphology; that is, of changing proportions between weight and stature.

[2] Atkinson and Greenwood (n.d.) have subsequently estimated moa body weights using a method based on measurement of femoral circumference. Their results were (mean and range, nearest kg): *M. didinus* 24 (17–34), *A. didiformis* 41 (32–59), *E. crassus* 75 (46–120), *Eu. geranoides* 96 (49–140), *P. elephantopus* 146 (97–247), *D. torosus* 96 (82–115), *D. novaezealandiae* 144 (100–200), *D. giganteus* 178 (134–273).

Allometry

It has been commonly assumed that moas were not merely unusually diverse in size and shape but in some species were outlandishly so. In stark contrast to tall slender moas were 'absurd looking creatures nearly as broad as high, with short, heavy stumpy legs, on which they could hardly waddle' (Hutton 1892c:98). But whether there were actually such morphological extremes is a question which depends upon removing to one side size-dependent variations in shape to allow residual differences to be perceived.

Cracraft (1976b:498, 517–22) studied the allometry of the moa leg by comparing legs from 36 moa skeletons against their body size, defined as the linear summation of thorax, pelvis and leg lengths. Taking moas as a single group, he found that the relationship of all femoral measurements to body size was essentially isometric (variation at a constant rate). Removing *Dinornis* from the sample, however, revealed positive allometry in all characters except femoral length: that is, bone breadth increased at a proportionately greater rate with increasing body size. Conversely, in the *Dinornis* sample, no variables, including length, exhibited positive allometry, and all except length fell below the regression line against body size fitted for the non-*Dinornis* data. Similar results were obtained in the cases of tibiotarsi and tarsometatarsi.

Cracraft concluded that the hindlimb morphology of all the non-*Dinornis* moas was quite uniform, and such differences of shape as existed simply expressed an allometric accommodation to size. It was not the Anomalopterygids which were unusual, but *Dinornis* which had leg bones remarkably slender for its size. The theory of elastic similarity predicts that in biomechanical structures length should scale as diameter to the two-thirds power (McMahon and Bonner 1983). In non-*Dinornis* moas the diameter exponent for moa femora was very close at 0.64, but in *Dinornis* it was 1.08, and 1.12 for the *Dinornis* tarsometatarsi. Tibiotarsi were slightly thinner than expected (0.84 and 0.87).[3]

Alexander (1983a) tackled the allometry of the moa hindlimb in a different way – by comparing bone length and shaft diameters against inferred body mass. Although the latter inferences involve substantial margins for error, they provide a more direct expression of the relationships between weight and size than Cracraft's choice of a linear measure. In relating bone length to mass the general relationship is mass approximates length cubed, or length is proportional to (body mass) 0.33; but elastic similarity predicts that the relationship should be (body mass) 0.25 for length, and (body mass) 0.375 for diameter (McMahon and Bonner 1983:38–53, 222).

Alexander found that the actual body mass exponents for flying birds and mammals averaged 0.35 for length in both, and 0.36 and 0.41 respectively for diameter. Turning to Anomalopterygidae he found, by comparison, that the tarsometatarsus is significantly short at 0.26, although very close to the theoretical relationship; the femur is slightly short at 0.31, and the tibiotarsus slightly long at 0.39. The Anomalopterygid toe length is slightly shorter than for flying birds in general. The exponents for the Anomalopterygid bone diameters were: 0.59 (femur), 0.44 (tibiotarsus) and 0.47 (tarsometatarsus). All are therefore comparatively stout. Alexander gives no exponents for *Dinornis* but the results showed that leg-bone lengths and diameters were similar to the mean for flying birds. Compared with Anomalopterygids the *Dinornis* femur was slightly thinner in relation to body mass, but the tibiotarsi and tarsometatarsi diameters were very close.

Alexander concluded that the leg bones of *Dinornis* were longer than would be predicted by comparison with Anomalopterygids of similar mass and the femur is slightly more slender. *Dinornis* leg bones are about the length which would be predicted by the mean exponents for flying birds and the Anomalopterygid bones would still fall within the range for flying birds. In comparison with modern ratites, the Anomalopterygids have tibiotarsi and tarsometatarsi which are in proportion, both shorter and thinner.[4]

In another study, Alexander (1983b) considered whether the leg bones of *P. elephantopus* were unnecessarily stout in terms of locomotion. He found that even running at slow speeds would produce levels of bone stress in the tibiotarsus comparable with those in other ratites and mammals, but that the femur and tarsometatarsus had wider margins of safety in their strength (below). Even so, in

---

[3] To explain the disproportionate slenderness of *Dinornis* leg bones Cracraft (1976b) suggested adaptive re-modelling of the micro-architecture of the bones which enabled them to withstand greater stress.

[4] McMahon and Bonner (1983:132) note that because structural relationships are different for volant organisms they should not be considered within the theory of elastic similarity. Nonetheless Alexander's (1983b) figures for flying birds are very similar to those for mammals.

proportion to body mass, 'the strengths of moa leg bones seem less remarkable than at first appeared' (Alexander 1983b: 374).

The main conclusion to be drawn from these studies must be that moas generally conformed to predictable relationships between size and shape, or height and mass. If Alexander is right about bone diameters, then it is only in the lower leg-bone lengths that moas scale diversely. Alexander's figures, although from a very small sample, show that *Dinornis* tibiotarsi are 26 per cent, and tarsometatarsi 85 per cent, longer than would be predicted for Anomalopterygids of the same mass. Since the kiwis scale as the Anomalopterygids and the large living ratites as *Dinornis* (and *Anomalopteryx* and *Megalapteryx*, although neither Cracraft nor Alexander divided their samples in this way in studying allometry), it is apparent that diversity in the moas was no greater than amongst the modern Australasian ratites. The weight and stature data plotted in Fig. 5.4 thus suggest that about half the moas scaled morphologically in a more or less geometrical relationship and the remainder were slightly tall for their weight.

Soft tissues

Another avenue for investigating the shape and appearance of moas arises from the existence of feathers and mummified portions of moa carcasses

(Table 5.2), most of which have been found in Central Otago.

Muscles and skin

Inference of musculature depends upon comparative deductions about the sinew attachment areas on bones. Numerous particular results of such research were reported by Owen and his contemporaries, but a recent investigation indicates that perhaps only the most general of conclusions are likely to be valid. McGowan (1979) examined the correlation between kiwi hindlimb musculature and attachment markings on the bones. He found that only 23 per cent of muscle origins and insertions could be identified by bone markings and that the latter provided no clear indication of the relative development of the muscles. In reference to moas, McGowan concluded that the 'possibility of being able to reconstruct the musculature of the kiwi from its skeletal anatomy, much less that of its extinct relatives, is remote' (1979:33).

Taking only his broad conclusions, then, Owen argued three points about the musculature of the moas. First, that the cranial muscles operating the jaw were very well developed, especially in *Dinornis*, where the 'depressions on the occiput for the insertion of the nuchal muscles indicate the force with which they must have habitually operated upon the head; and the unusual size and depth of the temporal fossae equally indicate the great

TABLE 5.2   Discoveries of moa soft tissues

Species with finder	Locality and date	Material	Museum	References
D. Robustus 'gold digger'	Tiger Hill, Manuherikia Valley, reported 1864	Flesh, skin and feathers attached to pelvic area. Part of sole on one foot. Some cartilage and ligaments on other bones.	York	Owen (1866a, 1869a, 1879aɪ:440–1), Dallas (1865), Buick (1931:246).
Mr S. Thomson	Junction Clutha and Manuherikia (Alexandra), reported 1871	Feathers, associated with moa bones	?National (N.Z.)	Hutton (1872b), Owen (1879aɪ:441–2)
'a digger'	Between Alexandra and Cromwell, reported 1871	Feathers		Hutton (1872), Owen (1879aɪ:442–3)
S. crassus and possibly other species, Mr Weir, Dr A. T. Thomson and others, Captain Fraser and son.	Earnscleugh Cave, near Clyde, 1872	Proximal portion of neck (last two cervical and first dorsal vertebrae) with flesh, skin and feathers. Femur with flesh attached. Pieces of skin and muscle. 'Rolls' of skin. A head with jaw and tracheae attached.	Otago	Fraser (1873), Hector (1872:111–15), Hutton and Coughtrey (1875b), Owen (1879aɪ:443–4)

Species with finder	Locality and date	Material	Museum	References
Mr W. A. Low	Alexandra district, reported 1871	Piece of moa flesh and feathers		Hector (1872:114)
D. ingens, M. G. E. Allen	Galloway Station, Manuherikia Valley, 4 June 1874	R. tarsometatarsus and phalanges (with other bones), flesh and skin.	Otago	Hutton and Coughtrey (1875a), Anon (1875)
M. didinus	Near Queenstown, in Old Man Range, reported 1878	Head and 14 cervical vertebrae plus both legs and feet. Flesh, skin and feathers cover most of the bones.	British Museum (Natural History)	*The Tuapeka Times* 23 November 1878, Owen (1885b)
?D. casuarinus Mr Taylor White	Mount Nicholas, Lake Wakatipu, reported 1875	Feathers, associated with ?moa droppings		White (1876, 1886); note by Hutton appended. Owen (1879aI:447), Russell (1877)
Mr Taylor White	Near Queenstown, reported 1875	Feathers, associated with ?moa droppings		White (1876, 1886)
M. didinus Mr P. McLeod	Waikaia district, reported 1894	Full left leg with flesh, skin and feathers	Otago	Hamilton (1895)
?M. didinus Mr A. Hamilton	Waikaia district, reported 1894	600–700 feathers		Hamilton (1895)
?M. didinus	Strath Taieri, reported 1893	Strip of skin and feathers, attached to portion of weka skin garment	Otago	Hamilton (1893b:487), Duff (1952:108)
?M. didinus Dr R. A. Falla	Takahe Valley, Fiordland, reported 1949	Feathers, ?moa droppings	?Canterbury	Duff (1952:93)
M. didinus	Cromwell area 1942	Head and neck with flesh and skin but no feathers. Ligaments on leg bones	National (N.Z.)	Oliver (1949:9, 153–4)
'small moa' found by 'rabbiters'	Tuapeka area	Feathers adhering to skull		*The Tuapeka Times* 16 July 1887
P. elephantopus Mr W. J. Branford	Nevis district 1884	L. tarsometatarsus with dried flesh and skin at proximal end. Separate patch of skin	Zoology Dept, Univ. of Cambridge	Buller (1888), Hutton (1892c)
Mr B. S. Booth	Shag Mouth, Otago 1875	Small piece of moa skin *c.* 2.5 × 4.0 cm		Booth (n.d.)
Mr P. J. O'Regan	Moonlight Creek, West Coast 1893	Leg bones with 'claws and scales'		Buick (1931:166)
A. didiformis Mr K. Hamilton	Lake Hauroko, Southland, 1975	Vertebrae with skin and ligaments	Southland	Beck (n.d.)
A. didiformis Mr. J. R. Murdoch	Lake Echo, Southland 1980	Skeleton with flesh, skin, feathers on pelvis, vertebrae and cranium	Southland	Forrest (1987)
–	Limehills	Piece of moa skin	Southland	Beck (pers. comm.)
M. didinus Mr P. Wopereis, B. Were and T. Worthy	Mt Owen, Nelson 1987	Leg, pelvis with flesh, skin, feathers	National	*The Otago Daily Times* 12 January 1987

strength . . . of the bill' (Owen 1849c:310). Second, the neck was extraordinarily strong. Some cervical vertebrae in *D. maximus* were almost equal in size to those of a horse so that when to the 'powerful neck muscles in *Dinornis*, were added their thick integument and covering of feathers, the neck must have been a feature of strength very different from the slender character of that lengthy part in the ostrich and the like living birds' (Owen 1877:161). Third, the legs in general, but particularly the lower legs and feet, were noticeably powerful, even in the smallest species, (Fig. 5.5, also Owen 1885a; Haast 1890b).[5]

The few relevant remains of soft tissues seem to support at least the latter two of these general conclusions. The base of the *E. crassus* neck from Earnscleugh Cave (Fig. 5.6) was 47 cm in circumference, even in a shrivelled state, and the *Megalapteryx* upper necks appear strongly made. The *Megalapteryx* leg from Waikaia has a large bunch of thick sinews arising from about the ankle joint, and the Queenstown leg, while lacking most of the soft tissue, impressed Owen with the apparent strength of the foot (Owen 1885b:260).

Kooyman's (1985:197–202) recent inferences of relative muscular strength are, however, somewhat at variance with these latter conclusions. He argued that attachment markings on the bones were weak for the *Megalapteryx* digital flexors, tarsometatarsal flexors and extensors, tibiotarsal extensors and the tissues associated with the rotation of the femur. These comparative deficiencies, he thought, probably excluded *Megalapteryx* from rapid locomotion. Kooyman also suggested that the *P. elephantopus* leg was not as heavily muscled as the size of the bones suggest, and that *A. didiformis* had a powerful lower leg and foot, possibly indicating a scratching or digging function as in the kiwi. Since Kooyman's conclusions are based upon evidence from dissections of kiwis they are worthy of respect, but it would be wise to regard them cautiously until further such research has been carried out.

Covering the flesh of moas was a thick and probably tough skin. On the Earnscleugh moa neck the dried skin was nearly 5 mm thick and reddish-brown in colour (Fraser 1873; Hutton and Coughtrey 1875b). It seems to have been at least as thick on the Galloway leg (*D. robustus*), where it was yellowish-brown in colour (Hutton and Coughtrey 1875a). The skin surface has the charac-

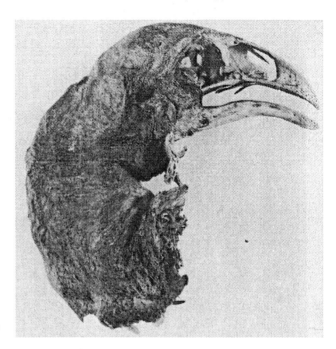

FIG. 5.5   Dessicated remains of *Megalapteryx didinus* head from Cromwell (see Table 5.2). (By courtesy of National Museum, NZ.)

teristic 'gooseflesh' appearance caused by small conical papillae for the insertion of the feathers. These seem to have been larger on the trunk and upper legs than on the neck and head. On the Galloway leg the tarsometatarsus is covered in a scalar pattern with thickened, subcircular patches of skin up to 12 mm in diameter, but there is no evidence of actual scales (Fig. 5.7). Both the sole and tarsometatarsus in this species and on the Queenstown leg (Owen 1885b:260) have a worn and scratched appearance, indicating that moas rested with their lower legs flat on the ground, as do the large modern ratites.

One further point of interest is that Owen (1879ai:453) thought that one of the series of footprints found near Gisborne (the prints he attributed to *D. dromioides*, i.e. *A. didiformis*), indicated a slightly webbed foot (Fig. 5.8). This feature, and also the comparatively long back toe would, he suggested, have provided a useful adaptation for traversing soft ground. *Megalapteryx*, as well, has a comparatively large foot (Worthy pers. comm.).

Feathers

There is no clear pattern of size or colouration represented amongst moa feathers. Structurally they are very flexible, filamentous, open-webbed and lacking in barbicels. Some, perhaps a minority, carry a shorter aftershaft.

---

[5] Muscular leverage was assisted by sesamoid bones behind the proximal and distal joints of the tarsometatarsus (Owen 1877:183).

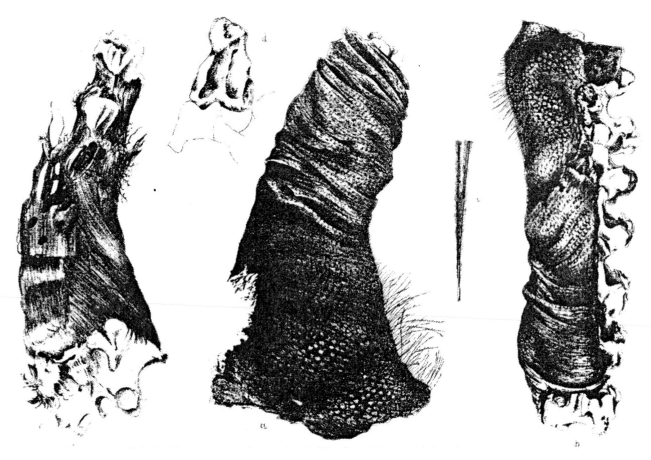

FIG. 5.6   Mummified moa neck from Earnscleugh Cave (Hector 1872). (By courtesy of Royal Society of NZ.)

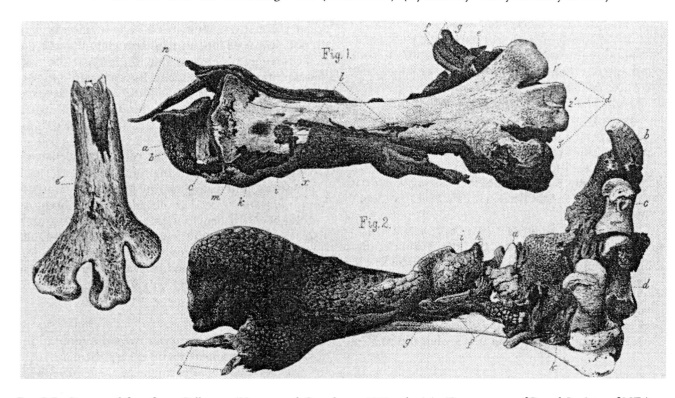

FIG. 5.7   Preserved foot from Galloway (Hutton and Coughtrey 1875a:pl. xix). (By courtesy of Royal Society of NZ.)

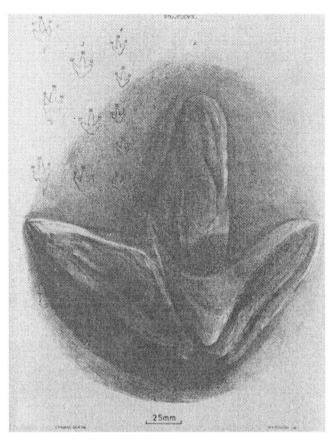

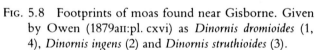

FIG. 5.8 Footprints of moas found near Gisborne. Given by Owen (1879aii:pl. cxvi) as *Dinornis dromioides* (1, 4), *Dinornis ingens* (2) and *Dinornis struthioides* (3).

FIG. 5.9 Mummified *Megalapteryx didinus* leg from Waikaia (see Table 5.2). (By courtesy of Otago Museum.)

The best specific evidence refers to *Megalapteryx didinus*, which was feathered from the base of the bill to the base of the ankle (Oliver 1949:47). The feathered tarsometatarsus is an unusual feature which, amongst ratites, is only otherwise found upon *Rhea darwini* and in the embryonic *R. americana* (Pycraft 1901). The lower leg feathers on the Queenstown specimen were 2.5–7 cm in length, single-shafted, without basal down and greyish in colour near the base altering to reddish-brown at the tip (Owen 1885b). On the Waikaia leg (Hamilton 1895), most of the feathers were in varying shades of brown with lighter brown tips (Fig. 5.9). One feather, found nearby rather than on the leg, was purple and about 55 mm long. No neck or head feathers were found on the *Megalapteryx* specimens, but the pits for their insertion were evident and these increased slightly in size on the neck and towards the occiput.

The feathers remaining on the back of the trunk in the Tiger Hill remains were reduced to basal shafts. They were·double-shafted, brown at the base and horn-coloured towards the top (Dallas 1865).

Few other collections of feathers can be attributed to any particular species, although there were a few chestnut-red feather barbs remaining on the Earnscleugh neck. Coughtrey observed that the insertion pits for these were small and about 2–4 mm apart on the dorsal surface, but larger and 5 mm apart on the ventral surface. He commented that, allowing for some shrinkage of the skin, this moa 'possessed not a very thick coat of feathers' (Hutton and Coughtrey 1875b:111).

The Mount Nicholas feathers were associated with some remains of *D. casuarinus* (*E. crassus*), but how well is not clear. They have been described rather differently on three occasions. Taylor White (1876) first saw them as double-shafted, greyish-brown and about 7.5 cm long; whereas Hutton, in a note appended to White's paper, described them as being pale yellow-brown and darker at the margins. The largest was 16.5 cm long. White (1886: 83) later saw most of them as being 'a bright transparent yellow, as of gum or resin, changing to dark purple brown on the outer margin'. Except for one large, pure white feather, the remainder were single-shafted of a dark-reddish or chestnut purple, with lighter reddish shafts. Reconstructing the plumage in imagination he suggested 'a foundation of shining yellow outwardly, shaded with dark purple brown, the breast a chestnut purple; and, to locate the white feather, say white on the afterpart of the back' (White 1886:83).

The Queenstown feathers found by White (1876) were described as double-shafted and brown, with light-coloured down near the shaft, but Hutton saw them as reddish-brown with a central longitudinal dash of dark-brown towards the apex. The basal down was brownish-white. White (1886) again described them as up to 15 cm long and belonging to three classes: long, double-shafted feathers with light coloured down along two-thirds of the shaft and dark purple-brown at the tip; a shorter, broader and more robust type with thick down which was darker in colour; and feathers 5–10 cm long of a more hairy texture varying in colour from yellowish-brown to nearly black.

The feathers found deep in river sand near the Clutha were double-shafted and up to 18 cm long by 2 cm broad (Fig. 5.10). They were brown, deepening upward into black, but with a narrow white rim at the apex (Hutton 1872, 1875).

It is difficult to glean much about moa plumage from these data. It is at least likely, however, that the strikingly short overall length of moa feathers – most of which seem to have been less than 10 cm long, and none over 18 cm – lent the plumage a juvenile appearance. This may have been enhanced by a rather thin coverage on the neck and head in some species, as well as by the lack of any tail or wing feathers to add elegance to an otherwise chicklike body. There is quite a range of colour, but reddish-brown shading down to light brown or grey, and up to deep red or reddish-purple, seems to have been the most common. It is impossible to tell in what combinations these colours may have been distributed through the plumage, but similar colours are found amongst the kiwis where there are both plain and checked patterns.

One matter which remains as unresolved as the appearance of the plumage is whether any moas carried a crest of feathers on the head. Parker argued that two groups of shallow pits on the roof of a *Mesopteryx* (*Pachyornis*) skull, and pits in other patterns on the skulls of *D. torosus*, *D. robustus* (Parker 1893a) and *A. didiformis*, 'indicate that the moas in which they occur possessed a crest of stiff feathers in the anterior frontal region' (Parker 1893b:5, Fig. 5.11). No other ratites possess such a feature, but if the casque on the cassowary head

FIG. 5.10   One of the moa feathers found at the Clutha–Manuherikia confluence (Owen 1879aII:pl. cxiv).

facilitates movement through thick foliage a crest might have served a similar function for forest-living moas. The difficulty at present is that the evidence of such a feature is neither particularly convincing nor sufficiently common.

Locomotion and other faculties

The conclusion that moas are unremarkable in their morphology is sufficient evidence to dispose of early beliefs that some moas found it difficult to walk, although Worthy (n.d.c.) has argued that the pelvic and leg bone geometry of *Euryapteryx* induced a waddling gait. But how fast moas in general could run is a more difficult matter to pin down. Alexander (1983b) made some preliminary investigations using the evidence of foot size and stride length in sequences of preserved moa footprints (Table 5.3). He calculated that the represented animals had been moving at between 2.9 and 7.2 km/hr, or still within walking speeds.

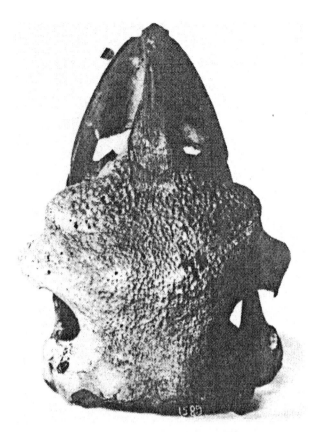

FIG. 5.11 *Dinornis* skull showing suggested feather pits of a crest (Buick 1931:224). (By courtesy of D. V. Avery.)

How fast a moa might have been able to run is a matter for greater speculation. In considering *P. elephantopus*, Alexander observed that fossil tracks of a bipedal dinosaur which had feet of about the same size have been estimated to show a speed of 43 km/hr. Adult humans with an equivalent hip height can run at up to 36 km/hr, and ostriches can reach 43–61 km/hr. Given the heavier build of *P. elephantopus* Alexander suggests a top speed in the range 11–36 km/hr. If so, the larger *Dinornis* species with their long slender legs could probably have run faster still.

Why they should need to do so is another difficult question. Given the scarcity of predators there would seem to be three possible answers. First, running at slower speeds may have been an efficient way of utilising widely spread and comparatively scarce food resources. Second, running could have been necessary for some other purpose – such as the kind of running-chasing agonistic behaviour observed amongst rheas (Cracraft 1976b:525). Third, a bodily conformation suitable for running might have been an incidental effect of selection for stature.

Moas probably also took to the water on occasion, if the evidence of other large animals is any guide, and the large modern ratites, especially the cassowary and rhea, have been recorded swimming strongly across rivers and estuaries. Rothschild (1901:127) recorded cassowaries inhabiting a small island 2.4 km offshore.

Other faculties

Other natural abilities of moas have been poorly regarded at times. A 'less delicate perception' than modern ratites, was Owen's (1849b:261) early opinion of their intelligence, judging by evidence of a narrow spinal canal; and he soon amended this to assert that moas were duller and more stupid than the dodo (Owen 1849c:326). Hutton (1892c: 98) also thought moas were small-brained, and consequently 'stupid and sluggish'. Possibly the only way in which such obvious prejudices might be tested, and then very indirectly, would be by a minute comparative examination of the interior surface of the cranial cavity.

Owen had taken a cast of this cavity in a specimen of *D. giganteus*, but his interest lay in the size of the optic lobes which he found to be relatively larger than in the kiwi. Together with evidence of relatively larger orbits, he concluded that moas possessed better sight and were diurnal, unlike the

TABLE 5.3 Estimates of moa locomotion speeds from footprints

Foot length (cm)	Foot width (cm)	Stride length (cm)	Estimated hip height (cm)	Estimated speed (km/hr)	Data source	Possible genus
20	18	100	60	5.04	Williams (1872)	*Anomalopteryx*
33	33	209	130	7.20	Owen (1879a)	*Dinornis*
19	–	87	60	3.96	Owen (1879a)	*Anomalopteryx*
38	38	132	150	2.88	Hill (1895)	*Dinornis*
30	46	152	150	3.60	Wilson (1913)	*Dinornis*

Note: Estimated after Alexander (1983b).

nocturnal kiwis. On the other hand, the kiwi olfactory cavities proved comparatively larger, suggesting that the moa sense of smell was not so well developed (Owen 1849c:311, 1872d:386, 1885b: 258). There is no clear consensus about this. Pycraft (1901:177) found that in both moas and kiwis 'the olfactory chambers are of enormous size, extending backwards nearly or quite as far as the optic foramina, thus so far encroaching upon the orbit as to obliterate the interorbital septum'. Hutton (1892c:97) regarded moas as possessing small eyes and well-developed olfactory organs, and Archey (1941:76) later concurred. Parker (1895:401) also remarked upon the small eyes of both moas and kiwis compared to those of other ratites. Upon these various authorities a good sense of smell seems more likely than otherwise, but perhaps moa eyesight was not of the same order. There may have been differences between species in these facilities. Worthy (n.d.c) argues that *Pachyornis* crania disclose about 30 per cent greater capacity in olfactory chambers than those of *Euryapteryx*.

As for the voice, if we leave aside the dubious 19th-century reports about moa cries, it becomes necessary to resort to analogy. Tinamous, young rheas and the kiwis all whistle, and the latter also scream. The large ratites have a wider repertoire, but the main sounds are hissing, grunting and a booming roar (Rothschild 1901:110, 127; van Tyne and Berger 1959:386–91). The larger moas, at least, possibly conformed to the latter style.

Feeding

In thinking about the likely diet of moas Owen (1849b:268) sought 'some peculiarity in the vegetation of New Zealand [which] adapted that island [sic] to be the seat of apterous tridactyle birds, so unusually numerous in species and some of them so stupendous in size'. From all that he knew it seemed that only ferns were sufficiently common and nutritious, and that they formed the basis of the moa diet appeared to be reflected by 'rhizophagous' characters in the moa skeleton. Thus, 'the unusual strength of the neck indicates the application of the beak to a more laborious task than the mere plucking of seeds, fruits or herbage'. The powerful neck was then regarded as the 'foundation of those forces by which the beak was associated with the feet in the labour of dislodging the farinaceous roots of the ferns' (Owen 1849b:269).

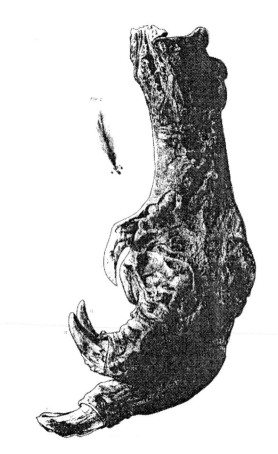

Fig. 5.12 Preserved foot of *Megalapteryx didinus* from Queenstown (Owen 1885b:pl. 60).

The powerful feet were, in the instance of the Queenstown *Megalapteryx* specimen (Fig. 5.12), thought to 'have possessed a certain grasping-power; and this may have been exercised by pulling . . . fern food up by the roots, after these had been exposed and loosened by the strong fossorial anterior digits' (Owen 1885b:260). The grubbing potential of the adze-like beak of *Dinornis* and evidence of a powerful musculature associated with it also contributed to Owen's views.[6]

This hypothesis gained some support from the discovery of probable moa droppings amongst moa feathers in the Wakatipu cave sites. White (1876:99) reported that the droppings largely consisted of 'branches and stalks of fern broken into short pieces of three-quarters of an inch in length'. But this evidence notwithstanding, the consensus

[6] F. G. Moore (11 August 1849) wrote to Owen that the Maoris believed moa 'lived upon Esculent Ferns and small Lizards'. Note also similar evidence of powerful grubbing capability in *Aptornis* sp. (Owen 1872c).

was already moving away from the view that ferns provided a dietary staple.

Haast (1872a:73, and see 1890a:174) had remarked that:

the greater proportion of the luxuriant vegetation of New Zealand is of comparatively little service to the present fauna, whilst it would produce more harmony in the household of nature if we imagined that the seeds of the *Phormium tenax* (the New Zealand flax), of the *Cordyline Australis* (the cabbage tree), of the large species of *Aciphylla* (spear grasses), the different species of *Coprosma*, and many other plants, had been at one time the favourite food of the *Dinornis*, whilst the roots of the *Aciphylla*, of the edible fern (*Pteris esculenta*), and several other plants, might have provided an additional supply of food when the seeds of the former were exhausted. Moreover, I have no doubt that the different species of *Dinornis* were omnivorous . . . and thus lizards, grasshoppers, and other insects might also have constituted part of their diet.

By 1885 Owen (1885a) had admitted buds and tree foliage to the probable moa diet, and only Hutton (1892c:98) continued to regard moas as generally feeding upon the produce of digging up the ground.[7]

Nevertheless the scarcity of tangible evidence was such that, despite a report by Hamilton (1892) of a preserved moa gizzard stuffed with *Leucopogon* and *Coprosma* seeds and twigs, the first and evidently superficial analyses of gizzard remains from Pyramid Valley swamp turned influential opinions upon moa diet in quite the opposite direction. Archey (1941:91) was told by C. E. Foweraker who examined these specimens, and who may have known of Forbes' (1892a:417) view that 'triturated grass' comprised the gizzard contents at Enfield, that 'the chief material in the gizzards was grass'. Duff (1941:335) also believed that coarse grass or tussock was, with twigs, the main component. These results doubtless seemed exactly what might have been expected from birds that had apparently been living in the open grasslands of the eastern South Island – where the major natural deposits of moa remains and the richest archaeological evidence of them was then located.

But a more thorough analysis had earlier provided different results. Falla (1941:341) had seen numerous *Coprosma* and *Podocarpus* seeds and twigs in several Pyramid Valley gizzard contents samples, and others, examined by R. Mason, also proved to largely contain fruits, seeds and leaves from a wide range of tree and shrub species (Oliver 1949:181). Mason's subsequent work on remains from two *Dinornis*, two *Emeus* and one *Euryapteryx* gizzard confirmed these results. Not grasses, but *Coprosma*, *Muehlenbeckia* and *Podocarpus spicatus*, amongst other woody plants, provided the fruits and foliage upon which the Pyramid Valley moas had last fed (Gregg 1972:156).

Quantitative results of comparative value did not become available, however, until the completion of Colin Burrows' (1980a, 1980b; Burrows *et al.* 1981) analysis of the plant remains in 11 gizzards from Pyramid Valley and three from Scaifes Lagoon, near Lake Wanaka. Although it is difficult to be certain about the generic identification, all of the samples are assigned to *Dinornis*. This may not be wholly correct, but the preliminary results obtained by Mason suggest that a number of genera shared the same basic food choices, even if *Euryapteryx*, for example, took in a much higher proportion of succulent than fibrous items, as compared to *Pachyornis* (Worthy, n.d.c.).

Burrows found that most of the moas had been consuming a wide range of food items; in the best-preserved gizzard samples there are some 20 plant species represented. These are very predominantly woody plants, and particularly shrubs of divaricating habit from which the twigs, leaves and fruit had been plucked. The main tree species were *Podocarpus spicatus* (matai) and *Plagianthus betulinus*, both of which are divaricate in the juvenile form. The main shrub species represented were *Coprosma* (including at least *C. rhamnoides* and *C. rotundifolia*), *Corokia cotoneaster*, *Myrsine divaricata* and *Olearia virgata*. The *Rubus* species of vines and the herb *Carex secta* were also commonly browsed.[8]

Interestingly enough, the moas at both Pyramid Valley and Scaifes Lagoon were exploiting the same plant species with almost the same pattern of preference amongst them (Table 5.4). Moreover, analysis of Burrows' results shows that the proportion of items and their relative abundance between forest and forest-fringe or open-ground species are also distributed in a nearly identical fashion between these distant sites. By frequency of choice, forest-fringe or open-ground species are more than

---

[7] That moas foraged along the shore or consumed shellfish etc., was raised by Thorne (1876:93); see also Owen (1879b:270).

[8] On the debate about whether a divaricating habit in about 10 per cent of woody plants was a response to moa browsing see, in favour, Greenwood and Atkinson (1977), Atkinson and Greenwood (1980), Lowry (1980), Mitchell (1980), and against, McGlone and Webb (1981).

TABLE 5.4   Occurrence of food items in moa gizzard contents

	Pyramid Valley								Main habitat		Scaifes Lagoon					
	Seed		Twig		Leaf		Other		(a)	(b)	Seed		Twig		Leaf	
Trees																
Carpodetus serratus									*		1	1				
Cordyline australis	2	2								*	3	3				
Elaeocarpus hookerianus	1	1							*		1	1				
Pennantia corymbosa	1	1							*							
Plagianthus betulinus	2	2	8	16			2	3		*	1	1				
Podocarpus spicatus	6	8			8	14			*		3	4				
Podocarpus dacrydioides									*				1	1		
Podocarpus cf. *hallii*									*		2	2			2	2
Pseudopanax ferox	2	3							*							
Pseudopanax sp.	1	1			1	1			*		1	1				
Shrubs																
Coprosma spp.	10	25								*	3	9				
Corokia cotoneaster	5	10								*	1	3				
Leptospermum scoparium					2	3	2	2		*						
Lophomyrtus obcordata	2	2							*							
Melicope simplex	6	6							*		3	3				
Myrsine divaricata	6	7			9	20				*						
Olearia virgata			10	14						*			3	4		
Pimelea sp.										*	1	1				
Teucridium parrifolium	2	4								*						
Phyllocladus alpinus							1	1		*						
Vines																
Muehlenbeckia australis	2	2								*	3	3				
Muehlenbeckia complexa	4	6								*						
Rubus spp.	6	8	9	17	6	14	1	2		*	3	8	3	9		
Tetrapathaea tetrandra	1	1							*							
Clematis sp.	1	1								*						
Herbs																
Carex secta	7	10								*	3	6				
Chenopodium cf. *allanii*	2	3								*	3	3				
Cyperaceae	4	4								*	3	6				
Phormium tenax	4	5								*	3	6				
Unid. grass or sedge					4	4				*						

Note: In each column lefthand figure is number of gizzard contents specimens in which item appears; righthand figure is abundance, derived as sum of relative abundance figures in Burrows (1980b). (a) = forest, (b) = forest margins or open ground.

twice as common in the diet as foods from inside the forest, while by approximate abundance they are about four times as frequent (Table 5.5). Thus, even allowing for some differences of opinion about my referral of food species to one or other category, and many do exhibit a sufficiently broad ecological distribution to have been obtained in either habitat (Burrows 1969), it seems that the preferred feeding habitat of the *Euryapteryx gravis* assemblage at Pyramid Valley, and also of the *Dinornis* component of the *Anomalopteryx* assemblage at Wanaka, was neither closed forest nor grassland but rather in ecotonal situations between forest and open country.

TABLE 5.5   Frequency of food items in moa gizzard contents by item type and plant species habitat

		Seed	Twig	Leaf	Other	Total
				Item type		
Pyramid Valley						
no. of cases		77	27	30	6	140
	%	55	19	21	4	
abundance		112	47	56	8	223
	%	50	21	25	4	
Scaifes Lagoon						
no. of cases		36	7	2		45
	%	80	16	4		
abundance		59	14	2		75
	%	79	19	3		

		Forest	Forest fringe or open ground	Total
			Habitat	
Pyramid Valley				
no. of cases		41	99	140
	%	29	71	
abundance		37	186	223
	%	17	83	
Scaifes Lagoon				
no. of cases		12	33	45
	%	27	73	
abundance		13	62	75
	%	17	83	

Note: No. of cases is number of times an item type occurs (above) or number of occurrences of item types associated with each habitat (below). Abundance is number of cases times relative abundance shown for each case by Burrows (1980b).

The relative volume of different foods is more difficult to estimate. Burrows notes that twigs are the dominant material, usually comprising about 80 per cent of the plant volume in the gizzards. However since they would have been more resistant to destruction in the gizzard than fruits, their actual contribution to the diet may be overestimated by the preserved remains. Most of the twigs were 10–30 mm long and 2–6 mm thick. They had been ripped and sheared off the branch by the sharp edges of the moa beak which, although some twigs were young and soft, had also coped with many which were old, fibrous and tough. Presumably birds with the food volume requirement of moas could not afford the time to select too delicately once they had found a bush with suitable browsing potential.

In combining a high volume of fibrous material with a wide variety of young twigs, herbs and fruit (and possibly invertebrates and other small animals) the moa diet seems to have been of a kind preferred by monogastric caecalids (Guthrie 1984:263–76). In lacking a rumen, these animals require a higher food volume for the same energy return as ruminants and have much less ability to degrade plant toxins. They feed mainly on plant parts low in toxic antiherbivory defenses – such as highly fibrous, but largely indigestible stems – and avoid being poisoned by their supplementary diet of more nutritious items through selecting a variety of species. If moas had this digestive adaptation, as Lowry (1980), Atkinson and Greenwood (1980) and Wardle (1985:780) suggest (and see also Davies 1978 on emus), then the diversity of plants which they would have required, and certainly consumed, probably acted as a significant constraint on population distribution and abundance.

Feeding mobility

Since moas were clearly putting a wide variety of foods together in each meal, and since it also seems that they were more physically adept and economical in moving about than was often thought to be the case, it is quite likely that their daily, and perhaps even seasonal mobility, was no less than amongst the modern large ratites (Davies 1978). In southern New Zealand, in particular, this might well have involved some segments of the moa populations, or some species, in transhumant migrations following the seasonal flush of foliage into the hills.[9]

Even so, additional evidence indicates that moa movements were measured in tens rather than hundreds of kilometres. Moas swallowed quantities of stones, from gravel-sized up to 10 cm in length, which were activated by a powerful gizzard musculature to form a mill for the reduction of fibrous twigs and similar foods. Two to 3 kg of stones was a normal quantity, but large *Dinornis* gizzards could contain 5 kg of pebbles (Chapman 1885; Hamilton 1892; Burrows *et al*. 1981). Haast (1872b:93), and later Duff (1941:335), argued that moas periodically disgorged gizzard stones when they became too smoothly rounded to retain their grinding efficiency, but Luckens (1983, 1984), whose researches show that 80 per cent of gizzard stones were incompletely worn, argues that the effectiveness of gizzard stones actually increased as

9 See Smith (1884:294) on possible transhumance.

they became smoother (because they presented a larger surface against the material to be crushed). Together with evidence that the highly resistant quartzes and similar materials which form the greater proportion of gizzard stones would probably take some years to wear entirely smooth, Luckens proposes that moas retained their gizzard stone complements for much longer periods.

The significance of this argument for moa mobility lies in the history of observations that moa gizzard stones reflected only local lithologies. This began with Haast (1872a:73), who gave as examples: 'in the caves of Collingwood, all the moa stones are derived from the quartz ranges close by, in the Malvern Hills from the amygdaloids of the same zone, and in Glenmark only from the chert rocks in the neighbourhood'. Chapman (1885:181) came to the same conclusion in examining the lithology of Mackenzie Country gizzard stones, and similar evidence was observed in the gizzard at Swampy Hill (Hamilton 1892), in those at Pyramid Valley and Scaifes Lagoon (Burrows et al. 1981) and, most recently, in a large number of examples examined by Luckens (1983, 1984; see also Smalley 1979). If, as suggested, there is a slow turnover of gizzard stones, then a relatively sedentary existence is indicated by the exclusive representation of local lithologies.

Another argument in favour of this conclusion was put forward by Scarlett (1974), who maintained that differences in the species spectra of sites close in time and space – for instance Marfell's Beach and Wairau Bar – implied the localisation of separate moa populations. However there are few cases where contemporaneity is sufficiently proven, or where cultural selectivity can be ruled out.

It would be fair to conclude that all the evidence and inferences which can presently be marshalled support the view that moas frequently moved short distances but were not given to the kind of long-distance mobility found amongst ostriches or emu. The reason is probably quite simple. The latter ratites faced periodic crises in water availability which, since they (and probably moas as well) required to drink about once a day, could only be solved by travelling substantial distances (a similar situation may have arisen occasionally in the eastern South Island, where seasonal drought is common enough).

Feeding adaptations

Consideration of feeding behaviour also raises the question of whether competition between species, even where there was little dietary variation, was involved in the evolution of different pieces of the feeding apparatus. Leaving aside the feet, which differ considerably in size but very little in shape, the main structures are stature, which is also related to ease of mobility, and the beak.

The functional significance of differences in beak shape is by no means as evident as the classificatory value of this source of variation might lead us to assume. In considering the matter it should first be noted that in the few cases where the keratinous sheath has survived, as in the Queenstown *Megalapteryx* head, it seems to follow the contours of the premaxilla and mandible, only furnishing them with sharp margins (Fig. 5.13). Some small, but potentially significant, variations in the cross-sectional shape of mandible and premaxilla margins between species have been noted by Atkinson and Greenwood (n.d.). Considering the shape of premaxillae, the most commonly used measure of beak form in moa research, it is apparent from Parker's figures (Table 5.6) that the overall plan shape is relatively invariant within moas, as compared to other ratites: moa beaks are broad and some are slightly broader than others both within and between species. There is also little variation

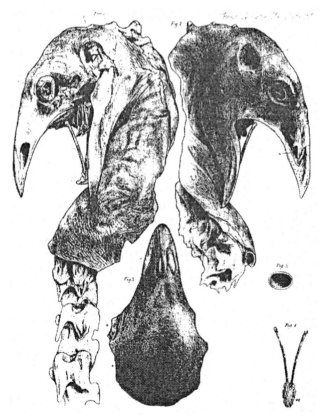

FIG. 5.13   Preserved *Megalapteryx didinus* head and neck from Queenstown (Owen 1885b:pl. 59).

TABLE 5.6   Comparative plan shape of moa premaxillae

Parker species	Max. length premaxilla	Body width premaxilla	Width/Length %	Cracraft species
D. maximus	157	71	45	D. giganteus
D. robustus	110–129	63–71	55–57	D. novaezealandiae
D. torosus	108–110	55–57	51–52	D. torosus
P. elephantopus	81–90	30–35	37–39	P. elephantopus
Mesopteryx γ	81	27	33	Eu. geranoides?
A. didiformis	73–76	30–35	41–46	A. didiformis
A. parva	68	22	32	A. didiformis
Emeus α	72	28–31	39–43	Eu. geranoides
E. crassus	80–88	37–41	46–47	E. crassus
Kiwi	144	4	2	
Emu	80	25	31	
Cassowary	90	14	16	
Ostrich	109	35	32	
Rhea	95	24	25	

Note: Length is apex to posterior edge of nasal process, width is between alveolar borders at posterior edge of prenarial septum (Parker 1895:407). Measurements in mm.

evident when the palatal shape of the premaxilla is compared between species, and only the blunt *Euryapteryx* form appears strikingly dissimilar from the modern emu plan (Fig. 5.14, in each outline the proximal terminations are at the point where the suture crosses the alveolar margin). Where beaks do vary significantly is in size, robustness, bluntness of the tip and in the marked downward deflection exhibited by *Dinornis* in particular.

In considering beaks together with other feeding structures it is possible to propose an adaptive change based upon food competition. If the earliest moa species were small, and if significant food competition arose because of population growth or environmental changes, there would be an adaptive premium upon the appearance of species which could browse more efficiently per patch by exploiting a greater height and depth range of foliage. Equally, these circumstances would favour cursorial adaptations which minimised energy output between feeding patches. Then, since larger species require more food absolutely, although not relatively, a longer beak, powerful muscles to operate it and perhaps a secateur-like action produced by curvature would produce more food per bite and the ability to shear thicker twigs, so increasing the relative amount of available foliage. Thus might we derive *Dinornis*.

There are, however, plausible alternative explanations of variation in feeding structures. There is a broad evolutionary tendency for increasing size with the passage of time, and both Hutton (1892b:590, 1892c:121) and Oliver (1949:1) argued

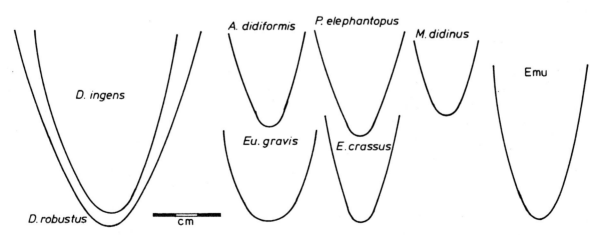

FIG. 5.14   Outlines, palatal view of moa and emu premaxillae. Data from Owen (1872a, 1885a), Parker (1895).

that some such genetic imperative coupled with a lack of predation and food abundance, not scarcity, ensured that moas simply got bigger. There was also the potential in New Zealand's wide latitudinal and altitudinal range for the operation of broad ecological principles related to ambient temperature differences (Bergmann's and Allen's Rules). At a specific level, some structural variations are probably connected to dietary selection. Thus, reduced temporal fossae (indicating weak jaw muscles), a gracile mandible and a comparatively small complement of gizzard stones in *Eu. gravis* may be related to a relatively less fibrous diet (Worthy n.d.c.).

It is not clear, therefore, whether variations in the size and shape of moas were adaptations to environmental constraints such as a relative scarcity of food, variations in temperature or intrinsic trajectories in the evolution of morphology.

A further issue in understanding feeding adaptations is sexual dimorphism, which often functions to ameliorate food competition and is general amongst ratites.

Females and eggs

The vexing question of distinguishing moa sexes has been commented upon at various points above. Briefly, Owen rejected, but Haast and Lydekker accepted, the likelihood of marked sexual dimorphism, although they never presented sufficient evidence to satisfy Hutton. He argued that if sexual dimorphism existed there should be a bimodal size distribution of adult bones and that the two size ranges should be geographically coincident and occur throughout any genus in which bimodality was perceived. Hutton found no convincing evidence of intra-specific bimodality in leg-bone lengths, although that might not be surprising given the degree to which his material was taxonomically divided and chronologically diverse (Hutton 1875:276, 1892c:102, 1896a:630).

Yet Hutton was not against the hypothesis as such, and argued on one occasion that two *D. maximus* skeletons of different sizes from Riverton Beach were male and female (in Ewen 1896: 654). To an association of the supposed female skeleton with eggshell, he added the evidence that certain features of the skull were very similar to those in the comparatively small *D. robustus* skeleton from Tiger Hill which was believed to have been found covering the remains of four chicks.[10]

But leaving aside the evidence of these (see below), it was pointed out by the ornithologist P. L. Sclater, as early as Owen's (1866a:343) first paper on this specimen, that amongst struthious birds it is generally males which tend the young. Furthermore the males tend to be slightly smaller, and the Tiger Hill cranium was one which Parker (1893a:3) found best exhibited the possible feather-pits of a male crest.

Withdrawing the Tiger Hill support leaves the Riverton case dependent upon no more than an association of shell and sternal fragments which was noticed only when the material had reached a museum. Only the Pyramid Valley *E. crassus* skeleton with an associated crushed egg (Fig. 5.15) is reasonably convincing, the more so because the other (male) half of the sexually-dimorphic pair comprises the smaller specimens assigned to *E. huttoni.*

Support for this particular conclusion has come from a recent study of citrate levels in moa bones. Citrate is differentially accumulated by females, and Dennison and Kooyman (n.d.) have shown that levels of it were slightly higher in samples from two of four *E. crassus* individuals, and equal in the remaining two, than in samples from four individuals of *E. huttoni.* Further evidence has been adduced (above) in support of the view that other moa species as well were sexually dimorphic, and that females were larger.

The identification of moa eggs is also based mainly upon relative size, but the sample is very small and many of the specimens were found broken. Only 18 complete eggs, or broken eggs able to be pieced together sufficiently for the main

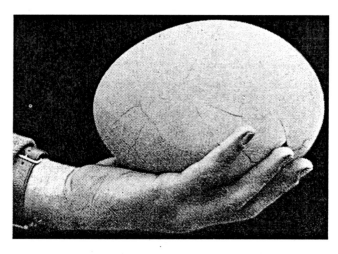

Fig. 5.15 Restored *Emeus crassus* egg from Pyramid Valley (Duff 1949:28). (By courtesy of Canterbury Museum.)

[10] Eggshell amongst *E. huttoni* remains was also cited by Benham (1935:87) as 'every reason to regard it as a female'.

dimensions to be ascertained, have been adequately reported in the literature. Half of these came from archaeological sites.

One egg has been a source of confusion. In examining Mantell's Waingongoro material, Owen (1879aɪ) found shell fragments which had evidently belonged to eggs of two or three sizes. For those of the largest size he compared the curvature of the shell pieces with fragments of an ostrich egg in order to predict that the original moa egg had measured 230 × 195 mm. *Dinornis elephantopus* was the species he suggested. Smaller fragments were re-fitted to construct most of an egg which measured about 190 × 152 mm (also given as 190 × 150 mm and 192 × 152 mm), and which was assigned to *D. crassus*. Although Owen (1879aɪ: 318) implies that the 'long and patient attempts' at restoration were his and that the material was also from Waingongoro, there is strong circumstantial evidence to indicate that it was actually Mantell who was responsible and that he did the work in 1856 using material from Awamoa. In following Hutton (1892c) and Archey (1941) who also took this view, it follows that references to a Waingongoro egg collected in 1847 should be disregarded.[11]

In Fig. 5.16 are shown dimensions of the 17 more or less whole eggs in Oliver's (1949:43) list and his suggested identifications, as well as some earlier views about identity. Also included are the dimensions of an egg recovered at Chatto Creek and thought to be from *Megalapteryx didinus* (Simpson 1955). There are two length measurements given for the presumed *D. maximus* egg – the larger measurement of 253 mm was corrected to 240 mm by Dell and Falla (1972:103; McCulloch 1983).

Oliver's identifications were largely achieved by an ingenious means. Noting that only the *E. crassus* egg from Pyramid Valley could be identified with certainty, he established ratios of egg length to the mean lengths of various bones in this species, building on a method used by Owen (1879aɪ), and then turned the procedure back-to-front to predict to which species eggs of known length probably belonged. *Dinornis* was excluded from this exercise because of its proportionately longer leg bones, but eggs were assigned to species of it by the comparative size of those not otherwise matched to non-*Dinornis* species. Oliver (1949:44) also argued that ratios of egg length to breadth and variations in the type of pore markings on the external surface of the shell supported his allocation of eggs to species.

In the absence of more certain evidence Oliver's method is at least objective, even if it is open to various sources of error; not the least of which is that the reference egg (Duff 1941:338) was found in a crushed state beneath an *E. crassus* sternum and might not have belonged to this individual, or may not have been restored to precisely the right dimensions. The earlier identifications of some eggs also reveal how much uncertainty exists in this area, particularly in distinguishing between *Euryapteryx*, *Pachyornis* and the smaller *Dinornis* species. Falla's (1942:45) view that all the Wairau Bar eggs could belong to *Euryapteryx* was based on his impression that this was the most common species in the site, while the *Megalapteryx* egg was identified according to Oliver's method of ratios. It was a green coloured egg, and Oliver (1949) had already suggested that eggshell of this kind, which was known to occur particularly in Central Otago, would prove to be from *Megalapteryx*. Similarly Archey's earlier ascription of the moa eggs found at Doubtless Bay to *Eu. curtus* was generally supported by Oliver's method.[12]

Turning to the fabric of moa eggs, the shell has a double structure comprising a thin interior prismatic layer overlain by a thick laminated layer. Through both layers extend pores, mostly of a simple conical form narrowing inwards, and the exterior surface is etched with round and slit-shaped pore openings which may form patterns specific to taxa, although the evidence is not yet very clear (Archey 1941:74–5; Oliver 1949:44–5; Tyler 1957). Moa eggshell varies from about 1.00 mm to 1.40 mm thick, which is thinner than

---

[11] Mantell (1872:96) describes unpacking his Awamoa collection in Owen's presence in 1856 and of restoring about 12 eggs, half of which went to the British Museum. Owen later (1879b:278) referred to the *D. elephantopus* estimate as his first acquaintance with moa eggs and described his comparison of it with the Kaikoura egg found in 1865. His only reference to a *D. crassus* egg is to Hector's description of the Cromwell specimen. Buick (1931:263) adds an egg 267 mm by 203 mm from Awamoa, refitted by Mantell and held in the British Museum. No egg of this size is now held there. The partly reconstructed eggs (A222, A222A, A222B) in that collection are provenanced, after Lydekker (1891:349), to Waingongoro, but his reference to A222 as the egg in Owen (1879aɪɪ:pl.cxv) is wrong, and it seems he had only followed Owen in this. The approximate sizes of these eggs are 200 × 150 mm (A222), 200 × 140 mm (A222A) and 215 × 150 mm (A222B).

[12] Note that the length of the *E. crassus* egg should be 179 mm (Archey 1941:74) and not 129 mm as shown in Oliver (1949:43). Benham's (1902:150–1) identification of one egg (see figure 5.16) could be either *Euryapteryx* or *Pachyornis* according to the synonymy of the species he cites. On *Megalapteryx*, Lockerbie told Simpson (1955:223) that the only archaeological site in Otago where green eggshell occurred in quantity was Pounawea, and *Megalapteryx* is, in fact, quite common amongst the MNI.

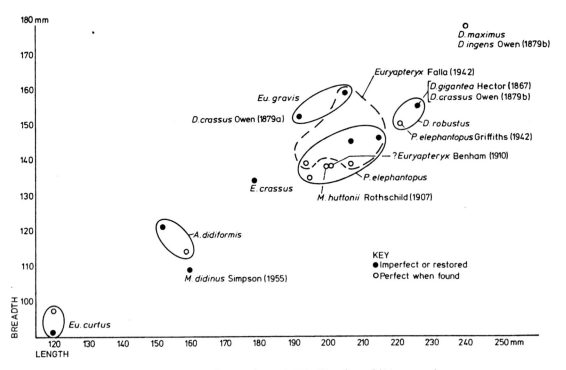

FIG. 5.16   Dimensions of whole moa eggs. Data from Oliver (1949:43), plus additions as shown.

ostrich but thicker than rhea eggshell. Apart from the green shell, the colour varies slightly from greyish-white through cream to a light buff shade. Mantell claimed to perceive 24 varieties of moa eggshell in his Awamoa collection, but Archey's (1941) examination of the same material distinguished only three different types based upon shell thickness and the configurations of the pore markings.

Clutch size and breeding behaviour

The most frequently adduced evidence of clutch size concerns the Tiger Hill *D. robustus* specimen which was found in sand by goldminers in the Manuherikia Valley about October 1863. It was obtained from them by Edmund Gibson of Oamaru who, once Hector had measured the remains, sent it to his brother Dr J. H. Gibson of the York Philosophical Society. In a letter preceding the arrival of the bones Edmund Gibson evidently described the collection as comprising a kiwi skeleton and eggs, in addition to the adult moa skeleton (Allis 1865a:50), but in notes found when the collection was opened at York Museum in May 1864 he wrote (in Owen 1879aɪ:338) that the adult had been accompanied by 'several bones of the young bird and . . . fragments of the shell of the egg, thus indicating that the parent bird was

brooding over its young when overwhelmed by the sand-drift'.

Dr Gibson and Thomas Allis presented papers on the bones in June 1864 in which they asserted, respectively, that 'four or five young birds' (Gibson 1865:22) and 'four distinct young birds of the same species' (Allis 1865a:50) had been found underneath the adult skeleton and were represented in the collection of remains. Owen, who had perceived some immature moa bone in sketches accompanying a letter about the Tiger Hill adult sent to him by Hector in February, and whose examination of parts of the adult lent to him in June had shown that it was smaller than others of the species, concluded in December 1864 that it was an example of 'a female which had perished with her chicks' (Owen 1866a:343). This opinion has been widely accepted and elaborated upon. Thus it evoked for Buick (1931:247) the 'silent suggestion of a mother bird which had died protecting her chicks from the rigours of a winter's storm. A snow-drift was her winding-sheet until the friendly summer winds gave her a mantle of golden sand'.[13]

---

[13] One possible, if garbled, account of the Tiger Hill discovery, which mentions several moas but no chicks, is in *The Otago Daily Times* (3 February 1904).

There are at least two severe obstacles to crediting this case at face value. The first is the association of adult and chick remains. Edmund Gibson's statement about the brooding position, repeated in his brother's paper, is a *non sequitur*, and Allis' (1864b:9196) description of the implicitly protective attitude of the adult skeleton was, as he admits, deduced from the differential decomposition of the bones (1865a:52), especially the cervical vertebrae. He later retreated from the conclusion that any of the bones had been found on the surface (1865b:140). The belief that the bones were found in a sand dune on the surface was later contradicted by Hector (in Owen 1866a:341), who wrote that the skeleton 'was met with in sinking a shaft on one of the terraces through a bed of dry incoherent sand-rock'. Haast (1872b:93) and Hutton (1892c: 167) later asserted that the discovery was made at 14 ft (4.2 m) down. If so, it is unlikely that any particular attitude of the adult remains or any specific association with other remains was recorded by the miners.

The second matter concerns the identification and number of the alleged chicks, and it is a problem which almost defies understanding. No chick remains were mentioned in a newspaper report of the discovery (*Nelson Examiner* 14 November 1863), or by Hector in his letter to Owen (1866a) or by Allis (1864a) in his first account of the adult skeleton, written the day the collection was unpacked. But immature bones in Hector's sketches were listed by Owen as half a sternum, an ilium '8 inches 5 lines long' (*c.* 21.5 cm) and an ischium and pubis 'about 6 inches long' (*c.* 15 cm). These are approximately 40 per cent and 63 per cent respectively of adult *D. robustus* dimensions as given by Archey (1941) and Oliver (1949), and they suggest juvenile to subadult rather than chick remains.

However, in a later discussion of the Tiger Hill adult, Owen (1879aɪ:320, 389–90; ɪɪ:pl. cxv) described and illustrated chick-sized remains of the same elements, plus an equally small scapulo-coracoid. Since the metric figures for the lengths of the ischium and pubis (4.5 cm) and the ilium (9.0 cm) are not too different from the imperial figures (above) it is possible that Owen simply made an error in understanding Hector's sketches. If so, he threw the matter into greater confusion by describing, elsewhere in the same work, exactly the same chick bones as embryonic remains more advanced than those in Hector's (1872) Cromwell example, and provenanced them to a *Dinornis crassus* egg (Fig. 5.17). Odder still, the chick bones are depicted in the same place as, and are clearly

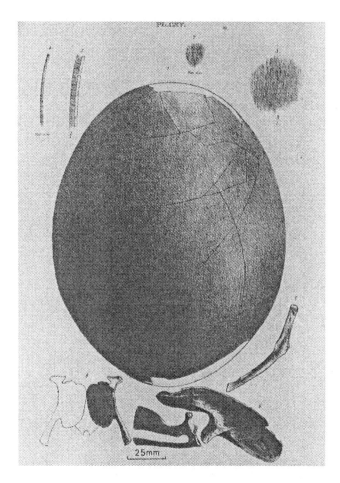

FIG. 5.17   Owen (1879aɪɪ:pl. cxv) described this as '*Dinornis crassus*: egg and sternum of embryo'. See text for comment.

implied to originate from, none other than the peripatetic egg of this species from Waingongoro (but see above).[14]

Leaving aside the particular association as clearly improbable, and Mantell mentions no such find at Waingongoro or Awamoa, it does seem more likely that the chick remains belonged to a smaller species than *D. robustus*. The Cromwell embryonic pelvis is of comparable length (*c.* 7.0 cm), but even the crude illustration of it cannot conceal its much less advanced development (Fig. 5.18). Since this egg is now tentatively identified as *D. robustus*, the supposed Tiger Hill remains are unlikely to be from the same species. It is possible, however, that they are not only the same species but the same individual and, moreover, actually the Cromwell specimen – that is, not two sets of bones, only one.

[14] It is curious that, in conjunction with the generally well-preserved Tiger Hill adult, the chicks should be represented not by leg bones but by a few pelvic and sternal remains.

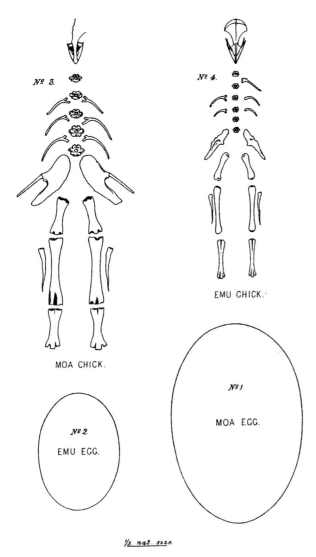

№ 3.

№ 4.

EMU CHICK.

MOA CHICK.

№ 1.

MOA EGG.

№ 2.

EMU EGG.

⅓ nat. size.

FIG. 5.18   Comparison of moa and emu eggs and embryonic bones (Hector 1872:pl. vi). (By courtesy of Royal Society of NZ.)

To complete the confusion Owen (1879b:279) claimed that his information about the *D. crassus* egg containing the bones of a partly-hatched chick (a sternum, pelvis and scapulo-coracoid) came from Hector.

Turning to Allis and Gibson provides no enlightenment. Allis (1865a:50) described the best-preserved chick bones as 'an ischium, an os pubis, a few ribs and a small cruciform bone [the immature sternum]'. This partly overlaps with Owen's list, but there is no indication of how four or five chicks are made out of it, or what elements were included in the remainder of the 'numerous' chick remains. There is also the question of whether, in his admitted inexperience with moa bones, Allis managed to misidentify the kiwi remains

mentioned by Edmund Gibson. There are no kiwi bones listed in the York Museum zoological acquisitions for 1864 (which include the Tiger Hill adult), but then there are no moa chick or egg remains listed either (Gibson 1865:26).

A speculative conclusion, which does not satisfy all the objections, might be that Edmund Gibson's comments and Hector's sketches indicate that a single moa embryo (which Gibson first thought was a kiwi) was found near the Tiger Hill adult; second, that Owen first mistook Hector's dimensions, was right later, and then confused matters by his own carelessness while writing the chapter on moa eggs for his 1879 work; and third, that Allis overstated the abundance of chick remains and simply counted each identifiable element as an individual. Whatever the truth of the matter, the four-chick episode should be suspended from the Tiger Hill case until more convincing evidence is discovered.

There are very few other data concerning the clutch size of moas. Hartree (n.d.; Falla 1962) found repeated evidence of only a single egg, or the remains of a single chick, in nests attributed to *A. didiformis* which he located in Hawke's Bay and Wairarapa rockshelters. Millener (1981:508) observed, similarly, that *Eu. curtus* eggshell was typically encountered in sand dunes in scatters indicating single eggs. Most of the natural occurrences of whole eggs also involved only a single egg in each case. The most notable exception was in the discovery of the egg containing chick remains at Cromwell in 1867 (Hector 1867). This egg was found 0.6 m below the surface in a fragile, chalky condition; 0.3 m away, and 0.08 m deeper, were the remains of another egg which were too decomposed to recover.

It might be tentatively inferred from these few cases that a single-egg clutch was common amongst the smaller moa species, and that two eggs were laid by larger species (Owen 1879aı:320), possibly because the mean egg size did not increase in proportion to body size. A one- to two-egg clutch is significantly smaller than amongst the other large modern ratites where the modal clutch sizes are: ostrich 3–8, rheas 4–5, cassowaries 3–5 and emu 8–9 (Winkler and Walters 1983:58). However since the weight of an ostrich egg, for example, is 1.3–1.6 kg, and that of a large moa possibly 4–7 kg, the investment in breeding is much more comparable than the clutch size alone would suggest. It is also important to recall that kiwi clutch sizes are only one or two eggs, and that the kiwi eggs are the largest in relation to body size of all birds.

Large eggs provided the energy and nutrient requirements for extended embryonic development of young moas, resulting in precocial young at hatching – that is, chicks covered in down, open-eyed and able to run about and feed themselves immediately (i.e. nidifugous). The evidence for this lies not only in the egg size and the ratite analogy but in one case – the Cromwell instance (above), in which a moa embryonic chick was compared with an emu chick at the same stage and found to be at least as well-developed (Hector (1867, 1872) also observed that the moa chick was only 12 per cent longer but its bones were already four times as heavy). Precocity is particularly suited to temperate regions in several ways. Seasonal food flushes enable the production of very large eggs and also provide some latitude in feeding for inexperienced chicks. Chick losses are also lower in temperate areas because predation is comparatively light. Cooler climates also favour precocity by placing a premium upon the early attainment of homeothermy in the young. In one of these points, the predation circumstances, New Zealand was unusually well served, and it is possible that the few and large eggs of moas, and perhaps other behaviour such as breeding at less than yearly intervals, were responses to that. Since the large ratites may live 30 years or more, and adult mortality rates are generally low, breeding can be a comparatively leisurely affair without seriously endangering the continuity of the population (O'Connor 1984).

The sequence of moa breeding behaviour is purely a matter of conjecture, but the patterns amongst other ratites are quite consistent and offer a reasonable source of analogy. Ratite males are territorial and engage in vigorous calling, chasing and fighting while attracting mates during the early months of the breeding season; monogamy is the rule. Taking the emu as an example, the usual breeding schedule thereafter is as follows: the adults, having built up their body-fat reserves over the late summer, mate during the early autumn and the female lays in April or May. The male is then left to incubate the eggs for about 56 days. During this time, mostly the winter, the male becomes torpid as his body temperature falls, and he makes only brief forays from the nest to drink and feed a little. The eggs hatch at the beginning of spring and the chicks bond to the male, now active and aggressive, whom they may follow until almost reaching adult size and plumage at about 12 months old (Eastman 1969; Grice et al. 1985). Similar breeding patterns, although with variations in timing within and between species, are

common amongst the ratites (Rand and Gilliard 1967; Davies 1976).[15]

Abundance

How common moas had once been was a question largely ignored until the discovery of the rich swamp sites in the later 19th century. These seemed to show the rapid deposition of large numbers of moas within very small sites and, consequently, that 'the number of individuals living together must have been very great' (Hutton 1892c:147). Earlier assumptions about the ready availability of presumed moa foods, especially ferns; some unspecified Maori stories about the abundance of moas which were told to Hochstetter (1867:190); the apparent evidence from Enfield that moas consumed grass; and the radiation of moa species in a predator-scarce environment – all helped to consolidate this conclusion to the extent that it remained virtually unquestioned until recent times. Duff (1977:280) suggested that moas might have been 'the teeming forerunners of our domestic stock', and less exuberant views were still expressed in such terms as 'plentiful' (Lockerbie 1959:82), 'numerous' (Simmons 1968:117) and 'in great abundance' (King 1984:25).

There is no direct evidence upon which these opinions could have been founded – nor any to falsify them. Instead it is necessary to appeal to analogical data of several kinds as a means of assessing their plausibility.

Some biomass density figures for mammalian browsing herbivores in temperate environments (Table 5.7) reveal a very wide range of possibilities. The highest figures, though, are from situations of game management that included providing supplementary feed. In addition, most of these animals are Cervids; fast-breeding, nutritionally-adaptable ruminants able to survive at high densities on a greater proportion of available browse than is the case with ratites. It is also relevant to note that the productivity of northern hemisphere deciduous-dominated forests is higher than that of New Zealand forests overall, and Nothofagus forests in particular. The latter point is reflected in the low

---

[15] There is little conclusive evidence about the form of moa nests, but rudimentary collections of sticks, ferns etc. in some cave or shelter sites, often associated with eggshell, are thought to have been moa nests (White 1876:98). Hartree (n.d.) and Scarlett (pers. comm.) found a cup-shaped depression in lapilli, inside a cave at Te Waka, Hawke's Bay. It was lined with moa eggshell, and was probably another form of nest; certainly hollows scraped in the ground are the usual form of nest amongst the large living ratites.

TABLE 5.7   Mammalian herbivore biomass density in temperate and cool temperate environments

Area	Vegetation	Herbivores	Biomass (kg/km²)	Reference
Germany	Mixed deciduous/coniferous	Three deer species plus boar	1500–2000	Mellars (1975:50)
Eastern USA	Mainly deciduous	White-tailed deer	430–690	Mellars (1975:50)
Western USA	Mainly coniferous	Black-tailed deer	77–81	Mellars (1975:50)
Czechoslovakia	Mixed coniferous/deciduous	Range of herbivores and diversivores	600	McCullough (1970:114)
Scotland	Mixed forest	Red deer	130	McCullough (1970:114)
USSR	Steppe	Saiga antelope	50	McCullough (1970:114)
Patagonia	Nothofagus forest	All mammalian herbivores	<100	Pearson (1983:489)

biomass of mammalian herbivores in Patagonian *Nothofagus* forest (Pearson 1983:489), and in figures which show that the number of bird-pairs in New Zealand's *Nothofagus* forest is only 40 per cent that of Danish *Fagus* forest (Cody 1973).

Data on the abundance and biomass densities of modern ratites (Table 5.8) provide a lower range of figures. As an analogy for moas, the ostrich figures are probably too high since ostriches flock in high densities, especially in managed game parks. The kiwi biomass figures are also probably too high since smaller animals can often survive at higher biomass densities than larger animals in the same range. The cassowary data are imprecise, but cassowaries seem to be fairly scarce in New Guinea

forests (Majnep and Bulmer 1977:155; Pratt 1983:283) although this might reflect low-level but long-term hunting pressure, as Diamond (1984) implies. There are considerable variations in the population density of emus which seem to be related to the availability of food in the breeding season, access to water and predation pressure from dingoes. Where these conditions are most optimal – in the eastern states – emu densities today are thought to be the highest attained since the arrival of Europeans.

In considering these various data as analogues for moa population densities it is possible to argue, by anticipating matters discussed in Chapter 13, that the extreme figures are very unlikely. If moas

TABLE 5.8   Estimated population and biomass densities of modern ratites

Species	Density number/km²	Mean adult biomass (kg)	Estimated biomass/km²	Comment	References
Struthio camelus Ostrich	0.83	100	83.3	Managed game park, Kenya. High density?	Davis (1976:116)
Casuarius casuarius Cassowary	0.19–1.66	45	8.6–74.9	Queensland. Vague density data	Crome (1976:76)
Apteryx australis Brown kiwi	17.1	2.3	39.3	Northland. Adults only. Medium to high density	Colbourne and Kleinpaste (1983)
Dromaius novaehollandiae Emu	0.066	35	2.3	Western Australia. Artificially high due to stock water	Davies (1976:116)
Dromaius novaehollandiae Emu	0.074	35	2.6	Western Australia. Average. Up to × 4 higher in places	Caughley and Grice (1982:257)
Dromaius novaehollandiae Emu	0.24–0.48	35	8.4–16.8	NSW/Qld/SA pastoral areas	Grice et al. (1985)
Dromaius novaehollandiae Emu	0.15–0.26	35	5.3–9.1	NSW/Qld/SA grain growing areas	Grice et al. (1985)
Dromaius novaehollandiae Emu	0.03–0.07	35	1.1–2.5	NSW/Qld/SA cattle pastoral areas	Grice et al. (1985)

had existed at biomass densities of many hundreds of kg per km², even 2000 kg per km² as I. McLean (*The Press* (Christchurch) 25 October 1986) has suggested, then the total population would be measured in some millions. Four million moas in the South Island, to take McLean's suggestion at face value (and given a mean moa biomass of 75 kg), would imply that an annual culling rate greater than the maximum sustained yield, let us say 5 per cent, would be 200,000 – a daunting task for a Maori population of a few thousands in such a large area. Moreover, if moas were as ecologically efficient as such densities suggest, then viable populations could have been maintained, at least for some species, in the substantial areas of forest and scrub which still remained at AD 1800 in the South Island – not to mention the North Island and Stewart Island.

If, on the other hand, moa population ·densities were as low as those of emu, perhaps 3000–10,000 in the southeast South Island, then they would hardly be large enough to maintain viable long-term breeding in most species (Anderson 1984: 731), and it is very unlikely that there would be any large or specialised butchery sites since moas would have been uneconomic to hunt, except opportunistically.

The orders of magnitude for the total moa population would then seem to lie between some tens of thousands and some hundreds of thousands. For the sake of argument – and archaeological speculation (Chapter 13) – I propose moa population densities based on the figures for emus. Amongst all the ratites, emus offer the most useful analogy because they are most common in environments which range from dry forest to grassland under 300 to 700 mm of annual precipitation. These conditions are comparable to those in the eastern South Island, where moas seem to have been most abundant judging by the density of moa-hunting sites (Chapters 8 to 10), and the concentration, in the same region, of remains from Haast's Eagle (*Harpagornis moorei*), the main pre-human predator of moas (Holdaway pers. comm.). Emus are less abundant in environments of either increasing humidity (and thus dense forest) or increasing aridity to either side of their preferred habitats. There are data which indicate the decline in emu

biomass density across environments of increasing aridity (Table 5.8; figures by Grice *et al.* 1985), but none which show the decline with humidity beyond the optimum habitats. I assume here that the gradient is the same, and I estimate hypothetical moa biomass densities for three environments of increasing humidity by multiplying the mean emu figures by × 5, on the ground that at least five moa species seem to have occurred in most areas, judging by archaeological catch data. This gives figures of 63 kg, 35 kg and 9 kg per km² for moas.

Three moa habitat zones of increasing humidity were established by estimating the areas defined by annual average water deficit contours on a map in Wards (1976:89). These were areas where the deficit was greater than 100 mm (i.e. relatively dry and probably under dry·forest, scrub and grassland originally; an optimum moa environment), between 50 and 100 mm deficit (fairly dry and open forest), and less than 50 mm deficit (dense, humid forest). The three zones were found to occupy 3 per cent, 27 per cent and 70 per cent respectively of the area of the North Island, and 19 per cent, 14 per cent and 67 per cent respectively of the area of the South Island.

When the hypothetical moa biomass density figures were multiplied by the areas of the habitat zones, and the data divided by a standard moa weight of 75 kg, the following results were obtained. In the North Island the driest zone carried 2500 moas, the next driest 15,000 and the wettest 9000. In the South Island the figures were 24,000, 10,000 and 10,000 respectively (in the case of the last figure, 15 per cent of the area was subtracted to allow for high alpine areas and lakes).

Various objections could be levelled at these estimates, but until we know a great deal more about moa ecology there is little point in dwelling on them here. All I want to argue is that if moa biomass densities were in the range × 2–10 those of emu, and were distributed with environmental gradients in a similar way, both of which seem fair assumptions, then the total population of moas in each island was measured in tens of thousands, the South Island population was about twice that in the North, and the greatest concentration of moas occurred in the eastern half of the South Island (Anderson n.d.e).

6

MAORI TRADITIONS

Most of the inferential superstructure of moa biology discussed in preceding chapters would count for little if only there existed some detailed observations of the living birds upon which we could rely. There have been, of course, various alleged sightings of moas by Europeans during the last 150 years, but none of these survive elementary tests of historiography (Anderson n.d.a, n.d.b), and even if they did would contribute, in most cases, no more than fleeting observations of large birds. Maoris, on the other hand, certainly knew moas very well at some stage and, according to this minimal criterion, traditions attributed to them warrant some attention here.

Virtually all alleged Maori traditions about moas were collected more than 80 years ago and it is now very difficult to evaluate them. With few exceptions they were published by Europeans and therefore at second-hand or greater from their original sources. In addition most informants, as well as the precise time and place of transmission, are anonymous. Even where the contexts are more completely known, most stories remain elusive. Take, for instance, the best known account of moa-hunting, said to have been told by Maoris in 1866 when Governor Grey, Taylor and McDonnell visited Waingongoro.

Taylor (1873:100) recalled hearing about moas being driven into a lake to be decapitated there from a canoe, but McDonnell (1889:439), quoting the Wanganui chief Kawana Paipai talking to Grey, described the use of teams of runners to bring moas to exhaustion by driving them into high fern. Almost certainly a third version of this alleged conversation, although probably the result of later confusion (Anderson n.d.a), is the Buller (1888:88) tale, attributed to Grey, of a small moa

being culled from a flock in Fiordland. It is possible, of course, that different accounts were given by different Maoris to the Europeans accompanying Grey, but lack of consistency is not the sole problem. Taylor died in 1873, but Grey lived until 1898 without publishing anything about these stories – even when he had most reason to do so, in his defence of recent Maori knowledge of moas (Grey 1870). Kawana Paipai (Fig. 6.1) died five years before his name was connected with the Waingongoro story, and was posthumously ridiculed because of it by his fellow chiefs of the district (Tregear 1889). As Duff (1977:301) observed, it is quite possible that he was never involved at all.[1]

The kind of questions raised by the Waingongoro stories – about their antecedents, the context of transmission, European interpretation and confusion – were very largely ignored during the 19th century, although Colenso's scholarship was a notable exception. Traditions were regarded as capable of describing with fair accuracy events and phenomena extending hundreds of years into the pre-European past. Even Tregear, who believed no living Maoris had seen moas, was prepared to defend traditions in general as having 'a value for accuracy beside which our current gossiping way of telling narratives or of compiling history [is] loose and valueless' (Tregear 1889:505). Thus, while specific assertions in the stories were challenged, there remained a consensus that traditions promised a broadly reliable and independent source of evidence about moas and moa-hunting.

[1] Field (*The Mataura Ensign* 1 October 1908), however, includes Paipai in a list of chiefs living about 1860 who told him about moa-hunting.

FIG. 6.1   Kawana Paipai (Buick 1931:288). (By courtesy of D. V. Avery.)

More recent surveys of the material have adopted different lines of approach. Beattie (1958), Richards (1986) and Brewster (1987) followed the 19th-century method of relying largely upon plausibility of content, together with the relative number of stories asserting a particular point. They concluded, for example, that since most Maori tales described very recent moa extinction, that was, in fact, likely to have been the case. Duff (1977), on the other hand, assumed at the outset that partiality on each side of the controversy about the moa-hunters, which Haast had raised in 1870, directly influenced the kind and content of Maori 'traditions' brought forward thereafter. His approach was to look for evidence of a context indicative of the direct transmission of a genuinely Maori story, however implausible its content.

This is a more sensible approach, for plausibility is no guide to validity. For one thing, those scientific inferences which guide plausibility may change quite radically, as in the case of the feeding preferences of moas; and for another, the moa stories which on grounds of context are most likely to have arisen in authentically pre-European traditions are those which describe manifestly mythological 'moa' beasts (below) and are the least plausible in terms of content.

Four matters are especially pertinent to the question of what biological knowledge Maoris may have retained from pre-European times about moas. These are: the early descriptions of 'moa', the word 'moa' in traditional Maori poetry and sayings, stories about moa morphology and behaviour, and the various sources of pre- and post-European confusion or encouragement in the context of moa tales. Maori traditions about hunting and extinction are reviewed in Chapters 11 and 13.

The mysterious bird 'moa'

The first recorded use of the term 'moa' was to Colenso at Waiapu in January 1838 (Colenso 1846: 81), on which occasion he heard about a creature that some Maoris thought was a bird, and others a man, 'in general appearance it resembled an immense domestic cock, with the difference, however, of its having a "face like a man"; that it dwelt in a cavern in the precipitous side of a mountain; that it lived on air; and that it was attended or guarded by two immense Tuataras'. At Turanga, J. W. Harris told the Rev. Taylor (Taylor, Journal 21 April 1839) a very similar story about a large bird which 'chiefly is found in the South Island but is occasionally seen in this part 2 days journey inland, it is said to be of a red colour . . . there is one said to always reside in a cave which is always attended by a large lizard or snake, the mountain is ascended and then looking down it is seen'. Williams (28 February 1842, to Owen 1879ai:75) reported essentially the same story, told to him in 1839, about a moa and lizard on Whakapunake Mountain; and Dieffenbach (1843i:140), in November 1839, was warned not to climb Mt Taranaki (Egmont) because 'there were ngarara (crocodiles) on it, which would undoubtedly eat me; the mysterious bird "moa" . . . was also said to exist there'. Further afield again, Watkins, at Waikouaiti in September 1841, reported fables about 'an immense serpent of the water species, and of immense birds which were formerly said to exist, and the bones of which are said to be often met with . . . these kinds used to destroy men' (in Duff 1977:295).

Taylor thus concluded in a letter to Owen (14 February 1844, in Owen 1879ai:136) that 'everywhere traditions of . . . [the moa's] existence are to be met with, coupled with that of an equally enormous Land-lizard'. This somewhat overstated the case, since no such stories came from Northland for example, but it still seems probable that while most of the missionaries had discussed moa myths amongst themselves before any were published these were, nonetheless, local manifestations of a genuine pan-Maori tradition containing the essential element of a giant bird-reptile association, and in which the bird-man characteristics were a subsidiary feature.

One of the obvious questions about these stories is why there is no earlier reference to them than the late 1830s, particularly since Europeans had been enquiring about other giant creatures recorded in Maori tradition since the 1770s, and were also interested in kiwis, the birds nearest to moas. One answer might be that earlier references were either not recognised or not associated with the term 'moa'. Thus Polack (1838:308) wrote of 'atuas [spirits] covered in hair in the form of birds, having waylaid native travellers', and he thought these were probably emu-like creatures. Similarly Yate (1835:59) heard at Waiapu in 1834, that kiwis were rare in the northern North Island but large and abundant on Mount Hikurangi, later one of the haunts of the 'moa'. This remark might just be the earliest published allusion to the moa.

Another reason might lie in a Maori conception of 'moa' as creatures which, though partly bird-like, were not birds like those living about them; that is, the large bones found in riverbeds and so on were not the bones of birds as such, but of 'moa'. It is very difficult to document this point, but the separation of dangerous mythological 'moa' from large birds used as food and easily hunted to extinction in Polack's (1838:303) description, and the lack of any comparable prosaic tradition about moas in most of the moa stories collected by missionaries, seems suggestive. Certainly it was the very lack of an unequivocal association between the term 'moa' and any straightforward account of large birds hunted and eaten by Maoris which formed the main flaw exploited throughout the long debate about what, if anything, Maoris had known about Dinornithiformes.[2]

Sayings about 'moa'

The largely dormant issue of what Maoris knew about moas was provoked into life by a letter from

Haast to Owen (20 October 1869) which proclaimed that he had 'no doubt that the species of *Dinornis* have been extinct many hundreds of years'. Haast's reasons were essentially geological of course, but Sir George Grey lost no time in taking him to task on other grounds:

the natives all know the word Moa as describing the extinct bird; and when I went to New Zealand twenty-five years ago, the natives invariably spoke to me of the Moa as a bird well known to their ancestors. They spoke of the Moa in exactly the same manner as they did of the kakapo, the kiwi, the weka, and the extinct kind of Rails in districts where all these birds had disappeared (Grey 1870:116).

Grey went on to instance five traditional references to moas in sayings. These were:

1. '*Ka ngaro, i te ngaro, a te moa*' ('lost as the moa is lost'. A saying attributed to a man, Ika-herengutu, on the loss of all three sons. Thus meaning something irretrievably gone).
2. '*Na hikuao te korohiko ko te rakau i tunua ai te moa*' ('from Hikuao came the korohiko, the wood with which the moa was cooked').
3. '*Ko te manu hou nei e, te moa*' ('the new bird here, the moa').
4. '*Ko te huna i te moa*' ('the destruction of the moa').
5. '*Ko te Moa kai hau*' ('the air-eating moa').

To these Colenso (1880:85–6) later added:

6. '*He mihiau te kowhatu i taona ai te Moa*' ('Mihiau was the (kind of) stone with which the Moa was baked'. Mihiau, according to Colenso, was probably a volcanic stone like obsidian. The name is possibly mimihau, the form of pitch used as a chewing substance in the South Island).
7. '*Na te Moa i takati te rata*' ('the rata tree trampled by the moa')..
8. '*He Moa oti koe, ina ka kore koe e kai?*' ('Are you a moa that you do not eat?')
9. '*He puku moa*' ('a moa's stomach or appetite').

Grey (1870) and Colenso (1880:87–9) also found some of these sayings incorporated into poems and, in addition, several legends which contained slight references to moas. In the story of Ngahue, otherwise a myth about the origins of nephrite, a moa is killed at a place called Te Wairere. A widespread tradition about Tamatea, a remotely ancestral figure who fired the New Zealand forests, also refers to the consequent destruction of all or most moas.

---

[2] There was also some confusion between *maero*, a mythical race of hairy men, sometimes described in avian terms (Polack 1838; Monro 1845, in Hocken 1898:263), 'moa' and *mamoe* (Ngatimamoe), an historical tribe (Rochfort 1862, Hochstetter 1867).

The term 'moa', however, is a very common Polynesian root and word. In New Zealand, in addition to its use for a bird-like creature, it had the meanings: a kind of stone or stratum; ironstone; a cultivated row of soil; a drill used on hard stone; a coarse coastal grass (*Spinifex* sp.); and the actions to jump up or forward and to oscillate or swing (Colenso 1880:93; Tregear 1888:295, 1892:420). Duff (1977: 291) observed that the earliest definition of 'moa' in Lee's *Vocabulary of the Maori Language*, published in 1820, is simply 'a stone, also a name of a person, and of a place'. Elsewhere in Polynesia 'moa' meant, amongst other things: a playing stick, a sledge and various plants (Hawaii); a spinning top, a mollusc, the middle of a road or river (Samoa); a whirligig, a bunch of miro leaves, a long, narrow face, the ankle joint and knuckles (Tahiti); a second-ranked priest (Marquesas); and so on (Tregear 1892:420). The one common element was 'moa' = the domestic fowl.

When the New Zealand references to 'moa' are considered, various possible meanings are therefore available; thus 'Lost as the moa is lost' could mean the 'moa' creature, Dinornithiformes, or the Polynesian fowl which either never reached New Zealand or soon became extinct here. Similarly many compound words are open to a variety of interpretations: for example, *papamoa* ('moa' flat, or spinifex flat, ironstone flat etc.); *moakura* (red 'moa' or red stone), and so on.

Place names like *Te Kaki o te moa* (the neck of the moa) or *Pukumoa* (moa's belly) clearly refer to a creature, but was it of Dinornithiformes? Here Tregear (1892:422) made the important point that many such compound words which included 'moa' had clearly been constructed before the Maoris reached New Zealand. *Tataramoa*, the prickly New Zealand vine (*Rubus australis*), is the same word as the Hawaiian *moakakala*, a sharp-spurred rooster; similarly the Maori word *Tautauamoa*, meaning a quarrel between a few people, has a similar meaning to Mangaian *taumoamoa* and Samoan *fa'a-moataulia*, where 'moa' clearly means the domestic rooster and the activity referred to is a cock fight. Even the example which seems most convincing as a reference to moa gizzard stones, *moamoa* = polished pebbles, is open to alternative explanations. Colenso (1880:96) considered 'moa' in this sense a generic term for anything spherical, and White (1895), although suggesting *he tutae moa* (moa excrement) as an explanatory allusion, noted that 'moa' was used to describe European oil-stones; hence, perhaps, stones used for, or polished.

It cannot, thus, be convincingly argued that apparent descriptions of moa localities, anatomy or behaviour have, necessarily, anything at all to do with Dinornithiformes. Perhaps the most striking omission in all such words or phrases is anything to express the size of the real moas. Tregear (1892:416) put it bluntly that 'so far as legendary mention goes, the moa might have been the size of a sparrow'.

The alternative names for moas are not at all convincing. *Te manu a Rua-kapanga*, *manu-whakatau* and *kuranui* came to light in a poem allegedly composed about AD 1400 (Davies and Pope 1907). This is very unlikely. The verse which includes these names appears to be an oblique comment on the modern moa dispute (in it we are advised to reject *manu-whakatau* and prefer *kuranui*, which perished in swamps etc.). The verse preceding it contains an apparent reference to an (introduced) turnip plantation. Furthermore the names contain no obvious traits of moas. *Manu-whakatau* may have meant singing bird, or perhaps, as Whatahoro insisted, 'deified bird' (Davies and Pope 1907), while *kuranui* has been translated as big red or, perhaps, great treasure. Downes (1916:428) also suggested that *manu-whakatau* implied a noble bird, while *kuranui* was a form of address to high-born women and could also refer to a treasured feather head-dress or anything valuable.

The emphatic assertion that these were actually names of moas came in the suspect Whatahoro manuscript published by Smith (1911). Here Rua-kapanga discovers a bird called *manu-whakatau*. The name is translated as referring to a bird the height of a man, although on what etymological ground is entirely unclear. When its wings proved to contain 200 red feathers it was re-named *kuranui*. It is difficult to accept this as anything but a later rationalisation of the kind of cryptic, and probably re-worked, data produced by Davies and Pope (1907). Post-European re-working of different legends about huge birds, very possibly as a consequence of a rapid deterioration in the transmission of oral traditions, seems even more evident in the names *poua* and *pouakai* (below). These were alleged by Tare te Maiharoa, an influential South Island chief about the turn of the 20th century, to be the true, ancient names for moas – which had been superseded by 'moa' in modern times, and then simply as a term for the bones (Beattie n.d.). This hypothesis was the second occasion on which moa bones were linked to ancient stories about huge flying birds, and it was equally mistaken in my view.

The first occasion was Rule's insistence to Owen (1839:16) that the bone he had acquired came from an eagle-like bird which flew periodically down to the coastal rivers from its mountain home. Rule called it 'A Movie', but his own paper (Rule 1843) unwittingly demonstrates that this was no more than a misunderstood reference to a common Maori name for the North Island, *Ika na Maui* (or 'Movie'), meaning the Fish of Maui (Anderson 1987a). But the name aside, the eagle story is almost certainly of pre-European origin and was later published in more specific forms by Taylor (1855:398), Wohlers (1876:110), Stack (1878:63) and Roberts (in Skinner 1912:146–7) in which accounts the bird was usually known as *pouakai*.

If Te Maiharoa had any specific source for his views it might have been the Chatham Islands tradition about very large birds of uncertain type known as *puoa* or *poua*, a name which Shand attributed to the emu-like call they were supposed to have made (Cockburn-Hood 1875:117). It was later argued by Forbes, however, that *pouwa* was the Morioriterm for the extinct Chathams swan, while Tregear suggested *poua* and *poouakai* were related (White 1897). Duff (1977:289) accepted this later speculation in attributing *pouakai* to the extinct mainland swan *Cygnus (Chenopis) sumnerensis*.[3]

This might seem confusing enough, but it is only a sample of the ramifications of the *pouakai* tradition. Called '*Pou-a-Hawaiki*' (Skinner 1912) by some Westland Maoris in 1897, its name intimated a crossover with another legendary Polynesian flying bird which had brought the ancestor, Pou, from Hawaiki to New Zealand. This bird, in turn, was referred to by early 20th-century Southland Maoris as *Manu-nui-a-Tane* (Beattie n.d.) and its characteristic colouration, black with a tuft of red feathers on the head, was shared with another large, eagle-like bird, the Hokioi, (Grey 1873:435; Cockburn-Hood 1875:494). From Hokioi, notable for its noisy wings in flight, it is but a short step to the Hakuwai, a seabird seen only momentarily against the moon over the muttonbird islands in Foveaux Strait but thought to have had very large wings which made a loud noise like a chain being lowered into a boat (see Tuckett 1844, in Hocken 1898 ('Breaksea Devil'); *The Otago Witness* 1 June 1910; *The Southland Times* 14 July 1931; Beattie n.d.). Both birds repeatedly cried their very similar sounding names as they flew. It is a moot point whether the name *hakuwai* was derived from *hokioi* to explain the frightening sound of the mysterious *hakuwai* in flight (once the eagle was extinct), as Miskelly (1987:103) suggests, or whether *hokioi*

has been adopted, as an imperfect rendition of *hakuwai*, to provide a name for the eagle legend. Another distinct possibility is that both words and their various alternatives are simply derived from the verb *hokio*, to descend, which is, after all, the principal action in which they were involved.

Considering this evidence of shared or transferred characteristics between a variety of flying and flightless mythological birds it seems sensible to refrain from identifying any of them as Dinornithiformes.

Feathers and food

Except to imply a general resemblance to the plumage of the domestic fowl or to note the existence of red feathers – one apparently seen by Harris (Taylor Journal 21 April 1839) – the first accounts of 'moa' did not specify any particular characteristics of the plumage. By 1847, however, it was apparently asserted to W. Mantell (letter 25 June 1847 to G. A. Mantell) at Waingongoro, that moas possessed long crest feathers prized by the Maori ancestors as ornaments. G. Mantell (1850) expanded his son's remark to include tail plumes, and later Thomson (1859I:33) declared that 'according to native tradition, moas were decked out in gaudy plumage . . . [like] a Cochin fowl'; Kawana Paipai was said to have compared moa plumage with that of the emu in 1866 (McDonnell 1889:439); and Stack (1872:108) recalled hearing, as a child, of beautiful moa plumes overhanging a cave on the East Coast. Soon after, John White insisted that he had heard from many East Coast chiefs (Travers 1876:81–2) 'who have seen the moa feathers worn in the heads of the old chiefs'. These feathers were described as being up to 60 cm long, with down along most of the quill and terminating in a flat feather like that of a peacock.

At about this point Colenso was told the story of *ko-te-rau-a-piopio* (the special plume of the piopio, a feather from the last surviving moa on Whakapunake Mountain which was said to adorn the hair of dead chiefs during funeral ceremonies). Enquiring further of his informant, Hawea, he was told that the feather 'was just like that of the Peacock, that it did not differ a bit in its glossiness and variety of colours, in its length and in its ocellated appearance'. Subsequently the feather was said to have an additional name (*Te Kowhakaroro*), and later again, to have been only one of 12 such 'beautiful round-eyed feathers' attached to the Moa of Whakapunake (Colenso 1880:84, and see Davies 1907). Smith (1911:58) described the moa under

---

[3] *Poua* was also a common term for grandfather, yet another source of potential bird–man confusion.

the name *kuranui* and as bearing twenty-four tail plumes, while Best (1942:186) reported an account of a moa-man creature which bore wing feathers, used as decorative plumes by chiefs, and which were known as *Rau-o-piopio*.

There is no need to pursue these obviously corrupted tales any further beyond noting that on the only two occasions when 'traditional' feathers asserted as those of the moa were actually produced they turned out to be, respectively, cassowary feathers (Mair 1893:534) and a horse-hair plume from a dragoon's helmet (Hamilton 1895: 233).

The earliest report of Maori views about the diet of moas seems to be in a letter from F. G. Moore to G. A. Mantell (11 August 1849) in which unspecified old men who apparently claimed to have captured moas in their youth said: 'that the bird had roaming habits, and lived upon ferns and small lizards'. Moore, a family friend, may have initially obtained this information from Walter Mantell and he, in turn, from the Maoris at Waingongoro, for Taylor (1873:98, 100) also mentioned the same two articles of diet, adding that he thought the disappearance of the tuatara (*Sphenodon punctatus*) probably contributed to the extinction of moas. Hochstetter (1867:193) also believed that fern roots formed the main constituent of the moa diet, as did Maning (1876:103, who implausibly connects moa fern root scratching with the definition of 'moa' as a cultivated area).

Leaving aside a possible confusion of stories about 'moa' guardians (i.e. giant lizards), with moa food, the suggestion that fern root was important (as it was in Maori diet, a possible source of the idea) is difficult to accept as unprompted Maori tradition because Owen (1849b:269, 1849c:310) had already expounded this idea in some detail and from a quite different source in 1843 and 1846. His argument stemmed not from traditional evidence but rather from an observation by Darwin, that New Zealand was particularly well-provided with ferns bearing palatable roots.

Later alleged traditions provided broader and quite different estimations of moa diet, possibly in response to Haast's (1872a:73) suggestion that moas had consumed the seeds and roots of various shrubs, ferns and trees as well as small animals. Thus John White claimed that young fern shoots (not roots), the sprouts of korokia and plants growing in damp areas were preferred (Travers 1876:79). Posthumous publication of his papers added the berries of some forest-edge shrubs and small trees (White 1925). Further implied tradition

suggested that nikau and other tree-ferns were especially sought after (Davies 1910:223) or that the diet comprised the fruit of forest trees such as tawa, hinau, and matai; a wild (introduced) turnip, and freshwater mussels, crayfish, fish and eels (Smith 1911:56; Downes 1926:36; Poynter 1932:97).

The opinions of the last-cited authorities and other views about moas expressed in Smith (1911), were said to have come from several named chiefs in the Poverty Bay area in 1839–40 which, if true, would certainly qualify them as evidence of considerable importance. However Simmons and Biggs (1970) have argued that almost all of this part (Te Kaue Raro) of 'The Lore of the Whare-Wananga' is a late compilation from diverse sources, only some of which is 'perhaps' as early as the 1840s in origin, and then only on the authority of a statement by J. M. Jury to Te Whatahoro in 1876.

Opinions equally as diverse as those about moa diet were expressed about other habits of the moas, and likewise upon alleged traditional evidence: they lived near the forest (White to Travers 1876:79), or in open country (White 1925:171), or in the forest depths (Davies 1910:223); they were the 'most stupid and sluggish birds . . . and would quietly allow themselves to be roasted alive without moving' (Maning 1876:102), or very swift of foot and dangerous (Graham 1919:108); were solitary (Davies 1910) or seen in groups (Smith 1911: 56), and so on. The possibility that some of these references were to different kinds of moas, and thus quite plausible, cannot be ruled out, but on no occasion was this point raised.

Possible sources

These references to the nature of 'moa' and aspects of their biology form only a part of an extensive historical literature which is claimed to arise from Maori traditions about moas in general. There is, though, very little about the contexts of the stories to indicate that they were handed down from the pre-European past. Indeed those Europeans who were most conversant with traditional evidence prior to 1870 when the major debate began were generally agreed that no detailed accounts had been passed on to them and sometimes no information at all. Stack (1872) could find no allusion to moas in Ngaitahu traditions, Colenso (1880) could obtain only mythological references, Mair (1890) encountered nothing about moas during his extensive experience with traditions and Wohlers sought, fruitlessly, for descriptions of moas in the Southland traditions. He went on to warn Haast, in 1884, that 'scientific men must not be misled by random talk of the present Maori who do not understand the old traditions, and whose fancy is led astray by talking with Europeans' (Wohlers 1884).

Nevertheless, early 19th-century Maoris certainly knew something about moas. They had mentioned very large birds, presumptively moas, to Europeans such as Polack and Watkins prior to scientific pronouncements about moa bones. But descriptions of aspects of moa biology, which in the 1840s were often quite bizarre and came progressively into line with scientific inferences during the late 19th century, seem to reflect a growing Maori acquaintance with foreign birds and European scholarship.

The domestic fowl to which moas were usually compared in the 1840s (rather than such obvious native models as kiwi or weka) were quite common throughout New Zealand by that time, and Williams, of course, had first identified moa bones as avian by comparison with those of a domestic fowl. Peacocks were first introduced in 1843, and peacock feathers were sometimes worn in the hair by Maori chiefs, for example Paora Matutera in

1859 (Hochstetter 1867). Governor Grey introduced emus and cassowaries to Auckland in 1867–68, although the former had been in Canterbury since 1864 and in North Otago since 1866 (*The Otago Witness* 10 February 1866; Thomson 1922). An ostrich farm was established in Canterbury in the 1890s (Anon 1898) and another near Auckland in 1900 (Boyd 1900). It is not at all difficult to see the characteristics of these various species reflected in the alleged traditional accounts.

In addition, as soon as scientific reports about moas became available, Europeans used them to prompt Maori 'recollections'. Mantell, for instance, showed Owen's first paper and plates to the Maoris at Waingongoro in 1847 (Archey 1941:96), although they concluded that the bones were of cows drowned in the Deluge. Colenso (1880) showed pictures of other ratites to East Coast Maoris in his search for information about moas.

There was thus no shortage of potential information from foreign sources when Maoris were relentlessly quizzed about moas in the 19th and early 20th centuries. If any had in fact retained genuine traditional lore about specific aspects of moa biology, it soon became submerged in the muddied pond of tainted assertion and cannot now be retrieved.

II

MOA-HUNTING, PROCESSING AND EXTINCTION

7

THE MOA-HUNTER DEBATE

That there had been some association of moas and people (Fig. 7.1) was acknowledged in the earliest reports, but it was by no means clear when it began or finished, and this uncertainty entailed an additional question about whether it had been Maoris at all who had hunted the moas. Nineteenth-century scientists in New Zealand had available three imprecise measures of past time. One was stratigraphical evidence, including assumptions about the age of sediments above or below sites. Another related means was analogical reasoning of the kind briefly adopted by Haast (below), in which remains of giant beasts and chipped stone tools in north European Pleistocene gravels suggested a possible age for giant bird remains and chipped stone tools in New Zealand – as indeed the European Neolithic furnished an alternative analogy for those who emphasised the polished stone tools found in association with moa bones. The third and most widely discussed means was provided by an ever-expanding body of alleged Maori lore which incorporated everything from myths and genealogies to purported first person accounts of moa-hunting. For more than a century, until the advent of radiocarbon dating – and then they were by no means entirely discarded – these circumstantial techniques were woven into arguments about the antiquity of the moa-hunters. Before the main chronological issues were tackled, however, there was a period of uncertainty about how far the early field evidence was to be interpreted as cultural.

FIG. 7.1 Otago University medical students, Wi Repa and Te Rangi Hiroa (later Sir Peter Buck), posed as hunters beside a 'restored' moa in the Woodhaugh Gardens, Dunedin, by Augustus Hamilton in 1903. (By courtesy of National Museum, NZ.)

Early discoveries

On 18 July 1843, below the Waingongoro Maori village (Taranaki) which later visitors knew as Ohawetokotoko, Taylor 'discovered a complete valley filled with moa bones . . . laid in several heaps as though the birds had died there, but most so fragile as to pulverize when touched' (Taylor, Journal 18 July 1843). No evidence of a cultural association was recorded by Taylor at the time but,

97

in a letter to Owen in February 1844 (Owen 1879ai: 135–6), he explained that each of the bone 'hillocks' contained remains from several kinds of moa 'as though their bodies had been eaten, and the bones of all thrown indiscriminantly together'. Taylor nevertheless qualified this suggestion with the observation that the loam surface on which the bones lay was, elsewhere than in the bone area, covered with several layers of marine and freshwater alluvia. It was only in his later description of Waingongoro, written after a visit in 1866 (below), that Taylor became fully convinced of the cultural origin of the bones.

Walter Mantell, who visited the site in January 1847, was also unsure at first about the cultural origin of the remains. Writing to his father (Mantell n.d., 3 February, 25 June 1847), he described an undulating sand flat, about 200 m wide 'covered with fragments of bones of men, moas, seals and what not'. Since this area still bore traces of Taylor's digging, Mantell decided to excavate to the side of it, at the foot of the slope below Ohawetokotoko. Here he found many moa bones, most of them undamaged until the local Maoris arrived 'trampling on the bones which I had laid out to dry . . . [so that] I was obliged to leave the digging to them . . . no sooner did one see a bone than a dozen were with him, scrabbling away for their lives and the bone of course came up in fragments'. This experience led Mantell into thinking that fireplaces observed in the vicinity must have been built by a recent shore party from *HMS Alligator* because unbroken bones, some in position of articulation would, it seemed to him, 'have required the absence of the natives' (Mantell n.d., 25 June 1847). Thus it was only on *other* parts of the sand flat, known as Te Rangatapu, that there were to be found 'small circular beds of ashes and charcoal and such as are left by native fires . . . fragments of obsidian, native flint, two fishing line stones and a whale bone mere [club]' (Mantell n.d., 25 June 1847).

In publishing a paper before receiving his son's June 25th letter, Gideon Mantell attempted to understand the geological status of the material which he had already received. Puzzled by the light colour and weight of the Waingongoro bones, and suspecting the site to be located in the upper reaches of the Wanganui River, he concluded that moa-bone deposits in general occurred in fluvial sediments which were composed of pure volcanic sand in higher situations (hence the lightness of the Waingoro bones) but of mud and silt in coastal areas, thus accounting for the dark, heavy, min-

eralised nature of other specimens (Mantell 1848a: 230–1). Mantell thus proposed an 'Age of Struthionidae' which preceded such recent geological changes as the uplift of gravel terraces. At the same time he conceded the probability that people had coexisted with, indeed exterminated, the last of the moas, and cited his son's observations at Waingongoro that charred moa, dog and human bones were all intermingled. But once he had received the more explicit letter about Waingongoro (Mantell n.d., 25th June 1847), his preference for a non-cultural origin for the bones surfaced more strongly. Until exposed by erosion, he argued, moa bones occurred in a sand layer between blue marine clays and deep overlaying conglomerates: 'There is also some doubt whether in the heaps of ancient native fires which contain bones of man, dog and moa, those of the colossal birds may not have been introduced by accident, and their charred appearance been occasioned by drying' (Mantell 1848b:241). The same year, however, he expressed some uncertainty, and two years later reported further evidence of the contemporaneity of moas and people at Waingongoro (Mantell 1850:339). Nevertheless uncertainty about the cultural status of the site continued for more than a century.

In 1872 Walter Mantell felt obliged to argue that he had formed, at the time of his excavations, 'a tolerably clear conviction . . . that the birds had been cooked, killed and eaten', but that he had enjoyed only partial success in impressing this view upon British scientists who, he suggested, were more impressed with the views of 'a gentleman of higher scientific and official position in the colony' (Mantell 1872:95).[1] His letters show this recollection to be not entirely accurate: he was, in fact, quite equivocal on the point, and much later commentators such as Archey (1941:94; and see his note on Walter Mantell's annotation of his father's paper) and Duff (1977:249) were also sceptical about the cultural status of the site.

Such later suspicions hardly seem justifiable in the light of observations during the visit to Waingongoro in 1866 by Governor Grey, Taylor, Lt Col. McDonnell and others. Taking Grey to the place where he had collected moa bones in 1843, Taylor (1873:100) was astonished to find that the wind had uncovered a lower stratum of ovens. Assisted by soldiers, Grey dug enthusiastically, uncovering many moa bones and moa eggshell

---

[1] A reference to Colenso, whom Mantell despised.

fragments, bones of kakapo (*Strigops habroptilus*) and kiwi, chert flakes and fragments of polished adzes. Taylor recorded a double line of ovens which must 'have been used for many years, as each layer of ash was separated by a thin stratum of sand from the one immediately below, and the number of them was very great'. McDonnell (1889:439) also recorded the clear association of ovens and moa bones: 'over and under the black- ened stones heaps of broken and partially charred moa bones – portions of skulls and huge thigh bones'. Yet as late as 1960 Buist and Yaldwyn (1960:77) felt required to outline the history of debate and argue that their uncovering of an oven containing the bones of a moa leg in a position of articulation provided the necessary proof that Mantell's excavations had occurred in a cultural site.

Elsewhere, however, the question of moa-hunting had long been decided. In 1852 Walter Mantell (n.d., 3 February 1853) had discovered a site at the Te Awakokomuka Stream, in north Otago. At the mouth he 'found a sandy deposit full of large broken burned boulders and with a few bones; a few yards up the stream . . . we found the same deposit continued and at intervals for forty or fifty yards with here and there sections of basins full of stones and skeletons of *palapteryx*'. His Maori guides each 'had a tent pole and each tent pole was immediately in such vigorously destruc- tive action . . . as would make you shudder . . . [but] having taken my degree at Rangatapu my patience did not fail me'.

The collection proved to contain some 40 moa skulls (*NZ Spectator and Cook Strait Guardian* 27 August 1853), very abundant moa eggshell, hun- dreds of vertebrae, 'myriads' of leg bones but few intact pelves 'it being next to impossible to extract them whole from among the huge stones and bones', and also bones of ducks, dogs, seals, kiwis and eels as well as charcoal and stone knives. A later report (in McDonnell 1889: 440–1) added remains of *Aptornis*, takahe, other small birds, rat, molluscs, porpoise, shark and other fish. Mantell observed that the ovens had been repeatedly used and contained remains of both large and small moas.

His evident good humour at the discovery of the site had also extended to a practical experiment. In one place he dug a hole to cook some pork and eels and came upon an ancient oven: 'rejecting the bones I made the boys use the same stones and charcoal for the cooking and I declare it could not have been fancy – we all noticed an exquisite moa

flavour . . . perhaps you might verify it . . . [he suggested to his father] by devoting one of the lumps of charcoal to boiling an egg'. Mantell was certain of the cultural status of this site, 'now there can be no mistake' he declared, and his stratigra- phic sketch makes this plain, although there were also moa bones in an underlying deposit of blue clay. Mantell's men jocularly named the site of their excavations Ruamoaamatara (Mantell's moa pit), and Mantell drew out the joke by re-naming the stream Awamoa (moa stream), an adjacent cliff Pani-moa and nearby caves Ana-moa (of which last he (Mantell n.d.) could not resist the comment (W. M. to G. M. 3 February 1853) that it meant not 'Anna Moore' (a reference to the daughter of his father's friend F. G. Moore) but 'moa cave'). Awamoa has stuck as the name of the site (Fig. 7.2).

In 1854 came a report from Opito (Coromandel) where N. E. Cormack (Owen 1862c:145–7) had recovered some moa bones from consolidated

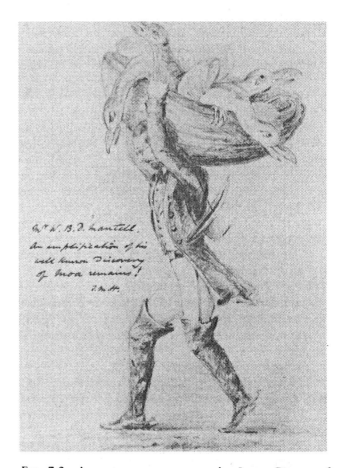

FIG. 7.2 A contemporary cartoon by James Brown of Walter Mantell carting moa remains from Awamoa. Comment by Thomas Hocken. (By courtesy of Hocken Library.)

sands, but beside a Maori oven. With this discovery the main provinces of subsequent moa-hunting research were described: the southwest coast of the North Island, the east coast of the South Island and the Coromandel district. So too was the central issue: how long ago was the age of moa-hunting?

The argument which had hitherto revolved around the question of whether various deposits of moa bones disclosed evidence of a cultural origin now focussed on the formative question of archaeology in New Zealand – who, Maoris or some other people, hunted the moas and when? This issue, which largely animated the so called 'Transactions' stage of moa-hunting research (Duff 1977:257), is often traced to the three papers read by Haast in 1871, but it had its origins somewhat earlier with Colenso and Mantell.

The transactions dispute

Even in the late 1860s there remained a common reliance upon Maori tradition as history. Thus Shortland (1869) observed that chiefly genealogies showed New Zealand to have been settled for only about 18 generations or some 500 years. But Colenso (1869), in a paper written in 1864, had already argued that other traditional and mythological evidence spoke of a pre-Maori colonisation. Colenso thought this population had the same origins as the Chatham Island Moriori and was inferior to the Maoris. It had come, he suggested, from the Americas, and was sufficiently ancient to be regarded as autochthonous. Colenso's argument of high antiquity also deployed, for the first time in New Zealand, a suite of archaeological arguments; the large number of hillforts and gardens long since deserted, the existence of large, deeply stratified shell middens, the existence of burial grounds unknown to present Maoris and the great number of nephrite artefacts in the North Island considering the remoteness of the sources. It was, he concluded, the more ancient aboriginals who had hunted moas, not Maoris.

Mantell (1869) proposed three stages of moa existence. Remains in caves and some alluvial sites were pre-cultural; remains in umu (Maori ovens) were associated with 'early aboriginals', not Maoris, who used chipped stone tools and had no nephrite implements. Mantell thought that their occupation was largely concentrated toward the inland districts, especially in Otago. Moas then became extinct in the third stage, very soon after

the arrival of the Maoris. Hector (1869) objected mildly that the negative evidence of the nephrite was insignificant since moa butchery, the main activity in the pre-Maori sites, required only rudimentary stone tools. It was not initially seen that this functionalist perception implied a means of refuting the entire argument and, by the time it did become clear to all, the trial of issues had descended into a clash of ethics and personalities (Fig. 7.3).

Haast, destined to stand at the epicentre of controversy, had asserted as early as 1862 that New Zealand was once inhabited by a pre-Maori people: 'this is proved by the discovery of stone implements, quite distinct from those of the Maoris, and found in swamps and below the roots of large trees' (H. F. von Haast 1948:228). In 1865 he investigated the Redcliffs (Sumner) sand-dune site, which had been reported in 1851 by Torlesse, and discerned a lower level of moa bones and oven stones separated by sterile sand from overlying

Fig. 7.3 Prominent figures in early research on moa-hunting, and in the 'Transactions' dispute (Buick 1931:96; 1937:64): James Hector (top left), Alexander McKay (top right), Julius Haast (bottom left), Walter Mantell (bottom right).

shell middens (Haast 1875a:75–8).[2] By 1868 his discovery of polished stone tools in shell midden situated deep beneath a primeval forest at Bruce Bay confirmed his view that the moa-hunting culture must have been very early indeed. In 1869 he visited a recently discovered moa-hunting site at the mouth of the Rakaia River and found it to consist of ovens and middens, largely of moa bone, strewn over an area of more than 20 ha. Amongst these remains were numerous 'rude stone implements' most of which were either 'primitive knives' or natural cobbles, possibly used as pounders to extract marrow from moa bones. But it was the discovery of more elaborately flaked implements 'which in every respect resemble those of the mammoth and rhinoceros beds of Europe' (Haast 1872a:85) which finally gave Haast the confidence to openly employ Lubbock's language and model as an analogy for the New Zealand evidence (Fig. 7.4).

The giant moas were, like giant beasts of Ice Age Europe, hunted by people at a Palaeolithic cultural stage. The only difference was one of approach: for while Boucher de Perthes had been obliged, some 20 years earlier, to demonstrate the contemporaneity of Abbevillian implements and Pleistocene megafauna, Haast faced almost the opposite problem – to demonstrate that moas had not been contemporary with the Neolithic Maoris, but with a different race, and that both had passed away long before the arrival of the Maori. Haast offered the following arguments. First, moa extinction must have preceded the arrival of the Maori since, on the authority of Stack and Colenso, mention of moas was exceedingly scarce in Maori traditions and, further, reports of moa bones being found on the surface of the ground could be explained by European disturbances to the landscape. Second, to Maori traditions of a pre-existing population, and to a general absence in moa-hunting sites of such Maori cultural traits as polished stone tools, nephrite and cannibalism, Haast added that two apparent Maori skulls (from dunes at Selwyn River mouth) which he had sent to the German anatomist Carus in 1868 had proven to belong to another, unknown race. Third, there were various considerations supporting the great antiquity of moa-hunting: the occurrence of *Dinornis* of very nearly the same species either side of Cook Strait

[2] However additional observations showed frequent intermixture of shell middens and moa-bone beds, which Haast (1875a:76) attributed to erosion.

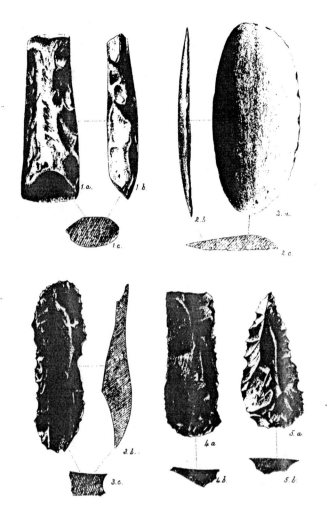

FIG. 7.4   Artefacts recovered at Rakaia Mouth by Haast (1872c:pl. vii). (By courtesy of Royal Society of NZ.)

showed that there must once have been a land-bridge, and its use by people seemed to be demonstrated by the existence of North Island obsidian in South Island sites since Palaeolithic moa-hunters, by definition, could not have had a maritime capability. It also followed that these pre-Maori people must also have been autochthones, and it seems very likely, as Law (1972a:11) has suggested, that Haast's receipt of a copy of Lyell's tenth edition of *Principles of Geology* in 1868 had set him thinking along the lines of an Australasian connection.

Five weeks later, Haast (1872b) elaborated further on several points. The word 'moa' had a variety of traditional meanings and its occurrence in tradition could hardly be relied upon as referring to *Dinornis*; while the sheer variety of form in the latter would surely, he thought, have elicited more than one Maori name. To the objection that polished stone tools had been found with a moa egg and human skeleton at Kaikoura in 1857 Haast replied, reasonably enough in view of the circumstances of discovery, that the association could have been purely accidental.

Haast had already attributed the occasional occurrence of polished stone implements at Rakaia Mouth to later Maori use of the site, but was obliged to narrow the focus of this proposition after another visit during the winter of 1871 when polished stone tools were found to occur all over the site, except actually within the moa-hunting middens. Haast (1872c) had also to report that the two skulls sent to Germany had proved, on examination by another expert, to be indubitably Maori, so that it became necessary to allow that the moa-hunters were, at least, probably of Polynesian origin. He did, however, find further evidence to support his view – based on the absence of gnawing on moa bones – that the dogs represented at Rakaia had been wild. Returning to the attack on traditional evidence Haast also pointed out that had the Maori any memory of large extinct birds they surely ought to have recalled the gigantic eagle, *Harpagornis* sp., a contemporary of moas. Haast then turned to recent criticisms of his earlier paper by Hector and Murison.

Hector (1872) had described moa remains from Central Otago which seemed to indicate the very recent survival of these birds – particularly the Earnscleugh Cave neck – but there was archaeological evidence as well. At Puketoitoi Creek, where moa bones and eggshell were very abundant, there later proved to be a row of Maori ovens in which, amongst moa remains and chert knives, there were fragments of polished stone implements. Murison (1872:124) argued that since moa-hunting was the only likely attraction of the spot for Maoris and, given the apparent freshness of moa remains in his district, it seemed most likely that 'the theory of palaeolithic and neolithic periods in New Zealand is unsustainable; that the *Dinornis* lived in comparatively recent times, and was hunted by the forefathers of the present aboriginals'. Haast (1872c:105) replied, unconvincingly,

that of a people possessing a very low standard of civilization, the generality used only very rough and primitive stone implements, but numbered a few favoured persons amongst its members, who were already in possession of fine polished ones, indicating a much higher state of civilization for them than for the mass of the tribes.

Thus, nine months after conception, did the European analogy drop stillborn from Haast's hypothesis, even if he still insisted in his summary of the

1871 papers that his 'probably Polynesian' autochthones used 'only' chipped stone implements.

In an attempt to cast more light upon the problem Haast (1875a) employed two men, one of them Alexander McKay, to excavate Moabone Point Cave. In the main or outer chamber occupational material was found up to 230 cm deep near the entrance and to 135 cm at the centre of the chamber. Most of this consisted of alternate shell and ash beds, usually three main shell beds, but with interleaved shell and ash lenses in the lowest. Below this 'upper series' was a thin dirt and ash bed, 10–20 cm thick, resting upon an agglomerate of roof spall fragments. Particularly in the southwest portion of the floor, however, there existed another thin ash bed below the agglomerate. These latter three layers formed a 'lower series', and it was within them that numerous moa bones, remains of whales, seals, dog, *Aptornis*, *Harpagornis* (see Duff 1977:256), shag, penguin and occasional freshwater mussel shells were found, together with wooden fire-making artefacts, post butts of a possible food store, wooden forks (probably combs) and fragments of spears and canoe timbers. The stone tools mainly comprised flake knives and blades as at Rakaia Mouth, but also some obsidian and polished stone tools. It was the existence of the latter in the lower series which sparked the most bitter and protracted dispute of the era (Haast 1875a).

A question of ethics

On 8 August 1874 Hector read a paper on the site, written by McKay, to the Wellington Philosophical Society. This, the first report of Haast's excavations, was partly devoted to the issue upon which Haast was most sensitive: 'whether the Moa-hunters were possessed of tools other than those of the rudest description' (McKay 1875a:98). McKay summarised the stratigraphy saying, as Haast was also to do, that 'the clear and distinct line of parting between the beds containing the Moa-bones and the overlying shell-beds . . . makes a very long blank in the history of the cave as a human habitation'. But McKay also suggested that evidence might be found elsewhere which would 'point to the gradual progression of the Moa-hunter into the fish-eater . . . [with local variation in timing, such that] many shell accumulations may be contemporaneous with existing mounds containing Moa bones'. This heresy was accompanied by the unequivocal statement that 'polished stone tools of high finish and keen edge were found in such positions as would lead to the inference that they . . .

are therefore contemporaneous with the Moa, whose bones are found in the same bed'.

Haast reacted swiftly. On 15 September he presented his own paper in which he admitted that there could no longer remain the least doubt that moa-hunters 'possessed polished stone implements, as well as chipped flint tools, probably employing the former for the building of their dwellings or manufacture of their canoes and wooden implements, whilst the latter were probably used for the chase or cutting up and preparing their huge game . . . I have to modify my former views' (Haast 1875a:72). He then described McKay as a simple labourer whom he had trained and encouraged and had subsequently recommended to Hector, only to be stabbed in the back:

It deeply grieves me, that a man for whom I have done everything in my power to help him on in the world, should thus, by betraying so shamefully the confidence placed in him, gain an unenviable notoriety, but I am still more astonished to see a person in Dr Hector's position, actually help my former workman in this business. This is incomprehensible to me . . . Dr Hector must know that the abettor of such a perfidious transaction, is as guilty as the perpetrator himself (Haast 1875d:530).

As later events would show, Haast undermined his case by seeking to give the impression that McKay was, as the latter described it, a 'mere mullock-turning machine examined and cleaned at stated intervals' (McKay 1875b:538). Had he been just that, McKay presciently suggested, then Haast was entitled only to the fruits of his labour, not any ideas that he may have formed about them. McKay was an intelligent man who knew very well the significance his discoveries at the cave held for Haast's theory, and he was planning as early as August 1873, just ten months after the excavation ended, to publish his own paper. The justification he gave was that he believed that Haast intended to suppress the evidence, partly because when it was drawn to his attention he 'replied, rather hotly, that he had no personal views to uphold, and that his object was the truth', and partly because Haast made no move to publish as soon as the artefacts were catalogued (McKay 1875b:537). Haast was slow by the standard of his times, but he was a busy man, and this was a proper excavation – indeed the first stratigraphical excavation in Polynesia, not a brief fossick such as he conducted at Rakaia Mouth and Shag Mouth. Haast's earlier concession to Murison's observations at Puketoitoi (above) and his claim (Haast 1875d:530) to have described the main results of his excavation to Hector, in

November 1872 – a claim never disputed – suggest McKay was quite wrong.

The charges against Hector, a fellow scientist, were correspondingly more serious. Hector's response was weak. As Manager of the New Zealand Institute he approved the reading of McKay's paper because it described the discoveries in general terms and contained McKay's views. To suppress the paper, said Hector, would have presumed on his relations with the author (thus ignoring the obligations which McKay might have owed to Haast, or his own duty to point them out). As to Haast's protest, Hector recommended to his fellow boardmembers that it be rejected since, amongst other reasons, Haast had obtained the prior publication that he regarded as his right by putting his own paper out as a pamphlet while McKay's paper was in press (Hector 1875). The Board, which included several other members opposed to Haast (Mantell, Travers), decided to publish both papers. This decision, and its carefully blinkered reasoning, went down badly in the South Island. 'Sheer nonsense' and 'a mischievous precedent' said *The Otago Guardian*, while *The Lyttelton Times* suggested that McKay's defense, such as it was, had been largely written by Hector, Mantell and Travers (H. F. von Haast 1948:729–39).

Haast resigned the presidency of the Canterbury Institute and his successor sought an opinion on McKay's action from Sir Joseph Hooker, President of the Royal Society. The reply was evasive and circular. Hooker took the view, which Haast had originally encouraged, that McKay was a simple workman who owed his employer only a description of the facts of the excavation; the Institute was right to publish McKay's paper on the grounds that it merited publication, and McKay was merely 'inconsiderate' in not advising Haast of his intentions. Hutton, no particular friend to Haast, described Hooker as 'very much given to gammon' (H. F. von Haast 1948:732).

Mantell, seeing an opportunity to exercise his sarcastic wit, then contrived to raise the controversy in the Legislative Council by moving that an inquest should be held on human remains found in the cave as 'a body found under suspicious circumstances'. The joke was eventually retailed in *Nature* (Anon. 1876), where Haast's reply so embarrassed Mantell that he tried to have the issue of the human remains raised seriously in Parliament, implying that Haast was that archetypal Victorian villain, the bodysnatcher. The Members persisted in regarding it as a joke (Fig. 7.5).

FIG. 7.5   Haast was made to ride a moa in a satirical poem (Chapter 7), but Mantell, one of his adversaries, did not escape the same fate; here in a James Brown cartoon. Comment by Thomas Hocken. (By courtesy of Hocken Library.)

Accusations and ill-humour dragged on for several years until the last public airing of the 'Sumner Cave' controversy in 1880, in the form of a satirical epic poem – probably written by McKay.[3] This publication, 'The Canterbury Gilpin or the Capture and Flight of the Moa, A Poem by Dinornis Sumnerensis', had Haast acquire a live moa, ride it about the town, and eventually disappear unwittingly upon it into the wilderness.

Haast's later views

At the end of 1874 Haast argued that six crouch burials found in dunes outside Moabone Point Cave, each associated with polished stone adzes of Archaic type, were of Moa-hunters; that there was

evidence of an hiatus between their burying and the deposition of a later 'shell-fish eaters' midden; and that the Moa-hunters were probably Melanesians known as Maero or Mohoao (Haast 1875b). Haast (1875c:93) also reported that his brief excavations at Shag Mouth revealed a similar situation (Fig. 7.6). The Maori and Moa-hunter beds generally:

are very distinct, and show clearly that a considerable period of time must have passed away before the Maoris, after the disappearance of the Moa-hunters, took again possession of that locality . . . the Maori or Shell beds are never found at a lower level than about 2 feet above high-water mark, while the Moa-hunter beds . . . [can occur] 2 feet below high-water mark, thus showing conclusively, that since the Moa-hunters . . . and before the shell-fish eaters . . . the country had been sinking considerably.

Several months later, Hutton sent Booth to investigate Shag Mouth. Booth's field notes show that he found 'immense beds of shells and fish bones on the top – not charred but steamed or boiled – moa bones immediately under – nearly all charred and broken . . . few shells or fish bones among the moas, but plenty of seal and a few dog bones' (Booth n.d.). Booth also noted an 'abundance of chipped implements, chiefly of the hill flint [silcrete] – none polished, no greenstone'.

This was, of course, more or less as Haast had argued, but Booth found no signs of the site having been abandoned between the moa-bone deposits and the shell beds; there were some moa bones in the upper shell layers and he argued that these were deposited at a time when moas were becoming extinct. Hutton (1876) accepted Booth's views in general but altered one important conclusion to state that moa bone was never unassociated with shell midden and that the one overlay as often as it underlay the other. Haast refused to accept this – with good reason as it turns out – and in a bristling rejoinder asserted precisely the opposite case: undisturbed moa-bone beds never contained shells, the two were only associated in places where 're-arranged beds have been mistaken for original ones . . . [which] simply proves that the excavators possessed insufficient experience to distinguish between them' (Haast 1877:672).[4] Hutton's frustration at this encounter was later made

---

[3] It is not clear whether McKay wrote the poem as Buick (1937:80) suggests, only drafted it, or if it was written by others (see The Otago Daily Times 16 May 1936).

[4] Haast (1877:670) 'Although my own excavations were on a more limited scale than those made by and for Captain Hutton, all the principal facts were nevertheless ascertained by me, and no further excavations, even had they been made under his eyes, could alter them in the least'.

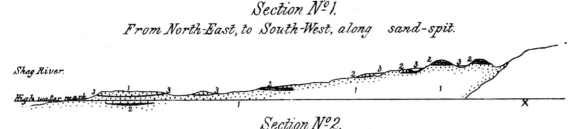

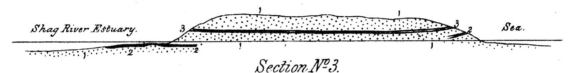

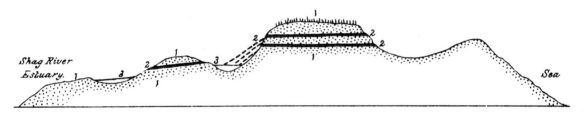

Section Nº 1.
From North-East, to South-West, along sand-spit.

Shag River.

High water mark.

Section Nº 2.
From West, to East, shewing Moa-hunter beds below high water mark.

Shag River Estuary.   *Sea.*

Section Nº 3.
From West, to East, shewing denudation of Moa-hunter kitchen-middens.

Shag River Estuary.   *Sea*

MOA-HUNTER ENCAMPMENT, SHAG POINT OTAGO.
REFERENCE.
Nº 3. *Maori kitchen-middens.*
" 2. *Moa-hunter kitchen-middens.*
" 1. *Blown sand. Marine sands. Estuary deposits.*
X *Tertiary rocks.*

To accompany Paper by Dᵣ Haast.

FIG. 7.6   Haast's (1875b:pl. iii) sketch of the stratigraphic relationships of Moa-hunter and Maori middens at Shag Mouth. (By courtesy of Royal Society of NZ.)

very plain in a letter to Hamilton, about 1890: 'Dr Haast's "facts" about Shag Point are all moonshine . . . Haast was only two or three hours at Shag Point, and part of the time was contained in emptying a bottle of Mr Rich's port wine . . . He has never altered . . . his opinions [of the age of the Moa-hunters] and would not even if you showed him a live moa' (Hamilton n.d.).

Chronology remained the crucial issue. Haast might have appeared impervious to contrary evidence and he 'had not the temperament which lets controversies drop', as his son conceded (H. F. von Haast to Duff n.d., c. 1950), but his persistence with an hypothesis which was slowly being stripped of its subsidiary assertions was based on the lack of any compelling evidence against his

central thesis that New Zealand has been occupied by people for many hundreds, possibly thousands, of years before the Hawaiki migration of Maoris.

He was not alone in this for, in addition to the trenchant anti-traditionalism of Colenso and a measure of support from Stack (1875), there were some geological considerations raised in the North Island. A tree stump, apparently chopped, was found in Tertiary clay beneath 8 m of stratified volcanic deposits in Auckland city and Goodall (1875) argued that it was a relic of pre-Maori aboriginal occupation. Cockburn-Hood (1875) used Goodall's stump, amongst other geological arguments, to propose a Maori (including Moa-hunter) occupation stretching back many thousands of years to a time when plains extended far towards the

Chathams. Such claims were not broadly accepted, but they indicate something of the latitude of scientific thinking at this time about human chronologies for New Zealand. Haast (1879) also reiterated an earlier argument (1875a:7) that the alignment and extent of moa-bone ovens in dunes north of Banks Peninsula indicated the existence of an ancient sand bar projecting towards the peninsula, and that at the time of occupation the peninsula might actually have been an island. Further arguments of great antiquity were found in the rockshelter drawings at Weka Pass. Their non-Maori appearance and the ascription of them to earlier traditional inhabitants of the South Island (Ngapuhi) by Maori informants (Stack 1878), together with their apparent contemporaneity with midden moa remains in the floor of the shelter, provided 'another proof, if it were needed, of the vast period of time during which New Zealand had been inhabited by man' (Haast 1878:45).

Yet Haast could feel the tide moving against his hypothesis. The argument of a disconformity between moa-bone and shell beds, maintained so dogmatically at Shag Mouth, was abandoned in the face of evidence from Kaikorai Mouth, where moa bones scattered within shell middens led him to the conclusion that even if pure moa-bone beds were probably to be found elsewhere in the site, the stratigraphy exposed on the shore indicated that 'the moas had already become so scarce that they only occasionally could be obtained, and the natives had to look towards getting other food as a regular means of subsistence' (Haast 1880:151). Furthermore at Brighton he found a site in which the unrefined forms of the implements, but the total lack of moa bone, suggested another manifestation of an intermediate stage (Haast 1880, n.d.). Later reflection also suggested that at Shag Mouth, as well, the Moa-hunters were 'also extensively shell fish eaters . . . [and that] the inhabitants of or visitors to this spot were already in a transition state, the Moa being on the point of being extirpated' (Haast n.d.). Haast had also to draw the obvious conclusion of considerable interbreeding between autochthones and Maoris, and he now resolved the difficulty of his implicit preference for a Melanesian or Australian ancestry of the former by emphasising a supposed Melanesian strain in the Maori racial character (Haast n.d.).

Additional evidence bearing on this issue was uncovered in 1889. At Monck's Cave – a site much like Moabone Point Cave, and situated about 1.5 km east of it – a wide range of items (including some of greenstone) and wooden artefacts carved in Maori styles were said to have been collected

from a floor upon which burnt and broken moa bones, moa eggshell and bones of the extinct swan, *Chenopis (Cygnus) sumnerensis*, were also found (Meeson 1889; Forbes 1891b). Since the site had been heavily fossicked there remained, however, an element of reasonable doubt until, in the summer of 1890–91, Chapman and Hamilton recovered a polished greenstone slab from amongst moa bones in an undisturbed stratified midden at Shag Mouth (Hamilton n.d.; Chapman 1892).[5]

This evidence was uncovered after Haast's death in 1887, by which time both the passion of debate and an emphasis on stratigraphical evidence had died away. Hutton (1892c), summing up the majority point of view of the time, canvassed most of the sources of evidence but appealed particularly to Maori traditions in asserting that it was Maoris, direct ancestors of the living people, who witnessed the extinction of moas 400–500 years ago in the North Island, and 300–400 years ago in the South Island. As if to rub it in, an old paper by de Quatrefages (1893), to which Haast had intended to reply upon its first airing ten years earlier, was then printed in the *Transactions of the New Zealand Institute*. This argued that in all imporant particulars Haast had been wrong, often repeatedly, and that traditions about moas were not to be denied. Colenso (1894), replying on behalf of his old friend, emphasised once more the unreliability of tradition as history. It was to no avail.[6]

Traditional and cultural typology

Between the excavations at Shag Mouth in 1891, and a resumption of systematic digging there some 30 years later, there was virtually no research

---

[5] Hector (1872) had earlier claimed that nephrite occurred at Puketoitoi moa-hunting site but Murison (1872) does not record it there.

[6] During the period of the moa-hunter controversy the arguments focussed on a small number of sites, but there was a growing list of discoveries, mostly remote from the epicentres of debate. They were reported at Miramar (Crawford 1873), Paekakariki (Enys 1873), Paremata (Chapman 1885:178) and Lake Grassmere (Robson 1876, 1877). Thorne (1876) discovered similar evidence at Pataua, despite popular wisdom that moas had not lived north of Auckland. Cheeseman, who had located equivocal evidence of a moa–people association at Ellerslie (1876) went back to Pataua with Thorne and found both natural and cultural sites. Moa ovens were also reported in the Mackenzie Country (Chapman 1885) and the South Canterbury downs (Smith 1884, 1891). Papatowai was discovered in 1889 (Buick 1937). Moa eggshell was reported in middens at Old Neck by Bollons about this time as well (Hamilton n.d.), and moa-hunter camps were recorded in Poverty Bay (Hutchinson 1898) and on the Waikaia Plateau (Hamilton 1895).

archaeology involving moa-hunting sites. Information about the distant past came, instead, from Maori traditions. It was different information, of course, and it had little to do with either moa-hunting, as such, or any associated material culture, but it was advanced with such authority that it swept the field of prehistory. When moa-hunter archaeology came to be studied again its agenda and concepts of organisation were, as a consequence, substantially set by the orthodox view of Maori traditional history. Central to this, and most influential for archaeology, was apparent traditional support for the idea that there was more than Polynesian in the Maori racial character.

The suggestion that Maoris had a proportion of Melanesian, Papuan or even Negroid blood had originated with Crozet in 1772. It was variously re-worked throughout the 19th century by D'Urville, Polack, Dieffenbach, and Haast, of course, amongst others, but it took a major step into the forefront of anthropological thinking when Professor Scott's craniometric measurements in 1893 of Maori and Moriori (Chatham Islands) skulls seemed to lend it a certain quantitative respectability (Sorrenson 1979). What was lacking, though, was a traditional description of the differences between an early – presumptively Melanesian – people and later – manifestly Polynesian – immigrants. By the early 20th century just such an account was in the hands of S. Percy Smith, the highly influential editor of the *Journal of the Polynesian Society*.

The Lore of the Whare-Wananga, as this dubious tradition was called, held that the original inhabitants of New Zealand were a dark-skinned, lazy and primitive people known as Maruiwi (or Mouriuri) who were either exterminated by, or married into, the Polynesian Maori, except for those who departed to the Chatham Islands and became Moriori. The efforts of Smith, Elsdon Best and Peter Buck ensured that this story became orthodox Maori history by the 1920s, and to a certain degree it still is (Simmons and Biggs 1970; Sorrenson 1979).

H. D. Skinner (Otago Museum), who had studied Oceanic material cultural under Haddon at Cambridge was sure, however, that Melanesian artefact types did not occur in the South Island, as traditional orthodoxy would demand. His first attempts (Skinner 1921) to resolve the matter thus removed South Island material culture and related assemblages from the east coast of the North Island to a 'Southern Culture' which, he suggested, had been brought by Polynesian migrants who settled these areas when they found most of the North Island occupied by people of a West Pacific cultural origin ('Northern Culture'). Fieldwork in the Chatham Islands soon showed that Moriori culture was also typically Polynesian. At the same time Skinner (1924a) began receiving the early results of renewed research in moa-hunter sites. In 1919 he had enlisted the help of David Teviotdale, a remarkably energetic digger, to find which artefact types were early – by their stratigraphic association with butchered moa remains. The evidence disclosed a 'Moa-hunter' assemblage which Skinner characterised as essentially similar to late Otago Maori culture on the one hand, but obviously derived from Polynesian culture on the other (see also Teviotdale 1932a, b; H. Leach 1972; Skinner 1974).

Encouraged by these results Skinner (1924b) then advanced the view that Maori culture in general was Polynesian, although he added the major qualification that it reflected an ancestral form of undivided Polynesian culture, probably as it had been in the West Pacific. That note of *de facto* compromise, though, was not enough to save him from the outrage of the traditionalists. Best called his hypothesis a 'quaint theory', and opposed unsuccessfully the awarding to Skinner of the Hector Memorial Medal in 1926 (Skinner 1974:15). The Maori traditionalists Buck and Ngata – who had, after all, most to lose – were even less restrained in their views, although they kept them private (Sorrenson 1986).

Skinner's protegé, Roger Duff, inherited his teacher's problem and, what is more important, his conceptual models. But culture-areas, and especially cultural conservatism and marginality, assumed in Duff's hands a considerably sharpened explanatory significance. The difference was essentially created by the discovery of one site.

In the 1940s Duff enjoyed the remarkable fortune to collaborate with Jim Eyles in investigating a series of richly furnished graves at Wairau Bar (below). The burial artefacts which they recovered formed a diverse assemblage of types from a single site and one which was, in addition, stratigraphically associated with abundant remains of an extinct avifauna. Duff (1963:30) thus formally decided, in 1949, 'to revive Haast's original term Moa-hunters to describe those settlers who began and probably completed the extermination of . . . moa, swan and eagle'. Duff was convinced that it was essentially only *Euryapteryx*, plus a small number of *Emeus*, that constituted the hunted moas. It was only in the second edition of his book (Duff 1956a: 280), and after Scarlett confirmed the identification of all six genera from Teviotdale's moa-bone collection obtained at Papatowai, that he was prepared to accept most of them as contemporary with people. He still doubted an association with *Dinornis*. This matter aside, Duff's first definition of 'Moa-hunter' closely followed the usages of Skinner and Haast. But when was the moa-hunting period and who were the moa-hunters?

In the case of the former, traditional evidence disclosed virtually no knowledge of moas amongst recent Maoris. It followed that if traditional history was correct in bringing the modern tribes to New Zealand about the mid-14th century, although only metaphorically as a fleet (Duff (1956a) later described 'The Great Fleet' of ortho-dox tradition as a concept, not a convoy), it must have been pre-Fleet people who were the Moa-hunters. This conclusion, in turn, suggested a chronology in which moa-hunting, and pre-Fleet people, disappeared together with the progressive expansion of post-Fleet tribes, largely from north to south, until 'the end of the moa and the Moa-hunter era [which can be] tentatively put as co-inciding with the overthrow of the [pre-Fleet tribe] Waitaha, about 1550 A.D.' (1956a:20). The upper limit was later revised to AD 1650 (Duff 1963:34).

On the issue of cultural identity, the artefacts from Wairau Bar and particularly those key types found repeatedly in the burials (notably his type 1A and 4A adzes and reel and whale-tooth necklace units) provided the essential line of evidence. Discoveries of these elsewhere in New Zealand disclosed a marginal geographic distribution, and the same seemed true of Polynesia where identical types were mainly found in marginal eastern archipelagoes. In terms of material culture, then, the Moa-hunters were also characterised as 'that portion of the first eastern Polynesian migrants to New Zealand whose culture remained largely static and did not obviously respond to the new environment . . . their conservatism suggests that they represent a single homogenous wave, where-as the marginal distribution of their culture within New Zealand suggests that they were its first human settlers' (Duff 1956a:16; 1956b). As Duff saw it, moa-hunter culture had once extended throughout the whole of New Zealand before the arrival of those elements – notably horticulture – which generated changes leading to historical Maori culture, 'in terms of the usual hypothesis that culture changes more rapidly in the heart or central area which is in this case the major land mass of the North Island' (Duff 1977:7). If there was any West Polynesian or Melanesian influence it must therefore have occurred after the Moa-hunter Period.

The success of this age–area hypothesis in link-ing Moa-hunters to the early East Polynesians was achieved, however, at the cost of a key piece of logic. It was not moa-hunting which demonstrated the association, but possession of a broadly com-mon set of domestic and decorative artefacts. Consequently, whereas Haast, Skinner and Teviotdale had defined moa-hunter material cul-ture by reference to contextual evidence of actual moa-hunting, Duff now reversed the emphasis to define Moa-hunters in terms of a material culture, and one originating far from any association with the moa.

Almost at the same time as he did so there arose cases which tested the model to the point of absurdity, no more clearly than at Takahe Valley. Here, in a site discovered in 1949, a *Megalapteryx* had been butchered, apparently in the 18th century (but see below). Having defined moa-hunting largely in terms of *Euryapteryx*, and moa-hunter culture as a period (pre-Fleet) and an artefactual assemblage, neither of which were relevant to the site, Duff was compelled to the conclusion that the 'anomalous survival of *Megalapteryx* until the arri-val of the Fleet tribes . . . neither makes the first a moa, nor the second moa-hunters' (Duff 1956a: 82). There was also the inverse anomaly: not only might non-Moa-hunters hunt non-moa Dinor-nithiformes, but 'Moa-hunter culture would undoubtedly outlast the extermination of the moa' (Duff 1956a:20).

Duff (1956a:21) dismissed these weaknesses on the grounds that his typological purpose was only 'to contrast the peak or zenith of Maori culture with the peak or zenith of the Moa-hunter culture phase', but others were not satisfied that a model of such inherent contradiction could provide an adequate cultural typology. Jack Golson (1959a, 1960) soon objected to the use of traditional history as a framework for archaeological classification and promptly dispensed with it altogether. His thoroughly archaeological solution to the prob-lems raised by Duff's model was to reduce 'moa-hunter' to its original status as a term appropriate to sites where there was actual evidence of that activity. In its place he proposed the 'Archaic Phase' (of New Zealand Eastern Polynesian Cul-ture), thus implying both a relative chronology and an ontological relationship with other phases (only one of which he specified in detail: the 'Classic Maori Phase', equivalent to Duff's 'Maori Culture'). The phases were defined by broad com-plexes of artefact types which were manifested in regionally-variable assemblages ('aspects').

Since the third edition of *The Moa-hunter Period of Maori Culture* (1977) was not substantially changed in the light of Golson's proposal and, where it was, only to offer a defence against it, it is widely assumed that Duff simply rejected the new model. In fact, in an important, but often over-looked address (Duff 1963), he tried to devise a compromise. Duff was hurt by the rejection of 'Moa-hunter' and, referring to 'the corner stone of the primary association of a cultural stratum with moa remains' admonished his listeners to 'recall the magnitude of the breakthrough towards clarity from the moment the Wairau burials made known the distinctiveness of the Moa-hunter pole of differentiation' (1963:30). Yet he bowed to Golson's argument on this point by accepting primary association with moa remains as the criterion for the Moa-hunter phase, and he adopted at least the terminology of a sequence of phases noting that the obvious consequence of his decision was a long post-moa transitional phase marked by what had earlier been called 'Moa-hunter' assemblages but which might now, with more accuracy, be designated 'residual'. Duff (1963:37) even tried to accommodate Green's (1963) developmental model, though with little conviction. Later (Duff 1977:xii) he defended 'Moa-hunter' as being simply a 'label of contrast' which, by nominating the most obvious game animal, picked up the primary difference between 'the first phase of ecological adaptation' and that of the Classic Maori. This merely evaded the point that it was material culture far more than subsistence economics which the competing cultural typologies were designed to describe.

In almost 20 years since the choice was offered, most archaeologists have opted for the Archaic–Classic Phase model, using it in a very broad and flexible way, but Moa-hunter, used in Duff's original sense, still holds sway in southern New Zealand where it is perhaps most applicable. Various other suggestions concerning cultural typology have been published since 1959, but none have won much support (e.g. Adkin 1960; Groube 1967; Anderson 1982b; Davidson 1984), nor have vehement denunciations of the preferred model been coupled with the disclosure of superior alternatives (Sutton 1987). It seems unlikely that there will be any major change unless a quite different element enters our present conception of Maori prehistory such as a greatly lengthened time-scale, or unless there is a return to the typological study of portable artefacts – an area of research which became, ironically, the first casualty of the widespread acceptance of Golson's proposal.

As for the term 'Moa-hunter' it has, in my view, outlived its usefulness. Even in the lower-case it implies something about cultural typology to which it is quite inappropriate. What we need to be concerned with, instead, is 'moa-hunting' as an activity set within (or without, if it should ever prove to be) the Archaic Phase.

8

NORTH ISLAND SITES

Adopting Golson's (1959a:36) suggestion, but emphasising moa-hunting and processing as activities rather than the definition of moa-hunting communities, seems a usefully simple definition to open a discussion of the more recent archaeological evidence. By 'moa-hunting' site, I mean only that there is some evidence of that activity, conceived in broad terms, manifest in the remains. In a context other than this volume a different adjective might be equally valid. This does away with the fair objection (Green 1975:611–13) that moa-hunting is an unreasonable descriptive term for a site which might also contain many more remains of seals, dogs or fish and which, in addition, might only have been the midden of a group engaged in a largely horticultural economy.

There are still difficult practical problems in the definition of moa-hunting sites. Nowhere is this more the case than in the northern region of the North Island, here defined as that long peninsula which extends at a right-angle from a base line drawn between the North Taranaki Bight and the eastern Bay of Plenty (see Fig. 2.2).

Northern North Island

One of the major issues in this region is the extent to which 'subfossil' moa bone (in this context meaning bone from birds which died naturally) has acquired a deceptively close association with cultural remains through dune deflation and other natural means. In northern Northland this is a particularly difficult problem because it is quite clear that subfossil bird bones, including moa remains, are a common element of the upper horizon of compacted Pleistocene dunesands overlain by later

mobile dunes in which archaeological sites are usually found (Millener 1981). Opinions about apparent moa-hunting sites are sharply divided. Millener (1981), like Archey (1941) and Duff (1956a:278), argues that most such localities result from deflation of post-moa archaeological sites onto moa-bone-bearing horizons. Millener (1981: 239–44) argues that only Houhora, one midden in Tom Bowling Bay and another in Matai Bay contain moa bone in secure cultural contexts. Scarlett (1974, 1979), however, believes that there is cultural moa bone in middens at Te Werahi, at several sites in Tom Bowling Bay, and also at Waikuku Beach, Tokerau Beach (and elsewhere in Doubtless Bay) and at Pataua. Davidson (1982:19) also accepts as cultural, sites with moa bone at Te Werahi, Twilight Beach, Tom Bowling Bay and Spirits Bay (Fig. 8.1).

One of the difficulties is, of course, that exposures are constantly changing in dune systems so that no two surface observations, nor occasional test pits, are likely to arrive at the same result. Fairfield's (1961) description of a moa-cooking site at Waikuku Flat is convincing at face-value; likewise the comments of E. T. Frost on evidence at Lake Ohia (Doubtless Bay). Although most moa remains were located on the compacted sand horizon, there were also 'their bones among the midden stones high up in the later sand dunes, mixed with seal bones' (E. T. Frost to W. R. B. Oliver (n.d.) 7 August 1932; Archey (1941) interpreted Frost's observations differently). Robinson (1963a) came to a similar conclusion and suggested possible evidence of a burial associated with a whole moa egg at Doubtless Bay. At Pataua, as well, Thorne (1876) and Cheeseman seem to have located at least four sites of moa-hunting amongst seven

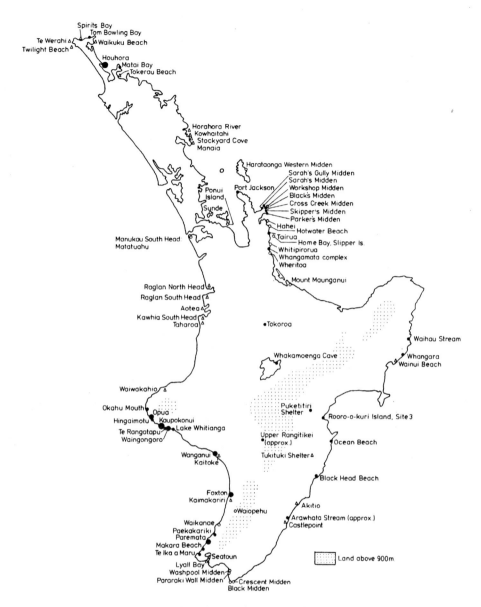

FIG. 8.1 Moa-hunting sites in the North Island. Filled circles are small, medium and large sites; open circles are sites to which moa bone was possibly imported; open triangles are sites where the cultural association of the moa bone is in question.

possible localities. At Kowhaitahi Beach, Thorne described ovenstones and broken moa bone in both loose sand and on a compacted surface. There were also moa-bone artefacts and Archaic adzes in association. Similar evidence was observed at Hora-hora River, Stockyard Cove and Manaia.

A second issue, and one which also brings in the Auckland and Coromandel sites, concerns the transfer of moa bones from any source (including midden remains) between one locality and another. At a site on Ponui Island (Nicholls 1963), where at least some of the moa bone appeared to have been fresh when used, it must have been imported;

similarly the *P. mappini* tarsometatarsus in the Sunde site (Scott 1970; Nichol 1981; Millener 1981:798), on Motutapu Island and unworked *Dinornis* bone at Home Bay on Slipper Island (Rowland 1978). Femoral and tibiotarsal fragments of *Eu. geranoides* at Harataonga, Great Barrier Island (Spring-Rice 1963; Law 1972b cf. Weetman 1886) are very probably in the same category unless there was a viable moa population there.[1]

---

[1] Polynesians often carried pigs, dogs etc. in canoes. They may have transported small, live moas to offshore islands.

Millener (1981:240) has also argued that *Anomalopteryx* leg bone in the Houhora site is significantly (and eponymously) anomalous in the district and was brought from another area, perhaps Coromandel. Nichol (n.d.) points out, however, that this genus is equally rare in Coromandel archaeological sites and suggests a Northland subfossil origin.

The importing of moa bones is frequently inferred by northern archaeologists when only sparse remains occur in a site, especially when they are the thick-walled leg bones favoured for industrial purposes (e.g. Leahy 1974; Davidson 1978; Harsant 1985; Prickett 1987; Nichol n.d.). This reflects, quite fairly, a conclusion about the general scarcity of moas in the north, but it also operates as an underlying working assumption which is precisely the opposite of that adopted in the South Island where any moa bone in a secure archaeological context constitutes *a priori* evidence of moa-hunting (notwithstanding Teviotdale's (1924) and Skinner's (1924a) more stringent guidelines on the matter). This too, of course, reflects a fair conclusion about the likelihood of local moa-hunting.

The northern assumption is odd in one respect – which is that scarce moas were perhaps more likely to be cut into small joints and distributed, as Smith (1985) has found with mammal remains from moa-hunting sites. The few remains at Ponui, for instance, were in association with large, retouched, flake implements of a kind common in undoubted moa-butchery sites, including Skipper's Midden. It is also fair to point out that it is the same bones chosen for industrial purposes which are least vulnerable to disappearance by rotting, trampling, gnawing etc., and their exclusive presence need not, thus, imply selection, only differential survival.

The northern assumption has the further consequence that bone thought to have been imported is also often ascribed to subfossil sources. Prickett (1987) takes this view of moa bone from Manukau South Head, and Nichol (n.d.) as well, of at least some remains from most sites containing moa bone in the whole region.

How much unequivocal evidence there might be to support this idea is hard to say because the identification of subfossil bone, without reference to its natural context, seems to rely on experience rather than any objective criteria. Scarlett (1974:3) points out that the degree of mineralisation is a very unreliable criterion, and that only something about the appearance of fractures or cut and saw marks is diagnostic. He could not, however, find words to describe how such damage appeared differently on

subfossil from green bone. Heavy mineralisation doubtless generally indicates subfossil material, and some kinds of cut marks (those associated with butchery) as well as obvious 'greenstick fractures' indicate cultural damage to fresh bone, but none are at all common amongst archaeological remains of moas. In addition, we hardly know anything about the range of appearance or any other qualities to be expected in moa bone subjected to a variety of exposure lengths in the highly diverse weathering conditions presented by New Zealand's soils and climate. Furthermore questions about the source of moa bone in sites are, it seems, not raised about the bones of other large birds, seals or whales, all of which might also have been exploited from traded joints, locally killed carcasses or other sources, including subfossil deposits.[2]

In the absence of taphonomic guidelines, most potential moa-hunting sites in this region must remain in a 'suspense list'. In Fig. 8.1 I have distinguished between two classes of potential moa-hunting sites: those which have moa bone in good cultural contexts but where the suspicion has been raised that the bone had been wholly imported to the site; and those in which the association of the moa bone with the cultural remains is at issue or has simply not been adequately established. Amongst the latter are sites on the West Coast between Raglan and Taharoa and at Mount Maunganui (Edson pers. comm.). Sites not shown, and not regarded here as 'moa-hunting' sites, are those in which the moa bone exists only in the form of artefacts or artefact-manufacturing debris. In some cases this is doubtless an unfair judgement, but to include all such cases would really beg the literal question – after all, moa bone was used for making fish hooks on the East Coast long after moas were extinct (Polack 1838).[3] Amongst the clear examples of moa-hunting sites, those with the most moa remains were Tairua (Rowland 1977, for midden analysis), Opito (Skipper's) and Sarah's Gully middens (Golson 1959a, 1959b; Green 1963; Calder 1972; Davidson 1979) and Houhora (Shawcross 1972).

---

[2] In addition to the belief that some sites were located on places where moa remains already existed (e.g. Taylor 1984:180; Nichol n.d.); Smart, Green and Yaldwyn (1962:259) suggest a moa died on Tairua site, *after* occupation.

[3] Nothing about the fragmentation, appearance, or subsequent use of moa bone informs about whether it came from direct hunting, meat exchange etc.

Houhora

The largest moa-hunting site (*c.* 1.5 ha) in the northern North Island, Houhora comprised 12 thin cultural layers separated by sand, indicating intermittent occupation. Shawcross estimated that there were 50 (± 10) moas represented in the excavated remains and that a preponderance of upper leg bones, especially femora, indicated 'that most of the moa were slaughtered and butchered at some distance from the settlement . . . and that consequently only the meat-covered upper legs were thought worth bringing back. Virtually no tarso-metatarsi and phalanges have been found' (Shawcross 1972:607). Moas, however, contributed relatively little, by quantity at least, to the diet of the inhabitants of Houhora. Smith (1985:290) calculated that only 6 per cent of the meat weight represented by the excavated faunal remains came from moas (cf. 57 per cent from fish, 28 per cent from seals).

Similar calculations concerning Coromandel sites indicate that moas provided about 25 per cent of the meat weight at Tairua (layer 2), Hotwater Beach (layer 5, but only 8 per cent in layer 4) and Parker's Midden (Smith 1985:246, 249–50, 257). Fish, at an average of 22 per cent, and seals, averaging 29 per cent of meat weight, were more productive resources. Nichol (n.d.) argues that the moa figures generally are too high, particularly since the meat-weight contribution of shellfish in most cases, and fish in some, is unknown. Specifically he reduces the Parker's Midden contribution to about 5 per cent and questions whether any moa remains were food wastes at Hotwater Beach.

Looking at the distribution of moa species in the northern sites it is apparent that the widest range occurs in the most convincing sites: six species each at Port Jackson, Skipper's Midden, Sarah's Gully Midden, Tairua and Houhora (Appendix C). Where quantified data exist they show an interesting difference, however, between Houhora, where most of the individuals were of *Eu. curtus*, and the Coromandel sites, where no single species stands out. In both areas sealing and fishing, perhaps also adze-making at the Tahanga quarry near Opito, were likely to have been more influential in the selection of localities than opportunities to hunt moas. The apparent specialisation at Houhora might reflect only the much greater availability in the hinterland of large expanses of sand dunes upon which *Eu. curtus* was accustomed to breed. In the Coromandel the relative unimportance of moas, compared to seals and artefactual stone, also seems to be implied by the absence of moa-hunting sites on the western (Firth of Thames) coast. There may have been fewer moas living there, but the total disparity is striking.

Southern North Island

Along the East Coast the familiar problem is raised of a coincidental association between cultural remains and subfossil moa bones in dunes, for instance near Castlepoint (Brodie 1950) and Waimu Beach (Hutchinson 1898), while Hill (1914) perceived no evidence of moa-hunting at all in Hawke's Bay. J. E. L. Simcox, a prominent collector, also observed no moa bone in middens on southern Hawke's Bay beaches. On the other hand, another collector, J. D. Buchanan, found moa bone and eggshell in 'restricted areas' in middens at Ocean Beach (Butts pers. comm.), and Scarlett (pers. comm.) found similar evidence there and at Black Head. Scarlett also excavated a moa-hunting rockshelter at Puketitiri and found moa remains in a midden at Arawhata Stream. To these few instances can be added burnt moa bone in a midden at Waihau Stream, Tolaga Bay (Jones pers. comm.) and circumstantial evidence of human occupation, including a desiccated gourd, in the Tukituki Shelter where an *Anomalopteryx* egg was located (*The Hawke's Bay Tribune* 16 October 1936).

More significant is a recent examination of dunes at Whangara which showed that there was a primary association between moa bone and cultural remains, including a prismatic core of chert (Jones and Moore n.d.). There is also an important site at Rooro-o-kuri where Bonica and Thorpe (1967) uncovered an Archaic midden which contained a whale-tooth pendant and evidence of fish-hook manufacturing 'using leg bones of small moas (which were probably hunted)'.

Poukawa

No discussion of Hawke's Bay could avoid mention of this site, excavated by Russell Price, beginning in 1956. The site lies in the same lacustrine depression as the Te Aute Swamp, 12 km to the south, and it has produced numerous moa bones and remains of other extinct avifauna including the swan, musk duck and pelican. Price (1963, 1965) claimed that broken moa bones, cut wood and other potential evidence of human activity were found below two ash and pumice layers, the upper of which was shown to be from the Taupo eruption at *c.* 1800 bp and the lower from the Waimihia eruption dated *c.* 3400 bp. This suggested 'implications almost too daring to be true' (Pullar 1965:11), which were nonetheless widely and popularly canvassed (e.g. Pullar 1970). McGlone (1978) showed, however, that extensive deforestation was not apparent in pollen from cores taken near the Poukawa Lake until a period beginning at about the 11th century AD, a strong indication that if local settlement had occurred earlier it could hardly have been much earlier. McFadgen (1979) then excavated part of Price's site and found that earlier farm discing had broken through the Taupo pumice in places and that deep cracks extended to below the Waimihia ash. It was only in such places that cultural material was located below these levels.

Though seemingly conclusive, these results have been challenged by Horn (1983) who argues that an analysis of the avian remains reveals such biasses in the representation of body parts amongst small birds that it actually furnishes 'tentative support' for Price's views (Horn 1983:76). This is equivocal evidence at best, and it seems far more likely that the explanation lies in such factors as variations resulting from Price's excavation and collection methods together with differential slippage of remains down cracks in the peat and other taphonomic factors operating in swamp sites.

Tokoroa and Whakamoenga

On the volcanic plateau are two moa-hunting sites, Tokoroa and Whakamoenga Cave. The former is an open site, and in this respect almost unique in the inland North Island. Limited excavations (Cook and Green 1962; Law 1973) revealed a few shallow ovens and some postholes and a shallow drain in no obvious pattern. Moa bone representing several individuals of *Eu. exilis* (i.e. *curtus*) and a considerable quantity of obsidian flakes were recovered. Tokoroa, like Whakamoenga Cave and other evidence cited by Law (1973:161) and Leahy (1976:32–3), shows clearly that forest and moas had subsequently colonised the area devastated by the 2nd century AD Taupo ash shower.

Whakamoenga Cave is a particularly interesting site because the materials are very well preserved and the moa-hunting remains were sealed by a rockfall, after which occupation recurred (Leahy 1976). The evidence indicates capture of perhaps three or four small moas (Nichol n.d. suggests a maximum of three) at a time when forest was abundant. Broadly associated with the moa bones, but with other bird remains as well, were two uni

laterally barbed bird-spear points (Hosking 1962: 7–8). Leahy (1976:68) suggests that the forest was largely destroyed by the end of the moa-hunting occupation and that subsequent inhabitants of the cave turned to freshwater mussels and imported marine molluscs, as well as bracken and cultigens.

The only other site which has been reported well into the interior of the North Island is on the Upper Rangitikei (Batley 1960). No details about it are available (Fig. 8.1).

Wellington sites

There were fragments of moa bone in four Palliser Bay middens, but the material may have been imported (Leach and Leach 1979:235–6; although one argument for this, the possible presence of *Eu. gravis*, no longer stands). A number of possible moa-hunting sites has been reported at Wellington, especially around the Miramar Peninsula where, however, there are natural deposits of moa bone in both swamp and old dune contexts. Crawford's (1873) early observations drew no conclusion about the relationship of moa bone to nearby evidence of Maori occupation, but later residents claimed moa bone and eggshell occurred in middens at Lyall Bay, Miramar and Seatoun (*The Dominion* 21 January 1937, 16 October 1937, 28 April 1939, 2 May 1939; H. M. Christie to Duff 14 July 1943, n.d.; McLeod 1919). Duff (1956a: 277) was suspicious of the decomposed nature of the bones, although he accepted Christie's account of the site at Lyall Bay, as does Jones (1986). Yaldwyn (1959), however, pointed to the lack of any direct evidence of a primary association between moa bones and the archaeological remains, and also argued that moa bones from Seatoun had a subfossil appearance.[4]

More convincing evidence of a moa-hunting site came from the discovery of a tibiotarsal fragment (*P. mappini* or *A. didiformis*) at 25 cm depth in an oven at Te Ika a Maru (Yaldwyn 1959). Later excavations turned up another piece of moa bone which had been cut while fresh, in Scarlett's opinion (Davidson 1976). The Makara Beach site produced more abundant moa remains including an immature bone, probably of *P. mappini*, which Yaldwyn (1959:22) regarded as 'decisive evidence of genuine moa-hunting'. Burnt and fragmented moa bone was found scattered in and around a cluster of ovens (Davis 1962; McFadgen 1980). Other sites have been reported at Paekakariki (Enys 1873) and Waikanae (Field 1892).

---

[4] See also Adkin (1948), McLeod (1919).

Paremata

The main site in the Wellington area seems to have been at Paremata (Porirua Harbour). Chapman (1885) located cut and burnt cervical vertebrae from moas, together with adzes, and later investigations found 'moa bone was ubiquitous in much of the excavation' (Davidson 1978:215). There seems to have been a single moa-hunting layer, (3), from which bone was later redeposited in upper layers, otherwise mainly of shell midden, as the result of successive occupations on the site up until European times. Ribs, vertebrae and tracheal rings indicate at least some butchery on the site as, perhaps, do the remains of six species, and virtually no evidence of bone-working, but there were few signs of ovens in layer 3 and stone flakes were also quite sparse for a moa-hunting site. Although the maximum MNI which can be calculated from Davidson's (1978:235) data is seven, there may be further individuals represented in the unidentified material or in Sinclair's (1977) collection. In any event it seems likely that the moa-hunting layer at Paremata, though shallow, extended over an area of perhaps 1000 m². An example of the kind of kill site which the Paremata hunters might have left was located by Adkin (1948:80) in the Tararua foothills at Waiopehu. It consisted simply of a heap of moa gizzard stones and a large, flint flake-knife. Adkin found a similar implement, with moa bones and gizzard stones, near Kaimakariri Lagoon.

Foxton

A medium-sized moa-hunting site, excavated by McFadgen (1967, 1978:38–40; McFadgen and McFadgen 1966), Foxton comprised a series of shell middens overlying, in the eastern part of the site, two layers rich in moa bone. The upper layer was associated with an oven, hearth and postholes indicating a rudimentary shelter. In the western part of the site moa bone was also abundant; over 50 bones being recovered from an area of about 4 m². These included vertebrae, phalanges and cranial remains, representing 11 birds of the species *A. didiformis*, *P. mappini*, *D. struthoides* and *Eu. curtus*; possibly also *Eu. geranoides*. The Foxton site is spread, discontinuously, over an area of nearly 6000 m² and was clearly an important moa-hunting station, possibly the kind of major site which might be expected from its location near the mouth of the Manawatu River.

There is little evidence of such sites at other major river mouths, except at Wanganui (Field 1877:222). However river courses change rapidly in the unconsolidated sediments of Manawatu and other moa-hunting sites may have been washed away (cf. Cumberland 1962).

Taranaki sites

There has also been rapid coastal erosion in Taranaki, particularly north of Mt Taranaki, but even on the south coast it has been estimated at a rate of 20 m per century (Grant-Taylor to Cassels 22 February 1980, Cassels n.d.). Even so, this is the richest area of moa-hunting sites in the North Island. In addition to a few sites about which little is known – Waiwakahio (Fyfe pers. comm.; possibly the site mentioned by Buist 1962:236), Rahotu or Okahu Mouth (Scarlett pers. comm.) and Hingaimotu (Smith 1985:492) – there are at least five which are of some importance. The Lake Whitianga site is in dunes atop a coastal cliff and contained burnt moa bone, large obsidian flake knives and other flaked stone pieces (Robinson 1961). Opua was discovered 90 years ago (*The Opunake Times* 11 December 1896), and the MNI listed in Appendix C are from bones collected in 1908. There were also numerous small birds, notably kiwis, and remains of people, dogs, fur seals, sea lions and an elephant seal (Fyfe pers. comm.). It is a very typical south Taranaki faunal assemblage.

Buist excavated about 40 m² at the famous Waingongoro site in 1960, finding an oven with the remains of a fully intact *P. mappini* leg lying in it. There was another oven as well, and numerous moa bones of at least five birds along with moa eggshell, a moa-bone needle and flakes of obsidian and chert. Taylor's (1873) double row of ovens was not located. One interesting point about the intact leg – apart from the fact that it *was* intact and is therefore no different from the kind of remains which are commonly regarded as 'subfossil' in other situations – is that it lay in probable life-position, that is, with a broad angle between femur and tibiotarsus and almost a right-angle between the latter and the tarsometatarsus (Buist and Yaldwyn 1960; they re-named the site Ohawe, from the name of the adjacent beach).

On the river bank, about 400 m west of the Waingongoro site, Canavan (1960) located ovens cut into compacted sand and conglomerate overlain by dunes. This has, of course, interesting implications for some of the northern North Island coastal sites. Small excavations at this site, Te Rangatapu, revealed several ovens packed with fragmented moa and seal bone and remains of small birds, dog, fish and shellfish, together with a few obsidian flakes (Canavan 1960).

If there has obviously been an extensive moa-hunting occupation at and near the mouth of the Waingongoro, one of the two largest rivers in South Taranaki, the same is also true of the other, the Kaupokonui.

Kaupokonui

In 1962 wind erosion exposed a large moa-hunting site in dunes at the mouth of the Kaupokonui River (Fig. 8.2). Initial excavations of about 34 m² by Buist (1962, 1963) and Robinson (1963b) disclosed three midden layers separated by sterile sand. The two lower layers, 4 and 6, contained moa bone and eggshell in and around ovens, together with the remains of birds and some seal, dog, rat and fish bone as well as bone and stone artefacts. A few fragments of moa bone were found in the upper layer (2), but were explained as material redeposited by the cutting of ovens which, in places, reached into layer 4.

Later excavations of about 45 m² in 1974 and 1979 by Cassels (n.d.; Foley 1980) were sited close to Buist's main area (Fig. 8.3), but the stratigraphic separation of his two lower layers was found not to be continuous and they were combined into a single cultural layer (4) of 10–40 cm in thickness. Within this it was possible to recognize a lower level at which moa bone was very abundant and where most reasonably intact skeletons were found, and an upper horizon where dog coprolites were particularly noticeable and moa bone was relatively scarce. The bone might have been scratched up by dogs. Alternatively Cassels (n.d.)

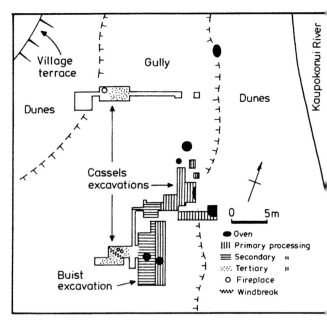

FIG. 8.3 Kaupokonui moa-hunting site, after Cassels (n.d.)

suggests that the coprolite horizon came to rest on the main bone midden by dune deflation. In the remaining dune areas scattered ovens and a higher layer (2) of ovens and fish bone and shellfish middens seems to correspond with Buist's layer 2.

Faunal data

Kaupokonui proved extraordinarily rich in avifaunal remains. Fifty-five species of birds other than moas are represented, including the extinct swan, giant rail, goshawk and crow. The main species are, however, weka (74 individuals estimated in combined Buist-Cassels data), pigeon (59), kaka (46), kiwis (46), tui (42), ducks (30+), kokako (21), parakeets (19) and takahe (16). More than 20 dogs, one elephant seal and 15 sea lions are represented, although the latter mainly by cranial bone, probably sought for ivory and other raw material (Cassels n.d.; Smith 1985). Fish and shellfish were very scarce in the moa-butchery layer.

The MNI of moas for the material recovered by Cassels was incorrectly calculated as 127 by Foley (1980). It is not entirely possible to calculate MNI correctly from her data, but a close estimate can be obtained, at the same time synonymising *P. septentrionalis* with *P. mappini* and *Eu. exilis* with *Eu. curtus*, species separated in her work. Taking the most common element and the highest number of it, by side, and adding together the figures for that element from each species in a synonymic pair,

FIG. 8.2 The Kaupokonui moa-butchery site, looking seaward. (By courtesy of Richard Cassels and Taranaki Museum.)

runs the risk of exaggerating the total MNI since, with fragmented bone, some pieces representing one individual in a divided sample could match other pieces in a combined sample. Because tibiotarsi are the most common elements, and one of the most fragmented, it is safer to take the numbers of femora, which are nearly all intact in these species, to give a more reliable, though lower, MNI. The results (Appendix C) indicate some 50 individuals. There are up to 10 further individuals, all *Euryapteryx* and mostly immature, which cannot be adequately dealt with; some may represent only further pieces of individuals already counted but at least seven seem acceptable. The total result, 50–57, agrees quite well with Cassels' (n.d.) view of the total MNI as 47, calculated irrespective of taxa.

Since the Buist data (from Scarlett in Foley 1980, app. 4) include bone fragment portions it is also possible to calculate MNI for this sample. The results (Appendix C) indicate almost precisely the same density of moas as in the Cassels excavations, about 1.3 per square metre. The species proportions are, however, quite different. *P. mappini* is entirely predominant, whereas *Eu. curtus* and *A. didiformis* dominate the Cassels sample which derives mostly from an adjacent part of the site (Fig. 8.3). This might indicate that several different catches are in evidence (below). Kooyman's MNI estimates (Appendix C) must reflect an incomplete analysis of the material since there was certainly more *Anomalopteryx* than he includes.

How many moas are represented at Kaupokonui can only be broadly estimated. The main butchery area and associated processing was largely confined to a band about 10 m wide along some 30 m of the eastern side of the site. On that basis about 400 moas might have been butchered if the moa density in the excavations obtained throughout that area.

Smith (1985:234) calculated the fleshweight contribution of moas at Kaupokonui as 73 per cent, but he used Foley's MNI data for moas. Recalculated according to my estimate of the MNI in Cassels' data, moas contributed about 51 per cent of meat weight, seals 19 per cent, small birds 15 per cent and dogs 12 per cent. These estimates make Kaupokonui appear more like other contemporary coastal middens in South Taranaki, such as Opua, than earlier seemed the case.

Organisation

The layout of the site (Fig. 8.3) can be described as a series of activity bands aligned along the course of the river. Ovens are concentrated in the river-front dune and behind them is a primary butchery area in which 'articulated skulls and necks, ribs, vertebrae and pelves occur. There are relatively few stone implements in this area [but] . . . some bone tools ("polishers" or "chisels") were found here' (Cassels n.d.:16). Immediately to the west is a secondary processing area characterised by numerous leg bones, notably tibiotarsi – many of which had been smashed – together with numerous stone tools. Around the inland periphery of this zone are discrete patches of stone tools and debitage and relatively sparse, but highly fragmented, moa bone. These seem to represent tertiary processing associated with living areas. In the northern part is a 'living floor' with bone tools possibly used in skin-working and evidence of pumice fashioning, including a pumice-reel necklace unit. In the southern part there is a low stone windbreak, a row of postholes – possibly representing a 'moderate-sized timber hut' – and two informal fireplaces (Cassels n.d.:17). Large quantities of chert and obsidian and also evidence of adze-flaking are associated with each area.

This pattern of features describes a complete moa-butchery camp, as will become clear once the Hawksburn site is described (p. 144–7). There is, then, no need to postulate a connection with a village site on a terrace beside, but about 7 m above, the Kaupokonui midden. Some moa leg bones at the latter may have been on the site as a result of the midden occupation, or were perhaps scavenged by the villagers for manufacturing fish hooks – one of their common activities. It seems most likely that the village, which has horticultural features and house remains associated with evidence of fishing and small-fowling, is later than the moa-butchery and possibly contemporary with the shell middens and ovens in the upper layer of the butchery area. At Waingongoro, of course, there was exactly the same spatial relationship between an ancient moa-butchery and a 19th-century village.

Hunting and processing patterns

Since the moa bones were abundant, largely intact and well preserved – including such fragile bones as the sternum, pelves and cranial elements – it is possible to delineate a clearer picture of moa processing at Kaupokonui than at any other site. So far as hunting is concerned, though, there are few clues in the data. The concentration of remains from smaller birds – notably the other ground-living species in the same areas as the moa bones, and mixed up with them in a way suggesting the processing of moas and small birds together – indicates that moa-hunting was pursued as part of a broader fowling strategy. What methods this might have involved, however, remains a mystery. The presence of a large number of dogs on the site and the historical use of dogs for hunting ground birds suggests one possible technique, but the use of snares is equally likely. One moa sternum was found with two holes in it which could have been from spears, and both Buist (1963) and Cassels (n.d.) speculated that some skulls and cervical vertebrae were lying in positions which indicated the wringing of moa necks, presumably of birds either taken in foot-snares or with their legs deliberately bound (Fig. 8.4).

The difference between a concentration of *Eu. curtus* and *A. didiformis* in the Cassels excavations, to either side of Buist's excavation in which *P. mappini* was wholly dominant, might indicate some patterning in the hunting or processing strategy. If it does not reflect a separation of species into different processing areas when the catch was returned to camp, it could arise from systematic hunting in different micro-environments. At Kaupokonui, the main hunting choices close to the site were either northwest into a large area of dunes extending to the Otakeho Stream or northeast onto terraces along the Kaupokonui River. Perhaps *Eu. curtus*, though nesting in the open, frequented light forest close to *A. didiformis* habitats, while *P. mappini* remained in scrub-covered dunes.

Processing of the carcasses generally began before transporting them to the site. There are not many gizzard stones in the midden, and only a few patches of them seem to have come from moas

FIG. 8.4 *Euryapteryx* vertebrae and cranium lying in a position which might indicate a wrung neck. (By courtesy of Richard Cassels and Taranaki Museum.)

butchered on the site – one heap lying under a sternum – so it seems that most birds were gutted in the field. Generally the feet were removed as well. Carcasses of the three main species were returned to the site with only about a fifth of the legs intact (judging by the frequency of tarsometatarsi compared to femora, the figures vary from 14 per cent to 22 per cent), but whereas nearly 30 per cent of *Eu. curtus* carcasses also had heads and about 20 per cent of *P. mappini*, *A. didiformis* was returned headless, possibly because it was generally caught deeper in the forest than the other species.

At the site no single processing sequence was followed, but the usual method was to cut off the head and neck as a unit, mostly at the base of the neck, cut off the feet at the joint between tarsometatarsus and tibiotarsus, and fling these pieces to one side (there was a small heap of them in one place). At that point the alternatives were to separate the sternum and/or the ribcage from the pelvis or to leave the body intact. The tibiotarsi were then removed, and finally the femora, the latter apparently cut from the dorsal side of the pelvis (Cassels n.d.).

It is difficult to be sure how this general process related to cooking and eating. The head-neck and feet were clearly discarded, and several instances of a whole skeleton minus only the legs suggests that some moa bodies were also left to rot. It was, in fact, Cassels' (n.d.:29) general conclusion that 'the waste is astounding', and that rather than a slow accumulation of well-chewed bones, the site represented a short-lived 'orgy of hunting and eating' (Cassels 1979:32).[5]

How long occupation of the site might have lasted is almost impossible to say, but there seems to have been one early expedition represented by Buist's (1963) lower midden layer and the lowest part of Cassels' (n.d.) midden layer, followed by a major 'blitz'. Cassels (n.d.) suggested that Kaupokonui was occupied in autumn-winter when the weather is generally less windy, and the number of weka, a species often caught historically in winter, could support that view. Over the whole range of birds, however, there is no obvious season represented (Foley 1980), and Smith (1985) could establish no seasonal pattern from the seal remains. Some features of the moa remains, on the other hand, do seem to suggest a seasonal bias. There

[5] The remarkable condition of even fragile bones also suggests a short span of occupation (by a lack of trampling etc.).

was a high proportion of immature individuals, especially of *Euryapteryx* sp. (*c.* 30 per cent), but also amongst *P. mappini* (*c.* 20 per cent) and, where it was possible to tell, these seemed to be from individuals close to the adult size but lacking epiphyseal fusion on the long bones. There were also remains of a few chicks and up to six eggs, taking the Buist and Cassels data together. At least part of the hunting, then, occurred during the breeding season, and if it is assumed that hunting beginning before, or at the beginning of, breeding would be likely to produce a much larger number of eggs and chicks as well as juveniles from the previous breeding season, then it can be speculated that the main hunting activity occurred from near the end of the breeding season onward – perhaps summer.

Moa-hunting and butchery obviously produced certain useful by-products, notably skins (perhaps also feathers) and bone. At Kaupokonui there were up to 15 moa-bone 'chisels' (Chapter 11), generally made from strips of tibiotarsal bone, sometimes with one end chopped to a point and then ground. Several of these artefacts were found closely associated with moa vertebrae and Cassels (n.d.) suggested that one of their uses may have been to wedge and split vertebral columns. The working surfaces are, however, smooth and unstriated and skin-scraping, or stripping meat from cooked joints, seems more likely (Cassels n.d.). Whether or not moa skins were used there were certainly plenty of dog skins to dress, and the only slight concentration of the bone chisels occurred in a dog-processing area.

The collection of moa tibiotarsi into a concentrated secondary processing area implies an intention to process them systematically. What products were sought is not, however, clear. They might have been joints from which the cooked meat was stripped. Many had smashed shafts (unlike femora or tarsometatarsi) and this could mean either, or both, access to marrow or to strips of flat shaft bone for manufacture into implements. The usual bone-sawing and drilling associated with fish hook manufacture were absent.

Some conclusions

Looking at the southern North Island sites as a whole it is obvious that moa-hunting was more important here than further north (Fig. 8.1), and that there exist several butchery sites rivalling those of the South Island. Amongst the major species, *P. mappini* and *A. didiformis* are noticeably more common in the southern region sites (Appendix C). The distribution of sites here, as in the northern region, appears to follow no obvious pattern. The Manawatu coast is generally prograding and the relative scarcity of sites there is puzzling compared to their size and abundance in South Taranaki where coastal erosion is occurring very rapidly indeed. The general lack of sites along the east coast as a whole and throughout the interior is also difficult to explain unless, in the case of the latter, there was little early penetration of the heavy forest and comparatively little reward from moas by doing so. It is, at any rate, most unlikely that the distribution reflects archaeological sampling patterns. Most moa-hunting sites recorded in the South Island were reported by local residents, and the North Island has been more densely settled for at least as long. We have to conclude that there was much less moa-hunting in the North Island. On grounds of species and ecology this is broadly understandable.

9

SOUTH ISLAND COASTAL SITES

The Southern Alps create much sharper climatic differences between east and west coasts in the South Island than occur in the North Island. The extremes are reached in Otago, where annual rainfall can exceed 8000 mm on the western slopes of the main divide but may be less than 300 mm in parts of the eastern interior, rising to about 800 mm along most of the east coast.

On the west coast, where dense rainforest was predominant, little evidence of moa-hunting has been reported, and almost none of it from the southern district (Fig. 9.1). G. J. Roberts mentioned 'split and charred moa bones' (Skinner 1912:146) but did not give any location. Three rockshelter sites in Fiordland contained a few fragments of moa bone and, at Southport, some moa feathers (Coutts 1972: table 3:53), but the *Eu. gravis* tibiotarsal and femoral fragments at Long Island were almost certainly brought from east of the main divide, and that might have been true of the other remains as well (Scarlett 1974). The scarcity of moa-hunting sites could reflect rapid coastal erosion (up to 350 m per century) and marked river mouth changeability in the unconsolidated coastal sediments north of Fiordland, together with beach-mining for gold in some areas, but a general scarcity of moas can also be assumed south of the Paringa River where beech is prominent in the forest composition (Hooker 1986). Wellman and Wilson (1964:716) record very large ovens and 'ox' bones at Martins Bay. If the ovens are pre-European in age, the bones may be from moas.

Northwest coast

Moa-hunting sites appear with greater frequency north of Cape Foulwind, where the annual coastal rainfall seldom exceeds 2000 mm. Moa bone oc-curred in sites at Little Wanganui, Oparara and Kohaihai (Anderson 1982e; pers. obs.), but the only systematic investigations have been at Buller Mouth and Heaphy Mouth. At the former, a site of about 2.5 ha, Orchiston (1974, app. 2) found a main occupation layer containing moa bone, amongst other midden.

Heaphy Mouth

Estimated at 3 ha prior to recent erosion, this site lies on the south bank of the Heaphy River estuary. Excavations of about 240 m² in 1962–63 revealed an unusual variety and abundance of features and artefacts. Over most of the excavated area there was a single occupation layer 25–60 cm thick, but at the seaward and estuary margins it was split in two by a thin layer of sand, which suggests two occupations close in time (Wilkes and Scarlett 1967). Prominent in the recovered artefact assemblage were 43 adzes, mainly of Duff types 2A and 4A, a moa-bone imitation whale tooth and 5000 flakes and flake tools, 50 per cent of them in Nelson argillite. Included were a number of retouched blades.

Inland of a band of 47 small ovens, and some shell middens, distributed along the estuary margin were artefacts and stone flaking areas concentrated about three stone pavements. The largest, 3 × 2 m, was subrectangular in shape, and had a kerb around three sides. Wilkes and Scarlett (1967; Scarlett 1982) interpreted the pavements as wet-weather working floors, possibly roofed, but evidence from other moa-hunting sites suggests that the pavements were probably along the margins of dwellings. Some postholes and at least one kerbed hearth can be interpreted in this way (Anderson 1986, n2; Anderson and Ritchie 1986).

FIG. 9.1   Moa-hunting sites in the South Island (for inset, see fig. 10.1). Filled circles are small, medium and large sites; open triangles are sites where the cultural association of the moa bone is in question.

Amongst the midden components, fish bone was scarce, fur seal remains were numerous and moa bone was also 'fairly plentiful' (Wilkes and Scarlett 1967:209). The latter was nearly all from *A. didiformis*, with one tibiotarsal fragment of *D. ?robustus* (although *E. crassus* was mentioned by Wilkes *et al.* 1963:89). Most of the pieces were from adult limb bones and neither crania nor vertebrae were represented. A few pieces of moa eggshell were recovered.

Not a particularly specialised moa-hunting site, Heaphy Mouth is still important for showing that patterns of site organisation and artefact assemblage typical of large eastern moa-hunting sites also prevailed on the west coast.

Tasman Bay and Marlborough Sounds

At Anapai a small beach-front midden, in which fur seal bones were predominant, also contained *A. didiformis* remains in the lower levels (Wilkes *et al.* 1963; Millar 1967). Elsewhere around Tasman Bay, moa bone has been reported from a number of early sites (Anderson 1966; Wilkes *et al.* 1963;

see Fig. 9.1) but only at Tahunanui, The Glen and Rotokura have there been systematic excavations. The first, primarily an adze and fish-hook manufacturing site, contained both hook tabs and midden remains of *A. didiformis* and some *Eu. gravis*, but as there was little evidence of either ovens or discrete middens it is probable that the bone had become dispersed from a food-processing part of the site lying outside the excavated area (Millar 1967, 1971). At The Glen moa bone was very sparse and most of it was thought to be subfossil (Walls 1979).

At Rotokura, a small, deep midden formed in a boulder beach, moa bones were concentrated in the lowest layer, and scattered amongst them were flake knives and blades of Nelson argillite. In the higher levels of this layer moa bone and seal bone were scarce and the upper middens were mainly of small bird remains, shellfish and fish bones (Millar 1967). Butts (1978) concluded that the spectrum of small bird and fish species (layer 4) indicated summer to autumn occupation in the early levels.

On D'Urville Island, Wellman (1962) argued that coastal sections often disclosed two occupation layers, in the upper of which there was fish bone but no moa bone, and in the lower of which moa bone was 'common'. If this latter view is consistent with his description of several bone fragments per 930 m² in an exposed occupation level at Greville Harbour as also being 'common', we might conclude, however, that moas were actually rather scarce, despite the number of sites in which remains occur (Fig. 9.1). A general scarcity of moas was also apparent to Prickett and Walls (1973) and Prickett and Prickett (1975). Similarly only scraps of moa bone occurred in a site in Kenepuru Sound (Rutland 1893).

The Sandhill site at Titirangi had three occupation layers, in the lowest of which moa bone occurred in association with evidence of adze manufacturing (Trotter n.d.a). This combination of activities seems to have been a general theme of moa-hunting sites throughout the South Island, but particularly in sites close to the Nelson-Marlborough argillite sources. Moas were mainly of the small species *A. didiformis* in the northwest region, and no specialised hunting or processing sites have come to light. Excavations at Awamoa and Whangamoa, two large and complex early sites in Tasman Bay might, however, tell a different story.

Northeast coast

Without doubt the eastern South Island was the main moa-hunting region, and the greatest number and largest sites are along the coast. The most important of these, in terms of the recent definition of 'Moa-hunter' culture, has been

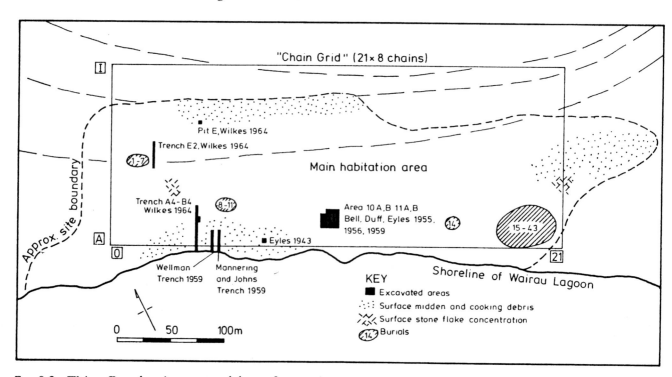

FIG. 9.2 Wairau Bar, showing areas and dates of excavation.

Wairau Bar, but what do we know of it as a moa-hunting settlement?

Wairau Bar

The stratigraphic history of the site has been described by Wilkes (1964; see also Trotter 1975a, 1977) from trenches dug in 1959 and 1964 (Fig. 9.2). The basal layers (1 and 2) of the site consist of bedded marine sediments overlain by lagoon mud and silt-cemented gravels to the south-west (trench A4–B4) and loose sand to the north-east (trench E2). It is in the latter material that the best-preserved burials are generally situated. Layer 3 is observable as a deeply-weathered fossil soil which has been saturated by comminuted charcoal near the lagoon edge, where it consists of a complex of inter-cut ovens and associated debris. At that point the layer extends well below high-tide level, and since ovens at the same level but not yet exposed at the lagoon edge show no sign of water-disturbance, a relatively lower sea level of about 50 cm was postulated by Wilkes (1964). Over some of the site the modern plough zone lies directly upon layer 3.

The main cultural layer (4) is largely composed of shell midden near the lagoon in trench A4–B4 (Fig. 9.3), but postholes and similar features, together with domestic artefacts and stone-knapping debris, predominate seawards. In trench E2 the postholes in layer 3 are sealed by ovens in layer 4, and also by shell midden, notably of the unfavoured species *Amphibola crenata* (mud snail). Layer 4 also extends across the adjacent burial area and since it is also underlain by lenses of layer 1 material, dug up during grave construction, burials 1–7 must date to layer 3 or earlier. Layer 5, the modern surface, contains thick lenses of river silt near the lagoon, indicating frequent flooding over the site.

Wilkes argues that there was a major change in the organisation of the settlement between the periods represented by layers 3 and 4. During the former occupation cooking areas were concentrated along the lagoon edge. During the latter occupation many structures were rebuilt, and cooking and refuse areas were largely relocated to the seaward margin of the site, partly over former habitation and burial areas.

Moa bone was quite abundant in the site, notably in middens along the main ridge and in the habitation areas where 'enormous quantities' (Duff 1956a:25), had been turned up by ploughing, only to disappear rapidly upon exposure during subsequent deflation of the surface by up to 30 cm.

FIG. 9.3   Trench B at Wairau Bar, 1963–64. (By courtesy of Canterbury Museum.)

Moa bone seems to have been especially abundant in layer 3 (Wellman was 'amazed at the relatively high proportion of moa bones' in this layer (Wilkes 1964:2), though see his comments in relation to D'Urville Island), but nowhere does there seem to have been the concentrated burnt bone middens of southern sites. Wilkes (1964) found most bone in the older (layer 3) ovens near the lagoon, while in the habitation area bone was largely confined to 'cache' holes (inferred stores for industrial bone, or possibly deposits of some ritual significance) and other small holes and depressions where it may have been swept by the inhabitants of the dwellings. Moa eggshell, though, was more abundant in this area.

Remains of the extinct swan were very common in this site (Falla 1942), and fur seal, dolphin and dog well represented. Shell and fish-bone middens were especially common in layer 4, and there is a suggestion (above) that exploitation of shellfish had depleted local reserves of the more-favoured species by this time.

Wilkes (1964) took column samples of 60 × 30 cm at 6 m intervals throughout his excavations and analysis of the recovered materials provides one of the few quantitative assessments of a moa-hunting site. The basic cultural components, averaged for the excavations as a whole and then scaled up to the present size of the site were: 1641 t of shell (86 per cent of it *Chione stutchburyi*), 33.5 t of bone, and 38.6 t of artefactual stone, nearly all of it argillite.[1] The bone proved to be 76 per cent moa in the samples, which scales to 25.5 t for the site. Nearly all the material was leg bone and, judging by Duff's (1956a) conclusions, mostly from *Eu. gravis* (possibly including some *P. elephantopus*) with small amounts of *E. crassus*. Scarlett (1974) also identified *A. didiformis* and *M. didinus* from Wairau Bar (appendix D). Taking *Eu. gravis* leg bone as weighing 2920 g per individual (Kooyman pers. comm.) provides an estimate of 8733 moas represented at the site. Since some of these were of smaller species, and at least part of the site has been eroded, the figure may be regarded as conservative within the limitations of its estimation. Wilkes (1964) also calculated that 2380 moa eggs had been consumed at the site (and see Millar 1967:8).

How big the site once was is clearly a pertinent question in estimations such as these. Wilkes (1964) argued that the arrangement and relative ages of the beach ridges at Wairau Bar, together with evidence of similar burials, artefacts and pits on the northern bank of the outlet, indicate that the river mouth was located south of the site during the main period of occupation and that settlement consequently extended over an area more than twice that known today.

Numerous postholes and some possible drains and formed floors were uncovered by Wilkes (1964) but no stone-kerbed hearths. What sort of dwellings his evidence discloses is thus unclear, but a plan of earlier excavations at area 10A to 11B (Fig. 9.4) seems to reveal, if uncertainly, a familiar pattern. A number of postholes which contained rotted butts are shown joined on Duff's plan (Fig. 9.4) to outline a structure about 5 m square. If it faced northwest, then the tendency for flint flakes to concentrate along the right-hand side (traditionally the women's side) and the possibility that a porch is somehow represented in the features

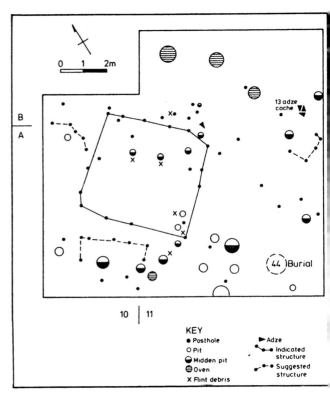

FIG. 9.4   Wairau Bar, area 10A to 11B, after Duff (n. d.).

(including the adze and flint flakes) along the northwest side, would suggest a small but typical Maori house. The lack of a hearth is quite common in this class of insubstantial dwellings (Davidson 1984:156). Given that conclusion, we might then see some cooking sheds or other domestic features, as well as open ovens, scattered about the dwelling, and a burial a few metres away.[2] Other than in this small area, and vague references to 'hut fireplaces' (?stone-kerbed hearths) mainly in the central area of the site (Duff 1956a), the pattern of habitation is not at all clear.

Most famous for its adzes and ornaments, Wairau Bar also produced numerous flake tools – amongst them large retouched flakes and blades of argillite. Since only six large silcrete blades were recovered it seems argillite was used instead. Neither obsidian nor limestone flint, both common at the site, were often knapped into large flakes or blades.[3]

Turning to the burials, the least-explored but most striking aspect of them is the variety amongst

---

[1] Millar (1967) calculated that 3000 adzes had been made, but the figure, based on 30.5 t of debitage, should be about 12,000.

[2] Wilkes (1964) accepts only one pit as an oven. Fewer postholes recorded in the southwest area of excavation are, he suggests, due to poorer recording in 1959.

[3] Wilkes (1964) observed that all the Wairau Bar argillite varieties could be found at Whangamoa quarry.

the grave-goods. Duff's (1977:61) explanation of this offered two hypotheses. Graves with relatively sparse assemblages, which were mainly in the 'southern cemetery', might have been:

made by people still bearing the moa-hunter culture, or at a period when the moas in the district had all been cleared out. [However] from the evidence of the inclusion of women and children, and from their various attitudes and orientation, I believe a more likely explanation to be that this area was to a greater extent a common burial ground, or perhaps the burial ground of a clan of lesser wealth and social importance . . . only point 3, Burials 1 to 7, appear to have been the exclusive resting place of men of superior rank.

Following Houghton's (1975) demonstration that the sex ratio amongst the burials is only 5:4 in favour of males, not 8:1 as Duff had it, B. F. Leach (1977) has argued that Duff's assumption that grave-goods were essentially the mark of high-ranking males is also largely wrong. There remains, though, some evidence of sexual bias in the distribution of the articles. Whale-teeth ornaments and reels occurred in seven male and three female graves, and moa eggs in eight male graves but only two female graves. Adzes were also more common in male graves and, in number, are three times as abundant as in female graves. But this source of bias aside, there is strong evidence of differentiation on chronological grounds.

If the earliest burials are numbers 1 to 7, which seem to be contemporary with layer 3, then these reflect an assemblage of grave-goods from a period when there was a major emphasis on moa-hunting. Table 9.1 shows that perforated moa eggs and moa bones, probably representing joints, were found in all these graves, and that bone or ivory whale teeth (real and imitation) and reels, together with Duff (1956a) adze types 1A, 2A, 4A and 3 (various sub-varieties), were particularly common.

The skeletons were in an extended form. A second set of burials in all of which perforated moa eggs were thought to have existed provides a quite similar pattern, though with some suggestion of a transition to a third set.

In the latter, burial styles were more various and most seem to have been in a trussed or crouched form. Grave-goods were much less abundant and more variable (and there is an additional 11 burials without any recorded grave-goods). No moa remains were included, the whale teeth and reel types were scarce and included different materials, shark-teeth necklaces appear, and the adze assemblage includes some rendered in nephrite but lacks the 4A type.

Since midden moa bone also occurs in layer 4, it cannot be argued that the latter burials are from a time when moa-hunting had ceased, although Wilkes (1964) argues that bone-caching reflects a growing scarcity of the resource. Nonetheless Duff's first hypothesis appears closer to the mark, and Wairau Bar can be regarded as a moa-hunting site which was occupied over some hundreds of years. Perforated moa eggs, not unexpectedly, and perhaps the 4A adze, seem to be types associated especially closely with moa-hunting (Duff 1977).

Other Marlborough sites

Between Wairau Bar and Banks Peninsula there are moa-hunting sites at the mouth of every major river, but none are comparable to Wairau Bar and their smaller size probably reflects a scarcity of wide valleys or coastal plains suitable for larger moas. To Robson's (1876) Grassmere site can be added two others in the vicinity: Mussel Point (Orchiston 1977a) and Marfell Beach – where Scarlett (1974 and see Duff 1956a:260 who lumps this site with Grassmere) found *Emeus* was much more

TABLE 9.1   Distribution of main types of grave offerings amongst burials at Wairau Bar

	Perf. moa eggs	Moa joints	Real and imitation whale teeth (bone/ivory)	Reels		Shark teeth	Bird bone tubes	Adzes					Use of nephrite
				bone/ivory	serpentine			1A	2A	4A	3	5	
Burials 1–7	100	100	71	71	–	–	–	57	86	71	43	14	–
Burials 14, 20, 30, 36, 38, 39,	100	17	67	33	14	–	–	67	50	17	67	–	–
Burials 9, 10, 12, 15, 16, 21, 22, 25–29, 32–35, 37	–	–	24	29	–	18	6	41	29	–	12	–	18

Note: Figures are percentage of burials in each group in which item occurs.

abundant than *Euryapteryx* (Appendix D). At Needles Point, a deflated dune site of 0.4 ha, a small sample of bone contained *Emeus* and *Aptornis* (Orchiston 1977a). There may have once been quite an extensive moa-hunting site to the south at the Clarence River where Trotter and McCulloch (1979:2–6) recorded moa bone and other midden scattered over 8 ha of dunes. Excavation produced a small bone reel, and surface collection other Archaic artefacts.

Avoca or Fyffes

Evidence of moa-hunting came to light very early at Kaikoura with the discovery of a burial, associated adzes and a drilled moa egg in 1857 (Dell and Falla 1972). In what is probably the same area Trotter (1980) investigated a site of 850 m² beside a coastal swamp. Shell midden occurred along the marshy edge with an adze-flaking area and seal and moa-bone midden behind. Moa eggshell was sparse. In a bone sample of about 11 kg, marine mammal bone comprised 71 per cent and moa 12 per cent. The latter represented five or six individuals of *Euryapteryx* and *Emeus*. Later excavations showed the site to be about twice as large as originally thought and to contain more abundant evidence of moa-hunting, but they also raised questions about the cultural status of some faunal remains. The site is located on beach ridges and some of the shell in the lower cultural layer is clearly of natural origin. McFadgen (1987) argues that the same could be true of seal and moa remains, or that carcasses cast up on the beach were scavenged by the inhabitants of the site. It is difficult to rule out the latter except to say that it seems unlikely that a number of more or less intact moa carcasses would fetch up, fortuitously, on the beach at the time of occupation. The former can be generally discarded on the grounds of a spatially concentrated distribution of seal and moa remains in association with ovens and flint tools including large, retouched flake knives (McCulloch and Trotter 1987). Adding to the likelihood that Fyffe's was a settlement of more permanence than reliance on scavenging suggests is the existence nearby of what is probably a contemporary cemetery where about 15 burials and Archaic artefacts have been found (McFadgen 1987).

Kaikoura – north Canterbury

Small moa-hunting sites have been recorded from South Bay (Fomison 1963), Lagoon Flat and Motunau Island (Trotter 1982); and larger sites at

Waiau Mouth (Parry 1961) and Hurunui Mouth (Duff 1956a:275).[4] A much larger site seems to have existed near the mouth of the Waipara where evidence is scattered over 9 ha, although it is mainly concentrated into 0.4 ha where moa bone occurred in some abundance together with numerous flake tools (Orchiston 1977b). The size of the site reflects, no doubt, the beginning of the huge plain, basin and downland hinterland which stretches 350 km south almost to Otago Peninsula, and which was clearly moa country par excellence.

Redcliffs

Haast (1875a) found evidence of moa-hunting widely distributed in the low-lying area north of Banks Peninsula. His map shows ovens and middens containing moa bones scattered for 3 km over dunes marking a former coastline east of Christchurch, and two moa-hunting and sealing sites (Palmer's and Wright's) were specifically mentioned (Fig. 9.5). Another site in this area has come to light recently at Bromley (Scarlett 1979). Compared with what seems to have been a very extensive, if discontinuous, occupational complex, the Sumner site area is quite modest. Even so, the Redcliffs dunes site is about 4 ha in area (Trotter 1975b). There are two cultural layers in some parts of it and ovens were used up to four times each (Trotter 1967a:253), but generally a fairly short and more or less continuous occupation by a large group of people was suggested to Trotter (1975b) by the lack of weathering or sterile layers within the cultural horizon, the very large size of the ovens (up to 3.5 m in diameter), the evidence of a single spatial organisation of the site into activity areas and the lack of remains from dwellings. On the other hand, the existence on the edge of this site of an Archaic cemetery (Haast 1875b) together with Moabone Point Cave, in which substantial postbutts occurred, are indications of longer tenure. Variation within the cultural layer from a level rich in moa bone at the bottom, to a greater abundance of shell midden towards the top, also suggests a fairly long occupation if, at the same time, it provides only partial confirmation of Haast's views (Trotter 1975b).

Moabone Point Cave had been badly damaged by fossicking, and Skinner (1923:102) argued that moa bone in the shell midden levels was simply industrial bone mined from a lower level. At

[4] Moa bone possibly subfossil at Lagoon Flat (Trotter 1982) and Whaler's Bay Cave (Scarlett 1979).

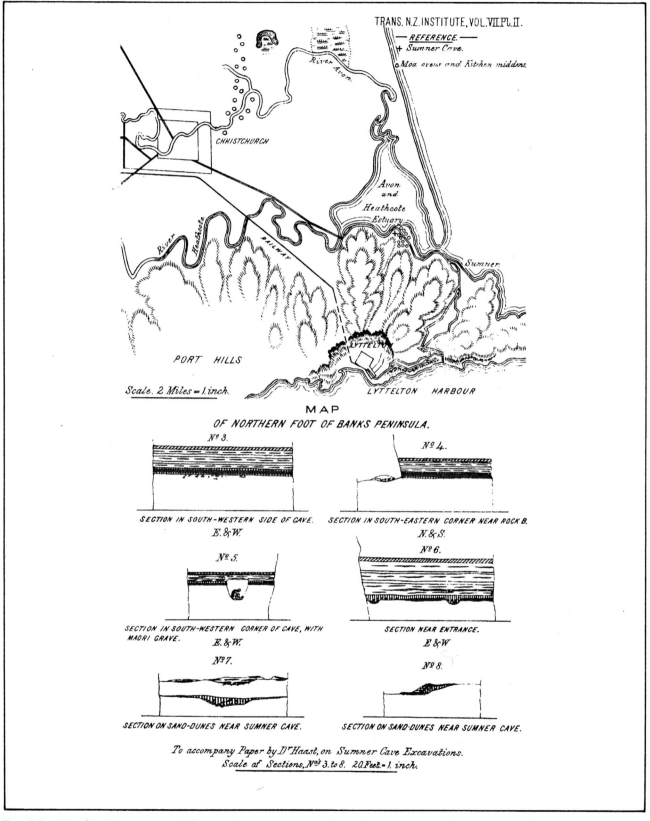

FIG. 9.5   Moa-hunting sites near Christchurch, and sections from Moabone Point Cave and Redcliffs Dunes sites (Haast 1875a:pl. ii). (By courtesy of Royal Society of NZ.)

Monck's Cave, Skinner (1924b) argued, similarly, that the upper levels had contained only industrial moa bone. Forbes (1891b:374), however, had personally recovered moa eggshell from an undisturbed part of the surface dust and stated emphatically that 'on the floor of the cave [were] numerous longish fragments of moa-bones, partly burned and partly broken, scattered around the last fireplace, or found on the floor of the inner caves'. There was also swan bone associated with it. On the face of it, this indicates that all of the rich assemblage of artefacts, excepting the carved bailer and paddle found on a ledge above the floor, are attributable to the moa-hunting era. Included are bird-spear points, sinkers, floats, an outrigger float, net fragments, fishing hooks and lines and a fern root beater; all otherwise scarce artefactual evidence of the real diversity of subsistence activities at many coastal moa-hunting sites. There were also ornaments – including a nephrite pendant and a lifelike wooden figurine of a dog, as well as adzes, chisels, a possible ulu and flake tools. Since similar material – particularly wooden combs, barracouta lures and beaters – came from the upper layers at Moabone Point Cave (Skinner 1923) it must still remain in question, however, whether Forbes' observations at Monck's Cave were in error, or the moa bone in the upper shell middens at Moabone Point Cave was midden in primary context.

On the basis of bones identified to species, but without MNI estimates, it is possible to derive an impression of the relative importance of marine mammals to moas, and of the moa species represented (Appendix D). From Moabone Point Cave, lower layer, seal bones were more abundant (54 per cent) than those of moas (36 per cent), amongst which the main species were E. crassus and A. didiformis. From the dunes site, seals were less abundant (32 per cent of bones) than moas (53 per cent), and the same two species were most common (Haast 1875a:84–5).[5] Trotter's (1975b) 1969 excavations in the dunes site showed that amongst the moa bone Eu. gravis was most common (83 per cent), followed by E. crassus (12 per cent), A. didiformis (4 per cent) and a few remains of D. maximus, and possibly P. elephantopus. Data from earlier excavations in the dunes site by Dawson and Yaldwyn (Trotter 1975b: app. II) also show a strong predominance of Eu. gravis (99 per

cent) but, in addition, that seal bone was twice as abundant as moa bone.

It might be generally concluded that the Redcliffs sites were the focus of a diverse subsistence strategy in which seals were as important as moas; and fishing, small-fowling, culling dogs and the gathering of roots also significant activities. Nevertheless moa-hunting was a major activity and it concentrated upon medium-sized, open-country species. The location of the sites, together with Haast's band of eastern Christchurch moa-hunting sites, suggests that the main hunting grounds were out on the Canterbury Plains rather than Banks Peninsula (the probable source of the A. didiformis remains, see Trotter 1975b) and, in turn, that an essential locational focus was a contemporary outlet of the Waimakariri River through the estuary in front of the Redcliffs site (McFadgen 1978:38).

Banks Peninsula

On Banks Peninsula, a number of small moa-hunting sites have been reported (Duff 1956a:70, 357; Mason and Wilkes 1963b; Wright and Bennett 1964; Allingham pers. comm.). Takamatua had swan bone and some moa-bone artefacts, but no midden moa remains, according to Trotter (1973a). Tumbledown Bay has recently been reinvestigated by Allingham (1987, pers. comm.) who found moa bone and eggshell in small quantities, but including tracheal rings and vertebrae. In the same layer was evidence of a circular hut, about 3 m in diameter, marked by postholes and a stone-kerbed fireplace and built in a shallow depression in the sand. There was also evidence of a former structure on the same place, and of similar hearths nearby. Immediately outside the northern margin of the hut were some unusual artefacts: shell discs with notched edges and what seems to be an early style of the rei-puta pendant.

Southern Canterbury

This district includes the greater part of the Canterbury Plains, along the coast of which the largest moa-hunting sites are located. There are some possible signs of moa-hunting along Kaitorete Spit (Lake Ellesmere) in the form of silcrete blades (Allingham pers. comm.), but the first certain site south of Banks Peninsula is on the north bank of the Rakaia.

---

[5] Assuming synonymisation of Haast's (1875a) identification with modern taxa after Archey (1941).

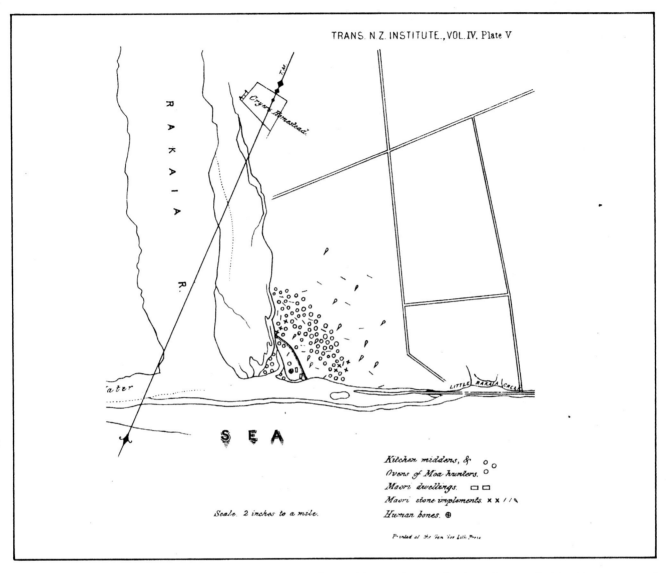

TRANS. N.Z. INSTITUTE., VOL. IV, Plate V

Kitchen middens, &
Ovens of Moa hunters.
Maori dwellings.
Maori stone implements.
Human bones.

Scale. 2 inches to a mile.

FIG. 9.6   Rakaia Mouth moa-hunting site (Haast 1872a:pl. v). This was drawn after Haast's second visit. (By courtesy of Royal Society of NZ.)

Rakaia Mouth

Haast (1872a) initially estimated this site at more than 20 ha in extent, within which about 8 ha was more or less entirely covered by ovens and middens. But a later visit, when more of the ground had been ploughed, showed that the area covered by these was considerably larger and that the full extent of the site was nearer 80 ha of which about half contained ovens and middens (Haast 1872c; see Fig. 9.6). The ovens appeared to be in five or six rows each extending a kilometre or so across a corner of the plains formed by the Rakaia River and a coastal lagoon. More ovens occurred on a lower terrace where, however, there was also evidence of several rectangular houses and associated burials which seemed to be post-moa-hunting in age. Haast (1872c) found the moa ovens were generally 3–4 m apart and in groups of five to eight separated by bare areas about 6 m wide, where he thought the moa-hunters had perhaps dwelt (Haast 1872a). The ovens were usually about 2 m in diameter, and revealed up to five layers of cooking debris. If we were to take these data literally, and it must be conceded that Haast was generalising from a modest acquaintance with the site, it could be calculated that the six rows of ovens would contain a total of about 1000 individual ovens.

Moa bones occurred both in ovens and refuse dumps nearby, along with seal and dog bone in some quantity and also small bird bone and sparse shell midden. Flat stones and accompanying boulders near the ovens had been used, Haast thought, to smash moa marrow bones (1872c). Generally these were tibiotarsi, whereas femora were often intact and tarsometatarsi had the ends broken, rather than the shaft. Leg bones were most common, but Haast saw numerous ribs, pelves, vertebrae, phalanges and some crania. *Emeus crassus* seems to have been the main species, but *Eu. gravis* was probably also common. Although cut marks were rare there were large quantities of flake tools including blades – several hafted – of porcellanite, silcrete and other materials, and cobble spalls of greywacke ('teshoa', see Chapter 10).

Later investigations showed that surface evidence could be seen over only 11.3 ha (Trotter 1972a:133). One oven (which seemed to have been used several times), was excavated at this time and the moa bone from it was found to be entirely of *Eu. gravis*, as was all the other moa bone which Trotter (1972a) collected. He also found moa eggshell to be reasonably plentiful.

Trotter also recorded oven sites scattered along the coast up to 5 km northeast of the main site (1972a). No moa bone was observed in these but they were associated with teshoa and other Archaic artefacts. On the south bank of the river, however, there was a large moa-hunting site scattered for 5 km through coastal dunes (Haast n.d.). Recent observations have traced it for at least a kilometre (Allingham n.d.), over which distance there occurred sparse remains of heavily eroded moa bone, numerous teshoa and silcrete flakes and blades. The site is eroding at the sea-front and it has, like the main Rakaia site, been badly damaged by ploughing and wind deflation (Trotter 1972a; Allingham n.d.) since Haast saw it.

On Great Island, situated between the two large sites, there are ovens, although without recorded moa remains. In the vicinity seven burials, each accompanied by adzes, were exposed in deflating sand dunes (McCully to Duff n.d., 30 November 1942). Large ovens with associated teshoa, and occasionally moa bone as well, are also strewn right along the low gravel cliffs of the Canterbury Plains and Waitaki delta (Trotter pers. comm.). Larger sites bearing remains similar to those at Rakaia Mouth have been briefly recorded on the south bank of the Hinds River and both banks of the Rangitata, but moa bone has yet to be confirmed from the latter (Trotter 1973b).

Wakanui

Enormous quantities of moa bones were reported by early settlers near the Ashburton River (Haast 1872c:103), although it is not clear that they were from a cultural site. The only recorded butchery site, located where an old branch of the Ashburton reached out to the sea, is at Wakanui. Midden, mostly moa-bone, was spread over an area of 2.7 ha (Burrage 1981), and test excavations of 150 m² revealed a site very like that at Rakaia Mouth. Moa bone was abundant in the centre of the site and about ovens elsewhere, and there were also a few remains of seals, small whales, dog, small birds, fish and shell midden. Teshoa comprised the most common artefact type, with 518 recovered by excavation (Hodgkinson 1981). Many had retouched edges and they were concentrated in areas of moa-bone midden. There were also many stone flakes and several retouched silcrete blades; also one each of an ulu, harpoon and lure fish hook. Some Archaic types of adzes and about 15 nephrite chisels have also come from the site. On higher ground, away from the ovens, a tamped clay floor was found (Scarlett 1971). Since this was also the area from which most adzes and other small finished artefacts were recovered, it is likely that dwellings of some form once stood here.[6]

Nearby, in a patch of clay, was an unusual structure. It comprised a deep pit, 1.5 m in diameter, joined by a channel to a shallow pit 1 m in diameter. Both pits had fire-hardened walls (Byatt 1972). The excavators could offer no interpretation, but I suggest that this may have been an apparatus for rendering fat from moa or mammal bones and blubber: the material being cooked by hot stones on the shallow pit, and the oil running into the deep collection pit. That some such process had occurred seems to be implied by the fact that the channel had been blocked with a removable baked-clay wedge (Burrage 1981).

Timaru district

The small site at Dashing Rocks (Patiti Point, in Duff 1956a:269) was largely a fishing and sealing camp in which teshoa were again particularly abundant (200 in 40 m² of excavation). The few moa midden remains were from *Euryapteryx* (Mason and Wilkes 1963a). At Normanby, two

---

[6] Postholes reported (*The Press* (Christchurch) 19 January 1972), but no details.

sites were recorded by Griffiths (1941, 1942). At
Site 1 were five hut sites and below them large
middens running down to a coastal swamp. Moa
bone, including whole femora, and moa eggshell
occurred amongst fish, whale and dog bone. At
Site 2 there were similar remains, in association
with 11 hut sites. Griffiths thought this the older
site, although it had significantly fewer silcrete
blades. A recent reappraisal (Holdaway 1981)
argues that the sites, only about 25 m apart at the
nearest edges, are actually parts of the same settlement. This makes sense of the spatial distribution
of features into several rows aligned the same way
in each area, with middens at the sea shore and
swamp edge to either side. Throughout the site,
but especially in the Site 2 area, teshoa were particularly abundant. Holdaway's inspection of a
sample of them revealed that they were generally
not butchery implements, however, but attrition
saws for bone or stone (see Chapter 10).

At Pareora a large moa-hunting site was spread
over an area of 18 ha, most of it concentrated into
about 8 ha. In one place there is a seasonal pond
around which Griffiths (1955) found evidence of
hut sites. Otherwise the site consisted of ovens and
moa-bone midden; 61 ovens were observed, but
since they ranged in size up to 14 m in diameter it is
probable that some were clusters of ovens. Teshoa
were less common than at Normanby, and silcrete
flakes and blades correspondingly more abundant.
Duff (1956a:271) was told the site was only 2 ha in
area and that another 'moa-hunter' site, 'Smith's',
lay about 2 km to the south.[7]

North Otago

Waitaki Mouth

Possibly the largest of all moa-hunting sites,
Waitaki Mouth is also one of the least known.
Very similar to the main site at Rakaia Mouth,
though not recorded until 1927, it comprised moa
ovens and middens scattered over a huge area.
Teviotdale estimated it at 61 ha, but recession of
the local coastline at the rate of a metre per year
since at least the 1860s (Teviotdale 1939; Gibb
1977) had already removed part of the site, and the
continuing process had reduced it to 51 ha by 1960
when it was first surveyed by theodolite (Knight
and Gathercole 1961). Since the main areas of

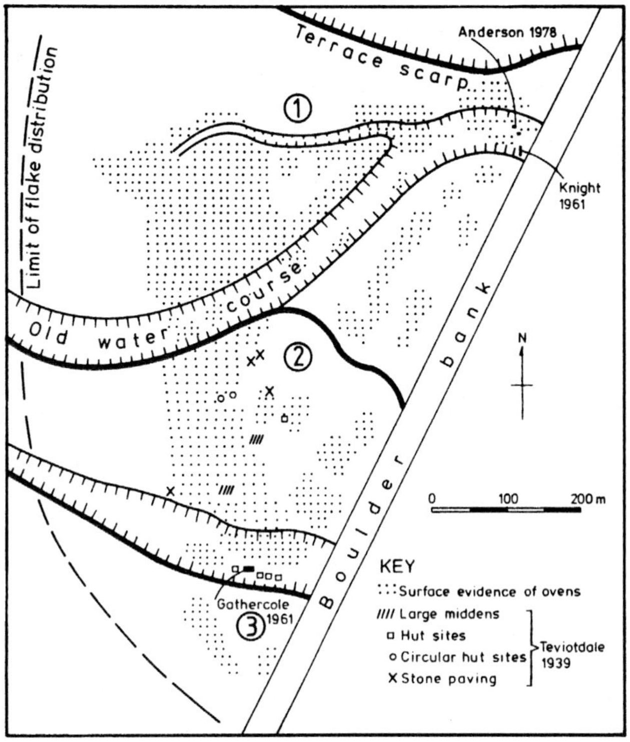

FIG. 9.7   Waitaki Mouth moa-hunting site, showing positions and dates of excavations.

ovens can be seen from the air to form a semi-
annular band truncated by the sea (Fig. 9.7), it has
been speculated that the site was originally twice
its size, about 120 ha, and broadly circular in shape
(Buick 1937; Knight pers. comm.).[8]

It now lies more than a kilometre south of the
Waitaki River, but the river is moving northward,
and it has been assumed that the distribution of the
site over three river terraces reflects the same process at an earlier period: initial settlement on
terrace 3 when the channel below it still held water;
movement to terrace 2 when that channel was
abandoned; and a later movement onto terrace 1.
The channel below the latter still holds stagnant
water, and since only stone anchors and sinkers
have been found between terrace 1 and the present
river bank, this probably indicates a substantial
elapse of time since the end of moa processing at
the site (Buick 1937:172; Knight and Gathercole
1961).

It can also be assumed that the importance of the
river channels along which the ovens are concentrated lay in their value as waterways for bringing

[7] Orchiston (1974:3.21:42) mentions a moa-hunting site at Seadown.

[8] Middens and artefacts lay well beyond the ovens (Willets pers.
comm.; Knight pers. comm.).

carcasses to the site, in the need for cooking water and in the deep deposits of silt along banks and abandoned channels which provided the best medium for cutting durable ovens. Elsewhere on the site the substrate is unconsolidated river gravel.

The cultural stratigraphy is poorly known, but it is apparent that two or three layers of cooking debris can occur, each separated by sterile river silt, as in the trench (Fig. 9.8) excavated by Knight (Gathercole n.d.). Teviotdale (1939:176) also observed three layers in a large midden, but if these reflect separate dumping episodes they were probably quite close in time. Over most of the site there is no known evidence of significant stratigraphy and the chronological dimension is doubtless represented by spatial expansion, as suggested above.

Judging by only one excavated example (Anderson 1978a) the ovens are large, 2–3 m in diameter, as at Rakaia Mouth. They are also very numerous. Since all the terraces have been ploughed repeatedly it is very difficult to estimate their size or numbers and, in addition, new ovens seem to appear with each ploughing, but some data were collected in 1962 by Gathercole (n.d.) after a ploughing on terrace 2. His team counted and measured 152 patches of oven debris. These varied from about 5 m² to more than 700 m² in size and covered, in total, about 8500 m². How many individual ovens this represented can only be guessed at, but if an oven of 2.5 m in diameter spreads to a patch 5 m in diameter (20 m²) when it is ploughed, then some 430 ovens are represented. The mean size of the patches, 56 m², would thus represent a cluster of three ovens. Since the area over which oven debris can be seen on terrace 1 is about twice as large, and there are also ovens on terrace 3, it could be tentatively estimated that there are at least 1200 ovens at Waitaki Mouth.

Quantified data concerning middens are similarly scarce, but there was an 'almost total absence of any other refuse except moa-bones' (Teviotdale 1939:177; McCully in *The Christchurch Star-Sun* 25 January 1951; Buick 1937:201 records scarce remains of seal, whale and dog and a little moa eggshell). These had all been burnt according to J. B. Chapman, an early owner of the site, and they were brittle and fragile (*The Evening Post* (Wellington) 9 September 1937; P. George to B. Allingham pers. comm.). Many had probably disappeared soon after scrub was removed from the site and stock introduced in the 1890's, as Teviotdale (n.d.) thought, but ploughing was certainly the major agent of destruction. Terrace 1 was first ploughed in 1927 and McCully described the ground as strewn with thousands of bones (Teviotdale 1932a:96). However, 'strong gales swept most of

FIG. 9.8   Moa-bone midden exposed above and below a silt layer at Waitaki Mouth. (By courtesy of Harwicke Knight.)

the soil away [so that] sun and wind have since destroyed them and nothing remains but a few scattered fragments' (Teviotdale 1939:168).

Teviotdale and his contemporaries therefore concentrated on terrace 2 where 'many middens' remained (Fig. 9.9). Two of these were particularly large and contained, together, 80–120 m³ of midden.[9] In these heaps the bones crumbled at a touch indicating that they had been burnt *in situ*, possibly ignited by hot ovenstones and charcoal mixed amongst them.[10] By counting pairs of tibiotarsi Teviotdale (1939:175) estimated that about 40 moas were represented in the smaller of the two middens, but my experience at Hawksburn (below), where the midden was also of burnt bone and oven debris, suggests this figure is far too low. Although only about a dozen moas could be recognised from the identifiable bones, there were actually about 400 moas represented in a 6 m³ midden at Hawksburn: this model would produce a figure of between 5000 and 8000 birds for the two Waitaki middens combined. Since there were numerous middens on terrace 2, including 'huge pits' of bone along the base of the terrace 3 scarp which were unknown to Teviotdale and were uncovered when S. Willets (pers. comm.) first ploughed terrace 2 (in 1952), then many thousands of birds must have been represented on this terrace alone. Willets (pers. comm.) described it as 'white with bone'.

Staying with the Hawksburn example, the ratio of number of ovens to the estimated MNI of moa there is 1:4 which, scaled to the estimated 1200 ovens at Waitaki (above), would suggest a total moa MNI of about 29,000, or more if the small size of ovens (c. 0.6–1 m diameter) at Hawksburn is taken into account. If Hawksburn is considered simply a miniature of Waitaki Mouth, a broadly fair assumption, and if camp size was strictly correlated with moa MNI, then Hawksburn scaled to the size of Waitaki Mouth would have a moa MNI of about 90,000. These more or less desperate attempts to put some sort of figures to frustratingly unquantified evidence may tell us little of fact, but the order of magnitude they suggest fits the anecdotal data.

The site was located, Duff (1977:70) thought, to form 'the terminal point of a vast cross-country drive' (cf. Haast on Rakaia Mouth). Chapman

FIG. 9.9 Lindsay Buick at Waitaki Mouth, where he dug with Teviotdale in 1936 (Buick 1937:236). (By courtesy of D. V. Avery.)

(*The Evening Post* (Wellington) 9 September 1937) subscribed to this view, noting that gizzard stones at Waitaki Mouth were often of a distinctive yellow quartz found in low hill country close to the site. Others laid a greater emphasis on the value of the swift-flowing Waitaki as a means of transporting carcasses from as far afield as the Mackenzie Country (Buick 1937:190; McCully in *The Christchurch Star-Sun* 25 January 1951).

Whatever the case, and Teviotdale (1939:178) simply regarded distant hunting and transport as consequent upon over-hunting locally, there is little to indicate more than temporary occupation of the site at any time. Teviotdale thought there were remains of both circular and rectangular huts on terrace 2. There is, however, little in his evidence to support this view (Anderson 1986), and even his co-worker, Buick (1937:204), was dubious about the alleged posthole (Teviotdale 1939:174) on which the dimensions of a large oblong hut were founded.[11] Gathercole's excavation of one of Teviotdale's hut sites under the scarp of terrace 3 revealed only a shallow linear depression in one place and a small hole (Gathercole n.d.; Knight and Gathercole 1961). Similar evidence was found beneath the oven I excavated there – it had obviously been caused by rabbit burrowing. Nevertheless some of the evidence, particularly the stone paving (Teviotdale 1939), probably does represent temporary shelters (Anderson 1986).

Impermanence of settlement is also indicated by relatively few domestic artefacts. Stone flakes and blades were very abundant and lay scattered

---

[9] Volume depends on assumptions about shape and cross-sectional area.

[10] Unburnt bone on terrace 2 as well (Knight and Gathercole 1961).

[11] Teviotdale (1939) found nephrite and moa bone cached in two 'house' sites elsewhere.

beyond the ovens, as did some caches of adzes (Willets pers. comm.; Knight pers. comm.), but despite Willets impressive collection of artefacts, Teviotdale (1939:177) was right in pointing to the general scarcity of adzes, bone implements or ornaments at the site compared with Shag Mouth. Furthermore most adzes were encountered in caches (Willets pers. comm.) as if they had been secreted by their owners.[12] It is also pertinent to observe that no evidence of burials has ever been uncovered at Waitaki Mouth (A. G. Hornsey to Duff n.d., 20 December 1942; McCully in *The Christchurch Star-Sun* 25 January 1951).

Teviotdale (1939:177) concluded that the site 'was never a permanent settlement, but simply a hunting camp occupied at one season in the year, when the inhabitants were occupied solely in securing the moa and preserving the flesh for future use' (see also Anderson 1982b).

Waitaki to Waihemo

Numerous moa-hunting sites have been recorded in this district, although very few have been systematically investigated. Between Waitaki Mouth and Shag Point (Waihemo), Trotter recorded examples at Cape Wanbrow and Kakanui (Trotter 1970a), Bewley Creek, Waianakarua, Waianakarua Bluff,[13] Hampden, Waiwherowhero Stream, North Beach, Katiki, Waimataitai north bank (where *D. torosus* bone may, however, be redeposited in the site), Katiki Beach (? subfossil bone) and Trotter's Creek (Trotter 1959, 1968a, 1970a; see Fig. 10.1).

Trotter's (1955) excavations at Waimataitai Mouth began on the south bank where moa bone, largely of *E. crassus*, was commonly found in the main (lower) cultural layer. At Hampden, a small excavation (10 m²) in a moa-hunting site estimated at about 1 ha in area (Trotter 1967b, pers. comm.) disclosed remains of three *Eu. gravis*, together with blades of silcrete amongst other artefacts. Elsewhere in the district, Harrowfield and Trotter (1966) found moa bone in a rockshelter midden at Totara, and Trotter (1965a) excavated another shelter at Ototara, where two individuals of *Eu. gravis* were represented amongst a wide range of coastal and open-country birds.

Anderson (1978b) recorded moa bone in a midden at Beach Road and excavated part of a largely

destroyed site at Waianakarua Mouth, where burnt and highly fragmented moa bone was sparsely scattered in a single, shallow layer. Silcrete and chalcedony flakes and blades were common, suggesting that moa remains had once been more abundant in the site (Anderson 1979a).

The two main sites north of Shag Mouth are Awamoa and Tai Rua. The former has been as sadly neglected by scientists as it has been a magnet to fossickers ever since Mantell's discovery. It is quite a large site (about 1.5 ha in area), and moa bone seems to have been both the main faunal material and generally abundant. Minor salvage excavations have revealed large ovens cut through earlier layers bearing cultural debris (Trotter 1979a, n.d.b).

Tai Rua, a site of about 2 ha, had one main occupation layer within which spatial variation was observed. Small fireplaces and postholes near the coastal margin indicated a habitation area, and behind this were shell and fish-bone middens in which moa bone was scarce. Beyond those again lay a dense moa-bone midden over an area of about 300 m². Here cervical vertebrae and tracheal rings often lay in position of articulation, while leg bones were generally broken and had also been gnawed by dogs and rats. Moa bone was abundant and formed, in places, almost the entire contents of the cultural layer. The main genera were *Euryapteryx* and *Pachyornis* in the approximate ratio of 11:4 by bone numbers. Unusually, there were no large ovens or many silcrete blades, but teshoa were common (Munro 1960; Trotter 1965b, 1979b).

Shag Mouth

At this site, uncommonly rich in Archaic artefacts, moa bones and ovens were found over about 2 ha of the sand spit at the mouth of the Shag River and across an area of waterlogged sand behind the dunes, which is of comparable size (Fig. 9.10). Moa bone was liberally strewn throughout the site and parts of the swampy flat were 'literally paved with moa bones' (Haast 1875c:94). It was, however, particularly concentrated in large middens up to 1.2 m deep lying along the inland edge of the dunes. These also contained significant quantities of seal bone, but few other remains. In 1890, Hamilton (1890) trenched one midden which was about 30 × 4 m × an average of 0.3 m deep (an estimated 30 m³) in which, from one small area, he recovered 50 moa crania each with associated cervical vertebrae. Teviotdale (1924) excavated another bone midden (30 × 15 × 0.5 m; about

---

[12] 318 adzes in Willets collection, cf. 336 in Otago Museum Shag Mouth collection.

[13] Site area *c.* 1 ha (Allingham pers. comm.).

FIG. 9.10 Shag Mouth as it was when Teviotdale dug there (Buick 1937:80). (By courtesy of D. V. Avery.)

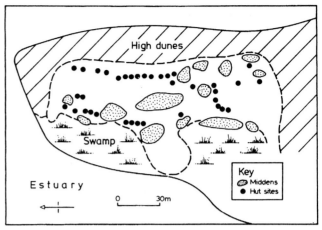

FIG. 9.11 Shag Mouth site, after Teviotdale (1924:5).

200 m³), and there was at least one other similar to it. In addition there was a very large 'central midden', a midden at the north end of the site which was 100 m long and 1.5 m deep at the centre and various smaller middens all of which contained some moa bone together with seal, fish and small bird bone, and great quantities of shell midden (Fig. 9.11).

All of these were surface features, but at the south end of the site there was evidence, not often reached by the early excavators, of underlying cultural layers rich in moa and seal bone which lay up to 3 m below the surface. Furthermore ovens and moa bone lay below the high-tide level well out into the lagoon, especially upon a low eroded ridge about 20 m from the shore. Skinner's (1924a:15) belief that 'the number of moas eaten at the site would have gone far towards supporting for sometime a village of respectable size' can hardly be doubted, and there is in fact evidence of this (below).

Shag Mouth is noted for its abundance of silcrete flake knives and blades, some being of the rare hafted form. These were found most often in the moa-bone middens (Teviotdale 1924). Teshoa were seldom recorded. The remainder of the richly diverse artefactual assemblage included several hundred adzes, large numbers of fish hooks and manufacturing tools and a wide range of ornaments. Two whole moa eggs were also found, one near a human burial (Teviotdale to Skinner 21 July 1944, Griffiths 1942).

These indications of non-transient settlement are reinforced by evidence of dwellings. Teviotdale's (1924) plan shows the position of 36 hut sites, each defined by a stone-lined hearth (mostly of sandstone slabs and 0.6 × 0.6 m), but Allingham's (n.d.) analysis of Teviotdale's diaries indicates at least 43 hearths. It is not clear that all these were contemporary, although the distribution of the huts suggests a single village – nor is it certain that they are of the same age as the bone middens, since moa bones also occurred in the shell middens. However, the huts were, at least, associated with some stage of local moa-hunting.

The ovens were quite small and shallow and Booth (n.d.) observed that they often contained only charcoal with moa bones lying upon it (no ovenstones), an indication of roasting rather than steaming. He also noted that moa bone sometimes occurred in heaps representing a number of individuals of the same species and suggested selective hunting of small flocks.

There was evidence of systematic butchery, with heads and necks discarded into one pile and pelves in another, 15 in one heap (Booth n.d.). Sterna were seldom broken but discarded with the sternal ribs attached. Tibiotarsi had been almost entirely smashed and most tarsometatarsi were broken, but 75–80 per cent of femora were intact – a familiar pattern (Booth n.d.; Haast 1875c; Hutton 1876). Much of the bone was unburnt or lightly burnt, but there were also heaps of heavily burnt bone 15–30 cm thick (Hutton 1876).

The scale of moa-hunting at the site was, thus, very considerable. If we were to adopt the density of moas in a midden of similar contents at Pounawea where Hamel (1980) found 1.2 individuals per square metre, disregard the probability that moa MNI were substantially higher in the Shag Mouth bone middens, and extend that figure over the area of the known surface middens (excluding the swampy flat, other areas between middens and the deeper layers) then about 6000 moas may have been processed at the site. The true figure was probably higher.

Pleasant River

Ovens and silcrete flakes and blades occur over about 8 ha at this site, but most of that area is now waterlogged and the main bone middens are located on 2.5 ha of low dunes. Elephant seal, fur seal and dog bones were common in a lower layer, but moa bones were predominant (Gathercole 1960; Munro 1960; Teal 1975; *The Otago Daily Times* 12 June 1982). Allingham (n.d.) found dense moa-bone midden in which all body parts were represented and many of the bones unbroken. Amongst this material were large silcrete blades and the pieces (later re-fitted) of a drilled moa egg. *Euryapteryx* and *Emeus* were the main genera and moa eggshell was quite abundant.

In places the lower layer disclosed stratigraphy, prompting Teal (1975) to argue a series of seasonal occupations. It extended all over the dune area and out into the present lagoon (Knight pers. comm.), and it contained moa bone, densely packed, up to a metre deep (Knight pers. comm.). In some places it was overlain by sterile sand and above that fish-bone and shell middens in which some worked moa bone occurred (Allingham n.d.).

As a moa-hunting site Pleasant River was probably as important as Shag Mouth, but apart from one burial with associated adze, moa bones and a possible egg (Allingham n.d.), there is little to suggest that it had been a permanent settlement.

Across the Pleasant River estuary another Archaic site, Tumai, is situated on the south bank. Excavated by Allingham (1988), this turned out to be mainly a fishing camp, but some remains of *Euryapteryx* were also recovered.

Waihemo to Otago Harbour

Sites in which moa remains are comparatively scarce have been reported from Shag Point (where there is some doubt about its midden status, Trotter 1970b), Stoney Creek (Allingham n.d.), Seacliff (Blake-Palmer 1956), Ross's Rocks (Till n.d.) and Purakanui (Anderson 1981a). At the latter, moa pelves and vertebrae are quite abundant in an eroded part of the site lying in the intertidal zone. A moa-butchery site existed at Waikouaiti on the estuarine shore (Knight pers. comm.; Allingham pers. comm.), there was possibly another in dunes above the natural site (Chapter 3) and a third at Omimi (Hamel 1977b). Other moa-hunting sites have been recorded at Murdering Beach (Lockerbie 1959; Skinner to Duff 16 February 1953) and Kaikais Beach (Lockerbie 1954). At Long Beach, moa bone was rare in the predominantly fish-bone midden excavated by Leach and Hamel (1981; Hamel pers. comm.), but it seems to have been encountered more frequently in a nearby area of Maori burials where moa and other bird remains were scattered over about 1.2 ha. Dawson (1949) and Dawson and Yaldwyn (1952), drawing on their North Island experience rather than any direct evidence of a non-cultural origin, argued, unconvincingly in my view, that the moa bone occurred naturally: 'broken moa bone legs, including worked pieces, have been taken from the midden layer. It is thought that their presence affords no evidence that the midden was laid down by a moa hunting community' (Dawson and Yaldwyn 1952:290). The main site immediately north of the Otago Peninsula was at Warrington.

Warrington

Small moa-hunting sites exist at Doctor's Point and Waitati Mouth (Allingham n.d.) on the south shore of the Blueskin Bay estuary, but a site of about 2 ha lies in dunes at the north (proximal) end of a sand spit between the sea and lagoon. Early reports described swan bone, moa bone and eggs 'almost complete' (? drilled) together with 'no end of fine implements' in association with stone floors (*The Otago Witness* 11 January 1894). A series of recent excavations (Allingham 1983, 1985, 1986; Kooyman 1984a; Anderson, Allingham and Smith n.d.) has revealed a stratified site containing three pre-European cultural layers. At the eastern end of the site a layer containing Classic phase artefacts lies above a middle layer, found over most of the site, in which frequent evidence of postholes and possible hearths suggests a settlement of some permanence. Moa bone occurs very sparsely and some has the appearance of subfossil material. Deeper again is a layer rich in moa remains and also containing the bones of sea lions, fur seals and dogs, amongst other components. The moa bones represent all body parts and come from, at least: *D. torosus*, *D. novaezealandiae* and *Eu. gravis* (Appendix D). They are associated with silcrete flake and blade implements, and ulus have also been recovered. Toward the western margin of the site the moa-hunting layer is split into a series of thin lenses separated by dune sand, indicating that the occupation as a whole was transitory and repeated, as the lack of postholes or any other evidence of structures also implies.

Otago Peninsula

South of Otago Harbour there are remains of moa-hunting at Pipikaretu (Teviotdale 1927, n.d. 7 November 1926), Papanui Inlet north (Knight pers. comm.) and south (Teviotdale n.d. 13 September 1929; *The Otago Witness* 7 July 1892) and MacKay's Beach, Hooper's Inlet 1, or Allen's Beach (Munro 1960; Knight 1965), Hooper's Inlet 2 (Knight 1965), Sandfly Bay and Anderson's Bay (Teviotdale 1932a: 101). These sites are generally quite small (0.25 ha at Allen's Beach and 0.05 ha at Anderson's Bay), but the Papanui Inlet site may be more extensive (pers. obs.; Fig. 10.1).

There are, however, two significant moa-hunting sites on the Peninsula, of which Harwood is the largest. Very little is known about it despite the fact (or perhaps because of it) that there was a minor industry in collecting moa bones from the Harwood dunes as early as the 1870s; Octavius Harwood advertising for sale at this time 'the bones of 40–50 birds . . . also a quantity of native knives found with them' (Harwood n.d.). An early map was also annotated in about 1863, 'moa remains and debris of native settlement of great extent'. These references are to the northeast and central areas of the dunes, but moa-bone middens are also found in the southwest area where Knight (pers. comm.) found a lower layer with small quantities of moa and seal bone and, above it, a thick layer containing 'masses of moabone'. Later excavations in the same general area showed shell middens overlying a layer rich in moa bone (Harsant 1980). Harwood is undoubtedly a very considerable moa-hunting site. Leaving aside an area in the centre, where remains appear to be less abundant, moa middens appear to extend over about 8 ha (Knight pers. comm.).

The other important Peninsula site, Little Papanui, was occupied during at least two phases, in the second of which it was probably a small village. Moa bone occurred sparsely in debris from this settlement phase but it was probably displaced from underlying layers. The lower layer, especially on the south side of the site, contained 'many fragments of moa bones, but all were from bones suitable for manufacture. Many of the fragments were of large size' (Teviotdale, in Simmons 1967:6). A charred moa pelvis in this layer satisfied Teviotdale of its moa-hunter credentials however, and it seems likely that most of the other bone was midden debris as well even if, as Teviotdale (1932a:100) suggested, it had come from the moa butchery at Kaikorai Mouth (below). Associated with the moa bone were large blades, mostly of silcrete, and three ulus were also recovered from the lower layer (Simmons 1967). If moas were important at this site in the early phase, it is still probably a more accurate appraisal to see it as an 'important summer fishing [and sealing, Smith pers. comm.] camp' (Skinner 1960:188). A small moa-hunting site also lies at the north end of Little Papanui Beach (Knight pers. comm.).

South Otago

Between Otago Peninsula and the Catlins district moa-hunting sites are uncommon. Moa bones, broken and with cultural materials, have been reported from the sand dunes at St Clair and St Kilda, but the extent of these sites, now under suburban housing, is unknown. At Haast's Kaikorai site Harding (1957) excavated a small area finding burnt moa bones, shell midden and silcrete blades in a thin layer which also contained a pumice carving remarkable for its resemblance, in miniature, to the great statues of Easter Island. The moa species represented was *Eu. gravis*. Another of Haast's sites, Otokia, has since proven to contain moa bone of several species (Anderson 1982c).

South of these, a stratified cave site near Taieri Mouth contained sparse moa remains (Teviotdale 1931) but the main site in this area is probably one of about 1.3 ha in dunes north of the river. Test excavations have indicated three cultural layers, the lowest of which contains moa bones, and there is also evidence of Archaic phase burials nearby (Allingham pers. comm.; Lockerbie pers. comm.). A smaller site (0.2 ha) containing moa bones lies at the mouth of the Tokomairiro (Allingham pers. comm.).

A large site might have been expected at the mouth of the Clutha, but the river outlet keeps swinging from north to south and it has probably removed any Archaic sites on the river bar (Lockerbie pers. comm.). Immediately to the south, however, Lockerbie (1945) recorded extensive but unconcentrated evidence of moa-hunting in the coastal dunes and George's (1944) excavations in this area revealed a stratified site with moa bone in the lowest of three cultural layers. Elsewhere along the Catlins coast little-known moa-hunting sites exist at Kaka Point, Nugget Point, Cannibal Bay, False Island, Waitangi Stream, Long Point, Tautuku and Hukihuki Stream (Lockerbie 1959:81, 88;

Hamel 1977a:184, 182–94, tables 4.9–4.12; 1977c).
A better-known site is at Kings Rock (Teviotdale
n.d.; Lockerbie 1940, 1954, 1959; Hamel 1977a:
185–6) where moa, whale and seal bones were
plentiful in the lower part of a site of about 250 m²
but were found, as midden remains, in the upper
levels as well. At Hinahina (Lockerbie 1959; Hamel
1977a:190–1) there is a site similar in stratigraphy,
size and contents to Pounawea, which is located
directly across the Catlins River estuary (Fig.
10.1).

Pounawea

Excavated by Lockerbie, and later Hamel, this site,
together with Papatowai, disclosed an assemblage
of Archaic artefacts and a sequence of strata which
have largely defined the technology and economy
of the southern Archaic phase (Lockerbie 1954,
1959; Golson 1959a; Hamel 1977a:189–91). For
our purposes, though, the important point is that
midden moa remains. occurred throughout the
sequence, though they were more abundant in the
lowest layer where silcrete and porcellanite blades
were also predominant and ulu occurred as well
(Lockerbie 1959:82–5; Hamel 1980).

Pounawea is unusual amongst southern moa-
hunting sites in disclosing abundant evidence of
postholes (Fig. 9.12). Lockerbie (pers. comm.)
found two lines of them, each a double row of
close-set posts. One line had been cut from the
bottom layer and lay along the lagoon edge of the
site, while the other, evidently cut from a higher
layer, lay across the site. No dwelling is indicated
by the pattern, and the posts of the former row
were much more substantial and close-set than a
drying rack would need: a palisade seems more
likely.

Hamel's (1980) analysis of the faunal remains
showed that in the 8.6 m² of undisturbed site
which she excavated there were 10 moas of 5 genera represented by all body parts, except in the case
of *Megalapteryx* (leg bone only), at least 9 moa
eggs, remains of 9 fur seals, 6 sea lions, 2 elephant
seals, 11 dogs, and numerous fish, small birds and
shellfish (Appendix D). The range of species represented and their ages at death (see also Smith
1985:172) indicated occupation of the site from
spring to mid-winter: year-round occupation cannot be ruled out. Smith's (1985:174) calculation of
relative meat weights represented by Hamel's data
showed that seals contributed 58 per cent and moas
25 per cent in the lower layer, but 30 per cent and
only 4 per cent respectively in the upper layer.
Lockerbie's impression (pers. comm.) was that

FIG. 9.12   Stratigraphy at Pounawea, showing upper shell
midden and lower black layer containing abundant
moa and seal bone. Postholes are also visible. (By
courtesy of Les Lockerbie.)

moa bone was not nearly as abundant at Pounawea
as at Papatowai, but notwithstanding this, or
Smith's calculations, the mean density of moas is
1.16 individuals per square metre, an unusually
high quantity.

Papatowai

Excavations, principally by Teviotdale (1937, 1938a,
1938b; Buick 1937) and Lockerbie (1953, 1959)
show this site to extend over an area of about
0.8 ha on the estuarine side of a coastal sand spit.
The site was formed by cultural refuse accumulating in at least seven large dune swales 2 m or more
deep (Fig. 9.13). The stratigraphy was analysed at
length by Hamel (1977a:199–228) and varied
between different parts of the site, but with few
exceptions it can be fitted into a standard sequence:
the basal layer, discontinuously represented, consists of a thin shell and bone (including moa bone)
midden sealed by clean sand from a more or less
continuous, deep, black sand layer containing
abundant moa and seal bones together with smaller
quantities of dog, bird and fish bone and occasional
lenses of shell. Above this is a stained sand layer,
apparently sterile in some places but in others containing abundant evidence of stone and bone-tool
manufacture. Above this again, and with a similar
distribution (suggesting the same occupational
phase), is a thick, dense, shell midden which also
contained some moa and seal bones.

This sequence suggests at least three occupations, the main one of which is represented by the
black layer. It was also the principal phase of moa-
hunting, and during it most of the dune swales

FIG. 9.13   David Teviotdale and Philip George excavating at Papatowai in 1936. (By courtesy of Otago Museum.)

became filled with cultural debris so that the later layers were deposited on a fairly even surface.

It is difficult to form any coherent picture of the spatial organisation of the site except to note that ovens and associated broken moa bones seem to have been more common around the northern and eastern edges of the site, while whole bones were frequently found in other areas (e.g. Teviotdale 1938b:115). One thing, at least, is clear. There was no evidence of a village as at Shag Mouth or Little Papanui: Teviotdale recorded only one 'hearth'.

Hamel's (1977a) small excavation at Papatowai (area TT1) provides the only quantitative faunal data of any precision (Appendix D). The excavation of 4.5 m^2 produced remains of 6 moas in the black layer, 3 in the working floor layer and 1 in the upper shell layer; a density of 2.2 individuals per square metre. There is no reason to think this grossly untypical of the site as a whole, except that MNI figures from small excavations, relative to large, are likely to be inflated. But even at half the density in the TT1 excavation (i.e. the density at Pounawea) 7000 moas would be represented at Papatowai.

Smith's (1985:162) estimation of relative meat weight for Hamel's TT1 data showed that seals contributed 70 per cent and moas 28 per cent in the lower layer material, but moas, at 45 per cent, made a more important contribution than seals (26 per cent) in the upper or shell midden layer.

The Catlins sites, though clearly well placed to

capture seals which colonised the rocky coast were, it seems clear enough, also major locations of moa butchery in which *Euryapteryx* and *Emeus* were the principle genera involved. Given the correlation of these moas with relatively open country, though, the Catlins sites appear something of an enigma. There are several likely explanations, one in particular. The sites exist mid-way between two of the major southern rivers, each with a huge inland catchment (Mataura and Clutha), and it might have involved relatively little extra effort to ship carcasses from them to village sites located primarily to take advantage of seals. More likely, I think, is the explanation implicit in Hamel's (1977a: Fig. 2.12a, 1980) reconstruction of forest patterns which showed that the Catlins River especially, but other major streams in the district as well, are so prone to spring frosts that a lower forest boundary is created leaving a corridor of grassland extending along the valleys almost to the eastern slopes of the Mataura watershed. This open ground doubtless offered the kind of habitats preferred by *Euryapteryx* and *Emeus* as well as access to the open country behind the Catlins hills. Support for this view may be found in the relatively high proportion of porcellanite, most likely from the Mataura quarries, at Pounawea (Hamel 1980).

Foveaux Strait

The frequency of moa-hunting sites declines west of the Catlins, a consequence no doubt of environmental conditions (swamp forest) being generally unsuitable for the common species. Nevertheless, in addition to small sites recorded at Haldane Estuary (Teal 1976), Waipapa and possibly Tokanui (Teviotdale 1932a), there was a group of larger sites at each of the Bluff and Pahia headlands. At the former, Teviotdale (n.d.) excavated sites at Bluff in 1942 (where moa bone occurred with 'basalt' (?argillite) and silcrete flakes) and at Greenhills in 1943 where he found moa bones and quantities of moa eggshell in several middens. On nearby Tiwai Point a later excavation disclosed 11 moas amongst midden debris in an adze-manufactory (Park 1969; Sutton and Marshall 1980). The contribution of moas to the represented meat weight (17 per cent) was much less, however, than that of seals (72 per cent), and not much more than the total meat weight of an unusually large number of muttonbirds (*Puffinus griseus*) and other small fowl (Smith 1985:144).

At Pahia, and the west end of Wakapatu,

Teviotdale (n.d.) found moa remains in sites, as did Higham (1968) at nearby Tihaka. Further west, Coutts (1970) recorded small quantities of moa bone in middens at Port Craig.

On the southern islands, moa eggshell in some quantity was recovered from Centre Island (Teviotdale 1932b) and eggshell associated with a large blade was recovered on Lee Island (Ruapuke) by Coutts and Jurisich (1972). On Stewart Island, moa bones associated with two large stone blades were reported from Mason Bay (Benham 1910). Traill reported various moa localities on Stewart Island (Traill to Ashton 6 September 1896, in Hamilton n.d.) of which Ruggedy Beach might be a site, and Native Island and the Neck certainly are (see also Bollons to Hamilton n.d.) along with the Ringaringa site (Knight 1970) nearby. Scarlett's notes from 1954 (Duff 1977:75) indicate that, while some moa bone occurred in the Native Island midden, the Neck was the major site. It is particularly notable for the number of Scarlett's *Euryapteryx* 'new species' represented there (Appendix D) – which indicates that it was a site of local hunting, and probably not formed by transport of carcasses from the mainland, which has to be counted a possibility in other cases.

Some conclusions

The distribution of sites in the coastal South Island is oriented very strongly to the eastern coast, the main province of moa-hunting in the country. This is clearly a reflection of the availability of moas, especially *Eu. gravis*, *E. crassus* and, to a lesser extent, other species of the '*Euryapteryx gravis* assemblage' (Appendix D) in the hinterland. Where areas of open woodland or scrub country were most extensive, as on the Canterbury Plains and inland Otago, the adjacent coast is most thickly dotted with moa-hunting sites.

Coastal processes have, however, probably removed a number of important sites, and significantly diminished the extent of others, along the gravel shores of Canterbury and north Otago. It is also possible that this factor accounts, to some extent, for the virtual absence of sites along much of the west coast, but an actual scarcity of moas was probably a more significant factor. Some coastal sites in the South Island are immense and must represent the butchery of many thousands of moas. There is, though, restricted evidence of sedentary settlement, and it may be assumed that moa-hunting was generally a temporary, perhaps seasonal, activity.

10

South Island Inland Sites

The inland South can be divided, north to south, into four districts, the first of which lies between the Wairau and Waiau (north Canterbury) valleys. This district is very mountainous and subalpine grassland, with beech forest at lower altitudes, was the main vegetation pattern at the arrival of Polynesians. No moa-hunting sites have been recorded.

From the Waiau to the Opihi valleys there is a narrow 'waist' of high country, about 150 km broad, in which there are small basins formed in the upper reaches of the main rivers. Forest, mainly of beech, occurred in these and on the alpine foothills, but subalpine grasslands and grassland, shrubland and open forest extending from the basins down to the coastal plains were the main elements of the pre-human vegetation pattern in this district. Small moa-hunting sites located in rockshelters have been recorded at Weka Pass (Haast 1878), the site now known as Timpendean (Trotter 1972b) and at Castle Hill (Trotter and McCulloch 1971:62). Other rockshelter sites, some exhibiting evidence of repeated occupation and 'prodigious numbers' of moa bones, were reported from the middle reaches of the Opihi and Tengawai rivers by Smith (1891, *The Taranaki Herald* (New Plymouth) 13 November 1936). Open sites were scattered over the downs in the same area (Smith 1884, 1901) and there was also one major site, about 0.8 ha in area, near the Tengawai Gorge (Smith *The Taranaki Herald* 13 November 1936), with possibly another at Arowhenua (Taylor 1952: 167). At Forest Creek, in the upper Rangitata Valley, Smith (*The Taranaki Herald* 13 November 1936) recorded two sites containing moa bone and eggshell, some of it burnt, together with stone implements. Similar sites were believed to occur in the hills between Forest Creek and the Opihi. It

seems very likely that systematic site recording would turn up more moa-hunting sites in the hill country of this southern area.

The third district comprises Central Otago and the Mackenzie Country.

Central Otago and the Mackenzie Country

Most inland moa-hunting camps are located in the triangular expanse of range-and-basin country east of six large lakes drained by the Clutha and Waitaki rivers. This is, overall, the driest area of New Zealand and McGlone's (1983) evidence shows that much of it was open country prior to the arrival of Polynesians. Beech and podocarp forest extended as a discontinuous band around the slopes of the ranges and more extensively about the lakes, but the broad basins were covered mainly in tussock grassland. Few moa-hunting sites have been recorded along the western margin and those which do exist comprise isolated ovens at Bolton's Gully (Trotter 1969) and Matukituki (Simmons 1966), and the remains of one or two moas in a camp at Dart Bridge where *ti*-cooking was the main activity (Anderson and Ritchie 1986). There is uncertain evidence of moa-hunting at Makarora and in the Lindis Valley. The main concentration of sites is in the middle Waitaki Valley, the middle and upper Taieri Valley and the central part of the Clutha watershed (Fig. 10.1).

Waitaki Valley

With the exception of moa remains at Tekapo, a site of uncertain status (Chapman 1885), at the Gray's Hills quarry site (Irvine 1943) and at

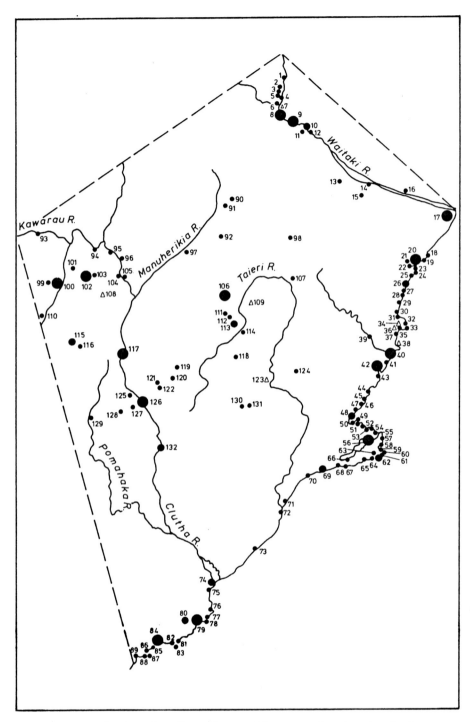

1. Hamiltons 2. Shepherd's Creek I 3. Shepherd's Creek II 4. Gooseneck Bend I 5. Gooseneck Bend II 6. Ahuriri 7. Junction Point 8. Te Akatarewa 9. Woolshed Flat 10. Stony Stream 11. Garguston 12. Waitangi 13. Otekaike 14. Takiroa 15. Maerewhenua 16. Ikawai 17. Waitaki Mouth 18. Cape Wanbrow 19. Beach Road 20. Awamoa 21. Totara 22. Ototara 23. Kakanui Road 24. Kakanui Point 25. Kakanui North Bank 26. Tai Rua 27. Bewley Creek 28. Waianakarua 29. Waianakarua Bluff 30. Hampden 31. Waiwherowhero Stream 32. North Beach 33. Katiki 34. Waimataitai North 35. Waimataitai South 36. Katiki Beach 37. Trotter's Creek 38. Shag Point 39. Glenpark 40. Shag Mouth 41. Stoney Creek 42. Pleasant River 43. Tumai 44. Waikouaiti 45. Seacliff 46. Ross's Rocks 47. Omimi 48. Warrington 49. Doctor's Point 50. Waitati Mouth 51. Purakanui 52. Long Beach 53. Murdering Beach 54. Kaikai's Beach 55. Te Waiparapara 56. Harwood 57. Pipikaretu 58. Papanui Inlet N. 59. Papanui Inlet S. 60. McKays Beach 61. Little Papanui N. 62. Little Papanui 63. Hooper's Inlet 64. Allan's Beach 65. Sandfly Bay 66. Anderson's Bay 67. St Kilda 68. St Clair 69. Kaikorai 70. Otokia 71. Taieri Mouth 72. Taieri Cave 73. Tokomairiro Mouth 74. Clutha Mouth 75. Kaka Point 76. Nugget Point 77. Cannibal Bay 78. False Island 79. Pounawea 80. Hinahina 81. Waitangi Stream 82. Long Point 1 83. Long Point 2 84. Papatowai 85. King's Rock 86. Tautuku North 87. Tautuku Point 88. Tautuku Peninsula 89. Hukihoki Stream 90. Homehill Runs 91. Hills Creek Upper 92. Rockyside 93. Owen's Ferry 94. Bannockburn 95. Rockfall I and II 96. Italian Creek 97. Ida Valley 98. Kyeburn 99. Nevis Spur 100. Schoolhouse Creek 101. Carrick Range 102. Hawksburn 103. Fraser 104. Clyde West 105. Muttontown Gully 106. Puketoi 107. Kokonga 108. Earnscleugh 109. Patearoa 110. Nevis Upper 111. Rocky Peak 112. Manson's 113. German Jack's 114. Loganburn 115. Glenaray 116. Upper Waikaia 117. Coal Creek 118. Great Moss Swamp 119. Lake Onslow 120. Onslow 121. Minzionburn Spur 122. Minzionburn Ovens 123. Matarae 124. Ross Creek 125. Moa Flat 126. Millers Flat 127. Millers Flat West 128. Wilden 129. Pomahaka approx. 130. Rocklands 131. Deep Stream 132. Beaumont.

Fig. 10.1   Distribution of small, medium and large moa-hunting sites in Otago.

Otekaike (another silcrete quarry), Maerewhenua shelter (Hamilton 1897), Takiroa shelter (SRF) and Ikawai (Vincent pers. comm.), the Waitaki sites are concentrated in and near the gorge. Some are rockshelters containing the remains of one or two moas, and flake and blade implements, together with the bones of small birds – particularly water-

birds and rails. Hamilton's, Gooseneck Bend I, Ahuriri and Junction Point are examples (Ambrose 1968, 1970). Small open sites with similar remains were located at Gooseneck Bend II (Duff 1977:271) and Shepherd's Creek I (Stevenson 1947) and II (Mason 1963; Trotter 1970a; Scarlett 1979). Larger open sites, though poorly known, were at Garguston, Waitangi and Stony Stream (Trotter 1970a). The two largest sites were at Te Akatarewa and Woolshed Flat.

At the former, sometimes called Hakatarewa, moa-bone ovens and silcrete knives were strewn over an area of about 4 ha. Four stone-kerbed fire-places were also recorded (Knight 1965; Trotter 1970a; Duff 1977). The Woolshed Flat site, about 0.6 ha in extent in 1970, had been severely eroded along one edge by the Waitaki River. Trotter (1966, 1970a) excavated one oven in which there occurred remains of three species of moas (Appendix D) and dog and tui (*Prosthemadera novaeseelandiae*) bones, together with chert and silcrete flakes.

Taieri Valley

None of the sites in this watershed has been excavated in modern times and few are known by more than brief reports. The main site is at Puketoitoi, where Murison (1872:122) reported a line of ovens beside the creek and 'great quantities' of moa bone and eggshell: the latter was 'found in layers, showing that a vast number of eggs must have been consumed as food'. On a low terrace behind the cooking area were many stone implements including knives and adzes as well as evidence of fires. This suggests a living area, and thus a site organised as at Hawksburn (below). Another site containing numerous stone tools was found nearby and there seems, in addition, to have been an extensive natural site at no great distance. At Patearoa, directly across the valley from Puketoitoi, was another site, uncertainly cultural, which also contained masses of moa eggshell (Hocken 1872).

In the headwaters of the Taieri a moa-hunting site of some importance, but badly damaged, was located by Gillies and Turnbull (1978) at German Jack's, and small sites at Great Moss Swamp, Loganburn, Rocky Peak and Manson's.

From the Strath-Taieri district, moa-hunting sites have been reported at Kyeburn and Kokonga (SRF) and at Rocklands and Deep Stream – where there are several quite substantial but little-known sites and a number of isolated ovens containing moa bone (Welch to Simmons n.d., 2 May 1966). Matarae shelter contains silcrete flakes, and possibly blades, and there are some pieces of bone which might be from moa (H. Leach pers. comm.). Teviotdale (1932a) records a moa-hunting camp and silcrete quarrying site at Ross Creek.

Overall the Taieri watershed is not as rich in moa-hunting sites as the Waitaki or Clutha valleys

and this might reflect, in part, the relative value of the rivers for transport (Chapter 11).

Clutha watershed

The Clutha watershed, below the lakes, is notable for four substantial sites (below). There are, in addition, smaller open sites. Below the upper gorge these are located at Beaumont, Onslow and Lake Onslow (Bagley 1973), Moa Flat (Hector 1872), Minzion Burn (Holdaway and Foster 1983), Muttontown Gully (Gilkison 1930), and directly across the river at Clyde (Hector 1872) and in the Manuherikia watershed (SRF).

In the Cromwell Gorge, the Rockfall II site consisted of a shallow oven in and around which were small pieces of leg, pelvic and neck bone from one individual each of *Dinornis* sp. and *Eu. gravis*. There was one large silcrete blade, several modified flakes, 96 waste flakes of silcrete and porcellanite and 25 chips of polished argillite, doubtless from adzes (Ritchie 1982b; Ritchie and Harrison 1981). The Italian Creek shelter contained a single cultural layer within which two shallow hearths were filled with blackened soil containing numerous fragments of moa eggshell, some freshwater mussel shells, small bird bone and several flake implements. Since most of the shell had been burnt, belonged to at least two species (one almost certainly *M. didinus*) and is very distinctly concentrated in the hearths, Ritchie (1982b) concluded that it was a cultural deposit.

Other small sites are located in the upper Clutha at Rockfall I (Ritchie 1982b) Bannockburn (SRF), Luggate (Teviotdale 1932a), Fraser River (Anderson 1979b), high in the Carrick Mountains (Hector 1872) and at several places in the Nevis Valley (George 1937). One of the latter, in the upper Nevis, consists of only a heap of gizzard stones and a stone blade and it is presumably a rare example of a kill-site, of which several have been reported in the North Island (Chapter 8).

Owen's Ferry, a more extensive site (about 180 m^2) contained two ovens, eight scoop hearths – evidently for cooking rather than dwellings – and a small butchery area and midden (Ritchie pers. comm.). Kooyman's (1984b) analysis of the moa bone showed that seven species were represented by just nine individuals (Appendix D), an indication that these moas were probably hunted as individuals. Since the bone was in good condition and largely unburnt, and since the site was almost fully excavated, it was possible for Kooyman (1984b) to infer that high-value meat-bones had been preferentially returned to the site (against femora at 100 per cent, tibiotarsi were represented at 67 per cent, ribs, fibula and tarsometatarsi at 33 per cent). Neck bones (vertebrae, tracheal rings) were very rare, and phalanges and cranial bones scarce; in other words, just the pattern suggested less certainly at many other sites. Tibiotarsi exhibited clear evidence of deliberate bone-smashing, and the fine cut marks showed that there had been severance points for muscle masses at each end of the tibiotarsus and on the pubis and ischial shafts, which suggests removal of meat from the rear of the pelvis.

Schoolhouse Creek

Turning to the major sites, there is not much recorded about the Schoolhouse Creek moa butchery or the site high on a spur about 3 km from it. The former once extended over an area of about 1 ha and moa bones were reportedly abundant. George (1937) found two stone-kerbed hearths, one with three ulu and a dagger-like implement associated with it. The spur site also had many moa bones and stone flake and blade implements, although no ovens were reported. The Schoolhouse Creek sites are close to a porcellanite quarry as at Coal Creek (below).

Coal Creek

Test excavations by Anderson and Ritchie (1984) show this site extended over an area of about 0.7 ha upon two terraces. One scoop hearth, numerous flakes and a nephrite ulu on an upper terrace suggest that this was a living area. On a lower terrace were ovens and a considerable quantity of moa bone, including drifts of heavily burnt and fragmented bone as at Hawksburn. Two cultural layers separated by silt were observed in one area and there was also a pit, re-cut at least once, and lacking the usual characteristics of a Maori oven. Even so, upon it lay numerous moa bones which had been partially burnt. Those about the periphery of the heap were least damaged and were mainly foot (tarsometatarsi and phalanges) and neck and head bones, in each case lying in position of articulation. There were also broken and sawn ends of tibiotarsi with the shafts missing. This was clearly a rubbish heap in which the refuse of both butchery and the secondary processing of bone had been dumped. The excavations were too limited in scope to provide evidence for an adequate estimation of the total number of butchered birds but the midden areas appear no less extensive than at Hawksburn (Appendix D).

Miller's Flat

Before this site was heavily eroded along the river edge and elsewhere covered by a deep layer of silt – the consequence of a major flood on the Clutha in 1878 – it was about 1.3 ha in extent, and there were many ovens observable on the surface. When the flood subsided, a line of ovens was seen sectioned along the river-edge and below them 'moa bones, not in hundred-weight, but in tons, were strewn in a continuous heap along the foot of the bank' (*The Evening Star* (Dunedin) January 1940). This important site, perhaps the largest in the Clutha watershed, has not been investigated by archaeologists.

Hawksburn

This moa-butchery site lies in a small valley, at an altitude of 660 m, in the Carrick Mountains (Fig. 10.2). There were excavations in 1955, largely unpublished (Lockerbie 1959; Hamel 1978), but the present analysis is based on excavations of 223 m² in 1979 (Anderson 1979b, 1983a, 1986). As shown in Fig. 10.3 the site can be defined by the distribution of stone flakes and blades which cover an area of 2700 m². They are concentrated into two bands: one lies behind the remains of a line of huts where it is unassociated with moa remains and appears to represent a tool-fabrication area, while the other lies alongside a double row of ovens amongst abundant remains of moa processing and bone midden. As at many other moa-hunting sites, the area over which stone tools and domestic structures are distributed is significantly greater than that which is readily apparent from the surface extent of the charcoal blackened soil.

FIG. 10.2 Hawksburn Valley. The moa-hunting site lies at the bend in the valley, centre left.

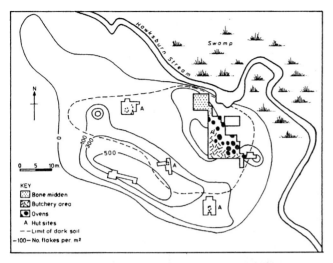

FIG. 10.3 Hawksburn moa-hunting site, showing areas excavated in 1979 (above) and view of excavations (below).

There are two cultural layers. The lower, consisting of two shallow ovens and sparse moa remains, is sealed from the main occupation layer by 15 cm of clean river silt. This might have accumulated in a day or two, and the radiocarbon dates indicate no difference in age (Chapter 13).

The 18 ovens were small, 0.6–1.0 m in diameter and 0.3–0.6 m deep. Some exhibited signs of recutting, and around the rims were remnants of micro-stratified lenses of silt and charcoal indicating repeated use. To the east of the bone midden was a refuse area for charcoal, ovenstones and silt discarded in the course of refurbishing the ovens.

Behind the ovens is a flat silt 'floor' on which moa ribs and sternal ribs and, and to a lesser extent, vertebrae, femora, tarsometatarsi and phalanges were concentrated. Taken together, the relatively low incidence of burning (9 per cent of fragments compared to 48 per cent of fragments in

the oven area and 98 per cent in the midden), the larger size of the bone fragments and the concentration of the stone flakes and blade tools in this area, suggest that it was a butchery floor (Fig. 10.4).

On the opposite side of the ovens is a dense bone midden in which most of the bone had been heavily burnt and fragmented to bone 'gravel'. Amongst identified elements phalanges, tracheal rings and cranial fragments were more common in the midden than elsewhere.

Butchery

Variations in the distribution of different bones can be explained in terms of carcass processing and to do so it is useful to rank the relative meat value of the carcass elements. To provide an appropriate analogy for moas in this regard, Kooyman (1985: 217–19) dissected eight kiwi (*Apteryx australis*) and weighed the muscle masses associated with each bone. These data provided the following ranking of relative meat values: head 3, neck 40 (in actual meat weight it is 80, but much of this is relatively inaccessible; moreover, it is unlikely that moas in general had quite as heavily muscled necks as kiwi), thoracic vertebrae 13, caudal vertebrae 1, ribcage 18, sternum 7, pelvis 28, femur 100 (per side), tibiotarsus and fibula 53 (per side), tarsometatarsus 1 (per side), phalanges 0 (see also Binford 1978:15–38 and Kooyman 1984b:49–50 on this ranking technique).

Initial butchery of a whole moa carcass probably began with the removal and discarding of the head-neck, feet and lower leg; the latter of which,

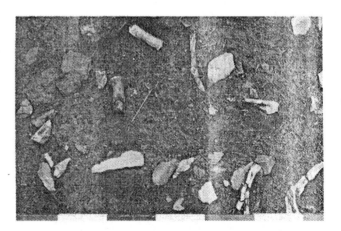

FIG. 10.4 Close-up of moa butchery area at Hawksburn, 1979, showing discarded moa ribs and phalanges, together with flake and blade implements.

at least, tended to remain in the butchery area at Hawksburn. Removing, and discarding in the same area, the ribcage and associated sternum and thoracic vertabrae, would leave the pelvis and upper leg. Since the femur was the meatiest bone but comparatively short, its relatively high occurrence in the butchery area at Hawksburn might have resulted from butchering it out to leave a boned joint (Table 10.1).

If this reconstruction of the butchery process is plausible, it is not as clearly revealed by the data as might be wished. Although there are doubtless biasses in sampling and identification involved, this is probably also due to the process not operating in quite the neatly prescribed and spatially segmented way I have described it. In addition to actual flexibility in the butchery, cooking and discard processes, there was probably also some 'wandering' in the location of the functionally separate parts of the site. If butchery began near the stream, for instance, it would have been progressively pushed away from it by the expansion of the midden and the construction of additional ovens, thus tending to obscure what might have been, initially, a clearer picture.

Further complication to a straightforward processing sequence was potentially caused by such secondary operations as the selective removal of bone for industrial purposes or for marrow extraction. Evidence of the former is very slight indeed – two possible saw cuts and a drill hole, and one ground bone point – but there are stronger indications of the latter, such as a 43 per cent incidence of long spiral fractures on unburnt bones in the butchery area. The fractured bones were mainly tibiotarsi, doubtless a reflection of their relative marrow capacity which, in medium and large moas, was twice or more that of femora (Kooyman 1985). Most of the clearly identifiable blunt-object blows (16) also occurred on tibiotarsi. Butchery cut-marks were seldom seen, but two of the three

heavy cuts to tibiotarsi were on distal shafts and may have been the result of removing the lower leg and foot. Probably for the same reason, six heavy cuts on fibulae were clustered in a small area at the distal end of the shaft. The distribution of fine cuts on tibiotarsi also supports this inference since 17 of 21 are on the distal shaft and may have resulted from severance of the strong ligaments in this area. Of fine cuts on femora, 13 of 15 are on the proximal shaft and probably result from separation of leg and pelvis. Two heavy cuts on tarsometatarsal fragments were located on the anterior distal shaft and were probably caused by removal of the foot (Kooyman 1985).

Although not common, these damage marks support the view that the main severance points were located at the proximal femur and distal tibiotarsus joints, with a secondary point at the distal end of the tarsometatarsus.

MNI and total number of moa

In Appendix D are the identified species and MNI of moas according to two analyses. Part of the difference is accounted for by Kooyman's preference for the Cracraft (1976a) taxonomy in which Scarlett's (1972) *Eu. gravis* and *Eu. haasti* are synonymised under *Eu. geranoides*, and *D. robustus* under *D. novaezealandiae*. The main real difference is in Kooyman's additional identification of *D. struthoides*, and his identification of *P. elephantopus* for fragments regarded as *Emeus* sp. by Scarlett.

If bone fragments identified to anatomy but not necessarily to species are considered, Kooyman's maximum MNI rises to 20 based on tibiotarsi, and 22 when size differences are considered. The percentage ratio of small moas (*M. didinus*): medium moas (*Eu. geranoides*, *D. struthoides*, *D. torosus*): large moas (*P. elephantopus*, *D. novaezealandiae*) in this sample is 14:68:18, but amongst moas identified by Kooyman (1985) to species the ratio is 25:50:25. Medium-sized moas are, therefore, probably under-represented in the latter sample.

How many moa carcasses had been deposited on the site can only be approximately estimated because of the highly fragmented nature of the material. Nevertheless from systematic test excavations over the total area of the site and collection of large whole samples in the excavated areas it is possible to calculate the total weight of moa bone. This came to 1795 kg which is an underestimate for several reasons, but mainly because it does not include bone fragments reduced to less than 2 mm in largest dimension which were sieved out with soil residue before calculating the bone content of

TABLE 10.1 Distribution of identified moa bone at Hawksburn by body part and site area (per cent)

Element	Butchery	Ovens	Midden
Head and neck	3	14	24
Back and pelvis	3	7	11
Ribcage	38	16	16
Leg	25	39	23
Foot	31	23	27
Total MNE	(65)	(110)	(177)

Note: MNE = minimum number of elements identified.

the whole samples. The figure can be conservatively rounded up to 1800 kg. Two estimates of total moa numbers are now possible. Given 22 individuals in the 112 kg of bone which Kooyman analysed, there would be 354 moas represented in the total amount of bone. Another approach is to establish the bone weight of anatomical elements in reference moa skeletons and divide the corresponding site total accordingly. This was done by using museum collections of selected leg bones from known species of different size. The bones were all whole, clean, dry, unburnt and unmineralised. The results were summed and scaled to the moa size ratio 14:68:18, as indicated above. On this basis an average moa in the Hawksburn site would produce 3.2 kg of dry leg bone (excluding fibulae, phalanges and sesamoids). Scaling the total weight of identified leg bones, as a proportion of all identified elements, up to 1800 kg, and dividing by 3.2 kg, produces an estimate that 443 moas are represented. This is close to an earlier estimate of 430 (Anderson 1983a:43) which used leg bone data from only five medium-sized moas.

Given the various sources of error in estimating the total bone weight discarded on the site and the fact that dry, burnt moa bone is bound to be lighter than dry, unburnt bone, the maximum MNI of moas at Hawksburn can be assumed to be 400 ± 50 for present purposes.

Pattern of return and food quantity

If the most commonly identified bone (tibiotarsus) is taken as the standard, the comparative percentage of other main elements is: femur 68 per cent, tarsometatarsus 37 per cent, quadrate and pelvis each 32 per cent, ribs and middle phalanges 20–25 per cent, and all others less than 20 per cent. It can be inferred from these data that if bone preservation factors have not operated differentially, then a fifth to a third of all moas were probably returned to the site as more or less whole carcasses.

Judging by the relatively low representation of the phalanges, tarsometatarsus and pelvis, most of the moas (about two-thirds of the carcasses), were returned to the site as leg joints. Hawksburn was, consequently, not primarily a kill site, if it ever functioned as that, but rather a depot for processing. It was essentially a moa butchery. Remains of 4 dogs, 29 small birds (8 ducks, 5 rails, 10 forest birds) several rats and freshwater mussels and approximately 3 moa eggs (number calculated according to data in Hamel 1980) complete the faunal inventory. Turned into edible meat weight (after data in Smith 1985) these represent a total of

46 kg. If moa carcasses were from species in the size ratio 14:68:18 (above), and two-thirds were returned as legs alone, then using Smith's (1985) edible meat weight estimates a total of 12,557 kg would be represented for 400 individuals. This is 99.6 per cent of the edible flesh weight represented.

Occupational span

Moa eggshell and some chick bone indicate that at least part of the occupation at Hawksburn occurred during the moa-breeding season, presumably spring. Other than that, there is little to be said about seasonality of occupation. The site may have been continuously inhabited for several years during the main occupation, but the lack of stratigraphy within this cultural level might only reflect the exceedingly slow soil development in the area: occupation gaps of some months or years are not represented by sterile sedimentary layers, except in one case (above).

Inland Southland

The upper watersheds of the southern rivers between the Pomahaka and the (Southland) Waiau define the fourth district. Most of it was under forest at about AD 1000, with beech the major component. The few moa-hunting sites in it are distributed around the inland margins, either near the western lakes or in the upper watersheds. The former group includes the small rockshelter site in the Takahe Valley, once thought to represent the killing of an individual *Megalapteryx didinus* as late as the 18th century (Duff 1952, 1977:75–82) but now regarded as an early site (Anderson n. d. a, and see Chapter 13). Others are little-known sites at Te Anau, Bullock Hills, Mararoa (Henry 1899; SRF), at Wilden, Upper Pomahaka (*The Otago Witness* 17 February 1904) and three sites in the headwaters of the Waikaia (Hamilton 1895, n. d.; Anderson 1986).

Glenaray

This site is on a plateau at about 1100 m in altitude in the upper Waikaia (Anderson 1980). There were 34 discrete patches of moa gizzard stones and three small middens of heavily burnt and fragmented moa bone. Flake and blade implements of porcellanite, and silcrete to a lesser extent, were strewn over an area of about 2600 m². The main importance of the site lies in what it reveals about settlement patterns on inland hunting camps. The distribution of the evidence (Fig. 10.5) discloses

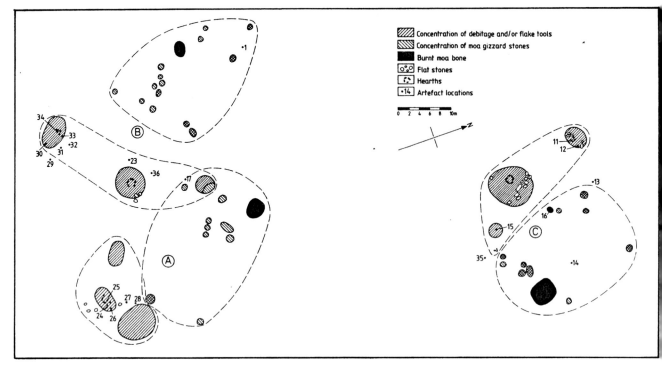

FIG. 10.5   Repeated domestic settlement pattern (A, B, C,) at Glenaray (Anderson 1986; Polynesian Society), above, and one of the main hearths, below.

three areas, in each of which there is the same pattern: the main component is a group of three more or less circular patches of flake implements and other tools, including fragments of adzes; each central patch also has a stone-lined hearth and flat stones set several metres to the east of it. In two of the areas (B, C) one other patch also has similar structures. These data have been interpreted as remains of groups of small huts – probably of the circular, tussock-covered, *whare porotaka* kind – known historically from Maori mutton-birding camps on the islands in Foveaux Strait. There, the usual domestic unit maintained a central dwelling

with working and storage huts to either side (Anderson 1986). In front of each group of presumed huts at Glenaray is a burnt-bone midden and 9 to 14 patches of gizzard stones.

A similar settlement pattern can be inferred at Hawksburn (above) and evidence of the same kind of dwellings can be found at Tumbledown Bay, Dart Bridge, Heaphy Mouth and Ringaringa (Anderson 1986; Anderson and Ritchie 1986; Knight 1970).

Some conclusions

Inland moa-hunting sites are concentrated into the basins and valleys of the Mackenzie Country and Central Otago. It is surprising that none have been recorded from either inland Marlborough, or the Waimea Plains and other lowland areas in the upper catchments of the Southland rivers. Closed forest probably covered much of these areas at the time of first human arrival, but it is unlikely that it was any more extensive than in, for example, the upper Waiau (Southland) or Pomahaka, where at least a few moa-hunting sites have come to light. The main species sought were of the '*Euryapteryx gravis* assemblage' (Appendix D) and it is noticeable that hunting sites have seldom been reported from the western valleys and lake shores of the interior where beech forests grew extensively. Moa-hunting in the interior was, thus, aimed at the same micro-environments as along the coast.

11

HUNTING STRATEGIES

In discussing the archaeological evidence detailed in preceding chapters, the first questions which arise concern how moas were hunted and in what way moa-hunting fitted in to the broader schedule of economic activities. Given the considerable variation, at a regional level, in the number of moas represented in early Maori sites, and the differences in access to alternative subsistence resources such as cultigens or seals, there can hardly be any satisfactory single answer. Where moas were relatively scarce or inaccessible anything more than the opportunistic pursuit of an economic bonus seems out of the question. In the eastern South Island, however, the quantities of moa bone in early sites are such that several alternative strategies seem possible. Whole communities might have organised their long-term economic arrangements around the continuous pursuit of moas, by mass-kill or individual hunting techniques. Alternatively there could have been a recognized moa-hunting season during which the whole of each community was involved in various associated tasks, much like horticultural harvesting or barracouta (*Thyrsites atun*) fishing, and with the same objective of accumulating a large reserve of stored food. Another possibility is that small groups regularly went moa-hunting throughout the year, largely consuming their catch during each expedition.

In sorting between these a number of elements need to be considered: hunting methods, the nature of the catch, the distribution and size of hunting sites in the landscape and evidence relating to the preservation of moa flesh, seasonality and material culture.

Hunting methods

Much of what we want to know about moa-hunting – its selectivity in terms of species, sex or age, its potential efficiency as a mechanism of predation, and so on – would become very much clearer if there existed reliable traditions about it.

Traditional evidence

Leaving aside the Tamatea tradition (e.g. Davies 1907) in which moas were all but destroyed by fires, in some versions said to have been lit for that purpose (Roberts 1875:548; Maning 1876:102), the earliest specific accounts of moa-hunting referred to the use of snares and nooses. Hamilton (1875:122) reported that, in 1849, a Southland Maori, Wera, told him moas had been caught by hanging nooses at cave entrances, and Roberts (1875:548) was evidently told, in 1856, about snares placed across moa trails. John White (Travers 1876:79) said that he heard of hunters placed along such trails to stab wooden spears into passing moas (see also White 1925:172; Graham 1919:108). Driving moas, as in the story attributed to Paipai (McDonnell 1889:439), the use of dogs (Davison 1870:604; Smith 1911:56; Downes 1926:37), hunting pits (Graham 1919:108) and driving moas into lakes (Taylor 1873:100) were also described. So was an unlikely tale about inducing witless moas to swallow heated pebbles (Best 1942:189).

Stories which tell of particular moa hunts are quite scarce and there are considerable drawbacks to accepting them as pre-European tradition, or as referring to moas. Best (1942:188) noted that Smith's (1911) dramatic tale about Ruakapanga and the hunting of giant birds (Chapter 5) was also known, in skeletal form, on Rarotonga (Cook Islands), where the phrase '*e manu-nui* [giant bird] *a Ruakapanga*' referred not to a bird, as such, but to an ancestor's kite. The story of Hape's encounter with a moa is also much less obvious than it seems. Travers (1876:80), in footnoting White's evidence, wrote that Karanga-na-Hape, a hill on the East Coast, commemorated the pursuit of a wounded moa by Hape, an Arawa chief, who struck at it with his fighting club and received a kick which broke his leg and sent him rolling down the hill. Mair (1890:72), however, explained on the authority of a named informant (Apanui Hamaiwaho, also White's informant) that Hape was a mythological figure and that the point of the story was that his heel struck a rock, opening the gorge for a local river. The tale then became hopelessly confused by a quite different but clearly related assertion: Buller said that Apahapaitaketake had stolen a pet moa belonging to another tribe and then fell over a cliff and broke his thigh, for which he was nicknamed Hapakoki (Hop-and-go-one). This implausible story which grew in the telling (Buller in Tregear 1888:304; Buller 1893:530; and see Tregear 1892:416, Davies 1910:223 and Best 1942:186 in which the moa is of the mythological man-bird kind) drew a dry response from Haast (11 April 1885, in Colenso 1894:501) who commented that 'the pet moa must have been very small or it could not have been retained by a man with a broken leg'.

Leaving aside such obviously corrupted tales, the assertions that moas were driven by men or dogs, caught in pits or speared in shrubland seem reasonable propositions, and even if they are late 19th-century speculations based upon scientific knowledge of moas or other large ratites and have no pre-European foundation, they are worth consideration in terms of archaeological evidence.

Archaeological hypotheses

The first point which must be made is that archaeological evidence has failed to disclose any particular artefact which might provide a solid clue about what technology existed at the sharp end of the hunting process.

Unlike some other Polynesians, Maoris did not have the bow and arrow (Colenso 1879) in the post-European era, and rare discoveries of what may have been stone arrow points (e.g. Kirk 1881) provide insufficient evidence that it existed prehistorically. Similarly there are few remains of large bone points, or of stone points which have the usual characteristics of spear heads. Blunt-tipped bone darts have been found, but rarely, and they can hardly have been effective against larger game, if they were used in hunting at all. Bone harpoon heads of open-socket form occur in early coastal sites, often in sites in which moa bone occurs, but they are not common and have a distribution which appears more obviously correlated with the remains of dolphins and other small whales, as one might expect (Smith 1985). So far as projectile implements are concerned, then, the field is narrowed to the possible use of slings, and wooden javelins and lances, all of which were used as weapons of war in the early post-European era (Colenso 1879).

Trapping pits might have been used. One suggestive example is a rectangular pit with a brushwood cover which was found on the margins of a swamp in Central Otago (Skinner 1934). Pits, however, were commonly used by the Maori as tuber stores or as large ovens for cooking *ti* (*Cordyline australis*). Whenever they have been investigated the characteristic structural features associated with these functions have usually been revealed. Also pits of any kind only occur rarely in the interior of the South Island and are far less common elsewhere in the eastern South Island, the main moa-hunting district, than in the horticultural regions to the north.

Driving moas into cul-de-sacs at the end of river-mouth bars, there to be dispatched by spears on land or in the water, was the method envisaged by most earlier writers. Thus Thorne (1876:92–3) advised of the Pataua sand spit that 'you will readily conceive how the wary Moa-hunter would skilfully drive the probably sluggish, stupid bird . . . on to the narrow sand dunes between the impassable swamp and sea as into the most cleverly contrived trap'. Duff (1951:25) likewise imagined 'young men spread out in a great circle in the Vernon Hills [driving] the moas towards the broad base of [Wairau] bar. Soon the birds would be helplessly rushing north along the narrow road of the bar, with the hunters behind them'. (See also Haast 1872a:86; Skinner 1924a:14; Teviotdale 1932a:92.)

This method appears plausible for small groups, if not to the extent of great moa drives, but its efficacy would depend on several factors which now seem less likely than hitherto. Driving of game usually occurs with herding or flocking species, principally grazers, on open ground. Since most moas were probably scattered in the scrub or light forest of the eastern South Island, and because it is unlikely that they formed large flocks, at any rate not of a single species, the effort required to gather and keep together a large flock of moas in tall vegetation would have required a very high investment of labour. Furthermore moas in general were probably more wary, mobile and aggressive than they are credited in mass-driving scenarios. Small groups of moas (perhaps six or seven birds, as Booth (Teviotdale 1932a:92) suggested in reviewing the distribution of patches of bone at Shag Mouth) driven short distances to convenient kill sites ought not, however, to be ruled out.

Another argument against large-scale moa drives is that archaeological evidence does not disclose the distribution of body parts which would be expected as a consequence. A marked imbalance between leg bones and most other elements – notably crania, cervical vertebrae, sterna and pelves, as for instance at Hawksburn – indicates that most moas reached large butchery sites as joints rather than as live animals.[1] These data are subject, it must be conceded, to unexplored questions of taphonomy and bone fragmentation, but at Kaupokonui, where bones were much less fragmented than at Hawksburn, a similar pattern of representation occurred: most moas (60–70 per cent of MNI) had lost heads or feet, or both, prior to arriving on the site (similarly at Wairau Bar, Wilkes 1964; Rakaia Mouth, Haast 1872a, 1872c; and in smaller sites such as Owen's Ferry, Kooyman 1984b). From this it can be concluded that moa-butchery sites in general were not also mass-kill sites. Further, in the few instances where kill sites can be inferred, they seem to represent the initial processing, but not cooking, of one or a few moas at a time, and the lithic inventory associated with them is restricted to only a few informal tools, as Kooyman (n. d.) predicted.

Another hunting technique which has been proposed is the firing of scrub or forest to drive moas into the open. This was, perhaps, quite likely in situations where the forest was in small patches, but otherwise it would have been a technique

requiring many people and with a low chance of success, since moas would presumably retreat further into the forest or become incinerated.

If moas were hunted as individuals or in small groups as the evidence suggests, then it is probable that the hunters as well were either individuals or in small parties, and used techniques to suit. Amongst these, two seem especially likely. The use of snares, set in shrubbery or on the ground, was a common Maori fowling technique for taking a wide variety of flying and flightless birds. The advantages of this method are that a large number of potential catching locations can be covered at the same time by one hunter, and that a snared moa would be far easier to dispatch than one able to flee or attack (Fig. 11.1). The use of dogs, also recorded ethnographically to run down flightless birds, represents another possibility. In the South Island particularly, Maori dogs seem to have been bred for a strong neck, forequarters and jaw (Anderson 1981b), which suggests their use to hold large game. This method would also have the advantage of extending an individual hunter's range of searching and pursuit, and render a kill more certain and less hazardous. It should be noted, though, that Maori dogs did not bark.

As in the case of moa biology, then, there are some points of agreement between putative traditional evidence and inferences from archaeological data, although the one does not validate the other. Individual or small-group hunting of small numbers of moas at a time, indirectly by using snares or directly with the assistance of dogs, seem the most likely methods. We now need to consider what they caught.

FIG. 11.1   A large moa snared and speared (Higham 1981:22).

---

[1] Recovering only leg and pelvic joints provides 70–80 per cent of available meat (35 per cent of liveweight) while 60–70 per cent of liveweight discarded (Kooyman n. d.). Reid (n. d.) found cassowary legs also provided c. 35 per cent of the total liveweight.

Characteristics of the catch

There has been a considerable range of variation in the methods by which moa bone was recovered from sites. Prior to the 1970s, bones were generally selected by hand, with a bias towards large or whole pieces, and the remainder discarded. Total recovery of bone, or sieving and the analysis of whole samples to estimate losses by that process, subsequently became standard practice, but comparatively few moa-hunting sites have been excavated in the last two decades. Moa bone identification has also been highly variable both in the methods and by quality. It would be unwise, therefore, to expect very much from the data in Appendices C and D.

Nevertheless some broad patterns of return, in terms of species selection, can be observed. Looking first at presence/absence data, it is apparent that many species occur in a fair number of sites, that is, there is no very strong evidence of concentration upon one or a very few species at a regional level. In the North Island (40 sites): *Eu. curtus* (30 sites), *P. mappini* (23), *D. struthoides/torosus* (24), *D. giganteus* (18), *A. didiformis* (17), *D. novaezealandiae* (13) and *Eu. gravis/geranoides* (10) were all quite widely caught. In the South Island (87 sites) there is a similarly broad spectrum throughout the region: *Eu. gravis* (53 sites), *E. crassus* (43), *P. elephantopus* (27), *A. didiformis* (26), *D. giganteus* (22), *D. struthoides/torosus* (20), *D. novaezealandiae* (19) and *M. didinus* (16).

Between the islands, however, there are some notable differences other than those caused by the island-specific distribution of species. Thus *Dinornis* is more widely spread in North Island sites. *D. struthoides/torosus* occurs in 60 per cent of sites compared to 23 per cent of sites in the South Island, and *D. giganteus* in 45 per cent as compared to 25 per cent in the South Island. *D. novaezealandiae* and *A. didiformis* are also more common, by this measure, in North Island sites. On the other hand, *Eu. gravis* and *Eu. geranoides* combined occur in 61 per cent of South Island sites but only 25 per cent of North Island sites.

There are some differences, as well, between coastal and inland sites in the South Island. *Emeus crassus* is nearly four times as common in coastal sites (76 per cent) as in the interior, and *A. didiformis* and *Eu. gravis* are slightly more common in inland sites (60 per cent) than along the coast. *P. elephantopus* is slightly more common in the interior.

In district terms the data reveal that *Dinornis* was encountered most particularly in two areas – the southwest North Island coast and the Otago coast south to the Catlins. *Euryapteryx*, *Emeus* and *Pachyornis* are, in the South Island, mainly from sites in north Otago, Canterbury and the interior.

In the relatively few cases where there are quantitative data they indicate that *P. mappini* was the principal species hunted in the North Island (average 50 per cent in combined MNI), followed by *Eu. geranoides* (18 per cent). The remaining species comprise 5–9 per cent of combined MNI. In the South Island, data on numbers of bones per species show an overwhelming predominance of *Eu. gravis* (75 per cent of all bones counted in sites where MNI have not been calculated). On the other hand, MNI data indicate a mean occurrence of only 29 per cent, compared to 23 per cent for *E. crassus*, 12 per cent for *A. didiformis* and 11 per cent for *P. elephantopus*.

Between South Island coastal and interior districts *E. crassus* stands out, on MNI data, as ten times more common in coastal sites, and *A. didiformis* twice as common. *Dinornis struthoides/torosus*, *M. didinus* and *P. elephantopus* are about twice as common in coastal sites where the MNI has been calculated.

Taking all these data together, one strong conclusion stands out. In all three islands the main focus of moa-hunting was on the 'Euryapteryx assemblage'; that is, the group of species which largely inhabited lowland open forest, scrub and grassland. The MNI data, few though they are, suggest that in the North Island 84 per cent of moas came from this assemblage, in South Island coastal areas 76 per cent, in the interior 50 per cent and on Stewart Island about 96 per cent.

Given the scarcity of MNI data, variations between regions may simply reflect sampling bias. It is possible, however, that they arise from the relative accessibility of moas in comparison with other resources. Where moas were regionally scarce and other protein sources (seals, fish, etc.) abundant, the early Maoris may have skimmed the accessible 'Euryapteryx assemblage' on the coastal margins of Stewart Island and the North Island and largely ignored the forest species which were more dispersed and less easy to hunt. Where seals, fish and other such resources were less accessible, as along most of the Canterbury coast, or did not exist, as in the interior, moa-hunting evidently proceeded beyond the 'Euryapteryx assemblage' and into the forest-dwelling species. Nonetheless it was the more open-country species which were, everywhere, the main focus of exploitation, and consideration of the broader aspects of hunting strategies can proceed on that basis.

Catchment strategies

Most moa-hunting sites are coastal in the South Island. They are concentrated along the coast of Otago, from Otago Peninsula to Cape Wanbrow, and on the Catlins coast. Since each of these areas has a coastal topography combining rocky shores and estuaries offering the widest range of marine resources to be found in the South Island (seals, fish, seabirds and shellfish), it may be assumed that such considerations formed a major locational factor. Moas, though, were clearly important and were probably accessible in quantity in the hinterland. Other eastern South Island shores, not substantially less rich in marine resources but where moas seem to have been significantly less abundant in the hinterland (south coast, Kaikoura coast), have many fewer moa-hunting sites. It is also noticeable that most of the largest coastal sites in the Catlins and north Otago are located at places where there was access through the coastal hills to inland valleys and basins (e.g. Shag Mouth, Pleasant River, Pounawea, Papatowai).

The distribution of the remaining eastern South Island sites can be divided into two patterns which reflect different catchment characteristics. The main rivers fall into two broad categories. There are comparatively short, fast rivers which run in straight courses across wide plains and which have no great extent of lowland in their upper courses. Their catchment areas below 600 m in altitude are about 1500 to 2500 km^2 in extent and approximately triangular in shape, on a broad coastal base. There are also long, winding rivers in which the middle and upper courses cross a series of almost self-contained basins and in which the total catchment areas below 600 m are more extensive (4000–10,000 km^2).

In the first case there are large butchery sites at or near the mouths of the rivers but very few moa-hunting sites inland. The Wairau, Waimakariri, Ashburton (Wakanui), Rakaia and probably Rangitata valleys exhibit this pattern. In the second case there are smaller butchery sites at the river mouths and numerous sites inland. The Taieri and Clutha catchments disclose this pattern. The Waitaki Valley seems to exhibit the first pattern, but in two sections: an upper area of plains (Mackenzie

FIG. 11.2 An example of a *mokihi*, the reed boat commonly used by Maoris on southern rivers and lakes.

Country) largely bereft of sites and crossed by fast tributaries converging on the gorge, where there are several large butchery sites; and a short, straight, lower course with a large butchery site at the mouth.

The difference between the two main patterns is explicable in terms of the relative costs of transport. In the first case the shape of the hunting territory would have meant that most moas were caught nearer the coast than the head waters and, in any case, the travelling time to the apex of the lowland hunting ground (the point at which the river emerges from the ranges) probably did not exceed two days (*c.* 70 km). Using *mokihi*, a type of boat built from bundles of reed or flax stalks (Fig. 11.2), the return trip to the coast would take only a day. The *mokihi* was a very stable, quickly-constructed traditional craft which could be built to carry loads of at least half a tonne, and Mantell (1853) found that on the lower Waitaki, for instance, it travelled at a rate of 7 km per hour.

In these circumstances it was probably easier to hunt in short trips from a river-mouth base to which gutted and partly-trimmed carcasses could be returned than to carry butchery gear, and build new ovens, shelters etc., only a day or so from such facilities at the coast. The economics of this hunting pattern, and the ability to keep carcasses in an edible condition, would have declined sharply, however, where travelling time in either direction exceeded a few days. It can hardly have been efficient to walk for a week to an inland valley, catch several moas, float the carcasses on a *mokihi* for three days or so to the coast, and then begin the process again. However, if the meat could be preserved, and particularly if it could be dried so that weight and bulk were substantially decreased, then the economics of this out-and-return hunting strategy would decline much less steeply.

Preservation

Preservation of bird flesh in fat (packed into containers, *poha*, fashioned from large blades of the bull kelp, *D'Urvillea antarctica*) was a common traditional activity associated both with mutton-birding (*Puffinus* sp.) in Foveaux Strait and weka (*Gallirallus australis*) hunting in inland Canterbury and Otago. In the case of weka, several tonnes of preserved birds were taken from the Mackenzie Country on each of a number of seasonal hunting trips recorded during the late 19th century (although they were transported at that time by horse and cart, Burnett 1927; Taylor 1952; Beattie 1954). There is some archaeological evidence of this activity in the form of spouted wooden bowls (used to pour melted fat) which have been found at various locations in Central Otago, and some examples of kelp bags recovered from rockshelters along the Clutha River (Anderson 1982d).

In open locations, which constitute the majority of moa-hunting sites, no such evidence could be expected to survive, and it is exceedingly difficult to test, by other means, the possibility of flesh preservation. The suggestive double-pit structure found at Wakanui (Chapter 9) is unique, and arguments based upon butchery patterns are open to various interpretations. Kooyman (n. d.) suggested that the scarcity of cut-marks on moa bones is an indication that joints were cooked and consumed on the site rather than the meat being stripped from the bones, prior to cooking, for preservation. The flaw in this argument, though, is that traditional Maori preservation techniques, both packing in fat and drying, were usually preceded by the cooking of carcasses or joints (Beattie n. d.), in which case the flesh could subsequently be stripped by hand. Sufficient fat for preserving the cooked meat could possibly have been obtained – as Kooyman (n. d.) suggests, on the basis of his kiwi dissections – from substantial subcutaneous deposits left on the skin. Otherwise there is little evidence of marrow extraction from moa bones on inland sites, and while it is possible to envisage a means whereby some melted fat could be collected by depositing hot stones in heaps of discarded body parts and butchered bones it would have been a difficult and inefficient procedure.

Preservation of moa flesh in fat, or by drying, cannot be ruled out, but it seems more likely that the proceeds of hunting at locations distant some days from the coast were mainly intended for consumption at the site.[2] It is noticeable in this connection that most sites in the Clutha and Taieri catchments are located away from the main river, and this is as true of the large sites as it is of the smaller; access to river transport cannot have been an important locational consideration in the case of Schoolhouse Creek, Hawksburn or Puketoi.

[2] In this I prefer Kooyman's (n. d.) analysis to that of Teviotdale (1932a, b) and Anderson (1983a).

Seasonality

Whether these various hunting strategies were pursued seasonally is a vital question but one about which there is little to say. It has occasionally been assumed that some inland sites (e.g. Hawksburn, Lockerbie 1959) could not have been occupied during the winter. Hawksburn is under snow for several weeks a year, and sites at higher altitude would almost certainly have been uninhabitable for much of the winter, but most inland moa-hunting sites lie below the level of anything but a light snowfall, and the inland valleys and basins are not significantly colder than coastal locations. Air temperatures are generally lower in winter, but wind chill factors are also lower than on the coast (Tuller 1977). Furthermore the main traditional activity concerning the inland basins was weka-hunting, a winter pursuit.

Archaeological evidence of seasonality is very slim indeed. Bones of chick or other immature moas have seldom been reported, although their scarcity is doubtless more apparent than real. Moa eggshell, however, was encountered in most excavations of hunting sites and in some it existed in considerable quantity (Wairau Bar, possibly Rakaia Mouth, Awamoa, Pounawea, Pleasant River, Greenhills, Puketoitoi and Italian Creek). This is sufficient evidence to argue that hunting commonly occurred in the incubating season, probably spring, and that it was, perhaps, concentrated into that period. If moas followed the common ratite pattern of a long incubation during which sitting males became torpid, then hunting at that time would be relatively well assured of success, and the collection of two products for the effort directed at one. This proposition is potentially testable in terms of the relative representation of sexually dimorphic species, but the data presently available reveal no pattern.

All that can be concluded about hunting seasonality is that a few sites could not have been occupied during the winter and that many were occupied for at least part of the time in the incubating season, some substantially so.

Material culture

Another approach to the question of whether moa-hunting sites were occupied either continuously or repeatedly, though not necessarily seasonally, is to compare the nature of material culture between sites.[3] In the eastern South Island, especially south

[3] Stratigraphy is another source of potential evidence, but there is very little accumulation of sediment or soil formation on 'inland focus' sites, and horizontal displacement of successive occupation has also been common.

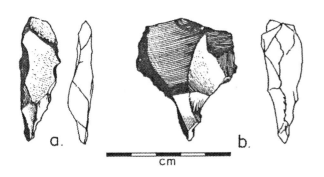

Fig. 11.3 Silcrete drill point (a) and awl (b) from Hawksburn.

of Banks Peninsula, moa-hunting sites can be broadly divided into two groups: those in the interior and along the coast of the Canterbury Plains which exhibit the characteristics of an 'interior focus' (Anderson 1982b), and those elsewhere on the coast which exhibit a 'coastal focus'. In the former group are sites in which moa-hunting was by far the most important subsistence activity represented; in the latter, the sites as a whole also contain substantial evidence of additional activities such as sealing, fishing, shellfishing and the exploitation of small birds. It could simply be asserted, of course, that settlements founded on such resource diversity are less likely to have been transiently occupied than those devoted to a single resource, but it is also possible, to some degree, to test that argument by comparing the relative diversity of domestic equipment. Sites occupied for longer periods at a time ought to contain a wider range of artefacts associated with habitations, craft work, clothing and ornamentation.

Evidence of dwellings provides less assistance in this matter than might have been expected. It is true that no large groups of stone-kerbed hearths and very few associated postholes have been recorded from sites of the interior focus, and that such evidence is more abundant in coastal focus sites, notably Shag Mouth; but many large sites of the latter group have also failed to reveal much clear evidence of dwellings (e.g. Pleasant River, Pounawea, Papatowai). It also remains an open question whether the informal style of dwelling inferred in the case of some interior focus sites (Dart Bridge, Glenaray, Hawksburn, Waitaki) was restricted to these, or could also have been the form represented at Shag Mouth as well (Anderson 1986).

There is very little evidence of most other domestic artefact types in interior focus sites. Teviotdale (1939:177) commented that at Waitaki

Mouth there is a 'scarcity of adze-heads, drill-points, polishers, fish-hooks . . . and the various other tools obtained from permanent village sites'. We might hardly expect many fish hooks, of course, but bone-working in general was evidently very uncommon. There were several sawn tibiotarsi at Coal Creek (Anderson and Ritchie 1984), and a few worked pieces of moa bone at Hawksburn (Lockerbie n. d.; Anderson 1979b) and Rakaia Mouth (Trotter 1972a), but drill points (abundant at such sites as Shag Mouth, over 400

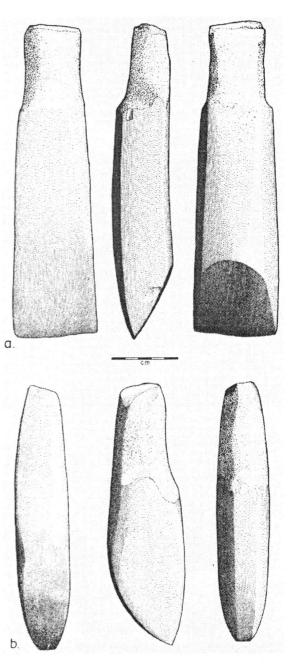

Fig. 11.4 Typical Archaic adzes of types 1A (a: basalt, Waitaki Mouth) and 4A (b: nephrite, Nevis Valley).

examples recorded by Teviotdale 1932a) and attrition saws are very rare: at Hawksburn eight drill points, one file and three polishers, and none at Owen's Ferry or Coal Creek. No drill points were recorded from Rakaia Mouth by Trotter (1972a), only one at Wakanui (Hodgkinson 1981) and very few at Waitaki Mouth (Teviotdale 1932a). Files and stone awls (two at Hawksburn) are similarly rare compared with collections from coastal focus sites (Fig. 11.3).

Adzes are less common on interior focus sites, judged at least by the relative size of sites. There were only seven at Hawksburn, and none from Coal Creek, Owen's Ferry and Minzionburn. Use of adzes, though, seems to have been common, since flakes from at least 50 different adzes were found at Hawksburn. The implication would seem to be that adzes were more often taken away from interior focus sites, or deposited on them in caches (especially Waitaki Mouth), than simply discarded or lost in domestic debris as seems to have occurred at many coastal focus sites (Fig. 11.4).

Bone artefacts used for domestic functions are also scarce. The moa-bone 'chisel', a strip of leg bone filed to a broad point or bevelled (both varieties are provisionally included) and which may have functioned as a skin burnisher, as Allo (1970) suggested, is a fairly rare form in general, except at Houhora (14 examples) and Kaupokonui (15 examples) (Fig. 11.5), but five examples were recovered at Shag Mouth and at least three at Papatowai (Otago Museum Collection). There was one at Paremata (Davidson 1978) and possibly another at Whakamoenga (Leahy 1976). In South Island interior focus sites, the only examples are

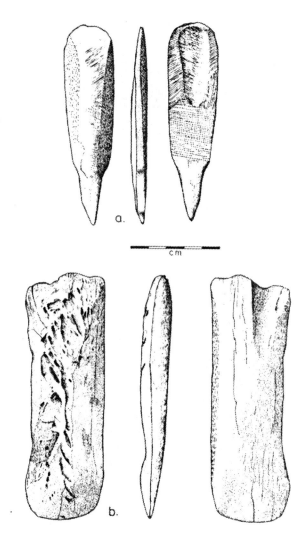

FIG. 11.6 Moa-bone chisels or similar artefacts from Papatowai (a) and Otago, unprovenanced (b).

one from Waitaki Mouth (Otago Museum Collection) and one from Hawksburn (Fig. 11.6).

Bone awls, probably used in working skins for clothing, are virtually non-existent in interior focus sites (one at Hawksburn), and no needles have been reported. The former is common in coastal focus sites (Fig. 11.7), the latter less so (Skinner 1924a; Teviotdale 1932a). Except for possible toggles at Rakaia Mouth (Trotter 1972a), neither these nor cloak-pins have been found in interior focus sites. Similarly neither marine nor freshwater mussel shells, or any other such implements which had possibly been used to dress flax for fibre, occur in more than a handful of interior focus sites, and then only in small numbers.

Of the various Archaic ornamental forms (Golson 1959a; Duff 1977), only reels occur reasonably often in interior focus sites (Rakaia Mouth, Waitaki Mouth, Junction Point, Gooseneck Bend,

FIG. 11.5 Moa-bone chisels from Kaupokonui. (By courtesy of Richard Cassels and Taranaki Museum.)

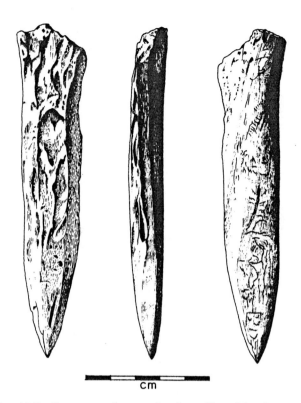

FIG. 11.7   Large moa-bone point from Shag Mouth.

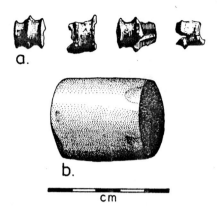

FIG. 11.8   Broken reels of seal ivory from Hawksburn (a), and unfinished stone reel (b) from Waitangi.

Waitangi, Gray's Hills and Hawksburn). Most of these sites are, however, restricted to the lower Waitaki Valley. Several pendants have also been recorded in the same area (Waitaki Mouth, Junction Point, Ahuriri, Skinner 1974; Ambrose 1970). The representation of ornaments on interior and coastal focus moa-hunting sites recorded in Anderson (1982b) is: reels 21 per cent and 56 per cent of sites respectively, and pendants 11 per cent and 52 per cent of sites, respectively (Fig. 11.8). No drilled moa eggs, nor any evidence of burials (except possibly at Rakaia Mouth, Chapter 9), have been recorded at any interior focus sites.

If this evidence, taken overall, is not as comprehensive as might be wished, it nonetheless seems to point to a significant difference in the quality of occupation between interior and coastal focus sites. The former do not seem to have been occupied for long periods at a time, and large sites were probably repeatedly occupied camps, as Teviotdale (1932a, 1939) and others have suggested.

Organisation of hunting

Moa-hunting was very probably an individual or small group activity in which snares, dogs and wooden spears were used (cf. cassowary hunting in New Guinea, Diamond 1984). Any single hunting episode probably resulted in a small mixed bag of species (Kooyman 1984b, n. d.). There is, at this time, no evidence of mass-kills having occurred. Hunting may have been more certain and productive during the incubating season, but there is insufficient evidence to rule out hunting throughout the year.

Moa-hunting seems to have been non-selective amongst species within the major habitats but to have concentrated on the 'Euryapteryx assemblage'. The distribution of hunting sites in areas where moas of this assemblage were most abundant in the eastern South Island, may be related to several broad patterns of strategic organisation. Most sites of the 'interior focus' (specialised moa-hunting sites) (Anderson 1982b) were probably occupied repeatedly for short periods by people whose main settlements were located at places where resources other than moas were at least as important. But when they were hunting moas, they seem to have adopted different strategies according to the practicability of river transport within each catchment for the recovery of carcasses to major butchery sites.

12

Processing Technology

Stone tools which seem to have been used in processing moa carcasses can be divided into four groups: flakes and blades, both struck from quarried cores; boulder spalls known as 'teshoa'; and polished stone knives known as 'ulu'. The most widespread and abundant are the first two, discussed below.

As for teshoa, the class is poorly defined and its intended functions unclear. Haast (1875c) gave the name (a Shoshone Indian word for similar implements) to subcircular spalls struck from the ends of water-rolled greywacke cobbles and boulders. These flake tools, sometimes retouched, were common at Rakaia Mouth, and Haast thought them skin scrapers. More recent examination of the Rakaia collection by Trotter (1972a) revealed light bilateral smoothing along the working edge indicative of cutting soft materials, possibly meat or even wood. Holdaway (1981) described very similar use-damage on the majority of 75 teshoa from Normanby which he examined, and suggested that they had been used as attrition saws on bone or stone. This matter needs further research in order to distinguish adequately between teshoa as knives and exactly the same kind of boulder spalls used, as many clearly had been, to saw bone, nephrite and other materials. Teshoa were largely confined to the coast of Canterbury where greywacke boulders are very abundant and other sources of good flaking stone rather distant (Figs. 12.1 and 12.2).

'Ulu' is an Inuit name given by Skinner (1974) to the thin, flat, polished stone knives, often of rectilinear or half-moon shape, which have been recorded from 70 localities in the South Island (Figs. 12.1 and 12.3). The distribution of ulus does not seem to have much to do with the distribution of slate sources as Duff (1977:195) argued, since it is now clear that they were commonly made in other types of stone, notably argillites and nephrite. Skinner (1974:115) suggested ulus were skin-cleaning implements, and Buckley's (1978) examination of edge-polishes adds weight to that proposition by showing that cutting and scraping skins and meat were the most probable functions. Ulus possibly served other, similar purposes, as suggested by a Maori remark to Haast about ulus as fish knives (Duff 1977:195) and the discovery of several ulus embedded in fish scales at a Catlins site (Lockerbie 1940:405), but the overall distribution of ulus closely follows that of moa-hunting sites (Fig. 12.1), and they are also particularly abundant in important moa-hunting sites (e.g. 27 ulus at Waitaki Mouth, 26 at Shag Mouth, 7 at Hawksburn, 5 at Pareora etc., Otago Museum registers).

Early attempts to group flaked stone tools into functional classes (Skinner and Teviotdale 1927; Knapp 1928, 1941; McCully 1941, 1948) failed because of a general lack of repeated forms and a scarcity of intentional retouch (Shawcross 1964: 22). Most Maori flake tools are primary flakes which appear to have been selected simply for the utility of their existing edges and only a few flake or core types can be readily recognised. Other than teshoa there are drill points, which probably constitute the most-common single class; stone awls or rimers of a concave-triangular plan shape; some possible burins and disc cores (Shawcross 1964); stemmed flakes or *mataa* (Jones 1981); hafted blades, some of which might have been spear points; and edge-retouched blades. All of these can occur in Archaic sites, irrespective of whether moa

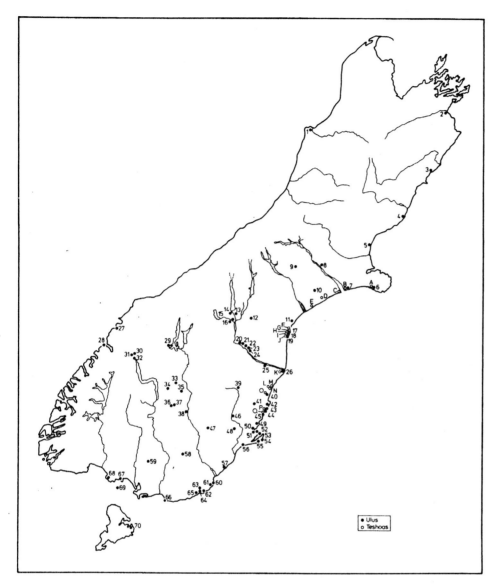

FIG. 12.1   Distribution of ulus and teshoa.

Data from site references in text plus Skinner (1974), Buckley (1978), Teviotdale (n. d.), Allingham (pers. comm.) and artefact register, Otago Museum. Ulu: 1. Buller Mouth 2. Wairau Bar 3. Rakautara Cave 4. Hurunui Mouth 5. Ashley Mouth 6. Tumbledown Bay 7. Rakaia Mouth 8. Te Pirita 9. Upper Hinds 10. Ashburton 11. Seadown 12. Grays Hills 13. Shelton Downs 14. Pukaki River 15. Ohau River I 16. Ohau River II 17. Normanby I 18. Normanby II 19. Pareora 20. Rugged Ridge 21. Akatarewa 22. Woolshed Flat 23. Stony Stream 24. Waitangi 25. Georgetown 26. Waitaki Mouth 27. Martin's Bay 28. Anita Bay 29. Matukituki 30. Camp Hill 31. Dart Bridge 32. Glenorchy 33. Upper Carrick 34. Schoolhouse Creek 35. Hawksburn 36. Glenaray 37. Upper Waikaia 38. Coal Creek 39. Kokonga 40. Waianakarua Bluff 41. Upper Shag 42. Waimataitai 43. Shag Point 44. Shag Mouth 45. Pleasant River 46. Middlemarch 47. Lammerlaws 48. Deep Stream 49. Puketeraki 50. Warrington 51. Doctor's Point 52. Long Beach 53. Kaikai's Beach 54. Little Papanui 55. Hooper's Inlet 56. Kaikorai Mouth 57. Tokomairiro Mouth 58. Waipahi 59. Hedgehope 60. Owaka 61. Pounawea 62. Jack's Island 63. MacLennan's 64. Papatowai 65. King's Rock 66. Waipapa 67. Riverton 68. Pahia 69. Centre Island 70. Stewart Island. Teshoa: A. Tumbledown Bay B. Rakaia North C. Rakaia South D. Wakanui E. Hinds F. Dashing Rocks G. Patiti Point H. Normanby I I. Normanby II J. Pareroa K. Waitaki Mouth L. Upper Totara M. Tai Rua N. Waianakarua O. Waianakarua Bluff P. Shag Mouth Q. Bobby's Head.

FIG. 12.2 Teshoa from south Canterbury, unprovenanced (a), (b) and attrition saw (c) from Waitaki Mouth.

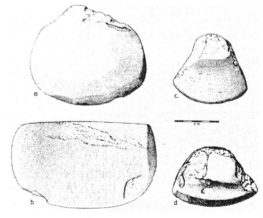

FIG. 12.3 Ulus: in red argillite (a) from Lammerlaws; in slate (b) and (c) from Pareora and unprovenanced; and in nephrite (d) from Coal Creek.

remains are present, but the latter two are especially associated with moa-butchery sites and are discussed in this chapter.

Before considering them, however, it is necessary to look briefly at two additional matters. These are the main sources of raw material, since there is a strong correlation between the availability of some and the distribution of blades, and also the wider flaked stone industry, within which recognisable types form only a small minority of pieces.

Raw materials

Flake tools occur, broadly, in three main raw materials: obsidian, cherts and silcrete (Table 12.1). Obsidian is available only in the northeast North Island. Cherts, widely defined by Moore (1977) to include both sub-aerial volcanic materials called siliceous sinter by Best and Merchant (1976) and also limestone flint, were found mainly along the eastern side of both islands from Northland to north Canterbury. In North Island moa-hunting sites, volcanically altered cherts are predominant (Moore 1977; Cassels n. d.). In the South Island, flint from the Amuri limestone is particularly common at Wairau Bar and in Kaikoura moa-hunting sites (e.g. Avoca). Other sources of cherts and chert-like rocks of some importance in the eastern South Island include red jasper, as pebbles, in south Canterbury rivers; *palla* (Haast 1872a:85) from Gawler Downs, a metasomatised tuff which was commonly used to make flake tools and adzes in south Canterbury Archaic sites (Orchiston

TABLE 12.1   Occurrence of lithic raw materials in moa-hunting sites (per cent)

Site	1	2	3	4	5	6	Reference
Tokoroa					100		Law 1973
Whakamoenga					100		Leahy 1976
Kaupokonui	23		11		66		Cassels n. d.
Avoca Point			98		2		Trotter 1980
Rakaia Mouth	47	2	29	x	5	17	Trotter 1972a
Waitaki Mouth	94	3	x	x	x	2	Knight 1965
Tai Rua	32	3		49	2	14	Trotter 1979b
Pleasant River	80				3	17	Knight 1965
Owen's Ferry	83	15				2	Anderson n. d. d
Hawksburn	26	72	x	x	x	2	Anderson n. d. d
Coal Creek	2	96				2	Anderson n. d. d
Pounawea	30	66	x	x	1	1	Hamel 1980

Note: 1 silcrete, 2 porcellanite, 3 chert, 4 chalcedony, 5 obsidian, 6 other.

1976); and various other rocks including one known, confusingly, as 'porcellanite' (see below) from Moeraki. Chalcedony, particularly from Moeraki sources, was another locally common flake material, found particularly in the Tai Rua site (Trotter 1979b). Argillite, primarily used for adzes, was also adopted for flake implements in the principal source areas: Nelson–Marlborough and Foveaux Strait.

The main materials for flake tools in moa-hunting sites were, undoubtedly, silcrete and porcellanite, especially the former. Silcrete ('quartzite', 'orthoquartzite') formed as a hard (Mohr 6.5–7.0) duricrust of siliceously cemented quartz sands and gravels of freshwater origin. Porcellanite ('jasperoid'), in the present sense (i.e. excluding the Moeraki material), refers to mudstones baked by contact with naturally burning lignite seams to a hard (Mohr 6.5–7.0) subvitreous material which, like silcrete, fractures conchoidally. A wide range of variation in colour and other qualities can occur in a single quarry of either material and neither discernable differences in hand-specimen nor trace-element spectra have proved useful as means of sourcing (Brown 1978; Mason pers. comm.).

Silcrete and porcellanite are confined to the southern South Island and occur in some 300 exposures of which only a few have been searched for quarry sites. Reporting by landowners and limited field sampling have, however, turned up 20 silcrete and 15 porcellanite quarries. Most of these are quite small (300–2000 m²), but the Bremner porcellanite quarry extends over approximately 1.5 ha, the Rough Block silcrete quarry over 2 ha and the Oturehua silcrete quarry is scattered discontinuously over an area of 20 ha (Fig. 12.4).

The extent of Oturehua, and its early radiocarbon dates (897 ± 24 bp, 927 ± 82 bp) are, perhaps, the result of its location on the northern tip of Rough Ridge, where the main routeways into the Clutha watershed from east (Shag Valley), southeast (Taieri Valley) and northeast (Dansey's Pass) converge.[1] The Bremner porcellanite quarry lies quite close by, on the southern flanks of the Hawkdun Range. In both cases, and perhaps more generally, the size of the quarries may reflect frequency of repeated use.

Quarrying of subsurface material was generally preferred to the working of boulders. The quarry

[1] The early dates have been accepted on the basis that the samples were from 'twig' sized pieces of wood charcoal. B. F. Leach (pers. comm.) is not, now, certain that this was the case.

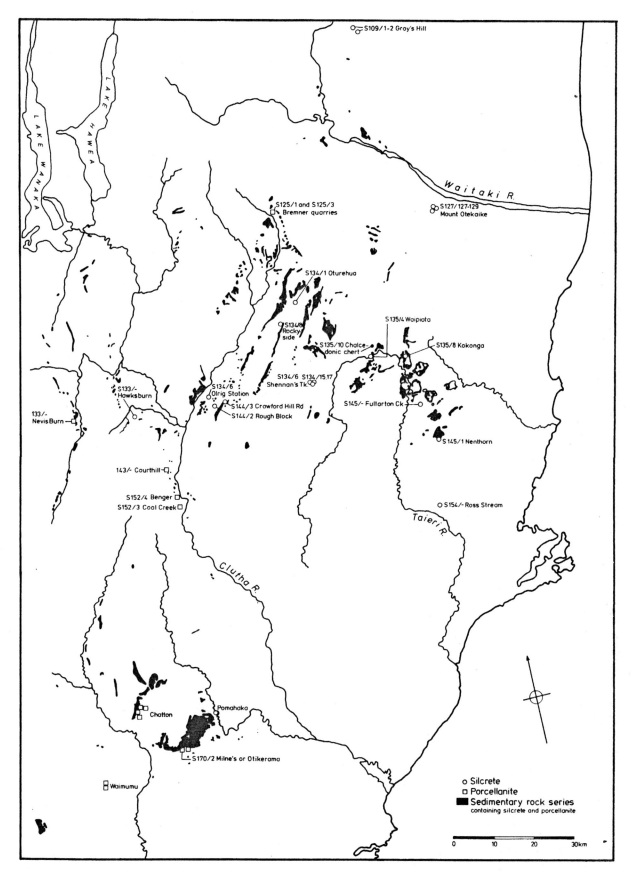

FIG. 12.4   Lithic series containing porcellanite and silcrete, and locations of prehistoric quarries.

pits are shallow, mostly only 0.25 m deep at Oturehua, although they are up to 2 m deep at Gray's Hills (Irvine 1943), but their existence indicates that quality rock was in relatively short supply despite an abundance of exposures.

Flaked stone tools

Large moa-hunting sites contain a remarkable abundance of flaked stone. At Hawksburn, the mean density of 153 stone flakes per m^2 in the excavations is more comparable with that in a stone-working floor at the Oturehua quarry, 233 per m^2, than with the figures from smaller moa-hunting sites or other site types. The implication, it seems, is that repeated hunting trips or concentrated processing of moa carcasses required an unusually large number of flaked stone implements.[2] What functions these performed is a question which has only been broadly investigated in the case of moa-hunting sites in Central Otago.

Kooyman (1985) argued that since carcass processing at a kill site has to be accomplished with those few tools a hunter has carried, he is likely to use them beyond the point at which they would have been discarded on an established butchery site (cf. Walker 1978; Tainter 1979). The incidence of broken and retouched tools, and those with severed use or retouch scars is, therefore, likely to be relatively high. But at Hawksburn, Coal Creek and Minzion Burn the incidence of these was uniformly low (< 15 per cent). Only at Owen's Ferry, where it was about 30 per cent, was there the character of a hunting rather than butchery camp.

Kooyman (1985) then carried out more than 100 use-wear experiments with newly knapped porcellanite and silcrete flakes. The silcrete experiments produced few useful results. Use-polishes formed, but slowly, and micro-flaking was both uncommon and unpatterned in relation to use on different materials. Porcellanite, however, rapidly acquired micro-flaking and use-polish in almost all the experiments. From the point of view of moa butchery, though, cutting meat (i.e. cutting flesh, not general butchery) with porcellanite produced virtually no observable damage, only faint 'nibbling' along the edge (cf. Bain 1979).

The experimental results were applied to the Owen's Ferry porcellanite assemblage, a 10 per

cent random sample from Minzion Burn and smaller samples from areas of apparently different function at Coal Creek and Hawksburn. They indicated that the main function of porcellanite tools, especially in the larger sites, was woodworking (Table 12.2). However it must be pointed out that the selection procedure favoured pieces apparently used against those apparently unused, in the ratio 3:1. The proportion of meat processing is, thus, probably underrepresented.

Kooyman (1985:138–40) discerned quite distinctive use-polishes on his experimental pieces of porcellanite but no use-polish on the archaeological pieces (although there was some soil-polish). The reason soon became apparent: alkalinity destroys the use-polish. He found that even a weak solution of NaOH not only removed the polishes from porcellanite but, in time, actually turned the stone back to mud. A total of 23 large silcrete pieces were examined for use-polish, but the incidence was very low.

Kooyman's experimental results and analytical methods were subsequently used to take a closer look at possible intrasite variation in the functions of the porcellanite tools at Hawksburn. From each of four excavation areas: A (stone-working area), C (midden), L and M (butchery areas), 24 tools were randomly selected in the apparently used : apparently unused ratio 2:1. These consisted of both flake and blade fragments. Retouch was uncommon on pieces from areas C (12 per cent) and L (16 per cent), but more significant in areas A (24 per cent) and M (38 per cent). The scar characteristics dominant on each used edge (Table 12.2) describe four quite different assemblages. In A, there are almost exclusively cutting tools of two kinds – some with comparatively low edge angles and scar characteristics indicative of use on fairly soft materials, but a majority with edge angles greater than 50° and scar characteristics associated with woodworking. In C, cutting tools are largely dominant, as are the characteristics associated with working soft or fibrous materials. In L, there is a significant component of scraping wood or some other quite resistant material, while in M, scraping wood seems predominant, particularly in light of the edge angles distribution.

These summary descriptions do not, on the face of it, fit entirely with other archaeological evidence from Hawksburn. That A was a fibre and woodworking area and C a repository of discarded tools associated with butchery are acceptable propositions, but the proportion of probable woodworking indicated in L and M is difficult to explain

---

[2] Some comparative figures: 1.3 flakes per m^2 at Owen's Ferry; 2.7 per m^2 at Whakamoenga; 15 per m^2 at Kaupokonui; 29 per m^2 at Coal Creek.

TABLE 12.2   Characteristics of use-damaged porcellanite implements from moa-hunting sites in Central Otago

Kooyman (1985) sample	Minzion Burn	Coal Creek	Hawksburn	Owen's Ferry
No. used edges	64	48	116	144
Use-wear – bone per cent	2	0	2	3
– not bone per cent	91	83	92	79
– not classifiable per cent	7	17	6	17
Non-bone Use-wear				
Wood per cent	14	58	62	35
Meat per cent	12	5	2	9
Hide per cent	0	0	2	3
Vegetable per cent	0	0	0	1
Non-specific per cent	74	37	36	52

| | Excavation Area | | | |
Hawksburn stratified sample	A	C	L	M
No. used edges	41	42	40	43
% bifacial damage	97	95	45	64
% medium and small scars	99	93	90	95
% medium and poor definition	98	96	90	25
% step termination	59	2	28	96
% feather termination	40	98	71	4
% straight-convex plan shape	65	48	50	56
% edge angles > 30°	100	86	91	90
% edge angles > 50°	60	58	54	72
% edge angles > 70°	24	34	28	38

– these were clearly butchery and cooking areas. It is possible that woodworking was an activity favoured by people sitting around the ovens, or that butchery tools struck bone more frequently than is apparent in the faunal remains. Inadvertent scraping or glancing blows softened by initial penetration through flesh might produce an effect similar to woodworking. Alternatively, damage caused by the severing of tough connective tissue or calcified sinews might have been similar to that associated with wood or bone (Fig. 12.5).

The southern blade industry

If blades form only a small subsample of the flaked stone assemblage in moa-hunting sites as a whole they are, nonetheless, the most characteristic tool type. Blades seem to have been the main product intended at silcrete quarries. They were also produced at porcellanite quarries but, judging by field observation (Mason pers. comm.; Brown pers. comm.), not in anything like the same numbers. Porcellanite is more brittle than silcrete and is frequently flawed by numerous small cleavage planes and vesicles. As a result, porcellanite blades are

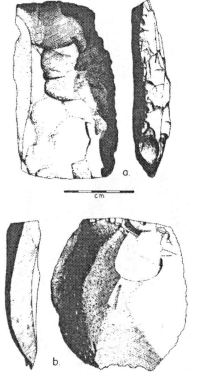

FIG. 12.5   Large silcrete flake implements from Hawksburn: (a) retouched, (b) unretouched.

both less common and smaller than those of silcrete (Fig. 12.6).

It seems strange that neither obsidian nor chert, both commonly employed for blade-making elsewhere in the world, were almost never so used in New Zealand. It cannot have been caused by a lack of models since silcrete blades were taken, if uncommonly, to sites as far north as Palliser Bay (Leach and Leach 1979) and Wairau Bar (Wilkes 1964), and silcrete cobbles to Kaupokonui (Cassels n. d.) – sites or areas well within the regions where good limestone flint was abundant and obsidian quite readily available. It might have to do, however, with the transmission or adoption of technological expertise, a matter worth briefly exploring here.

The antecedents of the New Zealand industry are unclear but the two preferred hypotheses are that it reflects an historical connection with another Oceanic blade-making culture, for instance in the Admiralty and Bougainville Islands (Skinner 1924a:18; B. F. Leach 1969:134) or that it developed soon after the time of the first settlement in New Zealand and out of pre-existing adze-working technology (H. M. Leach 1984). It would be premature to rule out the former hypothesis since discoveries of blades elsewhere in Polynesia add to the plausibility of an historical proposition, but there is also a good case for adaptation.

At both the Riverton argillite adze quarry and the Oturehua silcrete blade quarry the early stages of production were much the same: decortication, preparation of arrises, removal of corner blades and the reduction of overhanging edges on the core. The Riverton corner-blades had the shape (including a sinuous bulbar surface rising at the vertex to form the adze-bevel) desired for manufacturing adzes of triangular cross-section. Helen Leach (1984:117) argues that such adze-making techniques, already established in the technical repertoire of the Polynesian artisan, included all that was needed to quickly develop a separate blade industry if the need arose (see also Simmons 1967). This argument may be further illustrated by Knight's (1965) discovery of basalt blades, all apparently corner-blades but retouched as knives, at Warrington site 1, whereas only silcrete blades occurred in site 2, an apparently younger deposit nearby.

The blade-making techniques were relatively simple. At Oturehua, blades comprised 28 per cent of a total sample from one excavation area. They were struck by direct hard-hammer percussion, and often bipolar technique, from prepared cores. Otherwise the techniques were opportunistic rather than prescriptive; arris-straightening and platform preparation were generally avoided. The intended result of the production, detailed by H. Leach (1984:110), was primarily blades rather than cores, and it is assumed that 'packets' of blades and some cores were then transported to the moa-butchery sites (Fig. 12.7). In some cases these were not far away. Coal Creek moa butchery was only a kilometre from a porcellanite quarry, and there were reports of extensive scatters of ovenstones on the flat below Oturehua. Nevertheless the major butchery sites are often 30–50 km from the nearest-known quarries. In some cases there are a few silcrete boulders in the vicinity of the butchery sites, such as at Waikaia and Hawksburn, and in both cases these had been crudely worked in an attempt to obtain suitable material. It seems that

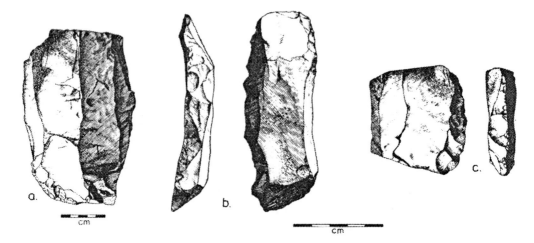

FIG. 12.6   Porcellanite core from Clyde (a); and, from Hawksburn, a retouched blade (b) and retouched medial section (c) of a blade (both porcellanite).

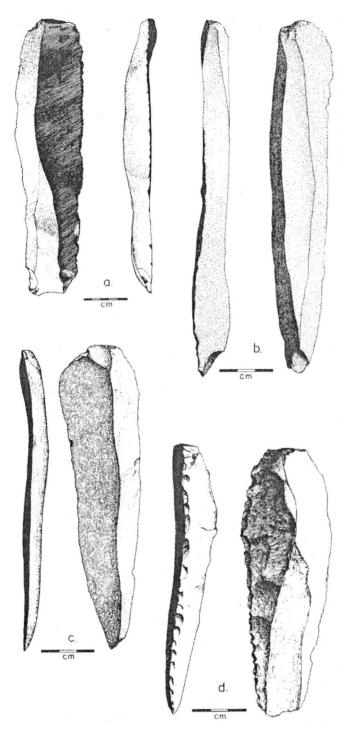

Fig. 12.7 Large silcrete blades from Berwick (a), Shag Mouth (b), (c), and Hawksburn (d).

a relative scarcity of material suitable for blades was generally accentuated by transport costs to the consumption sites. In order to elucidate what happened to blades at the latter localities I shall concentrate on the one intensively studied collection from Hawksburn moa butchery.

Used blades

Preference for silcrete in blade manufacture, evident at the quarries, is also apparent at Hawksburn. Silcrete blades outnumber those of porcellanite by 3:2 and, if the relative abundance of these materials in the site is taken as a basis for comparison, then silcrete blades are nearly three times as common as would be expected. This may not, however, reflect a manufacturing bias at Hawksburn so much as preferential importation of ready-made silcrete blades and thus a proportionately lighter weight of silcrete debitage. One piece of evidence which might support that view is the 1:8 ratio of silcrete to porcellanite cores.

A high proportion of the blades have been snapped, about 80 per cent (Table 12.3). This is typical of New Zealand blade assemblages in non-quarry sites (the figure is 90 per cent at Waitaki Mouth, Vincent 1980), and it has led to some speculation that deliberate breakage occurred. Shawcross (1964:21) argued that one of the main purposes of the silcrete blades at Waitaki Mouth 'was to provide blanks which·were snapped into sections, approximately as long as they are broad, then further altered by secondary retouching' (see also Anderson 1979b).

At Hawksburn, however, there is no regularity in the size or shape of the snapped blade sections. Some are merely transverse (latitudinal) slivers, others the whole blade minus what can only have been a very small piece at top or bottom, or both. The lack of any discernable pattern in the breakage suggests that, whether or not it was deliberate, it was not, at least, a systematically patterned technique. It seems unlikely, therefore, that Carty (1981:82) was on the right track in proposing that medial sections, from which inconveniently shaped proximal areas and curved distal tips had been snapped, were being created for side-hafted mounting in composite tools. Furthermore there is no other evidence of the side-hafting of blade sections such as notching, nor of a microblade industry.

It seems more likely that blade snapping was accidental. Patterson (1979:4) has shown that attempts to reduce the bulb of percussion frequently result in the blade snapping at a weaker point somewhere else. Bulb reduction, however, is rarely seen on the Hawksburn blades (c. 2 per cent of silcrete blades). Snapping as the result of bending forces during use is altogether more likely.

It has usually been assumed that the primary purpose of the blades was butchery of moas. Lockerbie (1959:90) argued that large flake knives

TABLE 12.3   Characteristics of blades from Hawksburn

Total sample	All blades					Used edges			
Material	Total No.	% Whole	% Prox.	% Med.	% Dist.	Total No.	% Unif. Dorsal	% Unif. Ventral	% Bifacial
Silcrete	426	17	35	30	18	169	59	14	27
Porcellanite	286	24	34	23	19	172	75	12	12
Total or Mean	712	20	35	27	18	341	67	13	19

Sample of whole blades

Size and retouch	Silcrete	Porcellanite
No. of blades in sample	$n = 45$	$n = 31$
Mean length : breadth (mm)	100:38	83:33
No. blades and no. edges retouched	17 (19)	8 (8)
No. shallow dorsal edges retouched	11	6
No. shallow ventral edges retouched	6	1
No. steep dorsal edges retouched	1	0
No. edges bifacially retouched	1	1
Use-damage – unretouched edges	$n = 17$	$n = 20$
Unifacial dorsal	7	7
Unifacial ventral	1	0
Bifacial (serial)	3	2
Bifacial damage	6	11
Nibbling	4	8
Crescent breaks	2	2
Small-medium scalar scars	5	7
Small step terminations/crushing	6	3

were found wherever there was evidence of active moa-hunting and that they became scarce as moa-hunting declined. Knight (1965) also observed that within large sites blades were not found in wood-working areas, as defined by the distribution of adzes. Both arguments led to the same conclusion: large blades were mainly, if not entirely, butchery implements, and had taken no significant role in woodworking.

In considering the function of the Hawksburn blades, the first point to make in the light of these views is that the evidence is less clear on the matter of spatial distribution than might have been pre-dicted. On the one hand, it can be argued that most of the blades were recovered from the oven and butchery areas (48 per cent of silcrete, 65 per cent of porcellanite blades) and the midden (29 per cent of silcrete blades, 21 per cent of porcellanite blades). On the other hand, if the question is whether blades were more common in some areas than others, relative to the frequency of other tools and debitage of the same materials, the results are much less significant. Scaled by abundance, blades comprise only 4 per cent of silcrete pieces in the butchery-oven area, 9 per cent on the midden and

3 per cent elsewhere. The figures for porcellanite blades are 1 per cent, 2 per cent and 1 per cent respectively. It could be concluded that silcrete and porcellanite tools, in general, were preferred for butchery, but not necessarily blades.

Turning to edge angles, it is apparent in Fig. 12.8 that at both Hawksburn and Waitaki Mouth only the edge angles of unretouched silcrete blades, in general, fall into the usual range occupied by stone butchery knives, that is, 26°–35° (e.g. Tainter 1979; Ferguson 1980). The distribu-tion of retouched edges at Hawksburn peaks at 55°, and at Waitaki Mouth at 58° (with 68 per cent of edges lying in the area above 55°). In both cases retouching has increased mean edge angles by 20°. Such results broadly imply non-cutting functions, and from the secondary peak in the Waitaki edge angles at 75° it seems rather likely that some such functions were involved. Nevertheless there is also evidence on the side of butchery at high edge angles. Jensen's (1986) analysis of use-polishes on unretouched blades indicated that it was those with edge angles of 40°–55°, that is to say, at the high end of the range for cutting tools in general (20°–55°), which had been used for butchery. A case of

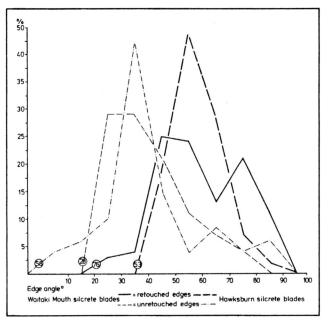

FIG. 12.8   Proportional distribution of edge angles on retouched and unretouched silcrete blades from Waitaki
Mouth and Hawksburn. Circled numbers are edges
measured.

practical support for the same conclusion comes
from Hayden's (1979:122) description of several
kangaroo butchering incidents in which stone tools
were used. These included large blocks of stone
with right-angled edges, in which the weight as
much as the edge snapped ribs and separated vertebrae; and the tools were retouched repeatedly
during the process. Hayden's (1979:123) cross-
sectional drawings of the tools indicate that the
final cutting-edge angles were between 60° and 75°.

The point to draw from these, I suggest, is that
butchery as a whole process – not simply skinning,
or slicing up muscular masses – was comparatively
heavy work in the case of large terrestrial animals.
It is quite likely that the heavy bipedal moas had
very tough connective tissues on the legs and possibly calcified tendons, as occur in large rails like
the pukeko (*Porphyrio melanotus*), and that they
presented a tough and awkward butchery proposition, especially in comparison with seals, for
example. Heavy tools with robust edges which
could be variously used to slice, rip, chop and
smash as necessity arose were probably the best all-
round implements, as some of Walker's (1978)
experiments in butchering marine and terrestrial
mammals suggest. These various tasks, as well as
working large blades into difficult joints, might
account for the high rate of breakage.

Finding evidence on the blades to show that butchery was indeed their primary function has, however, proven very difficult. The non-survival of
use-polish on porcellanite tools, and its scarcity on
silcrete (Kooyman 1985), largely confines analysis
to the problematical field of micro-flaking. Here
the main difficulties lie in distinguishing damage
caused by actual use from that which arose by tool
construction, retouching, hafting, prehension, soil
movement, excavation or handling. Retouching,
in particular, is a major problem. Within the
retouch scars on porcellanite and silcrete tools
from Hawksburn there is a common pattern of
small scalar and stepped scars and crushing. This
looks like use-damage, but it is almost certainly a
by-product of hard-hammer percussion as Keeley
(1980:26–7) has shown. It is, therefore, nearly
impossible to distinguish true use-damage on the
retouched blades except for occasional crushing
and rounding on the points between retouch scars.

Most unretouched whole blades exhibit some
form of micro-flaking (Table 12.3). It is, mostly
bifacial and includes 'nibbling', crescent breaks,
which vary in size from 2–10 mm across, and other
forms of damage (below) which are distributed
serially from one side of an edge to another. Bifacial damage, including the alternating pattern, is
generally characteristic of a cutting action (Odell
and Odell-Vereecken 1980:98), but so, too, may be
a concentration of damage on the dorsal surface,
the next most common site, especially on butchery
tools (Keeley 1980:54). As to the type of damage,
clusters of small scalar scars with feather terminations, as in the Hawksburn examples, are typical of
use on soft materials including meat and skin but
can also be caused by prehension (Odell and Odell-
Vereecken 1980:101, 107). Small step-terminated
scars and crushing which occur on silcrete blades
(Table 12.3), together with rounding of the projecting points, also suggests butchery but with
more frequent bone contact (Tainter 1979:465).
There is very little evidence of large (non-retouch)
well-defined scalar and stepped flake-scars such as
characterise bone-working (Keeley 1980:44–5). It
is difficult to rule out woodworking, however,
since small scalar scarring and crescent breaks are
typical of its use-damage effect (Keely 1980:38).
In the absence of more conclusive experimental
results than those which Kooyman (1985) could
obtain, and with such small archaeological
samples, it would be unwise to conclude that use-
damage patterns firmly indicate butchery, although they do not rule it out.

Retouched blades

Blades with retouched edges form an important and poorly understood group which deserves further consideration. Two basic characteristics of retouching are that it is positively correlated with blade size and that it seems, generally, to have preceded blade shaping. Thus, in a sample of 76 whole blades which I examined, all of them more than 40 mm in maximum length, retouching did not occur on blades less than 80 mm long. About half of blades 80–120 mm long were retouched and about two-thirds of those over 120 mm, all of which were silcrete (Fig. 12.9). Further, almost all broken blades in which the breadth exceeded 50 mm exhibited retouch. Vincent's (1980) Waitaki Mouth sample, all pieces from large silcrete blades, had a retouch incidence of 86 per cent.

In relation to snapping, 84 per cent of the retouched edges of silcrete blades at Hawksburn disclosed severed retouch scars, together with 73 per cent of comparable porcellanite edges. Knight (1965:233) implied that snapping generally occurred after retouching, while Vincent (1980) found both pre- and post-retouch snapping at Waitaki Mouth as well as one blade, in two pieces, which exhibited retouch before and after snapping. Except in such circumstances it can be difficult to unequivocally distinguish post-snapping retouch, but the main point is clear enough; retouching was commonly employed on blades before they were snapped.

Retouching might have had any one of a number of objectives: backing, edge rejuvenation, alteration of plan shape, etc.[3] It is not easy to decide between these, but some arguments can be advanced. Since the site of the retouch is predominantly the shallow edge on blades of asymmetrical cross-section, and since steep edges seldom disclose any signs of use on whole blades, backing can be ruled out.[4] Because most blades are asymmetrical in cross-section there is a steep edge which is naturally backed to some extent in any case. There has been no marked alteration of the plan shape of edges by retouch. Most edges are straight or slightly convex as on the blank blade and instances of created concavities are very rare in the blade collection as a whole.

[3] A more stable retouched edge probably resulted in fewer stone chips in the meat; a major consideration given the high mortality from dental problems.

[4] The steep edges of some medial sections of porcellanite blades have been used as scrapers.

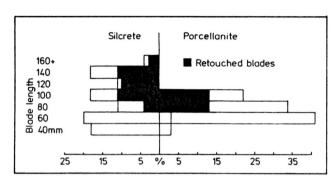

FIG. 12.9   Frequency of edge-retouch with blade length and material at Hawksburn.

This reduces the possibilities to edge form and rejuvenation. The former was the earliest hypothesis. Haast (1875c:96) described silcrete ('yellowish mottled flint') blades from Shag Mouth, where they were associated with moa remains, as having been retouched to form a kind of saw which 'was most probably used to cut or saw through the sinews, or other tough portions of the birds or seals'. Skinner and Teviotdale (1927) experimented with examples of Shag Mouth silcrete blades and concluded that the retouched blades were efficient wood saws, although of little use on bone. They noted, as well, the interesting fact that opposite surfaces, that is, dorsal and ventral, were usually chosen in cases where blades had been unifacially and bilaterally retouched. This is true in the few instances at Hawksburn and more clearly so in larger collections. Vincent's (1980) study of Waitaki Mouth blades shows 69 per cent of bilaterally retouched examples exhibited this 'under and over' pattern. If it has a functional origin it is probably that rotating the tool in the hand presents either edge to the task with the retouch scars facing the same way, certainly a practical advantage in a saw.

Amongst retouched blades, Skinner and Teviotdale (1927) found that those with 'steep retouch' would not work as saws but performed very well as spokeshaves. In their view, butchering functions were generally accomplished by large unretouched flakes and blades classified as 'knives and choppers', including those earlier regarded as spear points (Skinner 1924a). Except to observe that there is very little discernable use-damage on retouched blades, and that Skinner and Teviotdale (1927) found wood sawing with such implements much more difficult than their conclusions suggest, it is difficult to clearly reject their views. The only identifiable use-polish on a retouched silcrete blade (from Owen's Ferry) consisted of some patches of bone polish – perhaps reflecting contact during butchery (Kooyman 1985). If it is accepted, however, that the underlying assumption in relation to butchery – that it required blades with acute edge angles – can be discarded (above), the way is open to propose an alternative hypothesis.

If raw material was in relatively short supply, an efficient strategy of use would be to create a population of tools within which each cohort advanced through several functional stages (cf. Walker 1978:714). Unretouched blades could be used to cut and slice until broken or blunted. From that point, remaining whole blades might be retouched repeatedly to rejuvenate the edge, until they either

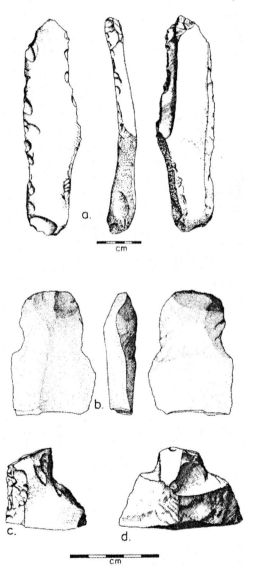

FIG. 12.10   Tanged silcrete blade from Kyeburn (a) and fragments of tanged blades from Shag Mouth (b), (d) and Hawksburn (c).

broke or the edge angle became too steep. Broken or steep edged blades could then be re-fashioned, or simply used as scrapers. In view of this there seems insufficient reason to argue that retouching was used to create formally different categories of tools (saws, spokeshaves, etc.), and the simple proposition of edge rejuvenation within the same broad functional class is preferable.

Retouching was also used to create apparent hafting reduction on the proximal end of some blades (Fig. 12.10). The purpose of this remains a mystery. It is not restricted to pointed blades, which probably rules out the suggestion (Skinner 1924a) that hafting was for spearheads (although some pointed blades, hafted or not, might still have been spearheads). In some cases, the reduction occurs on such a short section of the blade that it is difficult to see how it could have been used as a hafting area. There are also cases where the reduction appears very like edge damage from use as a concave side scraper, particularly on porcellanite blades. Whatever the functional utility of hafting, it is certainly not common. At Hawksburn it is discernable on only three silcrete and seven porcellanite blades. At Shag Mouth only three hafted blades were recorded (Skinner 1924a) and the form seems equally rare at Waitaki Mouth (Knight 1965:233) and in the large Catlins sites (Lockerbie 1959). Skinner and Teviotdale (1927:188) recorded one example as part of a *mataa* – a form of tanged knife reported from sites about Cook Strait and further north by Jones (1981) – but none of the hafted blades have the expanded body form of *mataa* and while they might be a related form it would be wrong to include them under that heading.

Distribution

Blades are rarely found north of Banks Peninsula. This is explicable, in part at least, by the scarcity of silcrete, the main blade material (Table 12.1). Where it does occur, as an imported material, there is usually some evidence of blades as in Palliser Bay (Leach and Leach 1979:170) and at Wairau Bar where one very fine silcrete blade was recovered (Wilkes 1964) and a few others as well. There is, however, an unusual quantity of silcrete at Kaupokonui but no silcrete blades. If the identification of this material is correct (Cassels n. d.), then since much of it arrived at the site as cobbles, rather than as cores or flakes, a direct voyage from a South Island moa-hunting region is suggested, which makes the lack of blades doubly odd.

The correlation of blades with silcrete and, to a much lesser extent, with basalt, chert and porcellanite, begs the question of why northern moa-hunters very seldom made blades of chert, obsidian, argillite or basalt. Obsidian is a classic blade-making material and it occurred in blocks of an eminently suitable size at Mayor Island, close to the Coromandel moa-hunting sites. The absence of large obsidian blades at North Island moa butcheries like Kaupokonui – where only one corner-blade was recovered (together with one possible quartz blade) – is a problem in more ways than one, although it may indicate, as Skinner (1924a:18) suggested, that there was no historical connection with Western Pacific obsidian blade industries.

Amongst possible solutions is the proposition that blades were an adaptation to butchering the larger moa species found predominantly in the South Island, or to the need to butcher large numbers of moas; that is, that some threshold of necessity for blades was exceeded only in the south. A less likely suggestion is that blade-making was either the discovery of a very small number of people, or that the technology arrived in the South Island with chance voyagers from a blade-making area and that they declined to teach the technique outside their immediate lineage. Whatever the reason, there are very few blades north of Banks Peninsula and no blade-making quarries.

It is fair to acknowledge, though, that blades are far from common in southern moa-butchery sites. At Owen's Ferry, 6.5 per cent of flaked stone pieces were blades, at Hawksburn 2 per cent and at Coal Creek only 0.7 per cent, a reflection of the porcellanite dominance. In view of these figures the scarcity of blades at Kaupokonui (0.3 per cent of flaked stone in Cassels' (n. d.) assemblage), and the total lack of blades in the small flaked stone assemblages from Tokoroa and Whangamoenga, do not appear so anomalous. It must also be remembered that the prominence of large blades in older assemblages – such as the Shag Mouth material, where blades comprise about 15 per cent of the pieces (Knight 1965:235) – is largely due to highly selective collecting.

Nevertheless if blades are not as abundant amongst lithic assemblages from moa-hunting sites as the earlier literature tended to suggest, nor by any means clearly butchering implements, they are still the most common and certain lithic indicator of moa-hunting, and must have functioned in some ways directly associated with it.

13

CHRONOLOGY AND EXTINCTION

It has been convenient to discuss moa-hunting up to this point as if it had been activity in which the passage of time was insignificant. This is, of course, not the case, but there are practical difficulties, discussed below, in merely retailing radiocarbon dates at face value, and to avoid repetition of these the radiocarbon chronology is discussed as a whole. Once a chronological framework has been outlined it is possible to examine those questions which are particularly dependent on it: the moa-hunting phase, the period of extinction and various hypotheses which are held to explain the extinction of moas.

Radiocarbon dating

All too frequently radiocarbon dates for moa-hunting sites have been reported without such essential details as stratigraphical provenance, sample type, secular correction or publication number. Lists of varying quality and completeness are available (McCulloch and Trotter 1975, 1976; Moore and Tiller 1975, 1976; McFadgen 1982, n.d.; Law 1974), but there is only one largely complete data base available from the New Zealand Laboratory (Institute of Nuclear Sciences). This was compiled by Mr H. Jansen, formerly a scientist of the Institute. It is referred to below as the JDB.[1]

From it I have taken all the charcoal conventional ages (Libby half-life, uncorrected) for moa-hunting

sites, plus standardised shell and bone dates, and have added a small number of published dates which are not in the JDB (Appendix E). Most JDB dates vary by up to ± 40 radiocarbon years from published results but some are very different indeed, and I have had these recalculated with respect to modern standards by the INS (Redvers-Higgins, pers. comm.).

The most important results are these: NZ 58 goes from 810 ± 60 to 1207 ± 65; NZ 136 from 630 ± 50 to 1192 ± 62; NZ 580 from 528 ± 45 to 874 ± 45; and NZ 1333 from 300 ± 40 to 705 ± 45. The same degree of change need not be anticipated in other cases, but since most published results vary to some degree from JDB dates, and a few JDB dates from those obtained by recalculation, it is apparent that a comprehensive review and recalculation of archaeological dates is needed.

Rejected dates

Out of the full list of dates a number have been rejected and do not appear in Appendix E. All moa bone carbonate dates have been discarded on the grounds that organic carbon in bone tends to exchange with modern atmospheric carbon (Jansen 1984). These were NZ numbers: 55, 138, 139, 140, 460, 514, 558, 751, 753, 755, 757, 759, 765, 917 or 918 (duplicated), 927, 929, 931, 1112. NZ 461 (Redcliffs Cave) given as 'red ash' by Trotter (1975b), but as moa bone carbonate in Trotter (1967a) is also rejected, but NZ 137 (Papatowai) given as carbonate by Hamel (1978) is confirmed as collagen on the JDB and is accepted. A seal bone carbonate date (NZ 56A) from Pounawea and a fish bone carbonate date (NZ 1298) from Hotwater Beach are rejected in favour of the respective

[1] The INS requests that this qualification about the use of the JDB be published. 'The radiocarbon dates presented here are taken from a preliminary compilation, by Mr Hank Jansen, of measurements made by the Institute of Nuclear Sciences from 1955 to 1985. The data have been released by the Institute on the understanding that they may be further revised to correct for errors in the compilation or in the age calculations.'

collagen dates from the same samples (NZ 56B, NZ 1299). I discarded, however, NZ 766 (Tai Rua), a contaminated moa bone collagen date from a sample used to test errors accruing from long storage and handling (Trotter 1979:227).

Freshwater shell is also suspect for similar reasons, especially that from lime-enriched environments, and I consequently reject NZ 893 (Timpendean), NZ 5014 (Pleasant River) and NZ 1377 (Awamoko). Mudsnail (*Amphibola crenata*) is another dubious material, but McGill (INS, to Allingham 7 December 1977) believes the aragonite dates from Tumai are acceptable; the conchiolin dates NZ 4434 and NZ 4437 are rejected. For the same reason I discard the keratin date NZ 580 (Waimataitai). Other shell samples rejected are NZ 4747 and NZ 4749 (Purakanui), because of significant calcite recrystallisation.

Other sample materials of unknown reliability and which have furnished dates considerably at variance with others from the same context are NZ 1171 (Hotwater Beach, 'soil grease'), NZ 2721 (Avoca Point 'palaeosoil matrix') and NZ 4544 (Waitaki Mouth 'graphitic sand'). All are rejected. Human bone collagen is another difficult sample material because of potential errors introduced by consumption of marine organisms (Law 1981; Jansen 1984). Rejected are NZ 1834 (Lagoon Flat), NZ 1835, NZ 4442, NZ 4443 and NZ 4444 (Wairau Bar).

Of the remaining dates, some had to be discarded on grounds of provenance. This included dates for levels without moa remains, although in moa-hunting sites: NZ numbers 221 (Pig Bay), 356 (Sarah's Gully Midden), 1876 (Tairua), 1029, 1031, 1036 (Whakamoenga Cave), 1478 (Foxton), 483 (Moawhitu), 4702 and 4703 (Long Beach). Dates rejected because they were insufficiently associated with moa remains elsewhere in the site, whether of the same apparent level or not, are: NZ numbers 1313, 1314 (Pararaki North), 1877 (Fishermans Bay, Makara), 3113, 3397 (Clarence Mouth), Motunau Island (no NZ no.), 804, 5323, 5325 (Dart Bridge), 2480, 4466, 4467, 4468 (Tiwai Point), 933, 934 and 935 (Wakapatu).

The stratigraphy of the Fyffe site (Avoca Point) remains controversial, but McFadgen's (1987) analysis of the sequence of beach ridge formation indicates that his dates NZ 6307, 6744, 6765 and 6779 should not be regarded as estimating the age of cultural events and are here rejected. I also discard the following dates thought to refer to natural deposits of bone: NZ 918 (Timpendean), NZ 4874 (Awamoa) and SUA 64 (Waihao Mouth).

Lastly, there seems little point in including dates of modern (< 250 bp) and 'post-bomb' age, the former on the grounds that their calendrical age cannot be adequately distinguished (McFadgen 1982) and because it is very unlikely that they date the death of moas. Rejected are: NZ 685 (Foxton), NZ 5327 (Dart Bridge), SUA 62A (Waihao Mouth) and NZ 4435 (Tumai).

It is almost certain that this cull has not removed all the dates which are dubious on any of the grounds noted above, but until full details become available for all New Zealand radiocarbon dates that will not be possible; Appendix E and Figs. 13.1 and 13.2 can at least be regarded as free of most of the problematical results.[2]

Sample type differences

One of the longstanding uncertainties concerning archaeological chronology in New Zealand is whether there is a systematic difference in the radiocarbon results obtained on charcoal samples as opposed to those obtained on bone collagen or marine shell. Trotter (1968b) and Trotter and McCulloch (1973) perceived a difference of about 300 radiocarbon years, charcoal providing the earlier dates, and Caughley's (n.d.) analysis of a sample of dates from moa-hunting sites disclosed a mean difference of 240 years. On the other hand, the variation is certainly not consistant. There are sites in which testing of this problem has shown no significant difference at all, for example, at Waimataitai (Appendix E), and Law's comprehensive comparison of charcoal and marine shell dates indicated that 'the oft-quoted difference between charcoal and other ages of 200 years, is shown on this larger sample to be less, at an average of 83 years. The modal difference, as opposed to the average, is close to zero' (Law 1984).

Calculation of best estimates (B. F. Leach 1972: 115) for all dates in Appendix E, pooled by sample types, showed that the mean difference for dates on moa-hunting sites was 26 years between collagen (best estimate of 577 ± 22) and marine shell (603 ± 26) and 77 years between the latter and charcoal (680 ± 15). A difference of about 100 years between collagen or marine shell and charcoal dates can be broadly assumed.

It is not possible, however, to determine what has caused the difference or which sample type

---

[2] Seven marine shell dates ranging from 600 bp to 780 bp, other details unknown, are reported from Pounawea (Moore and Tiller 1975).

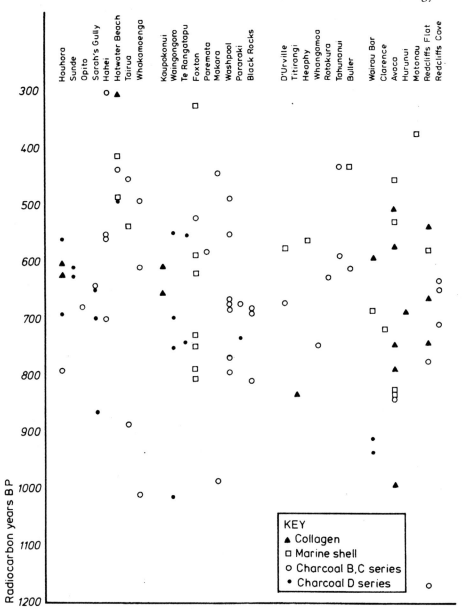

FIG. 13.1   Radiocarbon dates from moa-hunting sites, North Island and northern South Island.

provides the most accurate chronology in terms of calendrical age. One problem is that there are relatively few collagen or marine shell dates for northern North Island, southern South Island or inland sites and, consequently, the sample types might date different chronological sequences. Another difficulty is that while charcoal samples submitted before 1976 were not screened for old wood, and probably include a number with high 'inbuilt age' (McFadgen 1982), there are suspicions that collagen provides results which are too young (Mead and Meltzer 1984; Caughley n. d.) and that estuarine shell, a common material of marine shell samples, is subject to similar problems as freshwater molluscan shell (Law 1981). Until more is

known about these problems (see also Law 1971, 1974; McCulloch and Trotter 1975; McFadgen 1982; Caughley n. d.) it would be prudent to leave the matter of preference open and treat sample types as separate groups.

An age of hunting

How early moa-hunting began is a question depending on what view is taken of the early radiocarbon dates. Seven charcoal dates of older than 1000 bp survive the culling process (above). The oldest (NZ 359, 1700 ± 45) is from the basal level at Sarah's Gully. It is so much older than any

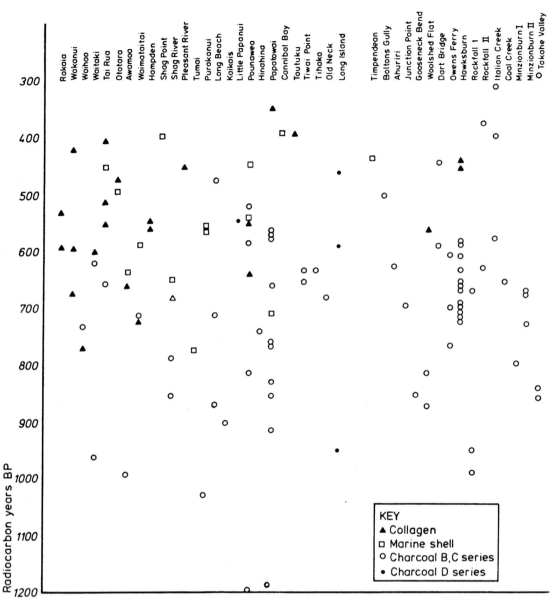

FIG. 13.2   Radiocarbon dates from moa-hunting sites, southern and inland South Island.

other date, and 900 years older than a charcoal date for the level immediately above it, that it can be reasonably discarded. The oldest dates at Pounawea (NZ 58, 1207 ± 65), Papatowai (NZ 136, 1192 ± 62), Whakamoenga (NZ 648, 1011 ± 62) and Hamilton's, Redcliffs (NZ 438, 1167 ± 91) are also from basal layers, and they are 300 to 600 years older than charcoal or marine shell dates for the same contexts. The Purakanui date (NZ 4637, 1030 ± 58), and the Waingongoro date (NZ 543, 1018 ± 49) are also about 500 years older than others from the same excavations. Since none of the charcoal samples producing these dates were screened for long-lived material, and since most

are from basal layers in which there must exist a possibility of contamination with natural charcoal, it would be unwise to regard them as sufficient evidence of occupation earlier than 1000 bp. That is not to say, though, that one or more of them might not actually provide an accurate age.

About twice as many dates fall into the period 900–1000 bp. Some, at least, are open to question. The only collagen date (NZ 3164 from Avoca, 992 ± 192) is from the same deposit as NZ 4155 which dated 743 ± 85. The Makara date (NZ 654, 987 ± 74) is from the same cultural layer as NZ 653 (442 ± 87), and the Long Island date (GaK 2393, 950 ± 80) is from a layer well above another dated about 500 years younger. The Awamoa charcoal date (NZ 926) is without context, but is more than 300 years older than several marine shell dates for the site. Similarly NZ 4543 from Waitaki Mouth (963 ± 86) is more than 300 years older than another charcoal date from the same oven feature, and two early dates from Rockfall I (NZ 4972 and NZ 4973) are also 200 years earlier than another date from the same oven. There is, however, no particular reason to challenge dates such as NZ 1332 (916 ± 88), NZ 4436 (773 ± 26) and others which give results similar to these on samples of other materials from the same archaeological contexts.

Many younger dates are, of course, similarly open to question (e.g. NZ 594, Tairua), but there seems no reason, given the consistency of repeated dates, to doubt that Pounawea and Papatowai were first occupied about 900 ± 50 bp. Various other sites – Titirangi, Wairau Bar, Avoca, some of the lower Waitaki sites, Shag River, Kaikais and Long Beach – were probably all first occupied in the period 800–900 bp.

It is, of course, impossible to say when moa-hunting actually began, although it is unlikely that it was before 1000 bp, but these data suggest that it was underway in the Catlins by 900 bp and elsewhere in the eastern South Island by 800 bp. Soon after that time moa-hunting sites were established throughout the country. Of the 73 dated sites, 32 per cent were occupied in the period 700–800 bp, 45 per cent in the period 600–700 bp and 36 per cent between 500 and 600 bp. Thereafter the rate of occupancy declined to 23 per cent in the period 400–500 bp, 14 per cent in the century 300–400 bp and to zero in the following century (Figs. 13.1 and 13.2).

Combining the dates (Appendix E) into cumulative probability curves for each radiocarbon sample type (Fig. 13.3) shows that the distribution of marine shell dates is complex and variable, with South Island dates tending to concentrate towards the younger end of the range and North Island dates towards the older end. The collagen and charcoal curves are leptokurtic and slightly positively skewed, suggesting that moa-hunting expanded less slowly than it declined, particularly in the South Island, and that there was a phase of relatively intensive hunting between 500 and 800 bp. Judging by the curves for charcoal dates this intensive phase occurred slightly earlier in the South Island, a conclusion which may also be reflected in the best estimates (after B. F. Leach 1972:115) for the pooled dates from each island:

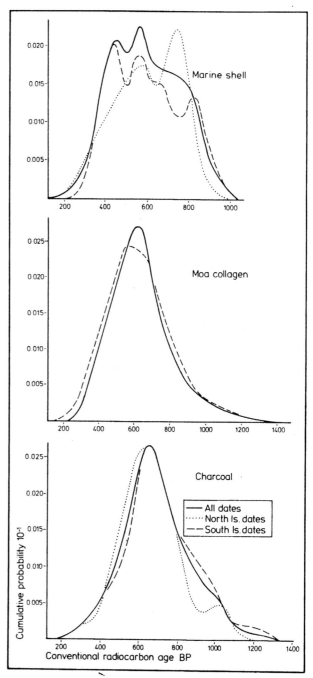

FIG. 13.3 Cumulative probability curves of radiocarbon dates from moa-hunting sites.

695 ± 18 (South Island) and 649 ± 24 (North Island). In addition, there is some regional variation within the South Island. The probability curve for inland charcoal dates peaks in the same place, but is more strongly leptokurtic, and the best estimate of the dates in that sample is 661 ± 24, compared to 725 ± 28 for the southern South Island

(south of Banks Peninsula) sample as a whole, and 740 ± 61 for the northern South Island. This suggests a slightly later and more concentrated phase of interior moa-hunting than occurred along the coast.

It would be as well to observe, though, that none of the differences which I have discussed can be regarded as anything more than interesting propositions, because the samples for radiocarbon dates were not taken randomly in terms of the universe of moa-hunting sites, the number of samples per site or with regard to stratigraphy. What we have is, at best, an approximate picture of moa-hunting chronology which is almost certainly biassed in directions which are not well defined (Anderson n. d.e).

A time of extinction

Various kinds of evidence have been canvassed concerning the period of moa extinction – alleged sightings by Europeans, Maori recollections or traditions, apparently recent remains of moas and archaeological evidence.

Of 46 European accounts alleging encounters with moas, 23 are in the form of direct sightings (listed in Anderson n. d. b; and see also Richards 1986; Brewster 1987). With the exception of several peculiar tales collected at a later date by Taylor (1855:238), not one concerns a possible sighting earlier than 1842; that is, the time when scientific knowledge of moas was becoming available. None of the various explorers, surveyors or missionary-travellers saw anything remotely resembling moas during the preceding 60 years, nor did they or any European scientists ever claim to see moas at any subsequent stage. Nearly all the alleged sightings, which concentrate into the era 1850–80, were made by recently-arrived immigrants and gold-miners. Having discussed most of these stories elsewhere (Anderson n. d. a, n. d. b), and concluded that they are not, in fact, sightings of Dinornithiformes, they need concern us no longer.

Maori evidence

In Appendix F are summarised 60 references, by Maoris, bearing on the period of moa extinction. I have left out derivative accounts (e.g. Westland 1848), European inferences concerning Maori poetry or songs (e.g. Downes 1916) and references to uncertain observations of moa tracks (Thomson 1858; Graham 1919) and skins (Field 1894; Buick 1931:282). A quarter of the references suggest that

moa extinction occurred in the remote past, often at the time of fires associated with Tamatea. These are lumped together in Appendix F as 'Tamatea Period'. It is impossible to offer a precise date for this. The mid 14th century was often suggested as the time of a Maori colonising fleet which brought Tamatea, amongst others, but recent appraisals of Maori tradition recommend caution and it would be fairer to think of any Tamatea Period as simply the Maori era prior to about AD1500. Another quarter of the references place moa extinction, so far as can be estimated, in the period early 17th to late 18th centuries.

Most accounts (26), however, refer extinction to the time between early European exploration, c. 1770, and extensive colonisation, in the 1840s. However, if mythological 'moa' are disregarded, some marked regional differences are apparent. In the East Coast–Bay of Plenty, disappearance of moas in the Tamatea Period was generally suggested; while in Wellington, Wanganui and Taranaki, survival of moas into the 19th century was evidently a widespread belief. In the South Island, moa extinction was assigned to the 17th century or earlier by Canterbury informants, but further south opinions were sharply divided between preference for the Tamatea Period on the one hand, and the 19th century on the other.

It is impossible to say whether these regional variations have any historical significance for understanding the course of moa extinction. They might represent a consensus of ancient traditions, widespread in each regional community; equally, they might reflect no more than random variations followed by local repetition.[3]

There are, of course, various other difficulties in accepting these accounts at face value. The duality of the concept 'moa' apparent in the early references – which at the same time allowed moas to disappear long ago, but mythological 'moa' to survive in certain places until the 19th century – was an obvious source of confusion. It might explain much of the apparent disagreement within and between stories since, by the later 19th century, the distinction had become lost to European enquirers. Another potential problem of translation lay in interpreting Maori references to the passage of

[3] My unpublished analysis of Southland and Otago moa traditions indicates that most are derived from a single source and subsequently spread amongst a group of related families. On European references to 'emu', 'cassowary', etc. in New Zealand see Anderson (n. d. a). Note also that where 'kiwi' and 'emu' are both mentioned this probably refers to the 19th-century differentiation of *Apteryx australis* (kiwi or tokoweka) from *A. haasti* (roa).

time. This seems to have been either by elapsed generations, or by reference to fathers and grandfathers. The latter, taken literally, could imply very recent extinction, but it depended greatly on which word was actually used – something very seldom recorded. On one occasion when it was, Hongi (1916:67) refers to Ngakuku saying moas became extinct 'as far back as the time of my grandfathers; "*I te wa ano ki tooku heinga*"'. The word *heinga*, however, is defined by Williams (1971:44) as 'parent, ancestor', which opens several additional interpretations to the one Europeans wanted to take from Hongi's translation.

The point of greatest difficulty, though, is to accept that moas could have survived into the period 1770–1840 without much clearer traditions about moa names, biology or associations with Maoris. Somewhere amongst the numerous references there may be one or two which are literally accurate but, as in other traditional evidence about moas, it now seems impossible to extract them. The period of moa extinction, or periods, if it occurred at different times between regions or species, can only be investigated, therefore, in terms of tangible evidence.

Surface remains and similar evidence

Evidence of desiccated moa soft tissues, possible moa trails and moa bones lying on the surface of the ground, has been adduced as supporting the proposition that moas survived into recent times (e.g. Hector 1872). There being no way to date the desiccated remains until the advent of radiocarbon dating, however, and with general agreement that they could easily be hundreds of years old, they proved of little value in this matter. The existence of trails through woody vegetation near Auckland, opened and maintained by the passage of moas until the arrival of European stock, was proposed by Graham (1919:109), who also claimed Maori authority for these including a name, *ara-moa* (moa paths). Hector (1872:19) had also attributed trails in alpine scrub near Jackson's Bay (Fiordland) to moas, but he qualified the matter of age by suggesting that the trails 'may have been for a long period in disuse . . . except by kakapo and takahe'. There is now no way of telling whether there was any substance to these assertions.

Similarly, modern claims that tracks worn into the soil along ridges or across slopes are relict moa trails (*awa-moa* in Brewster 1987:20–1) are virtually untestable. Finds of moa gizzard stones exposed along ridges (Brewster 1987) may only confirm the

expected selectivity of slope erosion, and since much the same routes were probably chosen in hill country by any large animal, moa or introduced mammal, the origin of the tracks is uncertain and of no obvious age.

The one really promising hypothesis of the mid-19th century, and one still proposed (Brewster 1987:38–40), is that moa bones found lying on the surface of the ground, and not apparently exposed by erosion, must indicate the very recent survival of the birds. In reference to Central Otago in the 1850s, Murison (1872:123) stated that 'the frequent occurrence of bones on the surface throughout the lower Clutha valley, and the freshness of the remains in many other parts of the province, is quite compatible with a belief that the bird was alive [about AD1800]'. Menzies, in 1861 (Beattie n. d.), reported many bones 'in a very perfect state' lying on the ground in western Southland with Maori cabbage growing in each patch of bones, and J. T. Thomson (1858:310) reported moa bones which 'do not appear above 30 years old' in the ruins of a Maori settlement in the same district (see also *The Otago Witness* 12 September 1871; Hector 1872:115; Hutton 1892c:166; Field 1894:563; McKay 1905; Beattie 1958:20, 22, 31, n. d.). Additional evidence pointing in the same direction was seen in reports of dogs gnawing moa bones (Gillies 1872:413) and the use of moa bones as firewood by early settlers (Pyke 1890).

Although Haast (1872c:103) and Hutton (1892c: 166) objected that they had seen no moa bones on the surface during their extensive travels in Canterbury and Otago in the early 1870s, except those clearly exposed by recent erosion, Hutton acknowledged that this could be interpreted as support for a conclusion of very recent extinction; in fact, that the survival span of moa bones exposed to the weather was only 15 years, in which case there must have been moas alive in the 1840s! Since that inference seemed altogether unlikely, Haast (1872c), Stack (1872) and Hutton (1892c) proposed that a more likely explanation was that increased burning and soil erosion had exposed old bones, which then rapidly decayed. Judging by later observations concerning bones exposed by ploughing at Wairau Bar and Waitaki Mouth (Chapter 9) this is a plausible proposition. Haast (1872c) also noted that moa bones dug up at Glenmark, and left on the ground, decayed rapidly, while Chapman (1885) argued that surface bones observed in the Mackenzie Country had been exposed by wind deflation and were rapidly decaying. Thomson (n. d.), one of the first Europeans to explore Central Otago and the upper Waitaki Valley in 1857, had also observed that the moa bones he saw on the surface were not fresh at all but 'in a very decayed condition'.

In the absence of more precise descriptions the historical argument can hardly be resolved, but so far as more recent cases go there is nothing in them to indicate the late survival of moas. Brewster (1987:39) regards the discovery of moa bones on a landslip at Haast in 1904 as 'strong evidence that a moa was alive . . . certainly in 1800', but there was 'young timber' growing on the slip, indicating that it had moved not long before, and it may have been that which exposed old bones. It is also likely that some bones, notably femora (Chapman 1885), can survive for a long period on the surface in dry conditions such as under rockshelters, or in the open in some localities, especially if they are intact and unburnt.[4] There was an eroded femur on the surface near Hawksburn moa butchery in a position where it may have lain for 600 years.

Other claims of late moa survival based on an association of bones with European artefacts, or cut-marks on bones suggestive of iron tools (Field 1882:45, 1892:560; Eyre Creek discovery, in Beattie n. d.), are open to question on stratigraphic grounds, (especially Field's discoveries in shifting sand dunes) or because it is apparent that stone implements could just as easily have wrought the same kind of damage (below).

Archaeological evidence

The period of moa extinction can, it seems, only be estimated in terms of archaeological evidence. Nine moa-hunting sites have produced dates later than 400 bp. The Hotwater Beach fish bone collagen sample (NZ 1299, 301 ± 92) is from the same layer as three results on charcoal and marine shell which date 415–485 bp, and the Hahei late date (NZ 4950) is, similarly, from a layer dated by three other results to 548–700 bp. NZ 1250 at Foxton is from layer 2 where, again, other dates consistently indicate a much older age (Appendix E), and NZ 5341 (376 ± 38) from Rockfall II is from an oven also dated to more than 600 years bp. As indications of late moa survival these data cannot be accepted.

The collagen date at Papatowai (NZ 137) is also much younger than a charcoal date from the layer above. It is, however, close to the single collagen date at Tautuku (NZ 146) and a marine shell date at Motunau (NZ 1538). Although single dates, in the latter two cases, should be regarded very cautiously, these results just might suggest survival of moas until c. 350–400 bp on the shorter chronologies of collagen and marine shell, and perhaps 400–500 bp on the charcoal chronology. The only site to produce two charcoal dates from the same feature which are later than 400 bp is Italian Creek (NZ 4714, NZ 4715), although there is also an older date (NZ 4716) for the same layer.

The very late date on a tussock sample from Takahe Valley (NZ 51), which has sustained numerous speculations about *Megalapteryx* surviving into the early European era, cannot be regarded as secure. There is no evidence that the sample was cultural and tussock was growing in the shelter at the time the sample was taken. The bark dates (NZ 52 and duplicate) were, on the other hand, on cultural material, and even if bark from long-lived trees is a poor material for radiocarbon samples, the results are more likely to express the approximate age of the site, c. 800 bp. Evidence that cut-marks on the *Megalapteryx* pelvis were produced by a metal implement has also been questioned (Duff 1977:79; Anderson n. d. a).

Since there are numerous dates on all materials which fall into the period 400–500 bp it may be concluded that moa-hunting, on present evidence, probably did not continue later than 400 bp. How much later all moas were extinct can only be guessed at (Anderson n. d. e).

I turn now to the question of causality.

Quantifying overkill

Amongst various explanations put forward to account for the extinction of the moas, overexploitation by hunters is the oldest (Polack 1838; Owen 1849b:270) and still the most widely preferred (Anderson 1983b, 1984, 1988a; Diamond 1984; Guilday 1984; Martin 1984; Trotter and McCulloch 1984). Its general plausibility depends on the conjunction of extinction with the first human colonisation of New Zealand, but since people engaged in activities other than hunting which were potentially inimical to moa survival, its particular plausibility depends on the quantification of the human–moa relationship. At a basic level of analysis there are three aspects to this: the natural abundance and Maximum Sustained-Yield (MSY) level of moas, the numbers of hunters or consumers and the number of moas actually killed. I

---

[4] McKay's discovery of chick bones (Brewster 1987:39) seems to have been in a rockshelter.

will discuss these largely in terms of the eastern South Island since, if the hypothesis fails there, it almost certainly fails elsewhere.

This region is approximately defined as the area east of a line joining Bluff, Queenstown and Picton. According to my estimates of moa density (Chapter 5) it would include most of the South Island's moas, a standing crop of about 37,000 birds. What proportion of this might have been available for culling without depressing the long-term viability of the population is a matter of conjecture. Nevertheless, given that moas were large, slow-breeding, equilibrium species in general, it was probably considerably less than 10 per cent, and possibly as low as 2 per cent, as amongst some pinniped seals, for example (Fowler and Smith 1981). For the sake of argument I take 5 per cent as the threshold of culling for maximum sustained yield.

Consumer population and culling rates

A second factor in the quantification relationship is the size of the consumer population at the peak of the hunting era, c. 700 bp. Duff (in Cumberland, 1962:159) estimated the moa-hunter population at a minimum of 15,000 in the South Island. Cumberland (Duff 1962:159) calculated a population of

10,000 at 700 bp by assuming a base population of 100 at 1200 bp and a growth rate rising from 0.1 to 0.9 per cent in the first century and 1 per cent thereafter. If we assume, though, that settlement began at about 1100 bp and that the base population was 100 at 1000 bp, it would have reached 2000 at 700 bp at an increase rate of 1 per cent. If the population was only 50 at 1000 bp, the total would have been 1000 at 700 bp.

These may be regarded as minimum figures. Had the population grown at 3 per cent for several generations, as occurred in the founding population on Pitcairn Island (Law, 1977), slowing to a rate of 1 per cent after six generations, then there would have been about 12,000 at 700 bp. For present purposes I take the conservative view that lower growth rates occurred and that the minimum population at 700 bp was 1000 and the likely size about 3000 ± 1000 (Fig. 13.4). This was the approximate size of the historical Maori population in the eastern South Island at the end of the 18th century (Anderson 1988b) when, of course, the terrestrial resource environment was much less attractive than it had been in the moa-hunting era.

Employing the above assumptions about prey and predator population sizes it is possible to consider culling rates and their implications. I look at

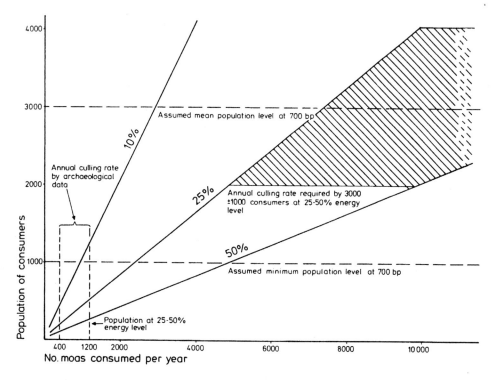

FIG. 13.4 Hypothetical relationship of number of consumers and number of moas consumed at three levels of moa-flesh energy contribution to annual food consumption.

this first in relation to the archaeological data from which the total size of the catch in the eastern South Island can be estimated, by extrapolating MNI density data over the known total area of moa-hunting sites.

MNI density data are few and variable (Table 13.1). If there is a pattern within them, it is that in large butchery sites the density is relatively high (0.14 to 2.2 MNI per m^2), while it is relatively low (0.06 to 0.37 MNI per m^2) in small sites. The densities at Pounawea and Papatowai might be artificially increased as a consequence of the small areas excavated, but they are not inconsistent with estimates from Kaupokonui and Hawksburn. Even so, it would be wise to err substantially on the side of caution. I take 0.1 to 0.2 MNI per m^2 as an overall range.

The total combined area of moa-hunting sites in the eastern South Island can only be derived from the 27 sites in which it has been estimated. These include, however, all the large sites, and the total area of all known sites may not be substantially greater. A more significant factor is the areas taken as having had moa remains strewn upon them at the two largest sites: Rakaia Mouth and Waitaki Mouth. For the former I take two figures: 40 ha (50 per cent of Haast's (1872c) revised estimate of the site area) and 11 ha (the area estimated as still exhibiting remains by Trotter 1972a). For the latter, also, I take 61 ha (the observed total extent of the site) and 30 ha (the area over which ovens were observed or surveyed in 1960). With these variations the total combined area of the 27 sites is 168 ha and 108 ha.

TABLE 13.1   MNI density of moa remains in archaeological sites

	Excavation area m^2	MNI moa per m^2
Large sites		
Kaupokonui	79	1.3
Wairau Bar	–	0.14
Hawksburn	223	1.79
Pounawea	8.6	1.16
Papatowai	4.5	2.2
Small sites		
Hampden	11	0.27
Tumai	8	0.37
Purakanui	12	0.17
Owen's Ferry	180	0.06
Rockfall II	35	0.06
Tiwai Point	181	0.06

At a moa density of 0.1 MNI per m^2 the total size of the moa catch is 108,000 to 168,000 and at 0.2 it is 216,000 to 336,000. These results are open to question on several grounds: the MNI density data might reflect particularly dense patches of bone and, what amounts to almost the same thing, there might not have been moa remains over the whole of the sites in question. Both are valid criticisms to an extent, but according to anecdotal data, at least, moa bones seem to have been both abundant and widespread in the large butchery sites. Furthermore, I have chosen clearly conservative MNI density ranges in the light of the available data. It must also be noted that not all known moa-hunting sites are included and that since most areas of the eastern South Island have not been systematically surveyed for archaeological remains, there are doubtless many more hunting sites to be recorded (not to mention a large number of known oven sites in the interior with flakes and blades scattered about them, which are almost certainly moa-hunting sites, but are not included here, e.g. Anderson 1982a). There exists, as well, the probability that a number of large moa butcheries on the south Canterbury coast have disappeared by very rapid coastal erosion (Anderson 1983b).

If the standing crop is taken as 37,000 birds, if 100,000 to 300,000 were killed between 400 and 1000 bp, and if the total catch had a normal frequency distribution in time, then during the peak century, 600–700 bp, 400 to 1200 birds were killed each year. This is a culling rate of 1.1–3.2 per cent which, I assume, was probably too low to represent a serious threat to the viability of moa populations.

Consumption rates

It is immediately obvious, however, that 400–1200 moas per year is much too small a catch to support the likely population of consumers. Taking the recovered flesh weight of an average moa at 37.5 kg (50 per cent of a 75 kg bird), assuming an energy value of 1100 kJ per 100 g (cf. raw turkey meat, Thomas and Corden 1977), and 11,000 kJ as the mean daily requirement per consumer (Thomas and Corden 1977), 400 moas represent sufficient food to support only 41 people for a year, and 1200 birds, 123 people for a year.

It would be necessary to assume that moas provided only 10 per cent of the annual energy requirement for 1000 people to bring the archaeological evidence into contact with the most minimal model of required consumption. Were that so, however, we would hardly expect the large number (200), size and evident specialisation of the moa-hunting sites in the eastern South Island. In most instances the faunal remains in them are very predominantly of moas, and even in those few cases where seals or fish are more important, moas usually represent 25 per cent or more of the estimated flesh weight. It should also be noted that vegetable foods were scarce in the South Island. Horticulture was impossible south of Banks Peninsula and marginal to the north of it, and fernroot (*Pteridium esculentum*) was seldom of economic quality. The production of sugar from the *ti* tree (*Cordyline australis*) was an important historical industry and it has archaeological antecedents extending to the moa-hunting era, but the distribution of *ti* cooking ovens is geographically restricted and the numbers are quite small.

The greater proportion of the food consumed during the moa-hunting era must have come from faunal resources and it seems very likely, in view of the archaeological evidence, that moas contributed 25–50 per cent of the total energy requirement at the peak of the hunting period. Taking that view, it follows that the annual catch required by a minimum population of 1000 consumers would have been 2500–5000 birds, and by 3000 consumers, 8000–15,000 birds (Fig. 13.4). These figures represent culling rates of 6.7–13.5 per cent and 21.6–40.5 per cent respectively.

It is possible, of course, that I have greatly underestimated the standing crop of moas, but equally, the number of consumers may have been substantially greater, as some have suggested. If there were 100,000 moas and 3000 consumers at a 25 per cent energy requirement level, the cull would still be 7.5 per cent, and about 25 per cent for 10,000 consumers. For the culling rate to fall to 5 per cent in this scenario a standing crop of 150,000 moas would be required and this represents a biomass density × 25 that of emus.

In summary, there is a considerable gulf between observed and expected rates of moa consumption, given the validity of the assumptions in my calculations. The archaeological evidence seems to represent only a fraction of the actual remains of moa-hunting. Either there were many more sites, as some evidence suggests, or the range of density figures which I have used is too low. To reach a minimum culling level of 2500–5000 birds per year at the peak of the hunting era (i.e. sufficient for 1000 consumers at a 25 per cent–50 per cent energy level) requires an MNI density in the known sites of about 0.5–1.0 per m². Such figures are, in fact, quite typical of large moa-hunting sites

in the few cases where they can be derived (Anderson n.d.e).

Overkill, though of necessity naively quantified, is, therefore, clearly a feasible hypothesis. The question raised now is by what means could it have been accomplished?

Blitzkrieg, rolling waves and serial overkill

In the lexicon of overkill hypotheses, 'blitzkrieg' is the proposition that explosive radial expansion of a hunting population occurred so rapidly, and the hunters killed with such efficiency, that prey extinction occurred at a moving front of population growth (Martin 1973; Mosimann and Martin 1975; Grayson 1984:811–12). One important consequence is that the rapidity of the activity is held to leave few traces such as kill or butchery sites in the archaeological record. Martin (1984:391–7) has argued that this may explain the relatively few moa-hunting sites in the North Island. This is, in my view, very unlikely. Had it occurred we might expect to find sites of the population which settled behind the front and evidence of widespread forest destruction marking the passage of the front. Neither occur. In addition, moa populations were probably much lower in the North Island and moas would certainly have been more difficult to locate under the heavy forest cover. There is, moreover, no evidence that the moa-hunting phase in the North Island was chronologically narrower than in the South Island. If blitzkrieg had occurred, the far more likely region would have been the eastern South Island. Here, though, both Martin (1984:392) and his critics (Grayson 1984:813–15; Marshall 1984:801) are agreed that, while overkill occurred, it was not in the form of a blitzkrieg.

Caughley (n.d.) has eschewed the term, in favour of 'rolling wave' colonisation, but argued that there was, nonetheless, something akin to blitzkrieg in the eastern South Island. He perceives a wave of colonisation, beginning on the northeast coast and accelerating southwards, at a population growth rate of 3 per cent per year. This was fuelled by an abundant supply of moa flesh which lasted for about a century in any district, after which moas were at, or close to, extinction. The proposition is similar to, and inspired by, Trotter and McCulloch's (1984:720) contention that moa-hunting occurred in a north to south expansion of colonisation, though they regarded the velocity of colonisation as constant.

The argument depends crucially upon radiocarbon dates. Trotter and McCulloch (1984:720) conceded that the pattern was 'not based on strong evidence, only a few dates from the far south would upset it'. Caughley (n. d.) calculated that three to six dates of 850 bp injected into the sample would render insignificant the linear regression of time against distance southward. There are, though, two ends to the sequence and both can be challenged. First, and considering only collagen and marine shell dates (as do Trotter, McCulloch and Caughley) there are now, in fact, several early southern dates: NZ 1333 (705 ± 45) at Papatowai, bottom layer, and on NZ 4436 (773 ± 26, Tumai). Both are on marine shell. Second, Caughley's dates for Avoca, the supposedly early northern site, are not those which I or McFadgen (1987) accept. The earliest date, NZ 3164, is a duplicate (above) of another (NZ 4155) which is 270 years younger. In addition, NZ 3164, now 992 ± 192, has a huge standard error. Furthermore to NZ 4155 can be added the moa collagen dates of 569 ± 42 (NZ 6496) and 785 ± 59 (NZ 6566), and the marine shell dates of 525 ± 40 (NZ 6472) and 454 ± 32 (NZ 6525). Taken together, these dates suggest that the moa-hunting horizon can be dated to somewhere between 500 and 800 bp, not 700 to 1000 bp. Caughley also conceded that if the nephrite adzes associated with those burials at Wairau Bar which he regards as post-moa-hunting in age were actually from within the moa-hunting period, thus implying exploration of the west coast before moa extinction occurred, then this would be fatal for his model. I suggest, in Chapter 9, that the evidence does indicate continuation of moa-hunting at Wairau Bar during the time nephrite adzes were used as burial goods and, even if that is not in fact the case, there are various instances of nephrite occurring in moa-hunting sites east of the main divide as both Lockerbie (1959) and I found at Hawksburn, for example. Furthermore silcrete blades, which must have come from the southern South Island, were also found, if rarely, at Wairau Bar. The rolling wave hypothesis is, therefore, unable to be sustained.

Nevertheless the underlying idea of some kind of sequential or serial exploitation of resource areas does appear likely (Anderson 1983a, 1987b). The hypothesis I propose is that there was rapid exploration and some colonisation throughout New Zealand prior to systematic moa-hunting getting underway, and that from localities favourable on other or additional grounds – notably places close to seal colonies, the most immediately obvious of New Zealand's big game resources to arriving Polynesians – there developed economies in which moa-hunting became of increasing importance. In the course of this process, overexploitation of moa populations close to the early sites led to expansion into areas where moas, but not other resources, existed in greater quantities.

As discussed above, there seems to have been 8 to 10 moa-hunting sites dispersed along the entire east coast of the South Island, and possibly one (Foxton) on the southwest coast of the North Island by 800–900 bp. Most of these were in areas of rocky coast where seals were abundant. The numerous later coastal sites, and the inland sites – which on the whole are slightly later again (above) – conform to a pattern of occupation which is at least consistent with the process proposed.

Extinction, in this model, can then be seen as a series of local events in which over-hunting in one valley was succeeded by over-hunting in another at a greater distance from the main settlement, the establishment of satellite settlements and, eventually, of substantial movements of population to other places, north or south, along the coast. As coastal valleys became worked out local economies began switching towards a greater emphasis on alternative resources (notably marine fish in the Catlins and east Otago as early as 600 bp, Anderson 1981b), but moa-hunting also expanded, probably in the form of seasonal expeditions, into more distant interior valleys and basins.

This model of serial overkill differs from the rolling wave hypothesis by assuming prior occupation of first-choice localities along the whole of one edge (the east coast) of the hunting grounds, only after which was there a series of broadly radial movements from one local hunting patch to another (Anderson n. d. e).

Predator–prey relationships

Whichever form of overkill hypothesis is preferred, there were elements of the predator–prey relationship which encouraged overexploitation. Moas were not broadly experienced as prey. Raptors preyed upon them, but determined terrestrial predation was entirely novel and they had little opportunity to develop effective behavioural responses to it such as nocturnal habits, increased breeding rates, etc. Second, terrestrial predation concentrated almost entirely upon moas because there were no animals of comparable size to deflect hunting attention.

Third, the hunters were naive; they had no experience of terrestrial big-game, and very little time to develop patterns of selective culling or territoriality before moa populations were depressed below the level of long-term viability. Whether it was an unplanned consequence of their methods or the result of deliberate policy, the catch seems to have been strongly focussed on adult birds, the population sector with the highest breeding potential. Eggs, also, were often intensively gathered.

Fourth, overexploitation was facilitated by the nature of the topography. Moas were slow-breeding, probably not habitually mobile beyond short distances, and were frequently compartmentalised into small populations by mountain ranges and deep, fast rivers. Although these can seldom have been total barriers, they were probably quite effective constraints on re-colonisation of over-hunted areas within the time-frame (100–200 years) of systematic hunting in any district. Topographical fragmentation of moa populations rendered them particularly vulnerable to a radial expansion of hunting pressure from settlements dispersed along the greater part of the coast (Anderson n. d. e).

Alternative hypotheses

Overkill is not the only possible means by which moas could have become extinct in the period 400–1000 bp. As Williams (1962:16) observed, the finding of moa bones in middens does not constitute a proof of extinction by overkill, 'the process could well have been going on independently of either hunting or habitat destruction'. Fauna of high evolutionary age or 'old endemics' are, by virtue of that status, closer to extinction and have frequently developed conservative life histories and habitat adaptations which restrict their distribution and render them more susceptible to environmental fluctuations (Falla 1942; Oliver 1949; Williams 1962; McDowall 1969; Mills et al. 1984). As an argument about vulnerability to extinction this is a valid hypothesis and, for some moas, adaptation to the kind of open environment which was decreasing in extent throughout the Holocene may have already reduced their populations to a dangerously low level (c. 500 breeding pairs or less, King 1984:139) by 1000 bp. Dinornis giganteus, the largest scrub and grassland moa, may have had territorial requirements of a size which had restricted it to two or three viable populations by that time, as its distribution in archaeological sites indicates. Other species, however, were clearly still abundant, and neither coincidental attainment of evolutionary senescence across all moa species nor natural habitat restriction generally can be advanced as explanations of extinction (Anderson 1983b:3). In the eastern South Island, at least, moa populations clearly withstood serious predation for hundreds of years prior to extinction and the Maoris certainly had to do more than 'merely [deal] the coup de grace' as Mills et al. (1984:67) assert.

Disease, dogs and rats

Serious population declines might also have occurred as the result of diseases – conceivably transmitted by the Polynesian fowl, if it ever reached New Zealand, or by migratory birds. Avian malaria occurs in New Zealand (Warner 1968:107), and birdpox – which often creates crippling lesions in the feet (Warner 1968) – is an interesting possibility given the high incidence of badly diseased phalanges noted at Hamiltons by Booth (1875) and other evidence of diseased bones (Hector 1893:557; Anderson and Sorenson 1944). On the other hand, pathological skeletal conditions seem to occur at a non-lethal level amongst cassowaries (Reid n. d.) and may be no more common in moa bones. Another possibility is that periodic outbreaks of botulism – which often occur in shallow, organically-enriched alkaline lakes (Ford 1982:123) during warm dry periods – occurred with lethal frequency in parts of the eastern South Island during the summers of a slightly cooler, and possibly drier, climatic phase between the 16th and 18th centuries.[5] There is, though, insufficient data upon which to test any of these speculations.

The introduction of dogs and the Pacific rat (Rattus exulans) with Polynesian immigrants was probably a contributory factor to moa extinction. Rats may not have directly attacked nesting moas, as Fleming (1969) speculated, but their impact on young chicks, and perhaps even more on the range of small vertebrates and invertebrates which otherwise offered high-protein food to moa chicks, may have been a significant factor (Holdaway n. d.). Whether dogs became feral is uncertain. It seems that they had in some inland South Island areas by the mid-19th century (Anderson 1981a), and they were potentially devastating predators on young moas (as dingoes are on emu), but it is not clear whether dog bones, which are common in moa-hunting sites, were from domestic animals or from a by-catch amongst feral populations.

---

[5] Possibly relevant to natural sites in alkaline swamps.

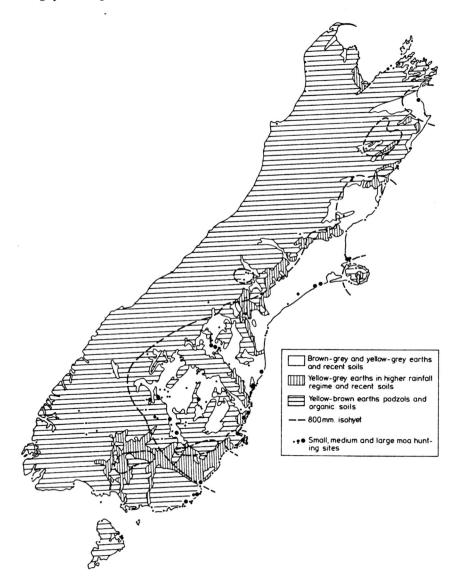

FIG. 13.5   Distribution of South Island moa-hunting sites in relation to soil types and 800 mm isohyet.

Habitat destruction

Transformation of the vegetation, especially in the eastern South Island, can be considered a major factor in moa extinction. The distribution of moa-hunting sites in the South Island, taken as an indication of the density distribution of the more commonly hunted moa species (Chapter 9), reveals a strong correlation with a range of drier vegetation types. The precise distribution of these at c. 1000 bp cannot be mapped as yet, but the broad features of the distribution are fairly predictable in terms of rainfall and soil distributions. The 800 mm isohyet (Fig. 13.5) provides a measure of the eastward margin of beech forest range, which does not extend into areas of less than 1000–

750 mm annual precipitation (Wardle 1984:135).[6] For most birds, including moas, beech forest provided a relatively poor habitat (McGlone n.d.). Areas of yellow-brown earths, podzols and organic soils in areas of higher rainfall were, within the altitudinal limits of forest, mostly heavily forested until the European era.

On brown-grey and yellow-grey earths and recent soils there was a range of drier vegetation types prior to the arrival of Polynesians. On fertile soils in lowland areas, under 600 to 1000 mm annual rainfall, there were stands of tall conifer-broadleaved forest. In inland areas of Otago and

---

[6] There are, however, areas of high rainfall in which beech forest is absent or rare (e.g. central west coast).

south Canterbury this contained a different association of species, but much of it had already given way to shrubland and tussock grassland, as the result of natural fires, by 1700 bp. On lighter lowland soils where the annual rainfall was 600 to 800 mm the forest contained numerous shrubby clearings, while on stony interfluvial areas of the Canterbury plains and on dry, inland hill country faces there was kanuka (*Leptospermum ericoides*) scrub (McGlone n. d.).

At 1000 bp much of the eastern South Island thus presented the appearance of a mosaic of conifer-broadleaved forests, within and around which were vigorous seral communities of shrubs and small trees, and areas of tussock grassland. All but the last of these were both important moa habitats and unusually prone to fire (Anderson 1982a; Hamel 1979; McGlone 1983, n. d.; Molloy 1969).

Between 1000 bp and 500 bp nearly all of the eastern South Island lowland forest and diverse shrublands in the drier districts (less than 800 mm annual rainfall) were destroyed by burning. The Wairau and adjacent valleys, the Canterbury plains, Mackenzie Country and Central Otago became extensive tussock grasslands dotted with patches of species-depauperate scrub and *Cordyline australis* (the cabbage or *ti* tree, an important source of sugar). Small stands of forest remained here and there along the upland fringes, but it was only in areas of higher rainfall (800 to 1600 mm) that more extensive forests survived: on the Kaikoura coast, Banks Peninsula, east Otago, the Catlins and central Southland (see maps in Anderson 1983b; McGlone 1983).

The scale of habitat destruction in the drier areas was such that few moa populations in the drier areas could have survived it. What is less clear, though, is whether large-scale burning occurred during the phase of increasing moa-hunting or only after the peak of hunting had been reached at about 700–650 bp. A series of radiocarbon dates on fossil logs (Molloy et al. 1963) groups fairly closely around 700 bp, in general, but older dates (c. 800 bp) occur on Central Otago samples and pollen analyses also suggest that shrubland was being converted to bracken and grassland in the eastern hills of that district as early as 700 bp (Anderson 1982a). On the other hand, a detailed study of the upper Waimakairiri Valley, in north Canterbury, indicates that devastating fires occurred there between 500 and 600 bp (Molloy 1977). Extensive burning prior to the main phase of moa-hunting can probably be ruled out, but there are not yet enough data to distinguish a

pattern of contemporaneous hunting and habitat destruction from a pattern of extensive burning once moa populations were already in substantial decline and alternative terrestrial resources had to be sought. Forest firing was a normal Polynesian practice which, because New Zealand's forests had few pyrophytic species, had unforeseen and irreversible effects in the drier districts. Even so, it increased the abundance of some valuable plants (notably *Cordyline* and *Pteridium* sp.) and the production of streams for freshwater fish (McGlone et al. n. d.)

In the western South Island the forest cover remained virtually intact, as it did to a considerable extent in the North Island. There were, however, some important areas in the North Island – notably in the extensive dune country in the far north – where burning after about 1000 bp was highly destructive (Millener 1981). There was also widespread forest firing in the early Polynesian period in the lowlands of the southwest coast, Hawke's Bay and Bay of Plenty (McGlone 1978, 1983, n. d.).[7]

Course and causes of extinction

Whether some genera or species of moas became extinct before others is a question with important implications for our understanding of moa ecology and behaviour, as well as hunting methods. Duff (1951) suggested a sequence of extinction (Fig. 13.6) and Cracraft (1980:36) has asserted that 'species of *Dinornis*, *Emeus* and *Pachyornis* were the first to be exterminated, probably within several hundred years after human colonization' but that *Euryapteryx* survived until 300–400 bp. I can see no evidence of this in the archaeological data. On the grounds that it was the largest species, occurred in fairly open country and was probably not as common as most others, we might expect *D. giganteus* to disappear early in the piece. However, it is reported from Makara (possibly c. 450 bp), Tairua (c. 550 bp) and Kaupokonui (c. 600–650 bp), amongst other sites. There is no apparent temporal order in the disappearances of other North Island species.

[7] There were some minor climatic variations after 1000 bp (Burrows 1982), but not on a scale significant for moa extinction. The degree and direction of their potential impact on vegetation patterns is unclear but, again, is not likely to have had a significant bearing on extinction. Amongst possible consequences of deforestation Melvin (1871) suggests that an increase in the abundance of the poisonous berry-shrub, *tutu*, may have contributed to moa extinction.

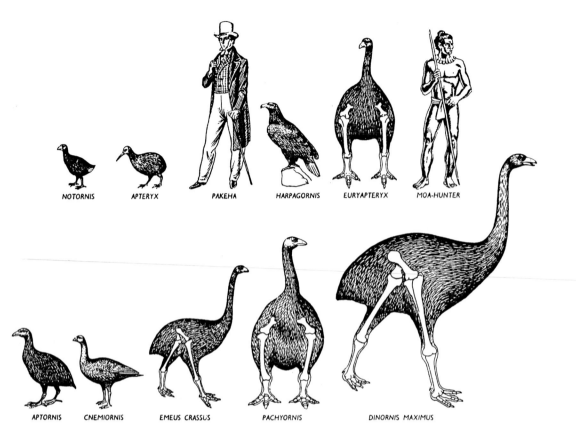

NOTORNIS   APTERYX   PAKEHA   HARPAGORNIS   EURYAPTERYX   MOA-HUNTER

APTORNIS   CNEMIORNIS   EMEUS CRASSUS   PACHYORNIS   DINORNIS MAXIMUS

FIG. 13.6   The approximate order of extinction (running from lower right to upper left) amongst large New Zealand birds, as suggested by Duff (after Duff 1949:24–25).

In the South Island, *D. giganteus* seems to occur mainly in sites with early horizons, but since most of these also have later moa-hunting layers (Pounawea, Papatowai, Shag Mouth, etc.) and the precise provenances of its remains are unknown, there are no grounds for inferring an early extinction. In any case, *D. giganteus* occurred at Owen's Ferry (*c.* 700 bp) and Purakanui (*c.* 500 bp). All other South Island genera occur in sites dated up to 400–500 bp, as do the remaining species of *Dinornis*.

The broad implication would seem to be that moas were hunted more or less proportionately to their natural abundance, that is, non-selectively, so that the decline towards extinction was a fairly even process across the genera. In the few instances where there are stratigraphic data from single sites, as at Pounawea (Hamel 1980) and Papatowai (Hamel 1977a), the genera which persist longest are, as might be expected, those thought to have been generally most abundant in the eastern South Island – *Emeus* and *Euryapteryx* (although the least accessible genus, *Megalapteryx*, is also represented in the upper layer at Pounawea).

Whether the various causes of extinction (above) operated differentially amongst species or regions is another important question which is difficult to answer precisely. Both hunting and habitat destruction were concentrated, in each main island, on areas where species of the '*Euryapteryx* assemblage' were most common, and may be regarded as the most likely explanations of extinction throughout this suite of species. Overkill, I have argued, is an adequate explanation for extinction in the eastern South Island. Given the smaller extent of habitat for '*Euryapteryx* assemblage' species in the southwest North Island, yet a comparable density of coastal hunting sites, it is, perhaps, equally sufficient there as well. Habitat destruction is less convincing as a single explanation because, in both regions, some substantial areas of shrubland remained by about 500 bp and some moa species, if unpredated, could probably have survived. The reality of the situation was that the processes overlapped substantially and, together, were undoubtedly lethal.

Beyond these areas and in some smaller districts (Coromandel, northern Northland) where extinction by overkill also seems likely, it is difficult to see what caused the moa to disappear, particularly within the '*Anomalopteryx* assemblage'. The species are seldom as common in sites as those of the 'Euryapteryx assemblage' and, although they probably had lower population densities overall, they inhabited areas more difficult of access, often far from the coast, and which largely escaped severe forest burning. If it was not dogs and rats which were responsible, we may have to consider that even light and discontinuous hunting was sufficient – as Diamond (1984) suggests from his experience of large, naive game in seldom-visited regions of New Guinea. (That being so, it would reinforce the probability that overkill was easily attained in the main moa-hunting regions.)

Whatever the case there is an obvious correlation between the decline and extinction of moas and the growth of human population. Initially the latter may have occurred faster in the South Island where there were more abundant and accessible protein-rich resources (Cumberland 1962:166; McGlone et al. n. d.), but the main surge was certainly in the North Island. Calculated at conservative rates of 0.8 per cent (Cumberland 1962:159) or 1 per cent (Law 1977) per year from a base of several hundred people at 1000 bp, the growth curves are steepest between 750 and 450 bp, the peak moa-hunting years, during which the North Island population size moved from one order of magnitude (1000s) well into the next. Casual hunting by a rapidly expanding population may have been enough to exceed the MSY of North Island moas.

Clearly there is still much to learn about moa extinction, but that it was caused, in various ways, by the human colonisation of New Zealand, can hardly be in doubt.

14

CONCLUSIONS

Looking back on a century of moa research, Archey (1941:5) observed that it had not been possible 'to establish finality, either in fact or inference . . . for each new find or investigation, in solving some problem, has as frequently revealed new uncertainties'. In certain respects that assessment remains valid another half-century on. The phylogenesis of moas is still an open question, both in their relationships to other palaeognaths and in their arrival and development in New Zealand. Vastly different implications, furthermore, hang on the choice between competing hypotheses. Systematic relationships at the familial and subfamilial levels, which have been explained by the operation of selective forces arising from vicariance and other environmental factors, would be viewed quite differently were it possible to show that moas were descended from several different flying ancestors – a view which is currently gaining ground. The importance of discovering fossil evidence of moas dated to earlier than the Pliocene can hardly be overstated.

Considerable progress has been made, however, at the generic and specific levels. The currently accepted pattern of the genera was set by Archey in 1941 and, since then, the main issue has been synonymisation of species. In this, Cracraft's comparative method supplied the objective measure of discrimination which had eluded researchers in more than a century of unrewarding manipulation of leg-bone dimensions. There have been minor changes to Cracraft's taxonomy, but recent analyses of leg-bone morphological traits, particularly by Worthy (n. d. b), have disclosed a substantial measure of agreement.

A certain stability in systematics, so long sought, has provided the platform upon which

other aspects of moa biology could be more confidently addressed. These have included further resolution of morphological distinctions between gracile and robust species, a problem which goes back to Owen's second definition of *Palapteryx*, and new estimations of weight and stature. It is now apparent that moas generally conformed to relationships of size and weight common to other birds and that none were grossly stout or awkward, as early opinion suggested. To the extent that there is deviation from the norm, it is in the opposite direction, in the gracility of *Dinornis* species. Research on moa diet – one of the most important outcomes of excavation at Pyramid Valley swamp – and subsequently on habitat preference and distribution has also caused revision of earlier views of moas as uniformly inhabiting open country.

There are still many unresolved issues in these and other aspects of moa biology. For instance we do not have a clear picture of variations in posture and movement, for although there are anatomical reasons to think that moas generally carried the neck looped, not upright, and that Dinornithids moved in a different gait from Anomalopterygids, the data have yet to be detailed. Reflection of functional differences in variations of beak form and operating musculature is another open issue. Sexual dimorphism is not yet well defined nor clearly separated from environmental influences upon size and shape. In the case of some species, such as *M. didinus*, *P. mappini* and *Eu. geranoides*, there is clear evidence that diminution occurred in the Holocene, and it is also apparent that there is intraspecific variation in size with latitude. Moa digestion, breeding behaviours, clutch sizes, habitual mobility, social arrangements and abundance are further areas in which data remain scarce and equivocal. Dwelling no further on these deficiencies in the evidence, I propose the following summary of moa biology.

Dinornithiformes, known as moas, were a group of large, wingless, New Zealand ratites which became extinct prior to the arrival of Europeans. They were probably descended from flying birds, possibly of different taxa, which reached New Zealand during the Tertiary and subsequently developed common anatomical characteristics by neotenic convergence. No taxa ancestral to Holocene species are recognised.

Recent classifications group moas into one or two families (Dinornithidae and Anomalopterygidae), six genera and about 12 species. Common to both main islands were *Anomalopteryx didiformis*, *Euryapteryx geranoides* (including *Eu. gravis*) and *Dinornis struthoides*, *novaezealandiae* and *giganteus*. *Euryapteryx curtus* and *Pachyornis mappini* were North Island moas, while *Megalapteryx didinus*, *Emeus crassus*, *Pachyornis elephantopus* (also *P. australis* and *D. torosus* if recognised separately) were South Island species. At least one genus, *Euryapteryx*, occurred on Stewart Island.

Moas ranged in stature from about 70 to 190 cm (height of back), and in weight from about 20 to 200 kg. Dinornithids were tall and gracile, and had long tarsometatarsi and broad, flat crania; Anomalopterygids were short and stout bodied, with comparatively short tarsometatarsi and rounder vaulted crania.

It is probable that all moas were diurnal, lived in small groups rather than flocks and were locally mobile. As adults they were herbivorous, though omnivorous as chicks, and probably had monogastric digestive systems requiring a high volume of fibrous foliage supplemented by a wide variety of more nutritious items. Food competition was minimised by sexual dimorphism, interspecific size differences and other mechanisms.

Clutch sizes were very small, one or two eggs, and chicks nidifugous. It can be assumed that females were iteroparous, and that moas in general were long-lived and K-selected. Adults and chicks were predated by native raptors.

Moas were found in most potential habitats between coastal dunes and alpine grasslands up to about 2000 m in altitude. They can be divided, however, into two broad ecological assemblages. *D. giganteus*, *Euryapteryx*, *Pachyornis* (except *P. australis*, possibly a high-country species) and *Emeus* were found mainly in fairly open lowland situations: dunelands, forest fringes and forest, shrub and grassland mosaics. In these areas moa populations probably reached a density of several individuals per km². Other *Dinornis* species and *A. didiformis* seem to have lived. in dense lowland conifer-broadleaved forest, and also beech forest in limestone areas. At higher altitudes, often in beech forest, *A. didiformis* was replaced by *M. didinus*.

This summary, it should be pointed out, owes nothing to Maori traditional evidence. Much was asserted about moas, and moa-hunting and extinction as well, by those who espoused alleged traditions as historical evidence – particularly between 1870 and 1920, and again recently. But while the content of some of these stories is plausible, there are cogent arguments against accepting nearly all of them as genuine recollections.

Turning to moa-hunting, it was accepted at a very early stage of research that 'in the absence of any other large wild animals, the whole art and practise of the chase must have concentrated on these unhappy cursorial birds' (Owen 1849b:270). Until recently, though, there was almost no deliberate investigation of moa-hunting sites in terms of elucidating that activity. It was only incidental to his interest in Moa-hunters that Haast established some of the functional characteristics of butchery sites and in nearly a century after 1870 very little else came to light. Evidence of moa-hunting held virtually no intrinsic interest and was regarded as simply the minimal definition of a cultural phase, all the importance of which resided in matters of material culture and culture history. Indeed in his influential monograph, *The Moa-hunter Period of Maori Culture*, Duff (1950) had even less to say about moa-hunting than had Taylor, Mantell or Haast.

Systematic research began only with the development of quantified methods of analysis in the late 1960s. These reflected a growing interest in economic prehistory which was, in turn, a manifestation of the same disciplinary convergence upon ecological models which fostered new approaches to the study of moa biology. Out of the latter emerged the means to better conceptualise moas as prey; not simply as 'the moa' but as a diverse group of birds which had exhibited particular characteristics of variability, distribution, behaviour and abundance.

The implications of these data for understanding moa-hunting cannot yet be fully realised. More than 300 sites have been recorded and about 50 of them investigated, but in general the excavations were very limited in extent and seldom occurred in major sites. As a result, quantitative faunal data are relatively few and variable in quality, and only tentative suggestions can be advanced about hunting and butchery.

The very small number and size of kill sites indicates that mass-kill episodes did not occur. Snares, dogs and spears were probably used, judging by ethnographic analogy and the lack of any remains of hunting artefacts in the archaeological evidence. Nevertheless, where moas were abundant, such individualised hunting was wasteful, and most kills were returned to butchery sites as upper-leg joints representing a third or less of the available meat weight. Present data indicate an emphasis on adults, with immature birds and chicks being seldom caught. Eggs, though, were frequently gathered. Tibiotarsi were selectively smashed, presumably for marrow, but there is little additional evidence of the collection of fat or of its use in flesh preservation. Butchery sites, generally, seem also to have been the localities at which catches were consumed.

Processing technology also remains rather poorly defined. Some artefacts, notably ulu and large blades, are clearly associated with moa-hunting sites, but only in southern New Zealand, and it is difficult to demonstrate that early confidence in their butchery functions was, in fact, well-placed. Use-damage patterns on flake and blade tools do not point unequivocally to butchery, and although the distinctive blade technology was probably developed in response to that need, blades are by no means as abundant in butchery sites as has often been assumed.

Research on the basic processes of hunting and butchery clearly has some considerable way to go. It is essential, especially in the North Island, to find a non-contextual means of distinguishing subfossil bone. There are also taphonomic questions to be answered about within-site and regional variations of bone survival according to element and maturity before we can be certain about patterns of return and processing. A better understanding of butchery technology depends, in part, on finding a more powerful means of functional discrimination than use-damage (as Newcomer *et al.* 1986 have argued). Perhaps residue analysis may hold the key. There is also a need to explain why there is such a marked difference in lithic assemblages between moa butcheries in the North and South Islands. These are also matters of some greater significance (below).

Looking at the distribution of sites overall, and evidence of the relative abundance of moa remains in them, it seems that there were marked variations in the regional importance of moa-hunting. Broadly speaking these can be attributed to the accessibility and probable abundance of different moa species. In the North Island (24 per cent of sites) there are very few, and small, inland sites. Closed forest covered most of the interior and moa-hunting was therefore largely confined to forest-edge and shrubland species around the coast, notably *Eu. curtus* and *P. mappini*, especially in the southwest district. In the South Island (76 per cent of sites) there was a similar concentration on species of the 'Euryapteryx assemblage' which inhabited the extensive vegetation mosaic of dry lowland forest and seral communities found east of the main axial ranges where 86 per cent of South Island sites are located. In this region there seem to have been two hunting strategies, which differed according to the practicability of transporting catches down-river to coastal butchery sites. These butchery sites, sometimes of very considerable extent, were probably repeatedly occupied sites which, like large inland butcheries, were temporarily occupied by hunters whose main settlements were located in those coastal areas where resource diversity was significantly higher.

The validity of this overview is substantially dependent, however, on whether the current pattern of sites is a fair reflection of their former distribution. On grounds of moa ecology, we might expect more sites to be discovered along the east coast of the North Island and in the northeast interior of the South Island. There is also a possibility that the much smaller and less-distinctive North Island lithic assemblages, coupled with regional variation in the survival of moa bone, have significantly influenced our present perception and explanation of the distribution of moa-hunting sites; that is, that the density of sites in the eastern South Island is, to some extent, a consequence of taphonomic factors and prehistoric access to certain lithic materials. Investigation of these matters might well subvert our present views.

In the matter of moa extinction, the extent to which overexploitation is implicated depends on questions of chronology and abundance. The radiocarbon chronology of moa-hunting sites is uncertain in several respects, including variation according to sample-type differences and with regard to calculation standards. In such a short prehistory these problems loom oppressively large. Nevertheless there is broad agreement that moa-hunting began about 900 bp, was most widespread and intensive in both main islands by about 650 bp and had ceased by 400 bp. It is very unlikely that moas survived much longer than that date. Alleged traditional evidence is thoroughly contradictory and clearly confused by naive interpretation of a complex ethno-ornithology, while arguments from surface remains of moas beg taphonomic questions.

The fairly long span of moa-hunting, the abundance of sites and the lack of any convincing evidence of radial expansion in hunting activities above the district level, seem to rule out overkill hypotheses of the blitzkrieg and rolling wave kind. Overkill by serial exploitation of topographically fragmented populations from a string of coastal settlements is the explanation I prefer for areas in which moas were abundant. It depends considerably, though, on what can only be regarded as crude estimations of moa abundance and productivity and of the number of moas actually killed.

Massive habitat destruction, which was broadly contemporaneous with moa-hunting, must have been a significant factor as well, but until there are many more radiocarbon dates which describe the progress of vegetation change, and of hunting, it is impossible to place these causes of extinction in a clear order of priority.

If it seems from these conclusions that 150 years of research has, indeed, raised as many questions as it has answered, it would be as well to emphasise that now they are, at least, different questions. Bound no longer to a study of moas and moa-hunters in which the characterisation of remains was a sufficient objective, we are beginning to file through conceptual shackles, fastened by the fact of extinction, towards a new understanding of once-living birds and their hunters.

BIBLIOGRAPHY

Abbreviations

AO = Archaeology in Oceania
APAO = Archaeology and Physical Anthropology in Oceania
HPT = New Zealand Historic Places Trust
JPS = Journal of the Polynesian Society
JRSNZ = Journal of the Royal Society of New Zealand
JZSL = Journal of the Zoological Society of London
NZAA = New Zealand Archaeological Association Newsletter
NZJA = New Zealand Journal of Archaeology
NZJE = New Zealand Journal of Ecology
PZSL = Proceedings of the Zoological Society of London
RAIM = Records of the Auckland Institute and Museum
RCM = Records of the Canterbury Museum
RNMNZ = Records of the National Museum of New Zealand
SRF = NZAA Site Record Form
TNZI = Transactions of the New Zealand Institute
TRSNZ = Transactions of the Royal Society of New Zealand
TZSL = Transactions of the Zoological Society of London

Adkin, G. L. 1948. *Horowhenua: Its Maori Place-names and their Topographic and Historical Background.* Internal Affairs, Wellington.

Adkin, G. L. 1960. An adequate culture nomenclature for the New Zealand area. *JPS* 69:228–38.

Alexander, R. McN. 1983a. Allometry of the leg bones of moas (Dinornithes) and other birds. *JZSL* 200:215–31.

Alexander, R. McN. 1983b. On the massive legs of a moa (*Pachyornis elephantopus*, Dinornithes). *JZSL* 201:363–76.

Allingham, B. 1983. Preliminary notes on a coastal Moa hunter site at Warrington, Otago. *NZAA* 26:228–30.

Allingham, B. 1985. Warrington moa-hunter site. Rpt. to HPT.

Allingham, B. 1986. Warrington moa-hunter site. Rpt. to HPT.

Allingham, B. 1987. Excavation notes on Tumbledown Bay. The author.

Allingham, B. 1988. Excavations on a moa-hunter period site at the mouth of the Pleasant River, North Otago. ms.

Allingham, B. n. d. Field diary. The author.

Allis, T. 1864a. Skeleton of a moa. *The Zoologist* (1st Series) 22:9114.

Allis, T. 1864b. The recent moa. *The Zoologist* (1st Series) 22:9195–7.

Allis, T. 1865a. Notice of a nearly complete skeleton of a *Dinornis*; presented by Mr Gibson to the Museum of the Yorkshire Philosophical Society. *Journal of the Proceedings of the Linnean Society* 8:50–2.

Allis, T. 1865b. Further note on a skeleton of *Dinornis robustus*, Owen, in the York Museum. *Journal of the Proceedings of the Linnean Society* 8:140–1.

Allo, J. 1970. The Maori dog — a study of the Polynesian dog in New Zealand. MA thesis, University of Auckland.

Allo, J. 1972. The Whangamata Wharf site (N49/2): excavations on a Coromandel coastal midden. *RAIM* 9:61–79.

Amadon, D. 1947. An estimated weight of the largest known bird. *The Condor* 49:159–63.

Ambrose, W. 1968. The unimportance of the inland plains in South Island prehistory. *Mankind* 6:585–93.

Ambrose, W. 1970. Archaeology and rock drawings from the Waitaki Gorge, Central South Island. *RCM* 8:383–437.

Anderson, A. J. 1966. Maori occupation sites in back beach deposits around Tasman Bay. MA thesis, University of Canterbury.

Anderson, A. J. 1978a. Waitaki Mouth excavation notes. The author.

Anderson, A. J. 1978b. A site survey of North Otago from Waitaki Mouth to Warrington. Rpt. to HPT.

Anderson, A. J. 1979a. Excavations at the Archaic site of Waianakarua Mouth, North Otago. *NZAA* **22**:156–61.

Anderson, A. J. 1979b. Excavations at the Hawksburn Moa-hunting site; an interim report. *NZAA* **22**:48–59.

Anderson, A. J. 1980. The rediscovery of a Moa hunting site in the Old Man Range. *NZAA* **23**:169–72.

Anderson, A. J. 1981a. A fourteenth-century fishing camp at Purakanui Inlet, Otago. *JRSNZ* **11**:201–21.

Anderson, A. J. 1981b. Pre-European hunting dogs in the South Island, New Zealand. *NZJA* **3**:15–20.

Anderson, A. J. 1982a. Habitat preferences of moa in Central Otago, A.D. 1000–1500, according to palaeobotanical and archaeological evidence. *JRSNZ* **3**:321–36.

Anderson, A. J. 1982b. A review of economic patterns during the Archaic phase in southern New Zealand. *NZJA* **4**:45–75.

Anderson, A. J. 1982c. The Otokia Mouth site at Brighton Beach, Otago. *NZAA* **25**:47–52.

Anderson, A. J. 1982d. Maori settlement in the interior of southern New Zealand from the early 18th to late 19th centuries A.D. *JPS* **91**:53–80.

Anderson, A. J. 1982e. West Coast, South Island. In *The First Thousand Years*, ed. N. Prickett, Dunmore Press, Palmerston North 103–11.

Anderson, A. J. 1983a. The prehistoric hunting of moa (Aves: Dinornithidae) in the high country of southern New Zealand. In *Animals and Archaeology*, eds. C. Grigson and J. Clutton-Brock, Vol. 2: Shell middens, fishes and birds, pp. 33–52. B.A.R., Oxford.

Anderson, A. J. 1983b. Faunal depletion and subsistence change in the early prehistory of southern New Zealand. *AO* **18**:1–10.

Anderson, A. J. 1984. The extinction of moa in southern New Zealand. In P. S. Martin and R. G. Klein, pp. 728–40.

Anderson, A. J. 1986. 'Makeshift structures of little importance': a reconsideration of Maori round huts. *JPS* **95**:91–114.

Anderson, A. J. 1987a. The first-recorded name for moa. *JRSNZ* **17**:421–2.

Anderson, A. J. 1987b. Supertramp science: some thoughts on archaeometry and archaeology in Oceania. In *Archaeometry: Further Australasian Studies*, eds. W. R. Ambrose and J. M. J. Mummery pp. 3–18. ANU, Canberra.

Anderson, A. J. 1988a. Moa extinctions in southern New Zealand: a reply to Sutton. *AO* **23**:78–9.

Anderson, A. J. 1988b. Mahinga kai: submission to Waitangi Tribunal. ms.

Anderson, A. J. n. d. a. On evidence for the survival of moa in European Fiordland. *NZJE*, in press.

Anderson, A. J. n. d. b. The beast without: moa as colonial frontier myths. In *Signifying Animals*, ed. R. Willis, in press.

Anderson, A. J. n. d. c. Salvage excavations at Mapoutahi Pa, Otago. Anthropology Department, University of Otago, Working Papers 1.

Anderson, A. J. n. d. d. Notes on central Otago lithic industries. The author.

Anderson, A. J. n. d. e. Mechanics of overkill in the extinction of New Zealand moas. *Journal of Archaeological Science*, in press.

Anderson, A. J. and N. Ritchie, 1984. Preliminary report on test excavations at a newly discovered moa-hunting site at Coal Creek, Central Otago. *NZAA* **27**:174–80.

Anderson, A. J. and N. Ritchie 1986. Pavements, pounamu and ti: the Dart Bridge site in western Otago, New Zealand. *NZJA* **8**:115–41.

Anderson, A. J., B. Allingham and I. W. G. Smith n. d. Notes on faunal remains from Warrington. University of Otago.

Anderson, C. C. and J. H. Sorenson 1944. Chronic osteomyelitis occurring in *Emeus crassus*. *TRSNZ* **74**:182–4.

Anonymous, 1875. The moas of New Zealand. *Nature* **11**:289–90.

Anonymous, 1876. Notes. *Nature* **13**:196.

Anonymous, 1898. *The Imperial Albumn of New Zealand Scenery*. McKee, Gamble and Wheeler, Wellington.

Archer, M. 1984. Earth-shattering concepts for historical zoogeography. In Archer and Clayton, pp. 45–59.

Archer, M. and G. Clayton 1984. *Vertebrate Zoogeography and Evolution in Australasia: animals in time and space*. Hesperian Press, Melbourne.

Archey, G. 1927. On a moa skeleton from Amodeo Bay and some moa bones from Karamu. *TNZI* **58**:151–6.

Archey, G. 1931. Notes on sub-fossil bird remains. *RAIM* **1**:113–21.

Archey, G. 1941. The moa: a study of the Dinornithiformes. *Bull. Auck. Inst. Mus.* no. 1.

Atkinson, I. E. A., and R. M. Greenwood 1980. Divaricating plants and moa browsing: a reply. *NZJE* **3**:165–7.

Atkinson, I. A. E. and R. M. Greenwood n. d. Moa-plant relationships. ms.

Augusta, J. and Z. Burian n. d. *Prehistoric Animals*. Spring Books, London.

Bagley, S. 1973. Clutha Valley HEP development: historical and archaeological sites in the Clutha Valley. Rpt. to HPT.

Bain, P. J. 1979. A functional analysis study of the porcellanite artefacts from the moa-hunting site of Hawksburn. BA hons. thesis, University of Otago.

Barnicoat, J. n. d. Journal 1844. Hocken Library, Dunedin, NZ.

Batley, R. A. L. 1960. Inland Patea. *NZAA* **3**:14–16.

Beattie, H. 1920. Nature-lore of the southern Maori. *TNZI* **32**:53–77.

Beattie, H. 1954. Our Southernmost Maoris, *The Otago Daily Times*, Dunedin, NZ.

Beattie, H. 1958. The moa: when did it become extinct? *The Otago Daily Times*, Dunedin, NZ.

Beattie, H. n. d. Collected papers. Hocken Library, Dunedin, NZ.

Beck, R. J. n. d. Moa bone investigation at Lake Hauroko. Southland Museum, Invercargill, NZ, ms.

Beddard, F. E. 1911. On the alimentary tract of certain birds and on the mesenteric relations of the intestinal loops. *PZSL* 1911, pp. 47–93.

Benham, W. B. 1902. Note on an entire egg of a moa, now in the museum of the University of Otago. *TNZI* 34:149–51.

Benham, W. B. 1910. The discovery of moa remains on Stewart Island. *TNZI* 42:354–6.

Benham, W. B. 1935. The skeleton of a small moa, *Emeus Huttoni* Owen. *TNZI* 63:87–103.

Best, E. 1896. The Maori and the moa. *JPS* 5:121–2.

Best, E. 1942. *Forest Lore of the Maori*. Government Printer, Wellington.

Best, S. J. and R. J. Merchant 1976. Siliceous sinter and the early Maori. *NZAA* 19:106–9.

Binford, L. R. 1978. *Nunamiut Ethnoarchaeology*. Academic Press, New York.

Blake-Palmer, G. 1956. An Otago coastal occupation site with *Dinornis* remains. *JPS* 65:161–3.

Bock, W. J. 1963. The cranial evidence for ratite affinities. *Proceedings of the Eighth International Ornithological Congress*, pp. 39–54.

Bonica, D. G. and N. Thorpe 1967. Notes on archaeological sites etc. Napier Boys High School, Napier, NZ.

Booth, B. S. 1875. Description of the moa swamp at Hamilton. *TNZI* 7:123–38.

Booth, B. S. 1877. On a second discovery of moa bones at Hamilton. *TNZI* 9:365–6.

Booth, B. S. n. d. Field notes kept for F. W. Hutton on excavations at Shag Mouth. National Museum of New Zealand, Wellington.

Boyd, M. S. 1900. *Our Stolen Summer*. Blackwood, Edinburgh.

Brewster, B. 1987. *Te Moa: the life and death of New Zealand's unique bird*. Nikau Press, Nelson, NZ.

Brodie, J. W. 1950. Moa remains at Castlepoint. *New Zealand Science Review* September, pp. 87–8.

Brodkorb, P. 1963. Catalogue of fossil birds (Pt 1). *Bull. Florida State Museum (Biological Sciences)* 7:208–18.

Brown, J. C. 1978. Report on porcellanite quarries. University of Otago.

Buckley, L. 1978. Microwear analysis of some stone artefacts with special reference to the New Zealand ulu. Research essay, University of Otago.

Buick, T. L. 1931. *The Mystery of the Moa: New Zealand's Avian Giant*. Avery, New Plymouth, NZ.

Buick, T. L. 1936. *The Discovery of Dinornis*. Avery, New Plymouth, NZ.

Buick, T. L. 1937. *The Moa-hunters of New Zealand*. Avery, New Plymouth, NZ.

Buist, A. G. 1962. Archaeological evidence of the Archaic phase of occupation in South Taranaki. *NZAA* 5:233–7.

Buist, A. G. 1963. Kaupokonui midden, South Taranaki N128/3. Preliminary report. *NZAA* 6:175–83.

Buist, A. n. d. Notes on Kaupokonui excavations. In Cassels, n. d.

Buist, A. G. and J. C. Yaldwyn 1960. An 'articulated' moa leg from an oven excavated at Waingongoro, South Taranaki. *JPS* 69:76–88.

Buller, W. L. 1869. Essay on the ornithology of New Zealand. *TNZI* 1:213–31.

Buller, W. L. 1888. *A History of the Birds of New Zealand*. The author, London.

Buller, W. L. 1893. Comment on Tregear 1893. *TNZI* 25:530.

Burnett, T. D. 1927. The Mackenzie Country. In *Natural History of Canterbury*, eds. R. Speight, A. Wall and R. M. Laing. Philosophical Institute of Canterbury, pp. 49–59.

Burrage, S. 1981. Wakanui report. Canterbury Museum, Christchurch. ms.

Burrows, C. J. 1969. Lowland and upland scrub. In *Natural History of Canterbury*, ed. G. A. Knox, pp. 212–17. Reed, Wellington.

Burrows, C. J. 1980a. Diet of New Zealand Dinornithiformes. *Naturwissenschaften* 67:n. p.

Burrows, C. J. 1980b. Some empirical information concerning the diet of moas. *NZJE* 3:125–30.

Burrows, C. J. 1982. On New Zealand climate within the last 1000 years. *NZJA* 4:157–67.

Burrows, C. J., B. McCulloch and M. M. Trotter 1981. The diet of moas. *RCM* 9:309–36.

Burrows, C. J., M. J. McSavenay, R. J. Scarlett and B. Turnbull 1984. Late Holocene forest horizons and a *Dinornis* moa from an earthflow on North Dean, North Canterbury. *RCM* 10:1–8.

Butts, D. 1978. Rotokura: An archaeological site in Tasman Bay. *J. Nelson Hist. Soc.* III:4–17.

Byatt, L. 1972. Wakanui fieldwork. *Cant. Mus. Arch. Soc. Newsletter* no. 26.

Calder, A. 1972. *Opito and Otama: Archaeological Report*. The author, Opito, NZ.

Canavan, T. 1960. Preliminary report on excavations at the Te Rangatapu site (Waingongoro River). *NZAA* 3:9–12.

Carty, V. L. 1981. Lithic analysis and activity areas: a case study from Hawksburn. BA hons. thesis, University of Otago.

Cassels, R. 1979. Whatever happened to New Zealand's moas? *Wildlife* 21:31–3.

Cassels, R. n. d. Kaupokonui N128/3B; a moa butchery and cooking site. A preliminary report on the 1974 rescue excavations. Plus associated notes. Taranaki Museum, New Plymouth. NZ.

Caughley, G. 1977. The taxonomy of moas. *Tuatara* **23**:20–5.

Caughley, G. n. d. The colonisation of New Zealand by the Polynesians. CSIRO Div. Wildl. and Rangelands Res., ms.

Caughley, G. and D. Grice 1982. A correction factor for counting emus from the air and its application to counts in Western Australia. *Aust. Wildl. Res.* **9**:253–9.

Chandler, A. C. 1916. A study of the structure of feathers with reference to their taxonomic significance. *University of California Publications in Zoology* **13**: 243–446.

Chapman, F. R. 1885. Notes on moa remains in the Mackenzie Country and other localities. *TNZI* **17**:172–8.

Chapman, F. R. 1892. On the working of greenstone or nephrite by the Maoris. *TNZI* **24**:479–539.

Cheeseman, T. F. 1876. Moa remains discovered at Ellerslie, near Auckland. *TNZI* **8**:427–9.

Clements, J. 1981. *Birds of the World: a checklist*. Croom Helm, London.

Cockburn-Hood, T. 1875. Comment, 3rd meeting Wellington Philosophical Society. *TNZI* **7**:493–5.

Cody, M. L. 1973. Parallel evolution and bird niches. In *Mediterranean Type Ecosystems*, ed. F. Di Castri and H. A. Mooney, pp. 307–38. Springer-Verlag, Berlin.

Colbourne, R. and R. Kleinpaste 1983. A banding study of North Island Brown Kiwi in an exotic forest. *Notornis* **30**:109–24.

Colenso, W. 1846. An account of some enormous fossil bones, of an unknown species of the class Aves, lately discovered in New Zealand. *Tasmanian Journal of Natural Science* **II**:81–107. Also published 1844 in *Annals and Magazine of Natural History* **14**:81–96.

Colenso, W. 1869. On the Maori races of New Zealand. *TNZI* **1**:339–423.

Colenso, W. 1879. On the ignorance of the ancient New Zealander of the use of projectile weapons. *TNZI* **11**:106–18.

Colenso, W. 1880. On the moa. *TNZI* **12**:62–108.

Colenso, W. 1892. Status quo: A retrospect . . . etc. *TNZI* **24**:468–78.

Colenso, W. 1894. Notes and observations on M. A. de Quatrefages' paper 'On moas and Moa-hunters' republished in Vol. XXV *TNZI*. *TNZI* **26**:498–513.

Cook, R. and R. Green 1962. An inland Archaic site. *NZAA* **5**:30–2.

Coutts, P. J. F. 1970. Archaeology in the Port Craig, Sandhill Point regions. *APAO* **5**:53–9.

Coutts, P. J. F. 1972. The emergence of the Foveaux Strait Maori from prehistory: a study of culture contact. PhD thesis, University of Otago.

Coutts, P. J. F. 1977. Archaeological studies at Dusky and Breaksea Sounds, Southwest Fiordland, New Zealand: a summary. *JPS* **86**:37–72.

Coutts, P. J. F. and M. Jurisich 1972. Results of an archaeological survey of Ruapuke Island. *Studies in Prehistoric Anthropology (Otago University)* no. 5.

Cracraft, J. 1974a. Phylogeny and evolution of the ratite birds. *Ibis* **116**:494–521.

Cracraft, J. 1974b. Continental drift and vertebrate distribution. *Annual Review of Ecology and Systemics* **5**:215–61.

Cracraft, J. 1976a. The species of moas (Aves: Dinornithidae). *Smithsonian Contributions to Paleobiology* **27**:189–205.

Cracraft, J. 1976b. The hindlimb elements of the moas (Aves, Dinornithidae): A multivariate assessment of size and shape. *J. Morphology* **150**:495–526.

Cracraft, J. 1976c. Covariation patterns in the postcranial skeleton of the moas (Aves, Dinornithidae): A factor analytic study. *Paleobiology* **2**:166–73.

Cracraft, J. 1980. Moas and the Maoris. *Natural History* 10/80:28–36.

Crawford, J. C. 1873. Notes on Miramar peninsula. *TNZI* **5**:396–400.

Crome, F. H. J. 1976. Some observations on the biology of the cassowary in northern Queensland. *The Emu* **76**:8–14.

Cumberland, K. B. 1962. Moas and men, New Zealand about A.D. 1250. *The Geographical Review* **52**:151–73.

Dallas, W. S. 1865. On the feathers of *Dinornis robustus* Owen. *PZSL* 1865, pp. 265–8.

Davidson, J. M. 1976. Survey and excavations at Te Ika-a-Maru Bay, Wellington 1962–3. *NZAA* **19**:4–26.

Davidson, J. M. 1978. Archaeological salvage excavations at Paremata, Wellington, New Zealand. *RNMNZ* **1**:203–36.

Davidson, J. M. 1979. Archaic middens of the Coromandel region: a review. In *Birds of a Feather*, ed. A. J. Anderson, pp. 183–202. B. A. R., Oxford.

Davidson, J. M. 1982. Northland. In *The First Thousand Years*, ed. N. Prickett, pp. 11–27. Dunmore Press, Palmerston North.

Davidson, J. M. 1984. *The Prehistory of New Zealand*. Longman Paul, Auckland.

Davies, F. J. 1980. The prehistoric environment of the Dunedin area: the approach of salvage prehistory. MA thesis, University of Otago.

Davies, G. H. 1907. The name moa. *JPS* **16**:106.

Davies, G. H. 1910. The moa. *JPS* **19**:223.

Davies, G. H. and J. H. Pope 1907. An ancient Maori poem. *JPS* **16**:43–60.

Davies, S. J. J. F. 1976. The natural history of the emu in comparison with that of other ratites. In *Proceedings of the 16th International Ornithological Congress, Canberra, Australia, 12–17 Aug. 1974*, eds. H. J. Frith and J. H. Calaby, pp. 109–20. Australian Academy of Science, Canberra.

Davies, S. J. J. F. 1978. The food of emus. *Aust. J. Ecol.* **3**:411–22.

Davis, S. 1962. Makara Beach (Wellington) excavation. *NZAA* **5**:145–50.

Davison, W. M. 1870. The *Dinornis*. *Nature* **1**:604.

Dawson, E. W. 1949. Excavations of a Maori burial, at Longbeach, Otago, with notes on associated artifacts. *JPS* **58**:58–63.

Dawson, E. W. and J. C. Yaldwyn 1952. Excavations of Maori burials at Long Beach, Otago. *JPS* **61**:283–91.

de Boer, L. E. M. 1980. Do the chromosomes of the kiwi provide evidence for a monophyletic origin of the ratites? *Nature* **287**:84–5.

Deevey, E. S. 1955. Palaeolimnology of the upper swamp deposit, Pyramid Valley. *RCM* **6**:291–344.

Dell, R. K. and R. A. Falla 1972. The Kaikoura moa egg. *Dominion Museum Records in Ethnology* **2**:97–104.

Dennison, J. and B. Kooyman n. d. The potential of nitrate estimation in determining the sex of moa and kiwi. ms.

de Quatrefages, A. 1893. The moas and the Moa-hunters. *TNZI* **25**:17–49.

Diamond, J. M. 1981. Flightlessness and fear of flying in island species. *Nature* **293**:507–8.

Diamond, J. M. 1984. Historic extinctions: a rosetta stone for understanding prehistoric extinctions. In Martin and Klein, pp. 824–62.

Dieffenbach, E. 1843. *Travels in New Zealand* (2 vols.). John Murray, London.

Downes, T. W. 1916. New light on the period of the extinction of the moa (according to Maori record). *TNZI* **48**:426–34.

Downes, T. W. 1926. Notes on the moa, as contributed by natives of the Wairarapa District. *JPS* **35**:36–7.

Duff, R. S. 1941. Notes on moa excavations at Pyramid Valley, Waikari. *RCM* **4**:330–8.

Duff, R. S. 1949. *Pyramid Valley*. Assn. Friends Cant. Mus., Christchurch, NZ.

Duff, R. S. 1950. *The Moa-hunter Period of Maori Culture* (1st edn). Internal Affairs, Wellington, NZ.

Duff, R. S. 1951. *Moas and Moa-hunters*. Government Printer, Wellington, NZ.

Duff, R. S. 1952. Recent Maori occupation of Notornis Valley, Te Anau. *JPS* **61**:90–119.

Duff, R. S. 1955. Further report on excavations at Pyramid Valley Swamp, Waikari, North Canterbury: Introduction. *RCM* **6**:253–5.

Duff, R. S. 1956a. *The Moa-Hunter Period of Maori Culture* (2nd edn). Government Printer, Wellington, NZ.

Duff, R. S. 1956b. The evolution of Polynesian culture in New Zealand. Moahunters, Maoris, Morioris. *New Zealand Science Review* **14**:147–51.

Duff, R. S. 1963. Aspects of the cultural succession in Canterbury-Marlborough with wider reference to the New Zealand area. *TRSNZ (Gen.)* **1**:27–37.

Duff, R. S. 1977. *The Moa-Hunter Period of Maori Culture* (3rd edn). Government Printer, Wellington, NZ.

Duff, R. S. n. d. Notes and correspondence. Canterbury Museum, Christchurch, NZ.

Easdale, S. and C. Jacomb 1986. Report on excavations at Nenthorn rockshelter. ms.

Eastman, M. 1969. *The Life of the Emu*. Angus and Robertson, Sydney.

Enys, J. D. 1873. Moa and Maori, comment. *TNZI* **5**:432.

Ewen, C. A. 1896. On the discovery of moa remains on Riverton Beach. *TNZI* **28**:651–4.

Fairfield, G. 1961. Artefacts from the far north of New Zealand. *Tane* **8**:65–8.

Falla, R. A. 1941. The avian remains. *RCM* **4**:339–53.

Falla, R. A. 1942. Bird remains from Moa hunter camps. *RCM* **5**:43–9.

Falla, R. A. 1962. The moa, zoological and archaeological. *NZAA* **5**:189–91.

Falla, R. A. 1974. The moa. *New Zealand's Nature Heritage* **1**:69–74.

Feduccia, A. 1980. *The Age of Birds*. Harvard University Press, Cambridge.

Feduccia, A. 1986. The scapulocoracoid of flightless birds: a primitive avian character similar to that of theropods. *Ibis* **128**:128–32.

Ferguson, W. C. 1980. Edge-angle classification of the Quininup Brook implements: testing the ethnographic analogy. *APAO* **15**:56–72.

Field, H. C. 1877. Notes on some ancient aboriginal caches near Wanganui. *TNZI* **9**:220–9.

Field, H. C. 1882. On the extinction of the moa. *TNZI* **14**:540.

Field, H. C. 1892. Discoveries of moa remains. *TNZI* **24**:558–61.

Field, H. C. 1894. The date of the extinction of the moa. *TNZI* **26**:560–8.

Fleming, C. A. 1963. A moa bone from the sea floor in Cook Strait. *Records of the Dominion Museum* **4**:231–3.

Fleming, C. A. 1969. Rats and moa extinction. *Notornis* **16**:210–11.

Fleming, C. A. 1974. The coming of the birds. *New Zealand's Nature Heritage* **1**:62–8.

Fleming, C. A. 1977. Review of S. Olson (ed.) *Wishbones for Wetmore*. *Notornis* **24**:144–6.

Fleming, C. A. 1979. *The Geological History of New Zealand and its Life*. Auckland University Press, Auckland.

Foley, D. 1980. Analysis of faunal remains from the Kaupokonui site (N128/3B). MA thesis, University of Auckland.

Fomison, T. 1963. Excavations at South Bay Kaikoura – site S49/43. *NZAA* **6**:100–2.

Forbes, H. O. 1891a. On avian remains found under a lava-flow near Timaru, in Canterbury. *TNZI* **23**:366–73.

Forbes, H. O. 1891b. Note on the disappearance of the moa. *TNZI* **23**:373–5.

Forbes, H. O. 1892a. Preliminary notice of addition to the extinct avifauna of New Zealand. *TNZI* **24**:185–9.

Forbes, H. O. 1892b. Evidence of a wing in *Dinornis*. *Nature* 45:257.

Forbes, H. O. 1892c. On a recent discovery of the remains of extinct birds in New Zealand. *Nature* 45:416–18.

Forbes, H. O. 1893a. The moas of New Zealand. *Natural Science* II:374–80.

Forbes, H. O. 1893b. Letter to the Editor. *Natural Science* III:318.

Forbes, H. O. 1893c. On *Anomalopteryx antiqua* Hutton, and other new species of moa from Enfield, New Zealand. *Natural Science* III:318–19.

Forbes, H. O. 1893d. Antarctica: a supposed former southern continent. *Natural Science* III:54–7.

Forbes, H. O. 1900. Catalogue of birds. *Bulletin of the Liverpool Museums* III.

Ford, M. J. 1982. *The Changing Climate: responses of the natural flora and fauna.* Allen and Unwin, London.

Forrest, F. M. 1987. A partially mummified skeleton of *Anomalopteryx didiformis* from Southland. *JRSNZ* 17:399–408.

Fowler, C. W. and T. D. Smith 1981. *Dynamics of Large Mammal Populations.* Wiley, New York.

Fraser, T. 1873. A description of the Earnscleugh Moa Cave. *TNZI* 5:102–5.

Fürbringer, M. 1888. *Untersuchungen zur Morphologie und Systematik der Vogel II.* Allgemeiner Theil Van Holkema, Amsterdam.

Gathercole, P. 1960. Fieldwork report. *Ann. Rep. Otago Museum* 1960, pp. 16–17.

Gathercole, P. n. d. Excavation diary and field notes, 1961–62, Darwin College, Cambridge, UK.

George, P. 1937. A Maori stone dagger from the Nevis. *JPS* 46:123–9.

George, P. 1944. Excavation at Kaka Point, Otago. *JPS* 53:72–3.

Gibb, J. G. 1977. Historical shoreline changes in New Zealand. In *Soil Groups of New Zealand. Part II, Yellow-Brown Sands.* Government Printer, Wellington, pp. 182–96.

Gibson, J. H. 1865. Donations. *Annual Report of the Council of the Yorkshire Philosophical Society for 1864.*

Gilkison, R. 1930. *Early Days in Central Otago.* Whitcombe and Tombs, Christchurch.

Gillies, K. B. and B. Turnbull 1978. A site survey of the Upper Taieri from Great Moss Swamp to the Lower Maniototo. Rpt. to HPT.

Gillies, R. 1872. Comment, 4th meeting of Otago Institute. *TNZI* 4:413–15.

Gingerich, P. D. 1976. Evolutionary significance of the Mesozoic toothed birds. *Smithsonian Contributions to Paleobiol.* 27:23–33.

Golson, J. 1959a. Culture change in prehistoric New Zealand. In *Anthropology in the South Seas*, eds. J. D. Freeman and W. R. Geddes, pp. 29–74. Avery, New Plymouth.

Golson, J. 1959b. Excavations on the Coromandel Peninsula. *NZAA* 2:13–18.

Golson, J. 1960. Archaeology, tradition and myth in New Zealand prehistory. *JPS* 69:380–402.

Goodall, J. 1875. On the discovery of a cut stump of a tree, giving evidence of the existence of man in New Zealand at or before the Volcanic Era. *TNZI* 7:144–6.

Gould, S. J. 1980. *The Panda's Thumb.* Penguin, Harmondsworth.

Gould, S. J. 1986. Of kiwi eggs and the Liberty Bell. *Natural History* 11/86:20–9.

Graham, G. 1919. Rangi-hua-moa. *JPS* 28:107–10.

Grayson, D. K. 1984. Explaining Pleistocene extinctions: thoughts on the structure of a debate. In Martin and Klein, pp. 807–23.

Green, R. C. 1963. Summaries of sites at Opito, Sarah's Gully, and Great Mercury Island. *NZAA* 6:57–69.

Green, R. C. 1975. Adaptation and change in Maori culture. In *Biogeography and Ecology in New Zealand*, ed. G. Kuschel, pp. 591–641. W. J. Junk, The Hague.

Greenwood, R. M. and I. A. E. Atkinson 1977. Evolution of divaricating plants in New Zealand in relation to moa browsing. *Proceedings of the New Zealand Ecological Society* 24:21–33.

Gregg, D. R. 1966. New dates for Pyramid Valley moas. *NZAA* 9:155–9.

Gregg, D. R. 1972. Holocene stratigraphy and moas at Pyramid Valley, North Canterbury, New Zealand. *RCM* 19:151–8.

Grey, Sir G. 1870. Letter. *PZSL* 1870, pp. 116–17.

Grey, Sir G. 1873. Description of the extinct gigantic bird of prey Hokioi. *TNZI* 5:435.

Grice, D., G. Caughley and J. Short 1985. Density and distribution of emus. *Aust. Wildl. Res.* 12:69–73.

Griffiths, C. 1941. The discovery and excavation of an old Maori (No. 1) camp near Normanby, Timaru. *JPS* 50:211–31.

Griffiths, C. 1942. Excavation of Maori No. 2 camp, near Normanby, Timaru. *JPS* 51:115–25.

Griffiths, C. 1955. South Canterbury Maori camps No. 3, investigations at Pareora. *JPS* 64:233–6.

Groube, L. M. 1967. Models in prehistory: A consideration of the New Zealand evidence. *APAO* 2:1–27.

Guilday, J. E. 1984. Pleistocene extinction and environmental change: case study of the Appalachians. In P. S. Martin and R. G. Klein, pp. 250–8.

Guthrie, R. D. 1984. Mosaics, allelochemics and nutrients: an ecological theory of late Pleistocene megafaunal extinctions. In P. S. Martin and R. G. Klein, pp. 259–98.

Haast, H. F. von 1948. *The Life and Times of Sir Julius von Haast.* Avery, New Plymouth.

Haast, J. 1865. Notes to a sketch map of the province of Canterbury, New Zealand, showing the glaciation during the Pleistocene and Recent Periods as far as explored. *Quarterly Journal of the Geological Society of London* 21:133–7.

Haast, J. 1869. On the measurements of *Dinornis* bones,

obtained from excavation in a swamp, situated at Glenmark, on the property of Messrs Kermode and Co., up to February 15, 1868. *TNZI* 1:80–9.

Haast, J. 1872a. Moas and Moahunters. Address to the Philosophical Institute of Canterbury. *TNZI* 4:66–90.

Haast, J. 1872b. Additional notes. *TNZI* 4:90–4.

Haast, J. 1872c. Third paper on moas and Moahunters. *TNZI* 4:94–110.

Haast, J. 1874. Remarks on the extinct birds of New Zealand. *Ibis* 1874:209–20.

Haast, J. 1875a. Researches and excavations carried on, in, and near the Moa Bone Point Cave, Sumner Road, in the year 1872. *TNZI* 7:54–85.

Haast, J. 1875b. Notes on an ancient native burial place near the Moa Bone Point, Sumner. *TNZI* 7:86–91.

Haast, J. 1875c. Notes on the Moa-hunter encampment at Shag Point Otago. *TNZI* 7:91–8.

Haast, J. 1875d. Proceedings, Philosophical Institute of Canterbury. *TNZI* 7:528–33.

Haast, J. 1877. Observations on Capt. Hutton's paper 'On the Maori cooking places at the mouth of the Shag River'. *TNZI* 9:670–2.

Haast, J. 1878. Address. *TNZI* 10:37–55.

Haast, J. 1879. *Geology of the Provinces of Canterbury and Westland.* Lyttelton Times, Lyttelton.

Haast, J. 1880. Notes on an ancient manufactory of stone implements at the mouth of the Otokai Creek, Brighton, Otago. *TNZI* 12:150–3.

Haast, J. 1884. Note on a new species of kiwi. *TNZI* 16:577.

Haast, J. 1890a. On *Dinornis oweni*; a new species of the Dinornithidae, with some remarks on *D. curtus*. Read 19/5/1885. *TZSL* XII:171–82.

Haast, J. 1890b. On *Megalapteryx hectori*, a new gigantic species of Apterygian bird. Read 2/6/1885. *TZSL* XII:161–9.

Haast, J. n. d. Notes to the collections, illustrating the ethnology of New Zealand exhibited by the Canterbury Museum, Christchurch. Canterbury Museum, ms.

Halliday, T. 1980. *Vanishing Birds: their natural history and conservation.* Penguin, London.

Hamel, G. E. 1977a. Prehistoric man and his environment in the Catlins, New Zealand. PhD thesis, University of Otago.

Hamel, G. E. 1977b. Salvage excavations at Omimi. Rpt to HPT.

Hamel, G. E. 1977c. Catlins archaeological site survey. Rpt to HPT.

Hamel, G. E. 1978. Hawksburn revisited: An ecological assessment. *NZAA* 21:116–28.

Hamel, G. E. 1979. The breeding ecology of moas. In *Birds of a Feather*, ed. A. J. Anderson, pp. 61–66. B.A.R., Oxford.

Hamel, G. E. 1980. Pounawea, the last excavation. Rpt to HPT.

Hamilton, A. 1889. Notes on a deposit of moa bones in the Te Aute Swamp, Hawke's Bay. *TNZI* 21:311–18.

Hamilton, A. 1890. Notes on excavations at Shag Mouth. Hocken Library, Dunedin, NZ.

Hamilton, A. 1892. Notes on moa gizzard stones. *TNZI* 24:172–5.

Hamilton, A. 1893a. On the fissures and caves at the Castle Rocks, Southland; with a description of the remains of the existing and extinct birds found in them. *TNZI* 25:88–106.

Hamilton, A. 1893b. Notes on some old flax mats found in Otago. *TNZI* 25:486–8.

Hamilton, A. 1894. Result of a further exploration of the bone fissure at the Castle Rocks, Southland. *TNZI* 26:226–8.

Hamilton, A. 1895. On the feathers of a small species of moa (*Megalapteryx*) found in a cave at the head of the Waikaia River. *TNZI* 27:232–8.

Hamilton, A. 1897. Notes from Murihiku. *TNZI* 29:169–78

Hamilton, A. n. d. Papers and correspondence. National Museum of New Zealand, Wellington.

Hamilton, J. W. 1875. Notes on Maori traditions of the moa. *TNZI* 7:121–2.

Harding, J. R. 1957. A carved pumice head from New Zealand. A preliminary note. *Man* LVII:99–101.

Harrison, L. 1916. Bird parasites and bird-phylogeny. *Ibis* 58:254–63.

Harrowfield, D. L. and M. M. Trotter 1966. A rock-shelter site in North Otago. *NZAA* 9:162–4.

Harsant, W. 1980. Report on Harwood Archaic site. Otago Museum, Dunedin, NZ.

Harsant, W. J. 1985. The Hahei (N44/97) assemblage of Archaic artefacts. *NZJA* 7:5–38.

Hartree, W. H. 1960. A brief note on the stratigraphy of bird and human material in Hawke's Bay. *NZAA* 3:28.

Hartree, W. n. d. Correspondence. Hawke's Bay Art Gallery and Museum, Napier, NZ.

Harwood, O. n. d. Papers and correspondence. Hocken Library, Dunedin, NZ.

Hayden, B. 1979. *Palaeolithic reflections: lithic technology and ethnographic excavations among Australian aborigines.* Aust. Inst. Ab. Stud., Canberra.

Hector, J. 1867. Notice of an egg of the great moa (*Dinornis gigantea*), containing remains of an embryo, found in the province of Otago, New Zealand. *PZSL* 1867, pp. 991–2.

Hector, J. 1869. Comment in Mantell 1869.

Hector, J. 1871. On recent moa remains in New Zealand. *Nature* 4:184–6.

Hector, J. 1872. On recent moa remains in New Zealand. *TNZI* 4:110–20.

Hector, J. 1875. Memorandum for the Board of Governors of the New Zealand Institute. *TNZI* 7:536.

Hector, J. 1889. Comment, 8th meeting of Wellington Philosophical Society. *TNZI* 21:504–7.

Hector, J. 1893. Summary report on moa, 1st meeting of Otago Institute. *TNZI* 25:555–8.

Helm-Bychowski, K. M. and A. C. Wilson 1986. Rates of nuclear DNA evolution in pheasant-like birds:

Evidence from restriction maps. *Proc. Natl. Acad. Sci.* (USA) **83**:688–92.

Henry, R. 1899. Moa farmers. *TNZI* **31**:673–7.

Higham, C. F. W. 1968. Prehistoric research in Western Southland. *NZAA* **11**:155–64.

Higham, C. F. W. 1981. *The Maoris.* Cambridge Introduction to the History of Mankind, Topic Book. Cambridge University Press, Cambridge.

Hill, H. 1889. Discovery of fossil moa-feathers in rocks of Pliocene age. *TNZI* **21**:318–20.

Hill, H. 1895. On the occurrence of moa-footprints in the bed of the Manawatu River, near Palmerston North. *TNZI* **27**:476–7.

Hill, H. 1914. The moa: Legendary, historical and geological: Why and when the moa disappeared. *TNZI* **46**:330–51.

Hjarno, J. 1967. Maori fish-hooks in southern New Zealand. *Rec. Otago Mus. (Anthropology)* no. 3.

Hochstetter, F. von 1867. *New Zealand: its physical geography, geology and natural history, with special reference to results of government expeditions in the provinces of Auckland and Nelson.* J. G. Cotta, Stuttgart.

Hocken, T. M. 1872. Report, 4th meeting of the Otago Institute. *TNZI* **4**:413–15.

Hocken, T. M. 1898. *Contributions to the Early History of New Zealand (Settlement of Otago).* Sampson Low Marston, London.

Hodgkinson, D. 1981. Notes on Wakanui. Canterbury Museum, Christchurch, NZ. ms.

Holdaway, R. N. n.d. A view of New Zealand's pre-human avifauna and its vulnerability. University of Canterbury, ms.

Holdaway, S. 1981. Normanby (S111/15 and 16): a re-assessment. University of Otago, ms.

Holdaway, S. and D. Foster 1983. Lower Clutha Valley Archaeological Survey. Rpt. to HPT.

Hongi, H. 1916. Kuranui as a name for the moa. *JPS* **25**:66–7.

Hooker, J. D. 1853. *The Botany of the Antarctic Voyage of H.M. Ships Erebus and Terror in the Years 1839–1843. Pt II: Flora Novaezealandiae.*, Vol. II. Lovell Reeve, London.

Hooker, R. H. 1986. The archaeology of the south Westland Maoris. NZ Forest Service, ms.

Horn, P.L. 1983. Subfossil avian deposits from Poukawa, Hawke's Bay, and the first record of *Oxyura australis* (Blue-billed duck) from New Zealand. *JRSNZ* **13**:67–78.

Hosking, T. 1962. Report on excavation of Whakamoenga Cave, Lake Taupo. *NZAA* **5**:22–30.

Houde, P. 1986. Ostrich ancestors found in the northern hemisphere suggest new hypothesis of ratite origins. *Nature* **234**: 563–5.

Houghton, P. 1975. The people of Wairau Bar. *RCM* **9**:231–46.

Hutchinson, F. 1898. On Maori middens at Wainui, Poverty Bay. *TNZI* **30**:533–6.

Hutton, F. W. 1872. On some moa feathers. *TNZI* **4**:172–3.

Hutton, F. W. 1873. On the geographical relations of the New Zealand fauna. *TNZI* **5**:227–56.

Hutton, F. W. 1875. On the dimensions of *Dinornis* bones. *TNZI* **7**:274–9.

Hutton, F. W. 1876. Notes on the Maori cooking places at the mouth of the Shag River. *TNZI* **8**:103–8.

Hutton, F. W. 1877. Remarks on Dr von Haast's classification of the moas. *TNZI* **9**:363–5.

Hutton, F. W. 1892a. On the origin of the Struthious birds of Australasia. *Report of the Fourth Meeting of the Australasian Association for Advanced Science* (Hobart) 1892, pp. 365–9.

Hutton, F. W. 1892b. The history of the moas, or extinct flightless birds of New Zealand, I. *Natural Science* ı:588–92.

Hutton, F. W. 1892c. The moas of New Zealand. *TNZI* **24**:93–171.

Hutton, F. W. 1893a. On *Anomalopteryx antiqua*. *TNZI* **25**:14–16.

Hutton, F. W. 1893b. New species of moas. *TNZI* **25**:6–13.

Hutton, F. W. 1893c. The moas of New Zealand. *Natural Science* ııı:317–18.

Hutton, F. W. 1895a. On the occurrence of a pneumatic foramen in the femur of a moa. *TNZI* **27**:173–4.

Hutton, F. W. 1895b. On the axial skeleton in the Dinornithidae. *TNZI* **27**:157–73.

Hutton, F. W. 1896a. On a deposit of moa bones at Kapua. *TNZI* **28**:627–44.

Hutton, F. W. 1896b. On the moa bones from Enfield. *TNZI* **28**:645–50.

Hutton, F. W. 1897a. On the leg bone of *Meionornis* from Glenmark. *TNZI* **29**:557–60.

Hutton, F. W. 1897b. The moas of the North Island of New Zealand. *TNZI* **29**:541–57.

Hutton, F. W. and M. Coughtrey 1875a. Description of some moa remains from the Knobby Ranges. With anatomical notes. *TNZI* **7**:266–73.

Hutton, F. W. and M. Coughtrey 1875b. Notice of the Earnscleugh Cave. With remarks on some of the more remarkable moa remains found in it. *TNZI* **7**:138–41.

Huxley, T. H. 1867. On the classification of birds; and on the taxonomic value of the modifications of certain of the cranial bones observable in that class. *PZSL* 1867, pp. 415–72.

Irvine, R. 1943. Quartzite quarry at Gray's Hills, Mackenzie Country. *JPS* **52**:90.

James, H. F. and S. L. Olson 1983. Flightless birds. *Natural History* 9/83:30–40.

Jansen, H. S. 1984. *Institute of Nuclear Sciences INS-R-328: radiocarbon dating for contributors.* INS, Lower Hutt, NZ.

Jensen, H. J. 1986. Unretouched blades in the late Mesolithic of Scandinavia: a functional study. *Oxford J. Archaeology* **5**:19–33.

Jolly, R. G. W. and C. J. Murdock 1973. Further excavations at site N40/2 Opito Bay. *NZAA* 16:66–72.

Jones, K. and P. Moore n.d. An archaeological survey and environmental interpretation of the Whangaroa dunes East Coast North Island. Rpt. to HPT.

Jones, K. L. 1981. New Zealand mataa from Marlborough, Nelson and the Chatham Islands. *NZJA* 3:89–108.

Jones K. L. 1986. *A guide to Wellington's Maori history*. Historic Places Trust, Wellington.

Keeley, L. H. 1980. *Experimental Determination of Stone Tool Uses*. University of Chicago Press, Chicago.

Kennedy, D. 1876. *Kennedy's Colonial Travel*. Edinburgh Publishing Company, Edinburgh.

King, C. 1984. *Immigrant Killers. Introduced Predators and Conservation of Birds in New Zealand*. Oxford University Press, Oxford.

Kinsky, F. C. 1970. *Annotated Checklist of the Birds of New Zealand*. Ornithological Society of New Zealand Inc. Reed, Wellington.

Kirk, T. W. 1881. Description of Maori comb and arrowheads. *TNZI* 13:436–7.

Knapp, F. V. 1928. Maori scrapers. *JPS* 37:113–24.

Knapp, F. V. 1941. Maori saws. *JPS* 50:1–9.

Knight, H. 1965. Flake knife in early New Zealand culture. *JPS* 74:231–6.

Knight, H. 1970. An assemblage from Ringa-Ringa, Stewart Island. *NZAA* 13:76–83.

Knight, H. and P. Gathercole 1961. A reconnaissance at the Waitaki River Mouth, Otago. *NZAA* 4:133–6.

Knox, G. A. 1980. Plate tectonics and the evolution of intertidal and shallow-water benthic biotic distribution patterns of the Southwest Pacific. *Palaeogeography, Palaeoclimatology, Palaeoecology* 31:267–97.

Kooyman, B. P. 1984a. Salvage excavations at Warrington moa-hunter site. Rpt. to HPT.

Kooyman, B. P. 1984b. Moa utilisation at Owen's Ferry, Otago, New Zealand. *NZJA* 6:47–57.

Kooyman, B. P. 1985. Moa and moa-hunting: an archaeological analysis of big game hunting in New Zealand. PhD thesis, University of Otago.

Kooyman, B. P. n. d. Moa hunting: communal or individual pursuit? University of Calgary, ms.

Kreuzer, G. and M. Dunn 1982. *Die Felsbilder Neuseelands*. Franz Steiner Verlag GMBH, Wiesbaden.

Law, G. 1971. Some errors with carbon 14 dating. *NZAA* 14:64–6.

Law, G. 1972a. Sources of moas and Moa hunters. *NZAA* 15:4–15.

Law, G. 1972b. Archaeology at Harataonga Bay, Great Barrier Island. *RAIM* 9:81–123.

Law, G. 1973. Tokoroa Moa hunter site N75/1. *NZAA* 16:150–64.

Law, G. 1974. C14 date-list – Eastern Polynesia, ms.

Law, G. 1977. Genesis in Oceania. *NZAA* 20:86–106.

Law, G. 1981. Radiocarbon dating, some guidance for users. *NZAA* 24:228–36.

Law, G. 1982. Coromandel Peninsula and Great Barrier Island. In *The First Thousand Years*, ed. N. Prickett, pp. 49–61. Dunmore Press, Palmerston North.

Law, G. 1984. Archaeological carbon dating using marine shell – the New Zealand experience. NZAA conference paper, 2–4 June, Oamaru.

Leach, B. F. 1969. The concept of similarity in prehistoric studies: a test case using New Zealand stone flake assemblages. *Studies in Prehistoric Anthropology (Otago University)* no. 1.

Leach, B. F. 1972. Multi-sampling and absolute dating methods: a problem of statistical combination for archaeologists. *NZAA* 15:113–16.

Leach, B. F. 1977. Sex and funeral offerings at Wairau Bar; A re-evaluation. *NZAA* 20:107–13.

Leach, H. M. 1972. A hundred years of Otago archaeology. *Rec. Otago Mus. (Anthropology)* no. 6.

Leach, H. M. 1984. Jigsaw: reconstructive lithic technology. In *Prehistoric Quarries and Lithic Production*, eds. J. E. Ericson and B. A. Purdy, pp. 107–118. CUP, Cambridge.

Leach, H. M. and G. E. Hamel 1981. Archaic and Classic Maori relationships at Long Beach, Otago: the artefacts and activity areas. *NZJA* 3:109–41.

Leach, H. M. and B. F. Leach 1979. Environmental change in Palliser Bay. In *Prehistoric Man in Palliser Bay*, eds. B. F. Leach and H. M. Leach. National Museum Bulletin 21:229–40.

Leahy, A. 1971. Preliminary report and carbon 14 datings on site N44/69, Hot Water Beach, Coromandel. *NZAA* 14:62–3.

Leahy, A. 1974. Excavations at Hot Water Beach (N44/69) Coromandel Peninsula. *RAIM* 11:23–76.

Leahy, A. 1976. Whakamoenga Cave, Taupo, N94/7. A report on the ecology, economy and stratigraphy. *RAIM* 13:29–75.

Lockerbie, L. 1940. Excavations at Kings Rock, Otago, with a discussion of the fish-hook barb as an ancient feature of Polynesian culture. *JPS* 49:393–446.

Lockerbie, L. 1945. Maori occupation of South Molyneux etc. Hocken Library, Dunedin, NZ, ms.

Lockerbie, L. 1953. Further excavation of the Moa hunter camp site at the mouth of the Tahakopa River. *JPS* 62:13–32.

Lockerbie, L. 1954. Stratification in Otago archaeological sites. *JPS* 63:141–6.

Lockerbie, L. 1959. From Moa-hunter to Classic Maori in southern New Zealand. In *Anthropology in the South Seas*, eds. J. D. Freeman and W. R. Geddes, pp. 75–110. Avery, New Plymouth.

Lockerbie, L. n.d. Report on Hawksburn excavation. Otago Museum, Dunedin, NZ.

Lowe, P. R. 1928. Studies and observations bearing on the phylogeny of the ostrich and its allies. *PZSL* 1928, pp. 185–247.

Lowe, P. R. 1935. On the relationships of the Struthiones to the dinosaurs and to the rest of the avian class, with special reference to the position of *Archaeopteryx. Ibis* **77**:398–432.

Lowry, J.B. 1980. Evolution of divaricating plants in New Zealand in relation to moa browsing. *NZJE* **3**:165.

Luckens, J. B. 1983. Moa gizzard stones: Some notes and comparisons of wear rates. The author, cyclost.

Luckens, J. B. 1984. Moa gizzard stones in the South Island of New Zealand. The author, cyclost.

Lydekker, R. 1891. *Catalogue of the Fossil Birds in the British Museum (Natural History).* Trustees, British Museum, London.

Lydekker, R. 1892. The history of the moas, or extinct flightless birds of New Zealand, II. *Natural Science* **I**:593–5.

McCulloch, B. 1982. *No Moa.* Canterbury Museum, Christchurch, NZ.

McCulloch, B. 1983. How big is a moa egg. *NZAA* **26**:271–3.

McCulloch, B. and M. M. Trotter 1975. The first twenty years. Radiocarbon dates for South Island Moa-hunter sites, 1955–74. *NZAA* **18**:2–17.

McCulloch, B. and M. M. Trotter 1976. South Island radiocarbon dates. *NZAA* **19**:110–11.

McCulloch, B. and M. M. Trotter 1979. Some radiocarbon dates for moa remains from natural deposits. *NZ J. Geol. Geophys.* **22**:271–9.

McCulloch, B. and M. M. Trotter 1987. Fyffe moa hunter site. *Te Karanga* **3**:8–11.

McCullough, D. R. 1970. Secondary production of birds and mammals. In *Analysis of Temperate Forest Ecosystems*, ed. D. R. Reichle, pp. 107–130 Springer-Verlag, Berlin.

McCully, H. S. 1941. Stone tools made and used by the Maori: suggested method of their manufacture. *JPS* **50**:185–210.

McCully, H.S. 1948. Stone tools: the flake. *JPS* **57**:46–56.

McDonnell, Lt Col. 1889. The ancient Moa hunters at Waingongoro. *TNZI* **21**:438–41.

McDowall, R. M. 1969. Extinction and endemism in New Zealand land birds. *Tuatara* **17**:1–12.

McDowell, S. 1948. The bony palate of birds. Part I. The Palaeognathae. *The Auk* **65**:520–49.

McFadgen, B. G. 1967. Foxton excavation results. *Wellington Archaeological Society Newsletter* **1**:3–4.

McFadgen, B. G. 1978. Environment and archaeology in New Zealand. PhD thesis, Victoria University, Wellington.

McFadgen, B. G. 1979. The antiquity of moa at Lake Poukawa, New Zealand. *JRSNZ* **19**:375–82.

McFadgen, B. G. 1980. Age relationship between a Maori plaggen soil and Moa-hunter sites on the west Wellington coast. *NZJ. Geol. Geophys.* **23**:249–56.

McFadgen, B. G. 1982. Dating New Zealand archaeology by radiocarbon. *NZ J. of Science* **25**:379–92.

McFadgen, B. G. 1987. Beach ridges, breakers and bones: late Holocene geology and archaeology at the Fyffe site, S49/46, Kaikoura Peninsula, New Zealand. *JRSNZ* **17**:381–94.

McFadgen, B. G. n.d. List of radiocarbon dates on marine shell and bone collagen, ms.

McFadgen, B. G. and B. McFadgen 1966. Excavation of Moa hunter site near Foxton. *Wellington Archaeological Society Publication.*

McGlone, M. S. 1978. Forest destruction by early Polynesians, Lake Poukawa, Hawke's Bay, New Zealand. *JRSNZ* **8**:275–81.

McGlone, M. S. 1983. Polynesian deforestation of New Zealand: A preliminary synthesis. *AO* **18**:11–25.

McGlone, M. S. n.d. The Polynesian settlement of New Zealand in relation to environmental and biotic factors. Department of Scientific and Industrial Research, Christchurch, NZ, ms.

McGlone, M. S., A. J. Anderson, I. Barber and R. Holdaway n.d. An ecological approach to the early settlement of New Zealand, ms.

McGlone, M. S. and C. J. Webb 1981. Selective forces influencing the evolution of divaricating plants. *New Zealand Journal of Ecology* **4**:20–8.

McGowan, C. 1979. The hind limb musculature of the Brown Kiwi, *Apteryx australis mantelli. Journal of Morphology* **160**:33–74.

McGowan, C. 1982. The wing musculature of the Brown Kiwi *Apteryx australis mantelli* and its bearing on ratite affinities. *Journal of Zoology* **197**:173–219.

McGowan, C. 1984. Evolutionary relationships of ratites and carinates: Evidence from the ontogeny of the tarsus. *Nature* **307**:733–5.

McGowan, C. 1986. The wing musculature of the weka (*Gallirallus australis*), a flightless rail endemic to New Zealand. *JZSL* (A) **210**:305–46.

McKay, A. 1875a. On the identity of the Moa hunters with the present Maori race. *TNZI* **7**:98–105.

McKay, A. 1875b. Correspondence with Hector and Haast. *TNZI* **7**:537–8.

McKay, A. 1882. On a deposit of moa bones near Motunau, North Canterbury. *TNZI* **14**:410–14.

McKay, A. 1905. Comment, 3rd Meeting Wellington Philosophical Society. *TNZI* **38**:585.

McLeod, H. N. 1902. On caves in the Martinborough District, and moa bones found therein. *TNZI* **34**:562–3.

McLeod, H. N. 1919. Maori occupation of Wellington district: notes on some archaeological remains. *JPS* **28**:1–17.

McMahon, T. A. and J. T. Bonner 1983. *On Size and Life.* Scientific American, New York.

Mair, W. G. 1890. On the disappearance of the moa. *TNZI* **22**:70–5.

Mair, W. G. 1893. On the antiquity of the moa. *TNZI* **25**:534–5.

Majnep, I.S. and Bulmer, R. 1977. *Birds of my Kalam Country*. Auckland University Press.

Maning, F. E. 1876. Extracts from a letter relative to the extinction of the moa. *TNZI* 8:102–3.

Mantell, G. A. 1848a. On the fossil remains of birds collected in various parts of New Zealand by Mr. Walter Mantell of Wellington. *Q. J. Geol. Soc.* 4:225–38.

Mantell, G. A. 1848b. Additional remarks on the geological position of the deposits in New Zealand which contain bones of birds. *Q. J. Geol. Soc.* 4:238–41.

Mantell, G. A. 1850. Notice of the remains of the *Dinornis* and other birds, and of fossils and rock specimens, recently collected by Mr. Walter Mantell in the Middle Island of New Zealand; with additional notes on the Northern Island. With note on fossiliferous deposit in the Middle Island of New Zealand. *Q. J. Geol. Soc.* 6:319–42.

Mantell, G. A. 1862. Notice of the discovery by Mr Walter Mantell in the Middle Island of New Zealand, of a living specimen of the *Notornis*, a bird of the rail family, allied to *Brachypteryx* and hitherto unknown to naturalists except in a fossil state. Read 12/11/1850. *TZSL* 4:69–73.

Mantell, W. B. D. 1844. The moa, or gigantic bird of New Zealand. *The Zoologist* 2:667.

Mantell, W. B. D. 1849. Outline journal Kaiapoi to Otago 1848–49. National Library, Wellington, NZ.

Mantell, W. B. D. 1853. Correspondence. In *A Compendium of Official Documents Relative to Native Affairs in the South Island*, pp. 274–80. The author, Nelson.

Mantell, W. B. D. 1869. Address on the moa. *TNZI* 1:5–7.

Mantell, W. B. D. 1872. On moa beds. *TNZI* 5:94–7.

Mantell, W. B. D. n.d. Letters to G. A. Mantell and other notes and correspondence. Hocken Library, Dunedin, NZ.

Marshall, L. G. 1984. Who killed cock robin? An investigation of the extinction controversy. In P. S. Martin and R. G. Klein, pp. 785–806.

Marshall, P. 1919. Occurrence of fossil moa bones in the lower Wanganui strata. *TNZI* 51:250–3.

Martin, L. D. 1983. The origin of birds and of avian flight. In *Current Ornithology*, ed. R. F. Johnston, pp. 105–129. Plenum Press, New York.

Martin, P. S. 1973. The discovery of America. *Science* 179:969–74.

Martin, P. S. 1984. Prehistoric overkill: the global model. In Martin and Klein, pp. 354–403.

Martin, P. S. and R. G. Klein 1984. *Quaternary Extinctions: a prehistoric revolution*. University of Arizona Press, Tucson.

Mason, G. M. 1963. Preliminary note on two Waitaki River sites – Mackenzie Country. *NZAA* 6:93–4.

Mason, G. M. and O. Wilkes 1963a. Dashing Rocks, Timaru; a preliminary note on excavations – site S111/1. *NZAA* 6:95–8.

Mason, G. M. and O. Wilkes 1963b. Tumbledown Bay – a Banks Peninsula Moa-hunter site S94/30. *NZAA* 6:98–100.

Mead, J. I. and D. J. Meltzer 1984. North American late Quarternary extinctions and the radiocarbon record. In Martin and Klein, pp. 440–50.

Meeson, J. 1889. The newly opened cave near Sumner. *TNZI* 22:64–70.

Mellars, P. 1975. Ungulate populations, economic patterns and the Mesolithic landscape. In *The Effect of Man on the Landscape: The Highland Zone*, eds. J. G. Evans, S. Linbrey and H. Cleene, pp. 49–56. Research Report 11, The Council for British Archaeology.

Melvin, J. 1871. Extinction of the moa. *Nature* 4:306.

Mildenhall, D.C. 1980. New Zealand late Cretaceous and Cenozoic plant biogeography; a contribution. *Palaeogeography, Palaeoclimatology, Palaeoecology* 31:197–233.

Millar, D. G. L. 1967. Recent archaeological excavations in the northern part of the South Island. *J. Nelson Hist. Soc.* ii:5–12.

Millar, D.G.L. 1971. Excavation of an Archaic site at Tahunanui, S20/2, Nelson. *NZAA* 14:161–72.

Millener, P. R. 1981. The Quaternary avifauna of the North Island of New Zealand. PhD thesis, University of Auckland.

Millener, P.R. 1982. And then there were twelve: The taxonomic status of *Anomalopteryx oweni* (aves: Dinornithidae). *Notornis* 29:165–70.

Millener, P. R. and R. J. S. Cassels 1985. Moa. In *Dictionary of Birds*, ed. B. Campbell and E. Lack, pp. 355–7. British Ornithological Union.

Mills, J. A., R. B. Lavers and D. G. Lee 1984. The takahe – A relict of the Pleistocene grassland avifauna of New Zealand. *NZJE* 7:57–70.

Miskelly, C. M. 1987. The identity of the Hakawai. *Notornis* 34:95–116.

Mitchell, N. D. 1980. A study of the nutritive value of juvenile and adult leaves of *Pseudopanax crassifolius*. *NZJE* 3:159.

Mivart, St. G. 1879. On the axial skeleton of the Struthionidae. Read 17/11/1874. *TZSL* x:1–52.

Mivart, St. G. 1893. Sir Richard Owen's hypotheses. *Natural Science* ii:18–23.

Molloy, B. P. J. 1969. Recent history of the vegetation. In *Natural History of Canterbury*, ed. G. A. Knox, pp. 340–60. Reed, Wellington.

Molloy, B. P. J. 1977. The fire history. In *Cass: History and Science in the Cass District, Canterbury, New Zealand*, ed. C. J. Burrows, Botany Dept., University of Canterbury, pp. 157–70.

Molloy, B. P. J., C. J. Burrows, J. E. Cox, J. A. Johnston and P. Wardle 1963. Distribution of sub-fossil forest remains, eastern South Island, New Zealand. *NZJ. Botany* 2:143–76.

Molnar, R. and M. Archer 1984. Feeble and not so feeble flapping fliers: a consideration of early birds and bird-like reptiles. In Archer and Clayton, pp. 407–19.

Moore, P. R. 1977. The definition, distribution and sourcing of chert in New Zealand. *NZAA* **20**:51–85.

Moore, P. R. and E. M. Tiller 1975. Radiocarbon dates for New Zealand archaeological sites. *NZAA* **18**:98–107.

Moore, P. R. and E. M. Tiller 1976. Radiocarbon dates for New Zealand archaeological sites: Errata and addenda. *NZAA* **19**:151–5.

Morrell, W. P. (ed.) 1958. *Sir Joseph Banks in New Zealand*. A. H. and A. W. Reed, Wellington, NZ.

Mosimann, J. E. and P. S. Martin 1975. Simulating overkill by Paleoindians. *Am. Scientist* **63**:304–13.

Munro, T. E. 1960. Fieldwork in Otago 1959–1960. *NZAA* **3**:13–18.

Murison, W. D. 1872. Notes on moa remains. *TNZI* **4**:120–4.

Newcomer, M., R. Grace and R. Unger-Hamilton 1986. Investigating microwear polishes with blind tests. *J. Arch. Sci.* **13**:203–17.

Nichol, R. 1981. Preliminary report on excavations at the Sunde site, N38/24 Motutapu Island. *NZAA* **24**:237–56.

Nichol, R. n. d. Draft ms. on moa-hunting sites, northern North Island. University of Auckland.

Nicholls, M. 1963. Preliminary report of excavations on Ponui Island. *NZAA* **6**:19–24.

O'Connor, R. J. 1984. *The growth and development of birds*. Wiley, Chichester.

Odell, G. H. and F. Odell-Vereecken 1980. Verifying the reliability of lithic use-wear assessments by 'blind tests': the low-power approach. *J. Field Archaeology* **7**:87–120.

Oliver, W. R. B. 1930. *New Zealand Birds*. Fine Arts (NZ) Ltd, Wellington.

Oliver, W. R. B. 1945. Avian evolution in New Zealand and Australia (2 parts). *The Emu* **45**:55–77 (Part I).

Oliver, W. R. B. 1949. The moas of New Zealand and Australia. *Dominion Museum Bulletin* no. 15.

Oliver, W. R. B. 1955. *New Zealand Birds*. Reprinted, Reed, Wellington 1974.

Oliver, W. R. B. n. d. Collected papers. National Museum of New Zealand, Wellington, NZ.

Olson, S. L. 1982. A critique of Cracraft's classification of birds. *The Auk* **99**:733–9.

Olson, S. L. 1985. The fossil record of birds. In *Avian Biology 8*, eds. D. S. Farner, J. R. King and K. C. Parkes, pp. 79–252. Academic Press, Orlando.

Orchiston, D. W. 1974. Studies in South Island, New Zealand, prehistory and protohistory. PhD thesis, University of Sydney.

Orchiston, D. W. 1976. Petrological studies in South Island New Zealand prehistory – 1. Maori use of Gawler Downs rhyolite tuff. *JRSNZ* **6**:213–19.

Orchiston, D. W. 1977a. Discovery of the bones of the extinct Giant Rail, *Aptornis otidiformis*, at an Archaic site near Needles Point, Marlborough. *NZAA* **20**:256–62.

Orchiston, D. W. 1977b. Prehistoric man in the North Canterbury Downlands. *NZAA* **20**:114–21.

Ornithological Society of New Zealand Inc. 1970. *Annotated Checklist of the Birds of New Zealand*. Reed, Wellington.

Owen, R. 1839. On the bone of an unknown Struthious bird from New Zealand. *PZSL* **VII**:169–171.

Owen, R. 1843a. No title. Read 10/1/1843. *PZSL* **XI**:1–2.

Owen, R. 1843b. No title. Read 24/1/1843. *PZSL* **XI**:8–10.

Owen, R. 1843c. No title. Read 10/1/1843. *PZSL* **XI**:19.

Owen, R. 1843d. No title. Read *c.* Nov. *PZSL* **XI**:144–6.

Owen, R. 1846. No title. *PZSL* 1846, pp. 46–9.

Owen, R. 1848. On the remains of the gigantic and presumed extinct wingless or terrestrial birds of New Zealand (*Dinornis* and *Palapteryx*), with indication of two other genera (*Notornis* and *Nestor*). *PZSL* **CLXXX**:1–11.

Owen, R. 1849a. Notice of a fragment of a femur of a gigantic bird of New Zealand. Read 12/11/1839. *TZSL* **III**:29–32.

Owen, R. 1849b. On *Dinornis*, an extinct Genus of tridactyle struthious birds, with descriptions of portions of the skeleton of five species which formerly existed in New Zealand. Read 28/11/1843. *TZSL* **III**:235–75.

Owen, R. 1849c. On *Dinornis* (Part II), containing descriptions of portions of the skull, the sternum and other parts of the skeleton, of the species previously determined, with osteological evidences of three additional species, and of a new Genus *Palapteryx*. Read 23/6/1846. *TZSL* **III**:307–29.

Owen, R. 1849d. On *Dinornis* (Part III): Containing a description of the skull and beak of that genus, and of the same characteristic parts of *Palapteryx*, and of two other genera of birds, *Notornis* and *Nestor*, formerly part of an extensive series of ornithic remains discovered by Mr. Walter Mantell at Waingongoro, North Island of New Zealand. Read 11/1/1848. *TZSL* **III**:345–78.

Owen, R. 1862a. On *Dinornis* (Part IV): Containing a restoration of the feet of that genus and of *Palapteryx*, with a description of the sternum in *Palapteryx* and *Aptornis*. Read Feb. 1850. *TZSL* **IV**:1–20.

Owen, R. 1862b. On *Dinornis* (Part V): Containing a description of the skull and beak of a large species of *Dinornis*, of the cranium of an immature specimen of *Dinornis giganteus*(?), and of crania of species of *Palapteryx*. Read 12/11/1850. *TZSL* **IV**:59–68.

Owen, R. 1862c. On *Dinornis* (Part VI): Containing a description of the bones of the leg of *Dinornis* (*Palapteryx*) *struthioides* and of *Dinornis gracilis* Owen. Read 14/11/1854. *TZSL* **IV**:141–7.

Owen, R. 1862d. On *Dinornis* (Part VII): Containing a description of the bones of the leg and foot of *Dinornis elephantopus* Owen. Read 8/4/1856. *TZSL* **IV**:149–57.

Owen, R. 1862e. On *Dinornis* (Part VIII): Containing a description of the skeleton of *Dinornis elephantopus* Owen. Read 8/4/1856. *TZSL* IV:159–64.

Owen, R. 1866a. On *Dinornis* (Part IX): Containing a description of the skull, atlas and scapulo-coracoid bone of the *Dinornis robustus* Owen. Read 13/12/1864. *TZSL* V:337–58.

Owen, R. 1866b. On *Dinornis* (Part X): Containing a description of part of the skeleton of a flightless bird indicative of a new genus and species (*Cnemiornis calcitrans* Owen). Read 23/5/1865. *TZSL* V:395–404.

Owen, R. 1866c. *Birds and Mammals. On the Anatomy of Vertebrates. Vol. 2.* Longmans Green: London.

Owen, R. 1869a. On *Dinornis* (Part XI): Containing a description of the integument of the sole, and tendons of a toe, of the foot of *Dinornis robustus* Owen. Read 28/11/1867. *TZSL* VI:495–6.

Owen, R. 1869b. On *Dinornis* (Part XII): Containing a description of the femur, tibia and metatarsus of *Dinornis maximus* Owen. Read 28/11/1867. *TZSL* VI: 497–500.

Owen, R. 1872a. On *Dinornis* (Part XIII): Containing a description of the sternum in *Dinornis elephantopus* and *D. rheides*, with notes on that bone in *D. crassus* and *D. casuarinus*. Read 25/6/1868. *TZSL* VII:115–22.

Owen, R. 1872b. On *Dinornis* (Part XIV): Containing contributions to the craniology of the genus, with a description of the fossil cranium of *Dasornis loninensis* Owen, from the London clay of Sheppey. Read 28/1/1869. *TZSL* VII:123–50.

Owen, R. 1872c. On *Dinornis* (Part XV): Containing a description of the skull, femur, tibia, fibula and metatarsus of *Aptornis defossor* Owen, from near Oamaru, Middle Island, New Zealand, with additional observations on *Aptornis otidiformis*, on *Notornis mantelli* and on *Dinornis curtus*. Read 10/3/1870. *TZSL* VII:353–80.

Owen, R. 1872d. On *Dinornis* (Part XVI): Containing notices of the internal organs of some species, with a description of the brain and some nerves and muscles of the head of *Apteryx australis*. Read 26/5/1870. *TZSL* VII:381–96.

Owen, R. 1873. The earliest discovered evidence of extinct struthious birds in New Zealand. *The Geological Magazine* 10:478.

Owen, R. 1874. On *Dinornis* (Part XVIII): Containing a description of the pelvis and bones of the leg of *Dinornis gravis*. Read 7/5/1872. *TZSL* VIII:361–80.

Owen, R. 1877. On *Dinornis* (Part XXI): Containing a restoration of the skeleton of *Dinornis maximus* Owen. With an appendix on additional evidence of the genus *Dromornis* in Australia. Read 7/6/1875. *TZSL* X:147–88.

Owen, R. 1879a. *Memoirs on the Extinct Wingless Birds of New Zealand: With an Appendix on Those of England, Australia, Newfoundland, Mauritius, and Rodriguez* (2 vols.). John van Voorst, London.

Owen, R. 1879b. On the extinct animals of the colonies of Great Britain. *Proceedings of the Royal Colonial Institute* X:267–97.

Owen, R. 1885a. On *Dinornis* (Part XXIII): Containing a description of the skeleton of *Dinornis parvus* Owen. Read 3/1/1882. *TZSL* XI:233–56.

Owen, R. 1885b. On *Dinornis* (Part XXIV): Containing a description of the head and feet with their dried integuments, of an individual of the species *Dinornis didinus* Owen. Read 20/6/1882. *TZSL* XI:257–61.

Owen, R. S. Rev. 1894. *The Life of Richard Owen* (2 vols). John Murray and Sons, London.

Park, G. S. 1969. Tiwai Point – a preliminary report. *NZAA* 12:143–6.

Parker, T. J. 1893a. On the classification and mutual relations of the Dinornithidae. *TNZI* 25:1–3.

Parker, T. J. 1893b. On the presence of a crest of feathers in certain species of moa. *TNZI* 25:3–5.

Parker, T. J. 1895. On the cranial osteology, classification, and phylogeny of the *Dinornithidae*. Read 14/2/1893. *TZSL* XIII:373–431.

Parkes, K. C. and G. A. Clark Jnr 1966. An additional character linking ratites and tinamous, and an interpretation of their monophyly. *The Condor* 68:459–71.

Parry, G. G. 1961. Moa hunters at the Waiau? *NZAA* 4:12–13.

Patterson, L. W. 1979. Limitations in uses of large prismatic blades. *Lithic Technology* 8:3–5.

Pearson, O. P. 1983. Characteristics of a mammalian fauna from forests in Patagonia, Southern Argentina. *J. Mammalogy* 64:476–92.

Polack, J. 1838. *New Zealand, being a Narrative of Travels and Adventures* (2 vols.). Richard Bentley, London.

Poynter, J. B. 1932. The Maori and the moa. *Proceedings of the Tairawhiti Maori Association* 1:95–107.

Prager, E. M., A. C. Wilson, D. T. Osuga and R. E. Feeney 1976. Evolution of flightless land birds on southern continents: Transferrin comparison shows monophyletic origin of ratites. *Journal of Molecular Evolution* 8:283–94.

Pratt, T. K. 1983. Diet of the dwarf cassowary *Casuarius bennetti* Picticollis at Wau, Papua New Guinea. *The Emu* 82:283–5.

Price, T. R. 1963. Moa remains at Poukawa, Hawke's Bay. *NZAA* 6:169–74.

Price, T. R. 1965. Excavations at Poukawa, Hawke's Bay, New Zealand. *NZAA* 8:8–11.

Prickett, N. 1987. The Bramley collection of Maori artefacts, Auckland Museum. *RAIM* 24:1–66.

Prickett, N. J. 1983. Waitotara ki Parininihi: aspects of the archaeology of the Taranaki region. In *A Lot of Spadework To Be Done*, eds. S. Bulmer, G. Law and D. Sutton. NZAA Monograph 14:281–329.

Prickett, N. and K. Walls 1973. D'Urville Island archaeological survey. Report to Lands and Survey Dept., Nelson, NZ.

Prickett, N. J. and K. E. Prickett 1975. D'Urville Island archaeological survey. *NZAA* **18**:108–31.

Pullar, W. A. 1965. Note on ash beds at Poukawa, Hawke's Bay. *NZAA* **8**:11–13.

Pullar, W. A. 1970. Pumice ash beds and peaty deposits of archaeological significance near Lake Poukawa, Hawke's Bay. *NZ J. of Science* **13**:687–705.

Pycraft, W. P. 1901. In Rothschild 1901, pp. 149–290.

Pyke, V. 1890. The moa (Dinornis) and the probable causes of its extinction. *The Otago Witness*, 18 September.

Rand, A. L. and E. T. Gilliard 1967. *Handbook of New Guinea Birds*. Weidenfeld and Nicolson, London.

Reichenbach, H. G. L. 1852. *Das natürliche System der Vögel*. Dresden.

Reid, B. n. d. Food intake and growth rate of cassowary chicks reared at Mendi, Southern Highlands, PNG. NZ Wildlife Service, ms.

Rich, P. and J. Balouet 1984. The waifs and strays of the bird world or the ratite problem revisited, one more time. In Archer and Clayton, pp. 447–55.

Rich, P. and G. van Tets 1984. What fossil birds contribute towards an understanding of origin and development of the Australian avifauna. In Archer and Clayton, pp. 421–46.

Richards, R. 1986. *Which Pakeha ate the Last Moa?* Paremata Press, Wellington.

Ritchie, N. A. 1982a. Two sub-fossil faunal deposits discovered near Cromwell, Central Otago. *NZAA* **25**:86–102.

Ritchie, N. A. 1982b. The prehistoric role of the Cromwell Gorge, New Zealand. *NZJA* **4**:21–43.

Ritchie, N. A. and A. R. Harrison 1981. Clutha Valley archaeology 1980–1981, an interim report. *NZAA* **24**:97–105.

Roberts, W. H. S. 1875. Letter on moa. *TNZI* **7**:548–9.

Robinson, D. W. 1961. A second Archaic site near Hawera? *NZAA* **4**:15–16.

Robinson, D. W. 1963a. A reconnaissance at Coopers Beach, Doubtless Bay. *NZAA* **6**:11–15.

Robinson, D. W. 1963b. Kaupokonui midden, South Taranaki N128/3. The artifacts. *NZAA* **6**:183–7.

Robson, C. H. 1876. On moa remains at Cape Campbell. *TNZI* **8**:95–7.

Robson, C. H. 1877. Further notes on moa remains. *TNZI* **9**:279–80.

Rochfort, J. 1862. Journal of two expeditions to the West Coast of the Middle Island of New Zealand in the year 1859. *J. Roy. Geog. Soc.* **32**:294–303.

Rothschild, W. Hon. 1901. A monograph of the genus *Casuarius*. With a dissertation on the morphology and phylogeny of the *Palaeognathae (Ratitae and Crypturi)* and *Neognithae (Carinatae)* by W. P. Pycraft. Read 20/6/1899. *TZSL* **xv**:149–290.

Rothschild, W. Hon. 1907. *Extinct Birds*. Hutchison, London.

Rowland, M. J. 1977. Tairua – results of midden analysis. *NZAA* **20**:223–43.

Rowland, M. J. 1978. Investigations of two sites on Slipper Island. *NZAA* **21**:31–52.

Rule, J. 1843. New Zealand. *The Polytechnic Journal* **7**: 1–13.

Russell, I. C. 1877. The giant birds of New Zealand. *The American Naturalist* **xi**:11–21.

Rutland, J. 1893. Did the Maori know the moa? *JPS* **2**:156.

Saiff, E. I. 1982. The middle ear of the skull of the kiwi. *The Emu* **82**:75–9.

Scarlett, R. J. 1957. Former faunal areas: Some sub-fossil evidence. *Proc. NZ Ecol. Soc.* **4**:17–18.

Scarlett, R. J. 1962. Interim list of moa species identified from North Island archaeological sites. *NZAA* **5**:245–6.

Scarlett, R. J. 1963. Comments on 'Excavations at South Bay, Kaikoura' S49/43. *NZAA* **6**:159–60.

Scarlett, R. J. 1968. A second North Island locality for *Pachyornis elephantopus* (Owen). *Notornis* **15**:36.

Scarlett, R. J. 1969. Moas and other extinct birds. In *Natural History of Canterbury*, ed. G. A. Knox, pp. 565–8. Reed, Wellington, NZ.

Scarlett, R. J. 1971. Wakanui salvage. *Canterbury Museum Archaeological Association Newsletter* **24** and **26**.

Scarlett, R. J. 1972. *Bones for the New Zealand Archaeologist*. Canterbury Museum, Christchurch, NZ.

Scarlett, R. J. 1974. Moa and man in New Zealand. *Notornis* **21**:1–12.

Scarlett, R. J. 1979. Avifauna and man. In *Birds of a Feather*, ed. A. J. Anderson, pp. 75–90. B.A.R., Oxford.

Scarlett, R. J. 1982. Archaeology on a shoe string: Excavations at Heaphy River Mouth 1961–63. *NZAA* **25**:180–2.

Scarlett, R. J. n. d. Identification of moa remains from Catlins and Stewart Island sites. Cards, Canterbury Museum, Christchurch, NZ.

Scarlett, R. J. and R. E. Molnar 1984. Terrestrial bird or dinosaur phalanx from the New Zealand Cretaceous. *NZ J. of Zoology* **11**:271–5.

Scott, S. D. 1970. Excavations at the 'Sunde Site' N38/24, Motutapu Island, New Zealand. *RAIM* **7**:13–30.

Shawcross, W. 1964. Stone flake industries in New Zealand. *JPS* **73**:7–25.

Shawcross, W. 1972. Energy and ecology: thermodynamic models in archaeology. In *Models in Archaeology*, ed. D. L. Clarke, pp. 577–622. Methuen, London.

Sherborn, C. D. 1893. Owen: Biographical notice. *Natural Science* **ii**:16–18.

Shortland, E. 1851. *The Southern Districts of New Zealand*. Capper Press, Christchurch.

Shortland, E. 1869. A short sketch of the Maori races. *TNZI* **1**:329–38.

Sibley, C. G. and J. E. Ahlquist 1981. The phylogeny and relationships of the ratite birds as indicated by

DNA-DNA hybridization. In *Evolution Today*, eds. G. G. E. Scudder and J. L. Reveal, pp. 301–35. *Proceedings of the Second International Congress of Systematic and Evolutionary Biology*. Hunt Institute for Botanical Documentation, Carnegie-Mellon University, Pittsburgh.

Sibley, C. G. and J. E. Ahlquist 1983. Phylogeny and classification of birds based on the data of DNA-DNA hybridization. In *Current Ornithology* no. 1, R. F. Johnston (ed.), pp. 245–292. Plenum Press, New York.

Sibley, C. G. and J. E. Ahlquist 1984. The phylogeny of the hominoid primates, as indicated by DNA × DNA hybridization. *Journal of Molecular Evolution* 20:2–15.

Simmons, D. R. 1966. Anthropology report in *Otago Museum Report for 1965 and 1966*.

Simmons, D. R. 1967. Little Papanui and Otago prehistory. *Rec. Otago Mus. (Anthropology)* no. 4.

Simmons, D. R. 1968. Man, moa and the forest. *TRSNZ* 2:115–27.

Simmons, D. R. n.d. Correspondence. Otago Museum, Dunedin, NZ.

Simmons, D. R. and B. Biggs 1970. The sources of the 'Lore of the Whare-Wananga'. *JPS* 79:22–42.

Simpson, L. O. 1955. A note on a green moa egg from Chatto Creek, Central Otago. *TRSNZ* 83:223–6.

Sinclair, E. D. 1977. Interim report of salvage excavations at Paremata (N160/50). *NZAA* 20:151–65.

Sinclair, K. 1983. The origin of the species. In *The Summer Book, 2*, B. Williams, R. Parsons and L. Missen (eds.), pp. 27–32. The Port Nicholson Press, Wellington, NZ.

Skinner, H. D. 1912. Maori life on the Poutini Coast, together with some traditions of the natives. *JPS* 21:141–51.

Skinner, H. D. 1921. Culture areas in New Zealand. *JPS* 30:71–8.

Skinner, H. D. 1923. Archaeology of Canterbury. Moa Bone Point Cave. *RCM* 2:93–104.

Skinner, H. D. 1924a. Results of the excavations at Shag River sandhills. *JPS* 33:11–24.

Skinner, H. D. 1924b. Archaeology of Canterbury. Moncks Cave. *RCM* 2:151–62.

Skinner, H. D. 1934. A pit in peat. *JPS* 43:292–4.

Skinner, H. D. 1960. Excavations at Little Papanui. *JPS* 69:187–98.

Skinner, H. D. 1974. *Comparatively Speaking*. University of Otago Press, Dunedin.

Skinner, H. D. n.d. Correspondence. Otago Museum, Dunedin, NZ.

Skinner, H. D. and D. Teviotdale 1927. A classification of implements of quartzite and similar material from the Moahunter camp at Shag River Mouth. *JPS* 36:180–93.

Smalley, I. 1979. Moas as rockhounds. *Nature* 281: 103–4.

Smart, C. D., R. C. Green and J. C. Yaldwyn 1962. A stratified dune site at Tairua, Coromandel. *Dominion Museum Records in Ethnology* 1:243–66.

Smith, I. W. G. 1985. Sea mammal hunting and prehistoric subsistence in New Zealand. PhD thesis, University of Otago.

Smith, S. P. 1911. The Maori and the moa. *JPS* 20:54–9.

Smith, W. W. 1884. On moa and other remains from the Tengawai River, Canterbury. *NZ J. of Science* II:293–5.

Smith, W. W. 1891. On the occurrence of moa and other remains at Albury. *NZJ. of Science* 1:193–8.

Smith, W. W. 1901. On ancient Maori relics from Canterbury, New Zealand. *TNZI* 33:426–33.

Sorrenson, M. P. K. 1979. *Maori Origins and Migrations*. Auckland University Press, Auckland.

Sorrenson, M. P. K. (ed.) 1986. *Na To Hoa Aroha – from Your Dear Friend: The correspondence between Sir Aparina Ngata and Sir Peter Buck 1925–1950*. Auckland University Press, Auckland.

Spring-Rice, W. 1963. Haratonga–Great Barrier Island. *NZAA* 6:25–7.

Stack, J. W. 1872. Some observations on the annual address of the president of the Philosophical Institute of Canterbury. *TNZI* 4:107–10.

Stack, J. W. 1875. Notes on the word 'moa' in the poetry of the New Zealanders. *TNZI* 7:app. xxviii–xxix.

Stack, J. W. 1878. Appendices to Haast 1878.

Stevens, G. R. 1980. Southwest Pacific faunal palaeobiogeography in Mesozoic and Cenozoic times: A review. *Palaeogeography, Palaeoclimatology, Palaeoecology* 31:153–96.

Stevenson, G. B. 1947. *Maori and Pakeha in North Otago*. Reed, Wellington.

Sutton, D. G. 1987. A paradigmatic shift in Polynesian prehistory: implications for New Zealand. *NZJA* 9:135–55.

Sutton, D. G. and Y. M. Marshall 1980. Coastal hunting in the subantarctic zone. *NZJA* 2:25–49.

Swinton, W. E. 1975. *Fossil Birds*. British Museum, London.

Tainter, J. A. 1979. The Mountainair lithic scatters: settlement patterns and significance evaluation of low density surface sites. *J. Field Archaeology* 6:463–9.

Taylor, M. 1984. Bone refuse from Twilight Beach. MA thesis, University of Auckland.

Taylor, Rev. R. 1855. *Te Ika a Maui*. Wertheim and MacIntosh, London.

Taylor, Rev. R. 1873. An account of the first discovery of moa remains. *TNZI* 5:97–101.

Taylor, Rev. R. n.d. Journal 1839–1843. Auckland Public Library, NZ.

Taylor, W. A. 1952. *Lore and History of the South Island Maoris*. Bascand, Christchurch.

Teal, F. J. 1975. Pleasant River excavations 1959–62. Research report, University of Otago.

Teal, F. J. 1976. Waikaia Harbour to Tokanui River Mouth site survey. Rpt. to HPT.

Temple, P. and C. Gaskin 1985. *Moa: the story of a fabulous bird*. Collins, Auckland, NZ.

Teviotdale, D. 1924. Excavations near the mouth of the Shag River, Otago. *JPS* **33**:3–10.

Teviotdale, D. 1927. Notes on artifacts found in a cache at Pipikaritu Beach, near Otago Heads. *JPS* **36**:292–3.

Teviotdale, D. 1931. Notes on the excavation of a cave near Taieri Mouth. *JPS* **40**:87–90.

Teviotdale, D. 1932a. The material culture of the Moa hunters in Murihiku. *JPS* **41**:81–120.

Teviotdale, D. 1932b. Notes on the Moa hunters. *JPS* **41**:239–41.

Teviotdale, D. 1937. Progress report on moa-hunters camp. *JPS* **46**:134–53.

Teviotdale, D. 1938a. Further excavations at the moa-hunters' camp at Papatowai. *JPS* **47**:27–37.

Teviotdale, D. 1938b. Final report on the excavation of a moa-hunter camp at the mouth of the Tahakopa River. *JPS* **47**:114–18.

Teviotdale, D. 1939. Excavation of a Moa hunters' camp near the mouth of the Waitaki River. *JPS* **48**:167–85.

Teviotdale, D. n. d. Excavation diaries. Hocken Library, Dunedin and Southland Museum, Invercargill, NZ.

Thomas, S. and M. Corden 1977. *Metric tables of composition of Australian foods.* Government Publishing Service, Canberra.

Thomson, Dr A. 1854. Description of two caves in the North Island of New Zealand, in which were found bones of the large extinct wingless bird, called by the natives, moa, and by naturalists, *Dinornis*; with some general observations on this genus of birds. *Edinburgh New Philosophical Journal* **LVI**:268–95.

Thomson, A. S. 1859. *The Story of New Zealand* (2 vols.). John Murray, London.

Thomson, G. N. 1922. *The Naturalisation of Animals and Plants in New Zealand.* CUP, Cambridge.

Thomson, J. T. 1858. Extracts from a journal kept during the performance of a reconnaissance survey of the southern districts of the province of Otago, New Zealand. *J. Roy. Geog. Soc.* **28**:298–329.

Thomson, J. T. n. d. Fieldbooks 1857–58. Lands and Survey Department, Dunedin, NZ.

Thorne, G. 1876. Notes on the discovery of moa and Moa-hunters remains at Pataua River, near Whangarei. *TNZI* **8**:83–94.

Till, M. n. d. Excavation notes, Ross's Rocks, East Otago, University of Otago.

Travers, W. T. L. 1876. Notes on the extinction of the moa etc. *TNZI* **8**:58–83.

Tregear, E. 1888. The Maori and the moa. *J. Anth. Inst. Grt. Britain and Ireland* **17**:292–305.

Tregear, E. 1889. Comment, 8th meeting Wellington Philosophical Society. *TNZI* **21**:504–5.

Tregear, E. 1892. The extinction of the moa. *JPS* **25**:413–26.

Trotter, M. M. 1955. First excavation of a Moa hunter camp site at Waimataitai Mouth, Katiki. *JPS* **64**:295–303.

Trotter, M. M. 1959. Archaeological investigations in North Otago. *NZAA* **2**:13–16.

Trotter, M. M. 1965a. Excavations at Ototara Glen, North Otago. *NZAA* **8**:109–14.

Trotter, M. M. 1965b. Avian remains from North Otago archaeological sites. *Notornis* **12**:176–8.

Trotter, M. M. 1966. Recording and rescue work in Canterbury and North Otago. *NZAA* **9**:119–26.

Trotter, M. M. 1967a. Investigations of a Moa hunter site at Redcliffs, Sumner. *RCM* **8**:247–50.

Trotter, M. M. 1967b. Excavations at Hampden Beach, North Otago. *NZAA* **10**:56–61.

Trotter, M. M. 1968a. North Otago archaeological sites. *NZAA* **11**:94–102.

Trotter, M. M. 1968b. On the reliability of charcoal for radiocarbon dating New Zealand archaeological sites. *NZAA* **11**:86–8.

Trotter, M. M. 1969. *Lake Pukaki survey.* Archaeology Department, Canterbury Museum.

Trotter, M. M. 1970a. Archaeological investigations in the Aviemore area, South Island. *RCM* **8**:439–53.

Trotter, M. M. 1970b. Excavations at Shag Point, North Otago. *RCM* **8**:469–85.

Trotter, M. M. 1970c. North Otago archaeological sites. *NZAA* **13**:135–42.

Trotter, M. M. 1970d. A Holocene section at Scaife's Lagoon, Wanaka. *RCM* **8**:463–7.

Trotter, M. M. 1972a. A Moa hunter site near the mouth of the Rakaia River, South Island. *RCM* **9**:129–50.

Trotter, M. M. 1972b. Investigations of the Weka Pass shelter S61/4. *NZAA* **15**:42–50.

Trotter, M. M. 1973a. Takamatua salvage, Banks Peninsula. *NZAA* **16**:74–7.

Trotter, M. M. 1973b. Prehistoric sites in the Ashburton district, South Island. *NZAA* **16**:137–42.

Trotter, M. M. 1975a. Further excavations at Wairau Bar, New Zealand. *Asian Perspectives* **18**:75–80.

Trotter, M. M. 1975b. Archaeological investigations at Redcliffs, Canterbury, New Zealand. *RCM* **9**:189–220.

Trotter, M. M. 1977. Moa-hunter research since 1956. In *The Moa-hunter Period of Maori Culture.* R. Duff, pp. 348–75 Government Printer, Wellington.

Trotter, M. M. 1979a. Investigation of Awamoa archaeological site, S136/4, ms.

Trotter, M. M. 1979b. Tai Rua: A Moa hunter site in North Otago. In *Birds of a Feather,* ed. A. J. Anderson, pp. 203–30. B. A. R., Oxford.

Trotter, M. M. 1980. Archaeological investigations at Avoca Point, Kaikoura. *RCM* **9**:277–88.

Trotter, M. M. 1982. Canterbury and Marlborough. In *The First Thousand Years,* ed. N. Prickett, pp. 83–102. Dunmore Press, Palmerston North, NZ.

Trotter, M. M. n. d. a. *Titirangi archaeology, an interim report.* Marlborough Sounds Maritime Park Board, Blenheim, NZ.

Trotter, M. M. n. d. b. Excavation diaries. Otago Museum, Dunedin, NZ.

Trotter, M. M. and B. McCulloch 1971. *Prehistoric Rock Art of New Zealand*. Reed, Wellington.

Trotter, M. M. and B. McCulloch 1973. Radiocarbon dates for South Island rockshelters. *NZAA* **16**: 176–8.

Trotter, M. M. and B. McCulloch 1979. *Prehistory at Clarence Bridge*. Kaikoura Coastal Reserves Board, Blenheim, NZ.

Trotter, M. M. and B. McCulloch 1984. Moas, men and middens. In Martin and Klein, pp. 708–27.

Tuller, S. E. 1977. Summer and winter patterns of human climate in New Zealand. *NZ Geographer* **33**:4–14.

Tyler, C. 1957. Some chemical, physical and structural properties of moa egg shells. *JPS* **66**:110–30.

van Tyne, J. and A. J. Berger 1959. *Fundamentals of Ornithology*. John Wiley and Sons, New York.

Vincent, B. A. 1980. Waitaki Mouth flake-blades. Research report, University of Otago.

Walker, P. L. 1978. Butchering and stone tool function. *Am. Antiq.* **43**:710–15.

Walls, J. Y. 1979. Salvage at the Glen – a late Archaic site in Tasman Bay. *NZAA* **22**:6–19.

Wardle, J. A. 1984. *The New Zealand Beeches*. NZ Forest Service, Christchurch.

Wardle, P. 1985. Environmental influences on the vegetation of New Zealand. *NZ J. Botany* **23**:773–88.

Wards, I. 1976. *New Zealand Atlas*. Government Printer, Wellington.

Warner, R. E. 1968. The role of introduced diseases in the extinction of the endemic Hawaiian avifauna. *The Condor* **70**:101–20.

Watkins, J. n. d. Journal 1840–1844. Hocken Library, Dunedin, NZ.

Weetman, S. 1886. Notes on some moa remains found at the Great Barrier Island during February 1886. *TNZI* **19**:193–4.

Wellman, H. W. 1962. Maori occupation layers at D'Urville Island, New Zealand. *NZ J. Geol. Geophys.* **5**:55–73.

Wellman, H. W. and A. T. Wilson 1964. Notes on the geology and archaeology of the Martins Bay district. *NZ J. Geol. Geophys.* **7**:702–21.

Westland, W. 1848. In *Letter from Otago 1848–1849*. Hocken Library, Dunedin, NZ. Victorian reprint series 4 (1978).

White, J. 1925. The moa in Maori tradition. *JPS* **34**:170–4.

White, T. 1876. Notes on moa caves, etc., in the Wakatipu district. *TNZI* **8**:97–102.

White, T. 1886. Remarks on the feathers of two species of moa. *TNZI* **18**:83–4.

White, T. 1895. On the bird moa and its aliases. *TNZI* **27**:262–73.

White, T. 1897. On the Poua and other extinct birds of the Chatham Islands. *TNZI* **29**:162–8.

Wilkes, O. 1964. Field notes and plans, Wairau Bar. Canterbury Museum, Christchurch, NZ.

Wilkes, O. R. and R. J. Scarlett 1967. Excavation of a Moa hunter site at the mouth of the Heaphy River. *RCM* **8**:177–208.

Wilkes, O., R. J. Scarlett and G. Boraman 1963. Two Moa hunter sites in North West Nelson. *NZAA* **6**:88–93.

Williams, G. R. 1962. Extinction and the land and fresh-water inhabiting birds of New Zealand. *Notornis* **10**:15–32.

Williams, H. W. 1971. *A Dictionary of the Maori Language*. Government Printer, Wellington.

Williams, W. L. 1872. Footprints of large bird found at Turanganui, Poverty Bay. *TNZI* **4**:124.

Wilson, K. 1913. Footprints of the moa. *TNZI* **45**:211–12.

Winkler, D. W. and J. R. Walters 1983. The determination of clutch size in precocial birds. In *Current Ornithology*, ed. R. F. Johnston, pp. 33–68. Plenum Press, New York.

Wohlers, J. F. H. 1884. Letter to Haast (Wohlers papers), Hocken Library, Dunedin, NZ.

Wohlers, J. F. H. 1876. Maori mythology and traditions. *TNZI* **8**:108–23.

Woodward, A. S. 1893. Sir Richard Owen's researches on the vertebrates. *Natural Science* **II**:129–34.

Worthy, T. H. 1987. Sexual dimorphism and temporal variation in the North Island moa species *Euryapteryx curtus* (Owen) and *Pachyornis mappini* (Archey). *Nat. Mus. NZ Rec.* **3**:59–70.

Worthy, T. H. 1988. A re-examination of the moa genus *Megalapteryx*. *Notornis* **35**:99–108.

Worthy, T. H. n. d. a. Draft ms on ecological distribution of moas. National Museum of New Zealand, Wellington.

Worthy, T. H. n. d. b. Draft identification guide to moa leg bones. National Museum of New Zealand, Wellington.

Worthy, T. H. n. d. c. Aspects of the biology of two moas. ms, National Museum of New Zealand, Wellington.

Wright, K. and B. Bennett 1964. Excavations at Smugglers Cave. *NZAA* **7**:133.

Yaldwyn, J. C. 1956. A preliminary account of the sub-fossil avifauna of the Martinborough Caves. *Records of the Dominion Museum* **3**:1–7.

Yaldwyn, J. C. 1958. Notes on the environment and age of the sub-fossil deposits of the Martinborough Caves. *Records of the Dominion Museum* **3**:129–35.

Yaldwyn, J. C. 1959. Moa remains from the Wellington district. *NZAA* **2**:20–5.

Yaldwyn, J. C. 1979. The types of W. R. B. Oliver's moas and notes on Oliver's methods of measuring moa bones. In *Birds of a Feather*, ed. A. J. Anderson, pp. 1–24. B.A.R., Oxford.

Yate, Rev, W. 1835. *An Account of New Zealand; and of the formulation and progress of the Church Missionary Society's Mission in the northern island*. Seeley and Burnside, London.

Appendix A

TAXONOMIES OF DINORNITHIFORMES

Owen 1843	1846 (1849c)	1858 (1862a–e)	1868 (1869b)	1882 (1885a, b)
January (1843b)	*Dinornis*	*Dinornis*	*Dinornis*	*Dinornis*
[*Megalornis*]	*giganteus*	*giganteus*	*maximus* (n. sp.)	*maximus*
Novae Zealandiae (n. sp.)	*struthoides*	*casuarinus*	*giganteus*	*giganteus*
	casuarinus (n. sp.)	*crassus*	*casuarinus*	*casuarinus*
July (1843c)	*crassus* (n. sp.)	*didiformis*	*didiformis*	*didiformis*
Dinornis (n. gen.)	*didiformis*	*curtus*	*curtus*	*curtus*
Novae Zealandiae	*curtus* (n. sp.)	*rheides* (n. sp.)	*rheides*	*rheides*
	D. (Palapteryx)	*gracilis* (n. sp.)	*gracilis*	*gracilis*
November (1843d)	*ingens*	*elephantopus* (n. sp.)	*ingens*	*ingens*
Dinornis	*dromioides*	*D. (Palapteryx)*	*dromioides*	*dromioides*
giganteus (n. sp.)		*ingens*	*geranoides*	*geranoides*
struthoides (n. sp.)	1848 (1849d)	*dromioides*	*struthioides*	*struthioides*
didiformis (n. sp.)		*geranoides*	*Palapteryx*	*crassus*
otidiformis (n. sp.)	*Dinornis*	*struthioides*	*crassus*	*elephantopus*
dromaeoides (n. sp.)	*giganteus*	*robustus* (n. sp.)	*elephantopus*	*robustus*
	casuarinus		*robustus*	*gravis* (n. sp.)
Added before	*crassus*			*altus* (n. sp.)
publication: (1849b)	*didiformis*			*Huttonii* (n. sp.)
Dinornis	*curtus*			*parvus* (n. sp.)
ingens (n. sp.)	*Palapteryx* (n. gen.)			*didinus* (n. sp.)
	ingens			
	dromioides			
	geranoides (n. sp.)			
	struthoides			

Reichenbach (1852)	Haast (1874)	Lydekker (1891)	Parker 1892 (1893a)	Parker 1893 (1895)
Moa (n. gen.)	Dinornithidae	Dinornithidae	Dinornithidae	Dinornithidae
giganteus	*Dinornis*	*Dinornis*	Gigantornithinae	Dinornithinae
Movia (n. gen.)	*maximus*	*novae-zealandiae*⊕	*Dinornis*	*Dinornis*
ingens	*robustus*	*maximus**	*giganteus*	*maximus*
Dinornis	*ingens*	cf. *robustus**	*maximus*	*robustus*
struthioides	*struthioides*	*struthioides*⊕	*robustus*	*torosus*
Anomalopteryx (n. gen.)	*gracilis*	*gracilis*⊕	*ingens*	species *a*
didiformis	*Meionornis* (n. gen.)	*Megalapteryx*	*torosus*	
Cela (n. gen.)	*casuarinus*	*tenuipes* (n. sp.)*	*struthioides*	Anomalopteryginae
curta	*didiformis*	*hectori**		*Pachyornis*
Syornis (n. gen.)		*Anomalopteryx*	Mesornithinae	*elephantopus*
casuarinus	Palapterygidae	*casuarina*⊕	*Emeus*	?*immanis*
Emeus (n. gen.)	*Palapteryx*	*dromaeoides*⊕	*crassus*	species α*

crassus	*elephantopus*	*didiformis*⊕	species *a*	species *β**
	crassus	*didina**	*Mesopteryx*	species *γ**
	Euryapteryx (n. gen.)	*parva**	*casuarina*	species *a**
	gravis	*oweni*†	species *a*	species *b**
	rheides	*curta*⊕	species *b*	*Mesopteryx*
		?geranoides⊕	species *c*	*casuarina*
		Emeus	*Anomalopteryx*	species *α*†
	Haast 1885 (1890a, b)	*gravipes* (n. nom.)*	*didiformis*	species *β**
	added:	*crassus**	*?curta*	species *γ**
	Dinornis	species *a**		*Anomalopteryx*
	˙*oweni* (n. sp.)	*Pachyornis* (n. gen.)	Pachyornithinae	*didiformis*
	Megalapteryx (n. gen.)	species *a**	*Pachyornis*	
	hectori (n. sp.)	*elephantopus**	*gravis*	Emeinae
		immanis (n. sp.)*	*ponderosus*	*Emeus*
		species *b**	*elephantopus*	*crassus*
			species *a*	species *α**
		Added in 1891 (1892):		species *β**
		Pachyornis		species *γ**
		rothschildi (n. nom.)		

Hutton 1891 (1892b, c)	Hutton 1892 (1893a, b, c)	Hutton 1894 (1895a, b)	Hutton 1896 (1896a, b; 1897a, b)
Dinornithidae	Dinornithidae	Dinornithidae	Dinornithidae
Dinornis (Dinornis)	*Dinornis (Dinornis)*	*Dinornis*	*Dinornis*
*altus**	*altus*	*altus*	*altus*
*maximus**	*maximus*	*maximus*	*maximus*
excelsus (n. sp.)†	*excelsus*	*excelsus*	*excelsus*
validus (n. nom.)*	*validus*	*validus*	*giganteus*
giganteus†	*giganteus*	*giganteus*	*robustus*
*robustus**	*robustus*	*robustus*	*firmus*
firmus (n. nom.)†	*firmus*	*firmus*	*ingens*
ingens†	*ingens*	*ingens*	*torosus*
potens (n. nom.)*	*potens*	*potens*	*struthioides*
Dinornis (Tylopteryx)	*strenuus* (n. nom.)*	*strenuus*	*dromioides*
gracilis†	*Dinornis (Tylopteryx)*	*gracilis*	*Megalapteryx*
torosus (n. nom.)*	*gracilis*	*torosus*	*tenuipes*
struthioides⊕	*torosus*	*struthioides*	*hectori*
Palapteryx	*struthioides*	*dromioides*	*Anomalornis*
dromioides†	*Palapteryx*	*Megalapteryx*	*gracilis*
plenus (n. nom.)*	*dromioides*	*tenuipes**	*didiformis*
Anomalopteryx	*plenus*	*hectori**	*fortis*
didiformis⊕	*Anomalopteryx*	*Anomalopteryx*	*parvus*
antiquus (n. sp.)*	*didiformis*	*didiformis*	*oweni*†
Cela	*antiqua*	*antiqua*	*Cela*
geranoides†	*fortis* (n. sp.)*	*fortis*	*curta*
curtus†	*Cela*	*parva**	*Meionornis*
Mesopteryx	*curta*	*Meionornis*	*didinus*
didinus⊕	*Mesopteryx*	*curtus*	*casuarinus*
Syornis	*didina*	*didinus*	*rheides*
*rheides**	*rheides*	*casuarinus*	*Euryapteryx*
*crassus**	*casuarina*	*rheides*	*crassa*
casuarinus⊕	*Emeus*	*Euryapteryx*	*ponderosa*
Euryapteryx	*crassus*	*crassa*	*gravis*
*elephantopus**	*Euryapteryx*	*ponderosa*	*exilis*†
ponderosus (n. nom.)*	*ponderosa*	*gravis*	*Pachyornis*

gravis*	gravis	compacta	immanis
pygmaeus (n. sp.)	compacta (n. sp.)*	?pygmaeus	elephantopus
	pygmaeus	Pachyornis	inhabilis
	Pachyornis	immanis*	rothschildi†
	elephantopus	elephantopus	pygmaeus⊕
	inhabilis (n. sp.)*	inhabilis	
	valgus (n. sp.)*	valgus	
	?geranoides		

Forbes (1900)	Rothschild (1907)		Oliver (1930)
Dinornithidae	Dinornithidae	Emeus	Dinornithidae
Dinornithinae	Dinornis	crassus	Dinornis
Dinornis	maximus	boothi (n. nom.)	giganteus
maximus	altus	gravipes	maximus
	giganteus	haasti (n. nom.)	ingens
Anomalopteryginae	ingens	parkeri (n. nom.)	novaezealandiae
Pachyornis	gracilis	exilis	dromaeoides
elephantopus	dromioides	Pachyornis	
Mesopteryx	novaezealandiae	elephantopus	Anomalopterygidae
casuarina	Megalapteryx	immanis	Megalapteryx
Anomalopteryx	hectori	rothschildi	didinus
didiformis	hamiltoni (n. nom.)	ponderosus	hectori
Megalapteryx	tenuipes	inhabilis	Anomalopteryx
hectori	huttonii	valgus	didiformis
	Anomalopteryx	pygmaeus	parvus
Emeinae	didiformis	compacta	antiquus
Emeus	parvus	Palaeocasuarius (Forbes)	curtus
crassus	antiquus	haasti (Forbes)	oweni
	fortis	velox (Forbes)	Emeus
	Cela	elegans (Forbes)	crassus
	curtus		casuarinus
	oweni		huttoni
	geranoides		exilis
	rheides		Euryapteryx
	casuarinus		elephantopus
			immanis
			ponderosus
			kuranui (n. sp.)
			gravipes
			pygmaeus

Archey (1941)	Oliver (1949)	Checklist (Kinsky 1970)
Dinornithidae	Anomalopterygidae	Anomalopterygidae
Dinornis	Emeinae	Anomalopteryginae
novae-zealandiae†	Pachyornis	Anomalopteryx
ingens†	(Mauiornis) septentrionalis (n. sp.)†	didiformis⊕
giganteus†	(Mauiornis) mappini†	oweni†
torosus*	(Pounamua) murihiku (n. sp.)*	Megalapteryx
robustus*	(Pachyornis) australis (n. sp.)*	didinus⊕
maximus*	(Pachyornis) elephantopus*	benhami*
	queenslandiae	Pachyornis

Anomalopterygidae
Anomalopteryginae
Anomalopteryx
didiformis⊕
antiquus*
Megalapteryx
didinus⊕
benhami (n. sp.)*
Pachyornis
elephantopus*
pygmaeus*
mappini (n. sp.)†
oweni†

Emeinae
Emeus
crassus⊕
huttonii⊕
Euryapteryx
gravis⊕
geranoides†
exilis†
curtus†

Emeus
huttoni*
crassus*
Euryapteryx
curtus†
tane (n. sp.)†
geranoides⊕
gravis⊕
Zelornis (n. gen.)
exilis†
haasti*

Anomalopteryginae
Anomalopteryx
oweni†
parvus⊕
didiformis⊕
antiquus*
Megalapteryx
hectori*
didinus⊕
benhami*

Dinornithidae
Dinornis
gazella (n. sp.)†
novae zealandiae⊕
torosus*
ingens⊕
robustus*
hercules (n. sp.)†
giganteus†
maximus*

elephantopus⊕
mappini†
septentrionalis†
australis*
murihiku*

Emeinae
Emeus
crassus*
huttoni*
Euryapteryx
curtus†
geranoides†
gravis⊕
Zelornis
exilis†
haasti*

Dinornithidae
Dinornis
novaezealandiae†
robustus*
giganteus†
maximus*
struthoides†
torosus*
hercules†
gazella†

Scarlett (1972)	Cracraft (1976a)	Cracraft Synonymy
Dinornithidae	Dinornithidae	
Dinornis	Anomalopteryginae	
giganteus†	*Anomalopteryx* Reichenbach 1852	*parvus* Owen 1883
hercules†	*didiformis* Owen 1844⊕	*antiquus* Hutton 1892
novaezealandiae†	*oweni* Haast 1885†	
struthoides†	*Megalapteryx* Haast 1886	
gazella†	*didinus* Owen 1883*	*hectori* Haast 1886
maximus*	*benhami* Archey 1941*	
robustus*	*Pachyornis* Lydekker 1891	*murihiku* Oliver 1949
torosus*	*elephantopus* Owen 1856*	*australis* Oliver 1949
n. sp.*	*mappini* Archey 1941†	*septentrionalis* Oliver 1949
Pachyornis	*Euryapteryx* Haast 1874	*Zelornis* Oliver 1949
elephantopus⊕	*curtus* Owen 1846†	*exilis* Hutton 1897
mappini†		*tane* Oliver 1949
septentrionalis†	*geranoides* Owen 1848⊕	*gravis* Owen 1870
murihiku*		*haasti* Rothschild 1907
australis*	*Emeus* Reichenbach 1852	
pygmaeus*	*crassus* Owen 1846⊕	*huttoni* Owen 1879
Euryapteryx		

gravis⊕
geranoides†
exilis†
curtus†
*haasti**
n. sp.*
Emeus
*crassus**
Megalapteryx
didinus⊕
*benhami**
Anomalopteryx
didiformis⊕
oweni†
*antiquus**

Dinornithinae
Dinornis Owen 1843
struthoides Owen 1844⊕
torosus Hutton 1891*
novaezealandiae Owen 1843⊕

giganteus Owen 1844⊕

Worthy (n. d. b)

Anomalopterygidae
Anomalopteryx
didiformis⊕
Megalapteryx
*didinus**
Emeus
*crassus**
Euryapteryx
curtus†
geranoides⊕
Pachyornis
mappini†
*australis**
*elephantopus**

Dinornithidae
Dinornis
struthoides⊕
novaezealandiae⊕
giganteus⊕

gazella Oliver 1949

ingens Owen 1844
robustus Owen 1846
hercules Oliver 1949
maximus Owen 1867

Notes on Classification Tables

1. The classifications are dated according to the year of compilation, with references in brackets. However, in Owen's case, and to some extent with Hutton, the changes were more or less continuous and I have simply taken convenient points in their careers. New generic and specific names or species are noted as follows: n. sp. = new species, n. nom. = new species name, n. gen. = new genus. Further details of early synonymy can be obtained from Lydekker (1891), Rothschild (1907), Archey (1941) and Brodkorb (1963).

2. Geographical attributions are marked as follows: South Island = *, North Island = †, both islands = ⊕. For Parker, and Hutton after 1891, I give only the attributions additional to those in Lydekker (1891) and Hutton (1892c).

3. Parker's 1893 scheme is that of his 1895 paper (in which he calls it his 1892 scheme). It differs slightly from his list on the basis of his earlier comments in the same paper, particularly about *D. potens* and *D. parva*. He was less dubious about *P. immanis* (p. 376), hence its inclusion.

4. There was an important change in the nature of *D. novaezealandiae* in 1954. Owen took a femur, tibiotarsus and tarsometatarsus as the type series of his *D. novaezealandiae*, but later allocated the tibiotarsus to *D. ingens* and the femur and tarsometatarsus to *D. struthoides*. Lydekker accepted the *D. struthoides* (*struthioides* after 1854) attribution but returned the tibiotarsus as the type of *D. novaezealandiae*. Archey in 1927 argued that Owen's second position was the correct one (femur and tarsometatarsus to *novaezealandiae*, tibiotarsus to *ingens*), but a decision of the International Commission on Zoological Nomenclature in 1954

accepted Lydekker's view, and also synonymised *D. ingens* with *D. novaezealandiae*. Thus, *D. ingens* of Archey and Oliver became *D. novaezealandiae* and their *D. novaezealandiae* became *D. struthoides*.

5. Rothschild (1907:187) refers to 38 species, and so does everyone else who reports him, but I have counted carefully through his list and can only reach 37 species.

6. The distribution of *Eu. gravis* in the 1970 checklist has been corrected after Caughley (1977), but I do not include *A. antiquus*, as he does, because that was only synonymised in the checklist.

7. *D. maximus* of Owen was in a paper read in 1867, but not published until June 1869, by which time Haast, who knew of the new name, had used it (in May 1869). Some writers attribute *maximus* to Haast, others to Owen.

8. Benham (1910) reported remains of *Euryapteryx crassa* (probably *E. crassus*) from Stewart Island, and Scarlett (1979) the remains of *Euryapteryx gravis* and his new species of *Euryapteryx* in middens near the Neck.

9. Archey (1931:115) retained *Cela* for *geranoides* and *curtus* because the proportions of the leg bones and skulls were intermediate between those of *Anomalopteryx* and *Emeus*.

10. Falla (1974) outlined a classification of moa which had six species of *Dinornis*, two of *Anomalopteryx*, one of *Megalapteryx*, four of *Pachyornis*, two of *Emeus* and four of *Euryapteryx*. The species were not named and the scheme does not resemble any other of the time.

11. *Euryapteryx curtus* also on Great Barrier Island and *Euryapteryx geranoides* on Stewart Island (Worthy n. d. a).

Appendix B

Radiocarbon Dates from Natural Moa Bone Sites

Lab. No.	Location	Material	Date BP old T½	Provenance
SWAMPS				
NZ 4871 C	Clevedon	Moa bone collagen	1315 ± 70	
NZ 764	Poukawa	*D. giganteus* tibia	5810 ± 60	Below Taupo Ash
NZ 3663	Poukawa	moa bone collagen	1806 ± 226	
NZ 2471	Poukawa	moa bone collagen	3125 ± 36	
NZ 2642	Poukawa	moa bone	7246 ± 248	
NZ 2640	Poukawa	moa bone collagen	1157 ± 79	
NZ 3689	Poukawa	moa bone collagen	1169 ± 107	
NZ 3698	Poukawa	moa bone collagen	2002 ± 93	
NZ 3535	Poukawa	moa bone	1566 ± 34	
NZ 3701	Poukawa	moa bone	586 ± 85	
*L 129	Pyramid Valley	*Dinornis* gizzard	1800 ± 150	*c.* 160 cm depth
*Y 129 A	Pyramid Valley	*Dinornis* gizzard	670	*c.* 160 cm depth
*Y 129 B	Pyramid Valley	marl-gyttja	1100	matrix of Y 129 A
*Y 129 B	Pyramid Valley	marl-gyttja	1550	matrix of Y 129 A
Y 144–1	Pyramid Valley	marl-gyttja	3500	yellow lake marl
Y 144–2	Pyramid Valley	marl-gyttja	4200	yellow lake marl
Y 144–3	Pyramid Valley	marl-gyttja	5100	blue-green pug
Y 144–4	Pyramid Valley	peat	3700	lower peat
Y 144–5	Pyramid Valley	wood	3600	yellow lake marl
NZ 619	Pyramid Valley	seeds and twigs	2620 ± 49	68–73 cm depth
NZ 620	Pyramid Valley	seeds and twigs	2930 ± 63	81–86 cm depth
NZ 621	Pyramid Valley	seeds and twigs	3720 ± 60	116–123 cm depth
NZ 622	Pyramid Valley	peat	4280 ± 62	160–170 cm depth
*NZ 609	Pyramid Valley	*Emeus* carbonate	1365 ± 58	100 cm depth
*NZ 610	Pyramid Valley	*Emeus* collagen	3600 ± 45	100 cm depth
NZ 623	Pyramid Valley	*Eu. gravis* gizzard	3450 ± 71	130 cm depth
NZ 624	Pyramid Valley	*D. maximus* gizzard	3640 ± 72	135 cm depth
*NZ 625	Pyramid Valley	*E. crassus* gizzard	3740 ± 72	100 cm depth
NZ 626	?Pyramid Valley	moa bone	3907 ± 44	
*NZ 3936	Pyramid Valley	*D. maximus* collagen	3480 ± 80	95 cm depth
*NZ 3937	Pyramid Valley	*D. maximus* gizzard	3590 ± 60	95 cm depth
NZ 1729	Glenmark	*P. elephan.* collagen	2730 ± 70	Haast collection
NZ 4943	Glenmark	moa bone	7110 ± 109	
NZ 1726	Albury Park	*Pachyornis* collagen	7390 ± 160	
NZ 1727	Enfield	*Eu. gravis* collagen	2020 ± 70	Forbes collection
NZ 4874	Awamoa	*Eu. gravis* moa bone	1670 ± 75	

214

Lab. No.	Location	Material	Date BP old T½	Provenance
NZ 1728	Pukemata	*Eu. gravis* collagen	9490 ± 200	
*NZ 762	Scaife's Lagoon	*Dinornis* collagen	1968 ± 71	Trotter collection
*NZ 1110	Scaife's Lagoon	*Dinornis* gizzard	2330 ± 60	
NZ 5233	North Dean	wood	1780 ± 68	*c.* 110 cm depth
NZ 5232	North Dean	bark	654 ± 57	*c.* 75 cm depth
NZ 4900	North Dean	*Eu. gravis* collagen	1445 ± 50	*c.* 60 cm depth

DUNES

NZ 4607	Northland	moa bone collagen	2950 ± 70	dune sand
NZ 4671	Northland	moa bone collagen	2090 ± 110	dune sand
NZ 4744	Northland	moa bone collagen	1840 ± 70	dune sand
NZ 4882	Northland	moa bone collagen	2170 ± 70	dune sand
NZ 4668	Northland	moa bone collagen	3020 ± 80	dune sand
NZ 4670	Northland	moa bone collagen	5320 ± 650	dune sand
NZ 4666	Northland	moa bone collagen	2400 ± 120	dune sand
NZ 4663	Northland	moa bone collagen	1210 ± 60	dune sand
NZ 4835	Northland	moa eggshell carb.	1595 ± 70	dune sand
NZ 4672	Northland	moa bone collagen	1050 ± 60	dune sand
NZ 4608	Northland	moa bone collagen	950 ± 60	dune sand
NZ 4620	Northland	moa bone collagen	2520 ± 70	dune sand
NZ 4691	Northland	moa eggshell carb.	2640 ± 40	dune sand
NZ 4611	Northland	moa eggshell carb.	2190 ± 70	dune sand
NZ 4612	Northland	moa bone collagen	1150 ± 70	dune sand
NZ 4616	Northland	moa bone collagen	2970 ± 80	dune sand
NZ 5065	Northland	moa eggshell carb.	3790 ± 100	dune sand

CAVES

NZ 4867	Waikiekie	moa bone collagen	2790 ± 80	cave sediment
NZ 4837	King Country	moa bone collagen	14900 ± 250	cave sediment
NZ 4838	King Country	moa bone collagen	24100 ± 450	cave sediment
NZ 4839	King Country	moa bone collagen	10750 ± 150	cave sediment
NZ 4840	King Country	moa bone collagen	10600 ± 200	cave sediment
NZ 4841	King Country	moa bone collagen	6150 ± 100	cave sediment
NZ 4842	King Country	moa bone collagen	3200 ± 60	cave sediment
NZ 4843	King Country	moa bone collagen	21200 ± 350	cave sediment
NZ 4844	King Country	moa bone collagen	10150 ± 150	cave sediment
NZ 4845	King Country	moa bone collagen	1090 ± 60	cave sediment
NZ 4886	King Country	moa bone collagen	4360 ± 80	cave sediment
NZ 5035	King Country	moa bone collagen	1860 ± 70	cave sediment
NZ 4150	Martinborough	*Pachyornis* collagen	1470 ± 50	in yellow clay floor
NZ 3184	Mount Owen	moa bone collagen	11850 ± 2250	loose stone/clay floor
NZ 3185	Mount Owen	moa bone collagen	2100 ± 60	loose stone/clay floor
NZ 6453	Honeycomb Hill	moa bone	15717 ± 209	
NZ 6480	Honeycomb Hill	moa bone	14234 ± 179	
NZ 6586	Honeycomb Hill	moa bone	14069 ± 176	
NZ 6526	Honeycomb Hill	moa bone	11478 ± 135	
NZ 6589	Honeycomb Hill	moa bone	14102 ± 176	
NZ 6569	Honeycomb Hill	moa bone	10918 ± 101	
NZ 7453	Gibraltar Rock	leaves, twigs, grass	8760 ± 115	ass. with moa eggshell
NZ 1725	Redcliffe, Rakaia	moa eggshell	663 ± 51	moa nesting debris
NZ 5321	Firewood Ck.	*Eu. gravis* collagen	1070 ± 60	schist cleft
NZ 5322	Cromwell Station	*A. didiformis* collagen	2530 ± 60	schist cleft

LOESS

NZ 3092	Cape Wanbrow	*Em.* + *Eu.* collagen	20300 ± 600	4.1 m depth
NZ 3093	Cape Wanbrow	*Em.* + *Eu.* collagen	32500 ± 2500	5.0 m depth

Lab. No.	Location	Material	Date BP old T½	Provenance
NZ 4743	Cape Wanbrow N.	wood charcoal	22600 ± 550	
NZ 4753	Cape Wanbrow S.	wood charcoal	26500 ± 1400	
NZ 5382	Banks Penin.	moa bone	27155 ± 1151	
OTHER				
NZ 3088	Custom St. Auck.	*A. did.* collagen	7300 ± 150	marine mud, 7.5 m depth
NZ 1724	Castle Hill	*Eu. gravis* collagen	1025 ± 60	shallow deposit
NZ 1128	Kawarau Valley.	*Dinornis* collagen	2330 ± 70	sandstone, 0.6 m depth
NZ 3455	Kawarau Valley	*P. eleph.* collagen	620 ± 60	silt, 2.0 m depth
NZ 3967	Kawarau Valley	*D. tor.* collagen	15750 ± 300	sand near basement schist
I 7794	Kawarau Valley	*P. eleph.* collagen	1000 ± 80	probably loess

Note: No error range for Y dates, * = dates from same specimen. Data from Deevey (1955), Gregg (1966, 1972), McCulloch and Trotter (1979), Burrows *et al.* (1981, 1984), Millener (1981), Ritchie (1982a).

Appendix C

Moa Species Identified from North Island Archaeological Sites

Species (see below)	1	2	3	4	5	6	7	8	9	10	11	12	13	Reference
COASTAL														
Tom Bowling Bay			x							x				Scarlett 1979
Spirits Bay										x				Scarlett 1979
Houhora		4a	7	4a						183		6	2	Scarlett 1974
Doubtless Bay										x				Scarlett 1974
Pataua				12						17			20	Oliver n. d.
Harataonga 1									x				?1	Law 1972b
Harataonga 2												?1		Law 1972b
Port Jackson		xa		xa						x		x		Davidson 1979
Port Jackson			1	1	1		5			2		1	6	Kooyman 1985
Sunde Site							1							Millener 1981
Parkers Midden			x							x		x		Simmons 1968
Parkers Midden	1									2		1		Jolly and Murdoch 1973
Skippers Midden		x	x	x						x				Simmons 1968
Skippers Midden		?x	x	x						x		x		Scarlett 1974
Blacks Midden										x		x		Scarlett 1974
Sarahs Gully		x	x							?x			?x	Simmons 1968
Sarahs Gully		?x	x									?x		Scarlett 1974
Ponui Island	x													Nicholls 1963
Tairua		x	x	x			?x					x		Simmons 1968
Tairua	1	?2a	?2a	2			6							Rowland 1977
Tairua			1		1								1	Kooyman 1985
Hot Water Beach	x						?x		x	x				Leahy 1971
Manukau Heads		xa		xa										Simmons 1968
Whangamata Wharf											?1			Allo 1972
Whangamata Wharf									x	x				Davidson 1979
Whiritoa			x	x			x			x				Scarlett 1974
Whiritoa			?x							x		?x		Davidson 1979
Whangara							x			x				Jones and Moore n. d.
Ocean Beach										x		x		Scarlett 1974
Dune Midden							x							Millener 1981
Opua			3				14			2		6	2	Prickett 1983
Rahotu Beach			x				x			x				Scarlett 1974
Kaupokonui		3	1				34					1		Buist n. d.
Kaupokonui		1					9			21	1	2	16	Cassels n. d.
Kaupokonui		1	1		1		13	1		3		5	3	Kooyman 1985
Waingongoro		1					3					1		Buist and Yaldwyn 1960

Species (see below)	1	2	3	4	5	6	7	8	9	10	11	12	13	Reference
Waingongoro		x	x	x			x			x		x	x	Prickett 1983
Te Rangatapu		x		x			x			x		x		Scarlett 1974
Foxton	x		x			?x	x			x		?x	x	McFadgen 1978
Paremata		20	9	5			9					9	63	Scarlett 1974
Makara Heads		x					x			x			x	Simmons 1968
Makara Beach		?x					?x						x	Scarlett 1974
Akiteo													x	Scarlett 1962
Te Ika a Maru									x				x	Simmons 1968
Washpool Midden							?3a				2	?4a		Leach and Leach 1979
Pararaki Midden Wall							?1a					?1a		Leach and Leach 1979
Black Rocks A	?1a									?1a				Leach and Leach 1979
Black Rocks B	?1a									?1a				Leach and Leach 1979
INLAND														
Tokoroa										?2				Law 1973
Tokoroa										1				Kooyman 1985
Whakamoenga							?1a			?1b		?2a	?1b	Leahy 1976
Puketitiri			x											Simmons 1968

Numbers **1** = estimated MNI, numbers 1 = number of bones or fragments, a = one or other species, ? = identification uncertain, x = present, no quantification.
Species: 1 = *Dinornis* sp., 2 = *Dinornis giganteus*, 3 = *Dinornis struthoides*, 4 = *Dinornis novaezealandiae*, 5 = *Dinornis torosus*, 6 = *Pachyornis* sp., 7 = *Pachyornis mappini*, 8 = *Pachyornis elephantopus*, 9 = *Euryapteryx* sp., 10 = *Euryapteryx curtus*, 11 = *Euryapteryx gravis*, 12 = *Euryapteryx geranoides*, 13 = *Anomalopteryx didiformis*.

Appendix D

Moa Species Identified from South Island Archaeological Sites

Species (see below)	1	2	3	4	5	6	7	8	9	10	11	12	13	Reference
COASTAL														
Heaphy River				?x										Wilkes and Scarlett 1967
Anapai											x			Wilkes et al. 1963
Greville Harbour				x									x	Scarlett 1974
Ohana	x													Scarlett 1974
Rotokura					x						x		x	Scarlett 1974
Tahunanui									x		x			Millar 1971
Mussel Point									?1	?1				Scarlett 1974
Wairau Bar									x		x	x	x	Scarlett 1974
Marfell Beach									14		40	1		Scarlett 1974
Cape Campbell											1			Scarlett 1974
Needles Point											x			Orchiston 1977a
Avoca Point								52a	3		52a	8		Trotter 1980
South Bay									x					Scarlett 1963
Waiau R. Mouth									xa		xa			Parry 1961
Hurunui Mouth									1					Scarlett 1974
Bromley									x					Scarlett 1979
Redcliffs	x						?x		?x		?x			Simmons 1968
Redcliffs		1					3		69		54	3		Scarlett 1974
Redcliffs Sewer		1							140		38	17		Trotter 1975b
Redcliffs School							?2		186		10			Trotter 1975b
Moabone Point Cave				x					x		x	x		Skinner 1923
Moabone Point Cave		3							x		x			Scarlett 1974
Moncks Cave											x			Skinner 1924b
Tumbledown Bay									x			x		Mason and Wilkes 1963b
Tumbledown Bay											?1			Scarlett 1974
Tumbledown Bay				x					x					Allingham 1987
Hikurangi									1					Scarlett 1974
Rakaia Mouth				x			x		x		x	x		Anderson 1982b
Wakanui									x		x			Anderson 1982b
Dashing Rocks								?x						Mason and Wilkes 1963a
Pareora								xa			xa			Griffiths 1955
Waitaki Mouth					1		18		64		22			Scarlett 1974
Waitaki Mouth				x	x		x		x		x	x		Anderson 1982b
Tai Rua		1		1	3	?1	3		6		1			Kooyman 1985
Ototara									x					Trotter 1965a
Kakanui							x							Trotter 1970c

219

Species (see below)	1	2	3	4	5	6	7	8	9	10	11	12	13	Reference
Awamoa		x		x			x				x			Anderson 1982b
Hampden Beach									3					Trotter 1967b
Waimataitai											x		?x	Trotter 1965b
Shag R. Mouth		2		5			3		88		4			Scarlett 1974
Shag R. Mouth				x	x		x		x		x	x		Anderson 1982b
Pleasant River	x						x		x		x			Anderson 1982b
Tumai									2					Allingham 1988
Seacliff				?1							1			Blake-Palmer 1956
Seacliff		x		x					x		x	x	x	Anderson 1982b
Omimi		1a		1a							4a	4a		Hamel 1977b
Warrington		5a	5a	1	5a		3		2					Kooyman 1984a
Warrington A						?1			?1			1		Kooyman 1984a
Mapoutahi	11													Anderson n. d. c
Purakanui		1									1			Anderson 1982b
Long Beach									?x					Dawson and Yaldwyn 1952
Long Beach											?4			Scarlett 1974
Murdering Beach											x			Davies 1980
Kaikais Beach									1					Scarlett 1974
Harwood							x		x		x	x		Anderson 1982b
Pipikaretu											x			Davies 1980
Little Papanui		2							4		3			Scarlett 1974
Little Papanui		x	x				x		x		x			Davies 1980
Papanui Inlet		x					x					x		Davies 1980
Papanui Beach									x					Davies 1980
Andersons Bay		x							x		x			Davies 1980
Hoopers Inlet									x		x	x		Anderson 1982b
Otokia Mouth									x		xa	xa		Anderson 1982c
Taieri Mouth		x												Anderson 1982b
Kaka Point									3		3			Scarlett 1974
Nugget Point							x							Anderson 1984
False Island									1	3	6			Scarlett 1974
Pounawea		1					14		36	10	20	?3	3	Scarlett 1974
Pounawea		1		2	2		1		28	1	18	8	5	Scarlett n. d.
Pounawea							1		3		5	2	2	Hamel 1980
Pounawea						?1	1		3		1	1	2	Kooyman 1985
Hinahina											x			Anderson 1982b
Papatowai		1		2					9		4	4		Teviotdale 1937
Papatowai		4		4			25		106		48	8	5	Teviotdale 1938a
Papatowai	2	5		4	3		44		366	72	157	23	?2	Scarlett 1974
Papatowai				1			3a		3a		?1	?3		Hamel 1977a
Papatowai				1	1		1		5	1	4	1	1	Scarlett n. d.
Kings Rock		?x		x					x					Simmons 1968
Tautuku Point		x					x		x		x	?x		Hamel 1977a
Tautuku Nth				x										Hamel 1977a
Tautuku Peninsula				x										Anderson 1984
Waipapa											x			Anderson 1982b
Tiwai Point									7		4			Sutton and Marshall 1980
Port Craig I							?1							Coutts 1977
Southport												x		Anderson 1984
Long Island I									1					Scarlett 1974

INLAND

Species (see below)	1	2	3	4	5	6	7	8	9	10	11	12	13	Reference
Timpendean									x					Trotter 1972b
Shepherd's Creek II									x			x		Scarlett 1979
Woolshed Flat							x		x			x		Trotter 1970a

Species (see below)	1	2	3	4	5	6	7	8	9	10	11	12	13	Reference
Ahuriri													x	Ambrose 1970
Gooseneck Bend							1							Ambrose 1970
Dart Bridge									?1			1a	1a	Anderson and Ritchie 1986
Luggate		x					x							Anderson 1982b
Owens Ferry		1	2	1	1		2		1			2		Kooyman 1984b
Hawksburn			1	3			1		5		1	1	3	Scarlett pers. comm.
Hawksburn			1	1	1		2		2				2	Kooyman 1985
Rockfall II	1								1					Ritchie 1982b
Italian Creek													x	Ritchie 1982b
Puketoi		x		x									x	Anderson 1982b
Coal Creek			2	1	3	?3	2		6		1			Kooyman 1985
Nenthorn									1					Easdale and Jacomb 1986
Takahe Valley												1		Duff 1977
STEWART ISLAND														
Native Island									1					Scarlett 1974
Old Neck								15	5	34		2		Scarlett n. d.
Mason Bay											x			Anderson 1984

Numbers **1** = estimated MNI, numbers 1 = number of bones or fragments, a = one or other species, ? = identification uncertain, x = present, no quantification.

Species: 1 = *Dinornis* sp., 2 = *Dinornis giganteus*, 3 = *Dinornis struthoides*, 4 = *Dinornis novaezealandiae*, 5 = *Dinornis torosus*, 6 = *Pachyornis mappini*, 7 = *Pachyornis elephantopus*, 8 = *Euryapteryx* sp., 9 = *Euryapteryx gravis*, 10 = *Euryapteryx* new sp., 11 = *Emeus crassus*, 12 = *Anomalopteryx didiformis*, 13 = *Megalapteryx didinis*.

Appendix E

RADIOCARBON DATES FROM MOA-HUNTING SITES

		Moa bone dates	
Lab no.	A date	Category	Site and provenance
NZ 5007	603 ± 56	A	Houhora N 3/6
NZ 5008	625 ± 46	A	Houhora N 3/6
NZ 3931	608 ± 49	A	Kaupokonui
NZ 3934	658 ± 57	A	Kaupokonui
NZ 4236	832 ± 148	A	Titirangi
NZ 1838	587 ± 58	A	Wairau Bar; *Euryapteryx*
NZ 6566	785 ± 59	A	Avoca Point; *Anomalopteryx*, outside wall
NZ 6496	569 ± 42	A	Avoca Point; *Anomalopteryx*, base of wall
NZ 4155	743 ± 85	A	Avoca Point
NZ 3164	992 ± 192	A	Avoca Point; duplicate of NZ 4155
NZ 1839	686 ± 85	A	Hurunui River Mouth; *Euryapteryx*
NZ 1162	662 ± 44	A	Redcliffs Flat; (Sewer Trench)
NZ 1113	741 ± 60	A	Redcliffs Flat; *Euryapteryx* (Hamiltons)
NZ 1376	537 ± 45	A	Redcliffs Flat; (Sewer Trench)
NZ 930	596 ± 71	A	Rakaia Mouth; *Euryapteryx gravis*?
NZ 932	527 ± 88	A	Rakaia Mouth; *Euryapteryx gravis*?
NZ 1767	598 ± 69	A	Wakanui; oven
NZ 1766	669 ± 58	A	Wakanui; oven
NZ 1768	423 ± 58	A	Wakanui; *Euryapteryx*
SUA 62b	770 ± 95*	A	Waihao Mouth
NZ 760	544 ± 70[†]	A	Woolshed Flat
SUA 61	600 ± 80*	A	Waitaki River Mouth; *Euryapteryx gravis*
NZ 59b	440 ± 55*	A	Hawksburn; oven
NZ 60	450 ± 60*	A	Hawksburn; *Euryapteryx gravis*
NZ 752	553 ± 36	A	Tai Rua; layer 5
NZ 578	513 ± 37	A	Tai Rua; layer 5
NZ 559	513 ± 37	A	Tai Rua; layer 5
NZ 766	403 ± 48	A	Tai Rua; layer 5
NZ 754	475 ± 70	A	Ototara; *Euryapteryx gravis*
NZ 4872	660 ± 54*	A	Awamoa; *Euryapteryx gravis*
NZ 5015	722 ± 173	A	Waimataitai; *Emeus crassus*
NZ 758	559 ± 60	A	Hampden Beach
NZ 756	543 ± 70	A	Hampden Beach
NZ 5016	681 ± 85	A	Shag River; prob. *Euryapteryx*
NZ 5013	448 ± 56	A	Pleasant River; *Euryapteryx*
NZ 4438	642 ± 47	A	Pounawea
NZ 137	349 ± 46	A	Papatowai; *Euryapteryx gravis*, middle layer
NZ 146	391 ± 59[†]	A	Tautuku; *Dinornis torosus*

		Marine shell dates	
Lab no.	A date	Category	Site and provenance
NZ 1296	415 ± 44	C	Hot Water Beach; above Loisels Pumice
NZ 1297	485 ± 44	C	Hot Water Beach; above Loisels Pumice
NZ 1875	538 ± 58	C	Tairua; oven, Layer 2
NZ 1480	589 ± 58	C	Foxton; Layer 1
NZ 1250	324 ± 68	C	Foxton; Layer 2
NZ 1347	793 ± 47	C	Foxton; Layer 2
NZ 1251	801 ± 84	C	Foxton; Layer 2
NZ 1479	619 ± 58	C	Foxton; Layer 2
NZ 1349	729 ± 45	C	Foxton; Layer 1
NZ 683	748 ± 60	C	Foxton; Layer 2
NZ 509	560 ± 100	D	Heaphy River; oven
NZ 482	576 ± 88[†]	C	D'Urville Is; lower occupation layer
NZ 1346	427 ± 44	D	Buller; northerly cooking area
NZ 1837	683 ± 41	D	Wairau Bar; aragonite
NZ 1836	719 ± 41	B	Clarence; early midden, aragonite
NZ 2719	827 ± 33	C	Avoca Point
NZ 2718	836 ± 29	C	Avoca Point
NZ 6472	525 ± 40	C	Avoca Point; beach ridge C
NZ 6525	454 ± 32	D	Avoca Point; outside wall
NZ 892	436 ± 50*	D	Timpendean
NZ 1538	374 ± 57	D	Motunau Beach; aragonite
NZ 1111	578 ± 42	B	Redcliffs Flat; (Hamiltons)
NZ 749	452 ± 37	C	Tai Rua; layer 5
NZ 560	492 ± 59	D	Ototara
NZ 4873	635 ± 56*	C	Awamoa
NZ 579	593 ± 32	C	Waimataitai; from 122 cm below surface
NZ 782	399 ± 59	D	Shag Point
NZ 5017	647 ± 33	C	Shag River; ash below shell midden
NZ 4436	773 ± 26	D	Pleasant River, Tumai
NZ 4746	553 ± 28	C	Purakanui; Layer 2
NZ 4748	561 ± 33	C	Purakanui; Layer 5
NZ 54	449 ± 63[†]	C	Pounawea; top layer
NZ 57	530 ± 64[†]	C	Pounawea; bottom layer
NZ 1333	705 ± 45[†]	C	Papatowai; bottom layer
NZ 147	390 ± 39	C	Cannibal Bay

		Charcoal dates	
Lab no.	A date	Category	Site and provenance
NZ 915	563 ± 61	C	Houhora; middle occupation
NZ 914	697 ± 49	C	Houhora; top occupation
NZ 916	796 ± 56*	C	Houhora; earliest occupation
NZ 1898	613 ± 58	D	Sunde Site; below Rangitoto Ash
NZ 1899	624 ± 85	D	Sunde Site; above Rangitoto Ash
NZ 354	689 ± 40[†]	C	Opito Beach Midden; below Loisels Pumice
NZ 355	656 ± 40[†]	D	Sarah's Gully Midden; area D
NZ 359	1700 ± 45[†]	D	Sarah's Gully Midden; lowest occupation
NZ 357	702 ± 50[†]	B	Sarah's Gully Midden; oven and moa pelvis
NZ 4951	556 ± 61	C	Hahei; firepit, Layers 3–4
NZ 4950	300 ± 45	C	Hahei; firepit, Layers 3–4
NZ 4953	700 ± 59	C	Hahei; firepit, Layers 3–4
NZ 4952	548 ± 59	C	Hahei; firepit, Layers 3–4
NZ 1169	437 ± 44	C	Hot Water Beach; oven, Layer 4

		Charcoal dates	
Lab no.	A date	Category	Site and provenance
NZ 595	449 ± 44	C	Tairua; oven, Layer II
NZ 594	885 ± 52	C	Tairua; oven, Layer II
NZ 648	1011 ± 62	B	Whakamoenga Cave; occupation 1:1
NZ 686	610 ± 61	C	Whakamoenga Cave; occupation 1:1
NZ 1030	485 ± 60	C	Whakamoenga Cave; occupation 1:2
NZ 717	552 ± 45	D	Waingongoro; river mouth
NZ 718	699 ± 61	D	Waingongoro
NZ 543	1018 ± 49	D	Waingongoro; oven
NZ 544	752 ± 60	D	Waingongoro
NZ 545	741 ± 48	D	Te Rangatapu; oven
NZ 723	542 ± 61	D	Te Rangatapu
NZ 684	523 ± 63	C	Foxton; oven, Layer 2
NZ 510	582 ± 48	B	Paremata; main layer
NZ 653	442 ± 87	B	Makara; oven C
NZ 654	987 ± 74	C	Makara; oven A
NZ 1509	554 ± 46	C	Washpool Sea Edge Site; Layer 2
NZ 1506	488 ± 44	C	Washpool Midden; Level II
NZ 1505	767 ± 45	C	Washpool Midden; Level I
NZ 1507	665 ± 44	C	Washpool Midden; Level II
NZ 1511	797 ± 45	C	Washpool Midden; Level I
NZ 1510	670 ± 44	C	Washpool Midden; Level II
NZ 1508	683 ± 88	C	Washpool Midden; Level II
NZ 1311	676 ± 86	C	Pararaki; midden wall
NZ 1312	737 ± 86	C	Pararaki; midden wall
NZ 1646	809 ± 59	C	Black Rocks; Black Midden
NZ 1647	687 ± 58	C	Black Rocks; Crescent Midden
NZ 1648	681 ± 58	C	Black Rocks; Crescent Midden
NZ 481	674 ± 90	C	D'Urville Is; Moawhitu
NZ –	743 ± 72	B	Whangamoa; oven
NZ –	625 ± 70*	C	Rotokura; Layer 4
NZ –	589 ± 70	C	Tahunanui; lowest level
NZ –	435 ± 70	C	Tahunanui
NZ –	611 ± 40	C	Buller Mouth
Y 204	935 ± 110*	D	Wairau Bar; upper layer
NZ 50	909 ± 48	D	Wairau Bar; upper layer
NZ 2716	840 ± 60*	B	Avoca Point
NZ 438	1167 ± 91	B	Redcliffs (Hamiltons)
NZ 459	777 ± 87	B	Redcliffs (Hines)
NZ 1378	505 ± 44	B	Boltons Gully
SUA 63	730 ± 75*	C	Waihao Mouth
ANU 47	625 ± 65*	C	Ahuriri
ANU 49	695 ± 135*	C	Junction Point; Layer 3
ANU 48	850 ± 150*	C	Gooseneck Bend; Layer 3
NZ 798	867 ± 40	B	Woolshed Flat
NZ 783	816 ± 61	B	Woolshed Flat
NZ 5324	587 ± 56	C	Dart Bridge; complex B
NZ 5326	442 ± 41	C	Dart Bridge; complex D
NZ 4636	620 ± 33	B	Waitaki River Mouth: D4/L1
NZ 4543	963 ± 86	B	Waitaki River Mouth; D2/L1
NZ 6039	699 ± 46	C	Owen's Ferry; Layer 10
NZ 6040	763 ± 34	C	Owen's Ferry; Layers 8 + 9
NZ 6038	607 ± 28	C	Owen's Ferry; Layers 8 + 9
NZ 5049	652 ± 33	B	Hawksburn; HB/L/5 Layer 3
NZ 5045	709 ± 33	B	Hawksburn; HB/H/8 Layer 1
NZ 5053	592 ± 33	C	Hawksburn; HB/E/2 Layer 1 hearth

		Charcoal dates	
Lab no.	A date	Category	Site and provenance
NZ 5047	611 ± 33	B	Hawksburn; HB/M/6 Layer 1
NZ 61	590 ± 50*	B	Hawksburn; bottom layer
NZ 5051	668 ± 33	B	Hawksburn; HB/FA/15 Layer 2
NZ 62	633 ± 65	D	Hawksburn; occupation layer
NZ 5046	714 ± 33	B	Hawksburn; HB/I/23 Layer 1
NZ 5048	691 ± 33	B	Hawksburn; HB/FB/8 Layer 1
NZ 5044	692 ± 33	B	Hawksburn; HB/H/14 Layer 1
NZ 5050	720 ± 33	B	Hawksburn; HB/M/14 Layer 1
NZ 5052	663 ± 28	B	Hawksburn; HB/L/10 Layer 3
NZ 4972	674 ± 59	C	Rockfall I; oven
NZ 4973	949 ± 57	C	Rockfall I; oven
NZ 5067	992 ± 58	C	Rockfall I; oven
NZ 5341	376 ± 38	B	Rockfall II; oven
NZ 5340	632 ± 45	B	Rockfall II; oven
NZ 4715	309 ± 82	B	Italian Creek; A2 hearth
NZ 4716	579 ± 96	B	Italian Creek; A4
NZ 4714	399 ± 88	B	Italian Creek; A2 hearth
NZ 750	657 ± 37	C	Tai Rua; layer 5
NZ 926	992 ± 49	C	Awamoa
NZ 1249	715 ± 45	C	Waimataitai
NZ 6855	655 ± 40	B	Coal Creek; oven
NZ 6659	792 ± 52	C	Minzion Burn I; oven
NZ 6653	727 ± 52	D	Minzion Burn II; scoop hearth
NZ 6657	671 ± 54	C	Minzion Burn II; test pit 2
NZ 6654	672 ± 52	B	Minzion Burn; Deb's test pit
NZ 605	788 ± 42	C	Shag River; oven
NZ 606	850 ± 61	C	Shag River; oven
NZ 1236	461 ± 86	D	Long Island; C/5 Layer 8B
GaK 2392	590 ± 150*	D	Long Island; B/4 Layer 8A
GaK 2393	950 ± 80*	D	Long Island; E/1 Layer 3
NZ –	900 ± 60*	C	Kaikais Beach
NZ 4637	1030 ± 58	C	Purakanui; Layer 2B
NZ 4705	865 ± 85	C	Long Beach; Layer 4B
NZ 4704	476 ± 56	C	Long Beach; Layer 4A
NZ 4701	710 ± 57	C	Long Beach; Layer 4C
NZ 6690	547 ± 49*	C	Little Papanui; south side
NZ 936	637 ± 59	C	Tihaka; oven fill
NZ 4469	656 ± 29	C	Tiwai Point; TW/X/W23/2 oven
NZ 4470	636 ± 33	C	Tiwai Point; TW/X/U23/2 area X
NZ 58	1207 ± 65	C	Pounawea; bottom layer
NZ 5031	582 ± 77	B	Pounawea; shell mound, Layer 1
NZ 5032	816 ± 78	B	Pounawea; lowest layer 2
NZ 55	520 ± 55*	C	Pounawea; middle layer
NZ 53	740 ± 75*	D	Hinahina; lowest stratum
NZ 1332	916 ± 88	C	Papatowai; bottom layer
NZ 4269	661 ± 71	C	Papatowai; middle layer
NZ 134	825 ± 41	C	Papatowai; bottom layer
NZ 4271	576 ± 57	C	Papatowai; oven 2 upper layer
NZ 4270	560 ± 57	C	Papatowai; shell lens upper layer
NZ 4267	853 ± 67	C	Papatowai; bottom layer
NZ 4268	760 ± 57	C	Papatowai; bottom layer
NZ 136	1192 ± 62†	B	Papatowai; bottom layer
NZ 135	762 ± 40	C	Papatowai; lowest occupation, duplicate of NZ 134
NZ 4272	577 ± 57	C	Papatowai; oven 1 upper layer
NZ –	680 ± 60*	D	Old Neck; oven

| Lab. No. | A date | Miscellaneous material | | |
		Sample type	Category	Site and provenance
NZ–	796 ± 56*	charcoal?	C	Houhora; earliest deposit
NZ 358	873 ± 40[†]	wood	D	Sarah's Gully Midden; second occupation
NZ 1170	492 ± 87	soil charcoal	C	Hot Water Beach; Layer 4
NZ 1299	301 ± 92	fish bone collagen	C	Hot Water Beach; Layer 4
NZ 2717	503 ± 156	bone (?moa/seal)	C	Avoca Point
NZ 512	706 ± 62	wood	B	Redcliffs Cave; inner post butt
NZ 511	633 ± 38	wood	B	Redcliffs Cave; outer post butt
NZ 437	642 ± 88	wood	B	Redcliffs Cave; post butt
NZ 52	857 ± 48	bark	B	Takahe Valley
NZ 52	840 ± 60*	bark	B	Takahe Valley; duplicate
NZ 51	289 ± 63	tussock	B	Takahe Valley
NZ 56	550 ± 55*	seal bone collagen	C	Pounawea; middle layer

Note: All dates from JDB except dates (*) from: Ambrose (1970), Butts (1978), Coutts (1972), Duff (1977), Hjarno (1967), Law (1982), Lockerbie (1959, pers. comm.), McCulloch and Trotter (1975), Orchiston (1974), Shawcross (1972), Trotter (1980, pers. comm.). ([†]): recalculated 1988 by INS. Category A = moa bone collagen sample; B = sample in close association with moa bone; C = sample from same layer as moa bone; D = sample from site with moa bone, closeness of association unclear.

Appendix F

Maori Views on the Period of Moa Extinction

NORTH ISLAND

Date	Source	Content	Periods of Extinction	Reference
1834–1857	East Cape M.	Very large birds in distant past	Long ago	Polack 1838:303
1838	East Cape M.	Moa alive at Wakapunake	extant	Colenso 1846:81–2
1839	East Cape M. to W. Williams	Moa alive at Wakapunake	extant	Owen 1879aı:75
1839	Poverty Bay M. to J. W. Harris	Moa alive locally and South Is.	extant	Taylor Journal 21 April 1839 (n. d.)
1839	Taranaki M.	Moa alive on Mt. Egmont	extant	Dieffenbach 1843:140
1841	Poverty Bay M.	Moa alive at Te Whaiti	extant	Colenso 1846:88
1839–44	East Coast M. to W. Williams	Moa alive South Is. and Tongariro	extant	*NZ Journal* 222:128 (1840)
1844	Haumatangi to Gov. Fitzroy	Saw moa *c.* 1800. Wellington	?extant	Hamilton 1875:121
?1840s	Te Apaapa, Kahutia Te Akiku (Poverty Bay) to J. M. Jury	Moa (Kuranui) killed in Tamatea fires	Tamatea Period	Smith 1911:58
1847	Wellington M. to W. Mantell	Saw moas *c.* 1800	?extant	G. A. Mantell 1848a:226
1849	An. M. to F. G. Moore	Moa captured *c.* 1800	?extant	Letter 11 August 1849 to G. A. Mantell (n. d.)
c. 1850	Wanganui M.	Moa alive Ruahine Ra.	?extant	Field 1894:567
c. 1860·	Te Marae, Paipai etc. (Wanganui M., named) to H. C. Field	Hunted moa *c.* 1820–1830	early 19th C.	*Mataura Ensign* 1 October 1908
1866	Waingongoro M.	Hunted moa *c.* 1800–1830	early 19th C.	Taylor 1873:100
1866	Kawana Paipai, Waingongoro	Moa hunted *c.* 1800	early 19th C.	McDonnell 1889:439
c. 1869	Apanui Hamai-waho	Hape killed last moa.	?Tamatea Period	Mair 1890:72
?*c.* 1870	An. M., Hikurangi to J. Hector	Moa seen by contemporary	?extant	Cockburn-Hood 1875:496
?*c.* 1870	Rewi Maniapoto to J. Hector	Moa killed by grandfather *c.* 1780	about 1800	Hector 1889:506
?*c.* 1875	An. M. ?Auckland	Moa almost extinct in great fire	?Tamatea Period	Maning 1876:102
1870s	Ngatiporou chiefs	Except two 'moa', extinct in great fire	Tamatea Period	Colenso 1880:81

NORTH ISLAND

Date	Source	Content	Periods of Extinction	Reference
1840–1875	?Apanui to J. White	Last moa killed at Whakatane	?18th century	Travers 1876:81
1879	Hawea and others, Hawke's Bay	Moa extinct in mythological flood	before Tamatea Period	Colenso 1880:82
c. 1880	Ngakuku, Northland	Moa extinct South Is. in grandfather's time	c. 1800	Hongi 1916:67
c. 1890	An. M.	Solitary moas recorded 15–16 generations ago	c. 1600	Mair 1893:534
1891	Waikanae M.	Kept pet moas c. 1830	early 19th C.	Field 1892:559
1892	Rangitikei M. to Sutherland	Pigs destroyed moa eggs	early 19th C.	Field 1894:565
1890s	Ngati-hau M., Wanganui	Moa extinct in distant past	Tamatea Period	Best 1896:122
1906	H. Potangaroa to R. J. Barton	Last Wairarapa moa killed in time of grandfather	c. 1760–1800	Buick 1931:283
1907	Hauka te Kuru	Moa extinct in Tamatea fires except at Whakapunake	Tamatea Period	Davies 1907
1910	Mereri, Waitemata	Last moa killed Auckland c. 1650–1700	c. 1700	Graham 1919:108
?1930s	An. M. various	Moas alive until 8 generations ago	c. 1750–1800	Best 1942:187

SOUTH ISLAND

Date	Source	Content	Periods of Extinction	Reference
?1823	Otago M. to E. Meurant	Moa(?) alive in interior	extant	Taylor 1855:238
1830s	Southland M. to Palmer to Chapman 1897	Last moa killed by contemporary	c. 1800	Buick 1931:301
c. 1840	Koroko, Waikouaiti, to Rev. J. Watkin. Reported E. Watkin to Chapman 1884	Saw moa c. 1770	c. 1800	Buick 1931:298
1841	Waikouaiti M. to Rev. J. Watkin	Giant birds alive until 4 generations ago	c. 1750	Duff 1977:295
1844	Otago M.	Moa alive in interior	extant	Barnicoat Journal 5 May 1844 (n. d.)
1844	Waikouaiti M. to ?J. Jones	Giant birds alive in interior	extant	W. B. D. Mantell 1844:667
1841–48	Motueka M.	Grandfathers hunted moa	c. 1750	Davison 1870:604
c. 1850	Nelson M. to F. Weld	Giant birds alive in interior	extant	Buick 1931:321
c. 1850	Rapaki M. to W. G. Brittan	Father hunted moa, Canterbury	late 18th C.	Hamilton 1875:122
c. 1850	Te Raki, Taieri	Moa may be alive in interior	extant	Davison 1870:604
?1850s	Canterbury M.	Moa extinct more than 10 generations ago	c. 1600	Stack 1872:10
1857	Riverton M.	Hunted moa in younger days	c. 1800	Beattie n. d.
1858	T. Brunner (M.) to J. Lockhart	Saw man-sized 'kiwi', Nelson	?c. 1800	Field 1894:564
1860	Ashburton M. to R. B. Booth	Moa 'remembered'	?c. 1800	Buick 1936:22

SOUTH ISLAND

Date	Source	Content	Periods of Extinction	Reference
1860s	Riverton M. to J. H. Menzies	Moa alive in Fiordland	extant	Beattie n. d.
c. 1875	M. Tiramorehu, Moeraki to J. Stack	Moa extinct in time of Ngapuhi	Tamatea Period	Haast 1878:46
c. 1880	Te Rauru to T. Kona c. 1880 to H. Beattie 1915	Father hunted last moa Hokonui District	c. 1780	*The Otago Daily Times* 18 October 1930
c. 1890	R. Te Maire, Waitaki	Last moa killed 8 generations ago	c. 1700	Downes 1926:36
1895	R. Te Maire to F. Chapman	Moa extinct in time of Waitaha	Tamatea Period	Buick 1931:299
1890s	Rakitapu, Molyneux	Moa killed in ancient times	Tamatea Period	*The Otago Daily Times* 18 October 1930
1900	An. M. heard at Patuki tangi	Moa hunted with nets, pits	?c. 1800	Beattie 1958:8
1910	J. Bragg (M.) to J. Drummond, Southland	Te Awha's father saw last moa	c. 1800	*The Otago Witness* 1 June 1910
?c. 1910	Taare te Kahu	Moa extinct in ancient times	?Tamatea Period	Beattie 1958:9
c. 1920	T. Te Maiharoa, S. Canterbury	Moa extinct before 'Fleet' Maori arrived	Tamatea Period	Beattie 1920:65
c. 1921	P. Matewai, Riverton	Moa killed out by fires	?Tamatea Period	Beattie 1958:10
c. 1930	An. M.	Moa alive, Takitimu Mtns until c. 1860	c. 1860	Beattie 1958:4
1952	E. P. Cameron (M.) Riverton	As boy, Patu saw last moa	?c. 1800–1830	Beattie n. d.
1920s–1950s	An. M., Southland	Moa killed in pit, Orepuki	?c. 1800	Beattie 1958:11
1920s–1950s	An. M., Murihiku	Moa nearly extinct Mataehu flood	pre-Tamatea Period	Beattie n. d.

Note: M. = Maori; An. M. = Anonymous Maori.

INDEX

Susan Leipa

Printed in the United Kingdom
by Lightning Source UK Ltd.
9697200001B